HISTORICAL DICTIONARIES OF SPORTS
Jon Woronoff, Series Editor

1. *Competitive Swimming*, by John Lohn, 2010.

Historical Dictionary of Competitive Swimming

John Lohn

Historical Dictionaries of Sports, No. 1

The Scarecrow Press, Inc.
Lanham • Toronto • Plymouth, UK
2010

Published by Scarecrow Press, Inc.
A wholly owned subsidiary of The Rowman & Littlefield Publishing Group, Inc.
4501 Forbes Boulevard, Suite 200, Lanham, Maryland 20706
http://www.scarecrowpress.com

Estover Road, Plymouth PL6 7PY, United Kingdom

British Library Cataloguing in Publication Information Available

Library of Congress Cataloging-in-Publication Data

Lohn, John, 1976-
  Competitive swimming / by John Lohn.
     p. cm. — (Historical dictionaries of sports ; no. 1)
  Includes bibliographical references.
  ISBN 978-0-8108-6775-8 (cloth : alk. paper) — ISBN 978-0-8108-7495-4 (ebook)
  1. Swimming--Competitions--Dictionaries. I. Title.
  GV836.3.L65 2010
  797.2'1—dc22

                                                    2010016926

Printed in the United States of America

Contents

Editor's Foreword

It is hard to imagine a more popular sport than swimming. Countless people around the world "swim" in one manner or another. So it is not hard to imagine that competitive swimming is also very popular, although this is something quite different. Indeed, competitive swimming has been in the Olympics from the very start, back in 1896. Over more than a century, it has always attracted the very best swimmers, coaches, and keen fans. It has also evolved along the way, providing room for women as well as men, and increasingly young people, with more strokes being added. Alongside swimming there is diving and water polo. But the part of this evolution that may not have been expected was that the swimmers have been getting better, or if not actually better, then certainly faster, as one record after another is broken, once every few years and now almost annually. This is seen at the Olympics and also the World Championships of the organization that manages the sport, the Fédération Internationale de Natation, as well as various regional and countless national and local meets. Alas, the competition is sometimes so intense that some swimmers or their coaches go too far, which explains the continuing bane of drugs, now paralleled by an entirely unexpected angle in swimwear. Still, no matter how you look at it, swimming is popular, will remain popular, and will also most certainly be competitive.

This *Historical Dictionary of Competitive Swimming* is the first in a hopefully long series of volumes on sports, with most of them devoted to the most popular sports around. And it makes an extremely good start. The introduction provides a suitable context for the other sections, reminding us of how competitive swimming can be, what its charms are, and what its challenges are. There are not that many important acronyms associated with this sport, but it is nice to find them on a handy list, as is provided in this book. But the chronology, or rather chronologies, are really precious since it is not easy to keep track of things, what happened when, and who broke what record at which meet. And that goes double for the numerous appendixes. The bulk of the book, of course, is the dictionary section, with literally hundreds of entries on the most significant swimmers of the past century plus. Other entries describe the various strokes, the main organizations, and the dozen or so national powerhouses, which have worked hard to produce good swimmers and win races. The last section is a bibliography, which is not terribly large because not that much has been written on competitive swimming. This is a great pity but it also makes this volume much more useful than otherwise.

This historical dictionary was written by John Lohn, who is the senior writer for *Swimming World Magazine* and former deputy sports editor of the *Delaware County Daily Times*. In these capacities, he has been covering numerous meets around the United States and abroad, including several U.S. Olympic Trials and National Championships, the World Championships, and the 2008 Olympic Games in Beijing. Although his interest lies mainly in competitive swimming today, he has done a masterful job in tracing it from its origins and also provided a very broad view of the situation around the world. Inevitably, he was attracted by all-time great Michael Phelps, whose career receives particular attention. But swimming is much bigger than even the best, and just how many have contributed can be judged by the multitude of other swimmers who are listed in this book. That alone makes it worthwhile to keep this book on hand.

Jon Woronoff
Series Editor

Acknowledgments

This book is dedicated to my family for its unending support through the years and during this project. To my lovely wife, Dana, each day we're together is better than the last. I'm so fortunate to have you in my life. To my mom and dad, I cannot thank you enough for all the guidance and encouragement you've provided, and for teaching me the importance of family. Thanks to Dr. Phillip Whitten, who in 2000 took a chance on a young kid pitching a story idea to *Swimming World Magazine*. You fostered my passion for the sport of swimming and have been a true mentor. Also, thanks to Lauren Nave, Delly Carr, and Steve Thomas for their generosity in providing photographs.

Acronyms and Abbreviations

THREE-LETTER NATIONAL ABBREVIATIONS

ALG	Algeria
ARG	Argentina
AUS	Australia
AUT	Austria
BEL	Belgium
BRA	Brazil
BUL	Bulgaria
CAN	Canada
CHN	China
CRC	Costa Rica
CRO	Croatia
CUB	Cuba
CZE	Czech Republic
DEN	Denmark
ESP	Spain
EUN	Unified Team
FIN	Finland
FRA	France
FRG	Federal Republic of Germany
GBR	Great Britain
GDR	German Democratic Republic
GER	Germany
GRE	Greece
HUN	Hungary
IRL	Ireland
ISL	Iceland
ISR	Israel

ITA	Italy
JPN	Japan
KAZ	Kazakhstan
KOR	South Korea
MEX	Mexico
NED	Netherlands
NOR	Norway
NZL	New Zealand
POL	Poland
POR	Portugal
PUR	Puerto Rico
ROU	Romania
RSA	South Africa
RUS	Russia
SCG	Serbia and Montenegro
SIN	Singapore
SLO	Slovenia
SUI	Switzerland
SUR	Suriname
SVK	Slovakia
SWE	Sweden
TRI	Trinidad and Tobago
TUN	Tunisia
TUR	Turkey
UAE	United Arab Emirates
UKR	Ukraine
URS	Union of Soviet Socialist Republics
URU	Uruguay
USA	United States
VEN	Venezuela
YUG	Yugoslavia
ZIM	Zimbabwe

OTHER ABBREVIATIONS USED

AIS	Australian Institute of Sport
ASADA	Australian Sport Anti-Doping Authority

CSCAA	College Swimming Coaches Association of America
FINA	Fédération Internationale de Natation
IM	Individual Medley
IOC	International Olympic Committee
ISHOF	International Swimming Hall of Fame
LEN	Ligue Europeene de Natation
MADD	Mothers Against Drunk Driving
NAG	National Age Group
NASA	National Aeronautics and Space Administration
NBC	National Broadcasting Company
NCAA	National Collegiate Athletic Association
PGA	Professional Golfers' Association
PMG	Premier Management Group
USADA	United States Anti-Doping Agency
USMS	United States Masters Swimming
USOC	United States Olympic Committee
USS	United States Swimming
WADA	World Anti-Doping Agency

Chronology of Swimming

1875   25 August: England's Matthew Webb becomes the first person to cross the English Channel, completing the course from Dover to Calais in just under 22 hours.

1896   6–15 April: The first Modern Olympics takes place in Athens with men's swimming events conducted in the 100 freestyle, 400 freestyle, and 1,500 freestyle. Hungary's Alfred Hajos is the gold medalist in the 100 freestyle and 1,500 freestyle.

1908   19 July: The Fédération Internationale de Natation (FINA) is founded in London and becomes the world governing body of swimming, diving, water polo, synchronized swimming, and open-water swimming.

1912   12 July: Australia's Fanny Durack wins the first Olympic gold medal in swimming by a female, defeating countrywoman Wilhelmine Wylie and Great Britain's Jennie Fletcher in the 100 freestyle. Fletcher is a member of the British squad that won the 400 freestyle relay, the first gold medal presented to women in relay competition.

1914   The swimwear company Speedo is founded by Scotland's Alexander MacRae, who had moved to Australia in 1910. The company is initially known as Fortitude, but later takes on the Speedo name in 1928.

1922   9 July: United States swimmer Johnny Weissmuller, later known for his repeated roles as Tarzan in the film industry, becomes the first man to break the one-minute barrier in the 100 freestyle. Weissmuller is timed in 58.6, taking nearly two seconds off the previous record of Duke Kahanamoku. Weissmuller registered a time of 57.4 in early 1924, a record that stood for a little more than 10 years.

1926 **6 August:** Gertrude Ederle becomes the first woman to cross the English Channel, accomplishing the feat in 14 hours, 31 minutes. Her time is the fastest in history, better than the five men who had previously made the crossing. At the 1924 Olympics, Ederle won three medals, gold on the United States' 400 freestyle relay and bronze medals in the 100 and 400 freestyles.

1937 Although the National Collegiate Athletic Association (NCAA) oversaw men's swimming beginning in 1924, it was not until 1937 that the organization recognized a team champion. The University of Michigan won the first NCAA title in the sport, outdistancing Ohio State.

1948 **29 July–14 August:** After the 1940 and 1944 Olympics were canceled due to World War II, the Games resume in London with the United States topping the swimming medal count with 15.

1952 The butterfly is accepted by the Fédération Internationale de Natation (FINA), swimming's international governing body, as a stroke unto itself. Previously, it was a variation of the breaststroke in which swimmers used the upper-body movement of the butterfly, but used the breaststroke kick to remain within the rules. The butterfly was first contested in Olympic competition in 1956.

1960 **29 June:** Lance Larson of the United States becomes the first man to break one minute in the 100-meter butterfly, recording a time of 59.0 in Los Angeles. **17 August:** Sweden's Jane Cederquist is the first woman to break 10 minutes in the 800 freestyle, covering the distance in 9:55.6. The time shaves more than 15 seconds off the previous record held by Australia's Ilsa Konrads.

1962 **27 October:** Australia's Dawn Fraser is the first woman to swim the 100 freestyle under one minute, registering a time of 59.9 in Melbourne. Fraser was long expected to be the barrier-breaker, having set eight world records in the event prior to her subminute performance.

1963 **4 August:** Japan's Satoko Tanaka sets the last of her 10 world records in the 200 backstroke, clocking 2:28.2 in a meet in Tokyo. From 1959–1963, Tanaka held the world mark for all but eight days, the period in which it took Tanaka to better the global record set by the United States' Lynn Burke in 1960.

1964   16 October: The United States' Thompson Mann becomes the first man to break the one-minute barrier in the 100-meter backstroke, posting a time of 59.6 at the Tokyo Olympics. **18 October:** The United States' Don Schollander helps the United States to the gold medal in the 800 freestyle relay, giving him four gold medals at the Tokyo Games. Schollander is the first swimmer to win four golds at one Olympics.

1965   27 December: The International Swimming Hall of Fame (ISHOF) is dedicated in Fort Lauderdale, Florida, with more than 4,500 spectators on hand for the ceremony. The venue is designed to be a shrine to the sport, featuring medals and other artifacts from highlight moments in swimming history. The Hall of Fame also includes an aquatic facility intended to host national-level competitions.

1967   25 June: The United States' Mark Spitz sets the first of 26 individual world records, swimming the 400 freestyle in 4:10.6. The record is equaled seven days later by France's Alain Mosconi and broken nine days later by the Frenchman. Spitz also set individual world records during his career in the 100 and 200 freestyles and the 100 and 200 butterfly events.

1971   12 December: Australia's Shane Gould covers the 1,500 freestyle in 17:00.6, simultaneously giving her the world record in every freestyle distance—the 100, 200, 400, 800, and 1,500.

1972   30 August: In the final of the 400 individual medley at the Munich Olympics, Sweden's Gunnar Larsson edges the United States' Tim McKee by two thousandths of a second. The finish prompts a rule change that measures times only out to the hundredth of a second, awarding ties if necessary. **4 September:** Swimming the butterfly leg of the United States' 400 medley relay, Mark Spitz wins his seventh gold medal of the 1972 Olympics in Munich. Spitz sets a record for the most gold medals won at one Olympics, a mark that stood until the United States' Michael Phelps captured eight gold medals at the 2008 Games in Beijing. Spitz wins the 100 and 200 freestyles, the 100 and 200 butterfly events, and contributes to the triumphant 400 and 800 freestyle relays, along with the 400 medley relay.

1973   31 August–9 September: The Fédération Internationale de Natation (FINA), the world governing body of swimming, holds its first

World Championships, conducting the meet in Belgrade, Yugoslavia. Led by Kornelia Ender, the German Democratic Republic (East Germany) women win 10 of the 14 events contested. **6 September:** The United States' Rick DeMont, a year after being disqualified from the Olympics for a positive drug test, the result of an asthma medication he was taking, is the first man to break the four-minute barrier in the 400 freestyle. DeMont wins the world title with a time of 3:58.18.

1976   19 July: The German Democratic Republic's (East Germany) Kornelia Ender registers the last of her 10 world records in the 100 freestyle, going 55.65 to win the Olympic gold medal. From 1973 through 1978, Ender was the only woman to hold the world record in the event. In the same race, the Netherlands' Enith Brigitha wins the bronze medal to become the first black swimmer to medal at the Olympics. **25 July:** En route to the gold medal at the Montreal Olympics, the United States' Jim Montgomery becomes the first man to break 50 seconds in the 100 freestyle, stopping the clock in 49.99. The world record lasts only 20 days as South Africa's Jonty Skinner goes 49.44.

1977   28 August: Christiane Knacke of the German Democratic Republic is the first woman to break one minute in the 100 butterfly, posting a time of 59.78 in Berlin. Knacke is one of several East German women suspected of being part of a systematic doping program implemented in the 1970s and early 1980s.

1980   21 March: President Jimmy Carter announces the United States, in response to the Soviet Union's invasion of Afghanistan, will boycott the 1980 Olympics in Moscow. Carter's decision angers many athletes, whose work toward making the Games is nullified. Among the swimmers denied the chance at winning gold medals are Rowdy Gaines and Tracy Caulkins. **22 July:** The Soviet Union's Vladimir Salnikov is the first swimmer to cover the 1,500 freestyle in under 15 minutes; his time of 14:58.27 wins the gold medal at the Olympics by a little more than 16 seconds.

1981   13 August: The United States' Mary T. Meagher sets the last of her five world records in the 200 butterfly, registering a time of 2:05.96 at the U.S. National Championships in Brown Deer, Wisconsin. Meagher's record stands for nearly 19 years, until Susie O'Neill lowers the mark to 2:05.81 at the 2000 Australian Olympic Trials in Sydney.

1982   18–20 August: The University of Florida captures the first National Collegiate Athletic Association (NCAA) women's swimming championship, nearly a half century after the NCAA first recognized a men's champion in the sport.

1984   28 July–12 August: In retaliation for the United States' boycott of the 1980 Olympics in Moscow, the Soviet Union leads a boycott of the 1984 Los Angeles Games. The Soviet Union and German Democratic Republic (East Germany) are the biggest athletic superpowers to skip the Games. Among the top swimmers who miss out on the chance at winning medals are the Soviet Union's Vladimir Salnikov and East Germany's Kristin Otto and Heike Friedrich.

1988   21 September: Suriname's Anthony Nesty wins the first Olympic medal for his country by claiming the gold medal in the 100 butterfly. Nesty is the first black male swimmer to win an Olympic medal.

1991   13 January: Hungary's individual medley star Tamas Darnyi swims the 200 individual medley in 1:59.36, marking the first time the event is covered in less than two minutes.

1993   2–5 December: As a complement to the World Championships, which are held in the Olympic-size pool (50 meters), the Fédération Internationale de Natation (FINA) introduces the World Short Course Championships, held in a 25-meter pool. The first edition takes place in Palma de Mallorca, Spain.

1994   1–11 September: In what is a precursor to a number of positive tests for performance-enhancing drugs, China's women win 12 of the 16 events contested at the World Championships in Rome. The gold-medal total is eight more than what China won at the 1992 Olympics. The only event in which China fails to medal is the 800 freestyle.

1996   25 July: Hungary's Krisztina Egerszegi wins the 200 backstroke at the 1996 Olympics, her third consecutive gold medal in the event. Egerszegi joins Australia's Dawn Fraser as the only swimmers to win the same event at three straight Olympiads. Fraser won the 100 freestyle in 1956, 1960, and 1964.

1998   15 January: Australia's Ian Thorpe, just three months removed from his 15th birthday, becomes the youngest male world champion in history when he tracks down countryman Grant Hackett in the closing strokes to win the 400 freestyle.

2000 16 September: For the first time in its Olympic history, the United States is defeated in the men's 400 freestyle relay. Australia's quartet of Michael Klim, Chris Fydler, Ashley Callus, and Ian Thorpe sets a world record of 3:13.67, bettering the American foursome of Anthony Ervin, Neil Walker, Jason Lezak, and Gary Hall Jr., which is timed in 3:13.86. The United States loses the relay again in 2004 when South Africa wins the gold medal.

2001 29 June: Russia's Roman Sloudnov posts a time of 59.97 in the 100 breaststroke, becoming the first man to go faster than a minute in the event. The breaststroke is the last event to see a man break the one-minute barrier. The feat was accomplished in the 100 freestyle in 1922, the 100 backstroke in 1964, and the 100 butterfly in 1960. **16–29 July:** For the first time, the World Championships include events in the 50-meter distances of the backstroke, breaststroke, and butterfly. This change is designed to showcase sprint specialists. Additionally, the 800 freestyle is added to the men's program, while the 1,500 freestyle is added to the women's schedule, raising the total number of events to 40.

2002 13 August: The United States' Natalie Coughlin becomes the first woman to break the one-minute barrier in the 100-meter backstroke, swimming a time of 59.58 at the U.S. Nationals in Fort Lauderdale, Florida. Coughlin also became the first woman to complete the event in under 59 seconds, accomplishing that feat at the U.S. Olympic Trials on 1 July 2008.

2004 17 August: The Ukraine's Yana Klochkova makes a claim for being the best individual medley performer in history when she repeats as Olympic champion in the 200 medley and 400 medley. Klochkova is the only woman in history to win both individual medley crowns at back-to-back Games.

2005 31 July: Australia's Grant Hackett defeats the United States' Larsen Jensen by five seconds to win his fourth consecutive world championship in the 1,500 freestyle. Hackett is the first athlete—man or woman—to record four straight victories in the same event at the

World Championships. **21 September:** Two months after the Fédération Internationale de Natation (FINA) voted to allow the dolphin kick in the breaststroke, the rule change is officially implemented. Swimmers are now allowed one dolphin kick after the start and turn, a response to the controversy that stemmed from the 2004 Olympic final in the 100 breaststroke. In that race, video footage revealed Japan's Kosuke Kitajima using two dolphin kicks, but the officials did not call the violation.

2006 20 March: Australia's Leisel Jones becomes the first woman to break the 1:06 barrier in the 100 breaststroke, taking an astonishing 1.11 seconds off the previous world record of 1:06.20, held by the United States' Jessica Hardy. Jones accomplishes the feat en route to the gold medal at the Commonwealth Games in Melbourne.

2007 25 March–1 April: Although overshadowed by the seven gold medals won by Michael Phelps, Australia's Libby Lenton wins five events at the World Championships in Melbourne, prevailing in two relays and individually in the 50 and 100 freestyles, along with the 100 butterfly.

2008 12 February: At various launches around the world, Speedo introduces the LZR Racer, a high-tech swimsuit that jumpstarts a new era in the sport. The suit was responsible for the majority of the 108 world records set in 2008 and led to rival companies scrambling to develop suits that could match up. The new suits, some with nonpermeable properties, were suggested to be forms of technological doping due to the drastic drops in time that followed their release. **17 August:** Already the oldest female swimmer in Olympic history at 41, the United States' Dara Torres earns the silver medal in the 50 freestyle, finishing a hundredth of a second behind Germany's Britta Steffen. It is Torres' third silver medal of the Games and the 12th Olympic medal of her career.

2009 26 April: France's Fred Bousquet, racing at the French Nationals, clocks a world record of 20.94 in the 50 freestyle, the first time under 21 seconds in history. Bousquet's time obliterates the previous world record of 21.28, held by Australian Eamon Sullivan. Bousquet races to his record by wearing a suit made by the company Jaked, not yet approved by the Fédération Internationale de Natation (FINA). **30 May:** It is reported that Mustapha Larfaoui, the president of FINA since

1988 and longest-tenured holder of that post, will not run for another term. On 24 July, Uruguay's Julio Maglione is elected president of FINA.

2010 1 January: Fédération Internationale de Natation's (FINA) ban on high-tech suits, announced in July 2009, officially goes into effect, much to the delight of the world's elite swimmers, coaches, and administrators. Since Speedo unveiled its LZR Racer in February 2008, leading to a suit war that led to the creation of polyurethane suits that aided buoyancy, more than 200 world records were set. FINA's ban requires male swimmers to wear suits that do not extend above the hips or below the knee and women's suits that are cut around the shoulders and thighs. In addition to banning bodysuits, FINA requires all suits to be made of textile fabrics, thus eliminating the use of polyurethane or other rubber materials.

CHRONOLOGY OF
THE FINA WORLD CHAMPIONSHIPS

1973 31 August–9 September: For the first time, the Fédération Internationale de Natation (FINA) holds the World Championships, debuting the event in Belgrade, Yugoslavia. The meet comes a year after the 1972 Olympics in Munich and features 47 nations and 686 athletes, absent Mark Spitz. After winning seven gold medals and breaking seven world records in Munich, Spitz had announced his retirement, opening the door for new stars to emerge. The United States wins the overall medal count with 32, ahead of the 25 won by the German Democratic Republic. Australia is a distant third with five. The United States' men lead with 19 medals and the East German women lead with 18 medals. There are 16 world records established, nine by women and seven by men.

One of the best storylines is the victory claimed by the United States' Rick DeMont in the 400 freestyle. After his triumph in the 400 freestyle at the Munich Games was voided when DeMont tested positive for a banned substance in his asthma medication, he wins the event in Belgrade in a world-record time of 3:58.18, history's first sub-4:00 performance.

East German backstroke great Roland Matthes, who swept the 100 and 200 backstrokes at the 1968 and 1972 Olympics, turns in that double. The United States' Jim Montgomery is the other individual double winner among the men, finishing first in the 100 and 200 freestyles. For the women, East Germany's Kornelia Ender claims gold medals in the 100 freestyle and 100 butterfly, and teammate Renate Vogel sweeps the 100 and 200 breaststrokes.

1975 19–27 July: The second World Championships, a prelude to the 1976 Olympics in Montreal, takes place in Cali, Colombia, with a slight drop in participation from the first version of the meet. There are

39 countries represented with 682 athletes competing. Only five world records are set, four by the women and one by the men. The United States repeats as the leading medal winner with 30, 17 by its men. The German Democratic Republic is second in medals with 23, its women pacing the competition with 19.

The United States' Tim Shaw becomes the first person to win three individual events at the same World Championships, prevailing in the 200, 400, and 1,500 freestyle events. He's joined as a double winner by Great Britain's David Wilkie, who claims gold medals in the 100 and 200 breaststroke events. East Germany's Roland Matthes, considered the greatest backstroker in history, captures his last major title by defeating the competition in the 100 backstroke to defend his crown from two years earlier.

Once again, the East German women are led by Kornelia Ender, who defends her championships in the 100 freestyle and 100 butterfly, setting world records in both events. Her countrywoman Hannelore Anke wins both breaststroke events and East Germans Ulrike Richter (100 backstroke) and Rosemarie Kother repeat as gold medalists. The top effort from a United States woman is Shirley Babashoff, collecting gold medals in the 200 and 400 freestyles.

1978   18–23 August: The third World Championships returns to Europe with Berlin, Federal Republic of Germany, serving as the host of a competition that featured 49 nations and 828 athletes, a sizable increase from the previous two meets. The United States tops all three of the medal counts, leading the overall total with 36. The American men rank first with 20 medals and the U.S. women win 16 medals. The Soviet Union finishes second in the medal count with 14. There are 14 world records set, 10 by women and four by men.

For the United States, this competition marks its last major international meet until the 1982 World Championships due to Jimmy Carter eventually announcing the United States would boycott the 1980 Olympics in Moscow.

The United States' Tracy Caulkins, a 15-year-old with vast versatility, is the undisputed star of the competition, capturing six medals, including five gold. Caulkins sets world records on the way to individual victories in the 200 butterfly, 200 individual medley, and 400 individual medley. She also helps the United States to gold medals in the 400 freestyle relay and 400 medley relay and adds a silver medal in the 200 breaststroke. Her teammate Linda Jezek doubles in the 100 and 200 backstrokes.

Two of the stars in the men's meet are the United States' Jesse Vassallo and the Soviet Union's Vladimir Salnikov. Demonstrating his range, Vassallo sets a world record while winning the 400 individual medley, captures gold in the 200 backstroke, and is the silver medalist in the 200 individual medley. Salnikov makes his presence known in the distance events, winning the 400 and 1,500 freestyles.

1982   29 July–8 August: The fourth World Championships is held in Guayaquil, Ecuador, with a record 52 nations and 848 athletes taking part. For the first time, the United States does not sit alone atop the medal count, as the United States and German Democratic Republic each win 25 medals. The United States' men edge the Soviet Union for the most men's medals, 13 and 12, respectively, while the East German women total 19 medals, far ahead of the 12 won by the United States. There are seven world records set, three by women and four by men. It's the first time at the World Championships in which more men's world records are set than women's standards.

Although it is later revealed she was using performance-enhancing drugs supplied by her coaches, East Germany's Petra Schneider is the star of the competition, winning the 200 and 400 individual medley events, to go with a silver medal in the 400 freestyle. Her winning time in the 400 individual medley, a performance of 4:36.10, stands as the world record for 15 years.

The Soviet Union's Vladimir Salnikov, as was the case at the 1978 World Championships and the 1980 Olympics, is the champion of the 400 and 1,500 freestyles. The Federal Republic of Germany's Michael Gross makes his first major international competition a coming-out party. Gross wins gold medals in the 200 freestyle and 200 butterfly, wins silver in the 100 butterfly, and is a member of West Germany's bronze-medal winning 800 freestyle relay and 400 medley relay.

1986   13–23 August: The fifth World Championships takes place in Madrid, Spain, with a record of 1,119 athletes competing from 34 nations. The German Democratic Republic wins the medal count with 30, on the strength of 24 medals from the women. In the women's meet, East Germany wins 13 of the 16 events contested. The United States finishes second with 24 medals, including a meet-high 13 from its men's squad. There are six world records set, all by women.

Heike Friedrich and Kristin Otto are the top performers for East Germany, Friedrich winning the 200 and 400 freestyles and helping a pair of relays to gold medals. Otto, who two years later won six medals at the Seoul Olympics, wins the 100 freestyle and 200 individual medley and is also a member of two gold-medal winning relays. Mary T. Meagher is the sole female winner from the United States, prevailing in the 200 butterfly.

The United States' Matt Biondi is the headliner among the men, claiming seven medals—four individual and three relays. Biondi wins the 100 freestyle, takes silver in the 100 butterfly, and is the bronze medalist in the 50 and 200 freestyles. The Federal Republic of Germany's (West Germany) Rainer Henkel is the champion of the 400 and 1,500 freestyles, the Soviet Union's Igor Polyansky sweeps the backstroke events, and Hungarian Tamas Darnyi is the gold medalist in the 200 and 400 medley events.

1991 3–13 January: The sixth World Championships is held in Perth, Australia, which also served as the host of the 1998 World Championships. Record numbers of athletes and nations participate, with 60 federation represented by 1,142 competitors. Due to the fall of the Berlin Wall, Germany competes as one nation and remains among the medal leaders, finishing second with 20. The United States tops the medal chart with 23, 11 from the men and 12 from the women. There are seven world records established, all in the men's meet.

Hungarian Tamas Darnyi continues his dominance of the individual medley events, repeating as the champion in the 200 and 400 medleys while setting a pair of world records in the process. His countryman, Norbert Rozsa, sets a pair of world records in the 100 breaststroke, first in the preliminaries and then in the championship final. Rozsa is also the silver medalist in the 200 breaststroke. Germany's Jorg Hoffmann joins Darnyi as a double champion in individual events, claiming gold in the 400 and 1,500 freestyles.

Although there are no world records in the women's competition, four athletes stand out above the rest, notably United States distance star Janet Evans. In addition to winning the 400 and 800 freestyles, Evans collects a silver medal in the 200 freestyle. Her American teammate, Summer Sanders, is the champion of the 200 butterfly, takes silver in the 200 individual medley, and is the bronze medalist in the 400 medley. Hungarian Krisztina Egerszegi sweeps the backstroke events, and China's Lin Li betters the competition in the 200 and 400 medley disciplines.

1994   1–11 September: The seventh World Championships, held in Rome, will forever be under a cloud of doubt due to the sudden emergence of the Chinese women as the premier nation in the world. After winning nine medals at the 1992 Olympics in Barcelona, a breakthrough in itself, the Chinese women win 19 medals at the World Championships, including gold medals in 12 of the 16 events. China boasts the winner of both backstroke events, both butterfly events, and both individual medleys. Many of the athletes who earn medals for China later test positive for performance-enhancing drugs.

The number of nations competing balloons to a record 102, with 1,400 athletes in action. Although China dominates the female competition, the country does not have a male medalist, and China finishes second in the overall medal count, just behind the 20 medals won by the United States. The meet features 10 world records, seven from the women and three from the men.

China's Le Jingyi is the winner of the 50 and 100 freestyles, and He Cihong doubles in the backstroke. Another Chinese double winner is Limin Liu in the butterfly events. Australia's Samantha Riley dominates the breaststrokes, setting a world record in the 100 distance and winning the 200 breaststroke. Germany's Franziska van Almsick prevails in the 200 freestyle, setting a world record that lasts nearly eight years. Janet Evans is the only champion for the United States' women, who have their poorest showing in World Championships history, totaling 11 medals—one gold, five silver, and five bronze. Evans' title is a repeat in the 800 freestyle.

The men's competition is highlighted by Russia's Alexander Popov and Australia's Kieren Perkins, regarded among the finest sprinters and distance freestylers in history. Popov holds off rival Gary Hall Jr. for victories in the 50 and 100 freestyles, while Perkins cruises to titles in the 400 and 1,500 freestyles, the shorter distance in a world-record time. The other double winner is Hungary's Norbert Rozsa, who repeats as world champ in the 100 breaststroke and also captures the 200 breaststroke.

1998 7–18 January: The eighth World Championships is the first held at a previous site, returning to Perth, Australia, which also played host to the 1991 event. There are 121 nations competing, consisting of 1,371 athletes. The 1998 World Championships is the first not to feature a world record and gets off to an auspicious start when several members of the Chinese National Squad are banned from the competition when they are caught at the Perth Airport with performance-enhancing drugs.

The United States again wins the overall medal count, reaching the podium 24 times, ahead of the 20 medals won by Australia. However, the Australians are tops among the men with 12 medals, two more than the total won by the United States. The American women collect 14 medals to the eight won by Australia.

The top performance of the competition is Ian Thorpe's victory in the 400 freestyle, making him the youngest world champion in history at the age of 15. Thorpe's teammate, Grant Hackett, wins the first of four consecutive world titles in the 1,500 freestyle, and Aussie Michael Klim is the top all-around performer with six medals, including victories in the 100 butterfly, 200 freestyle, 800 freestyle relay, and 400 medley relay. The United States' Lenny Krayzelburg sweeps the 100 and 200 backstrokes, a prelude to the feat he repeats at the 2000 Olympics in Sydney.

In the women's competition, the United States' Jenny Thompson is the champion of the 100 freestyle and 100 butterfly and contributes to a pair of triumphant American relays. Although several of her teammates are sent home for possession of performance-enhancing drugs, Wu Yanyan gives China a victory in the 200 individual medley. She later tests positive for doping and is suspended by the Fédération Internationale de Natation (FINA). Her countrywoman Yan Chen wins the 400 freestyle and 400 individual medley.

2001 16–29 July: For the first time, the World Championships is held in Japan, going to the city of Fukuoka. Although there are no women's world records for the second straight World Championships, the men total eight records. There are 134 nations competing, leading to 1,498 athletes. The United States leads with 26 medals, 14 from the men and 12 from the women. The Australian men tie the United States for the high total in that gender. For the first time, the Fédération Internationale de Natation (FINA) introduces championship races in the 50-meter distance of the backstroke, breaststroke, and butterfly.

Australian Ian Thorpe puts on one of the greatest displays in meet history, winning the 400, 800, and 1,500 freestyles, all in world-record time. Thorpe also wins three gold medals in relay action, becoming the first man to garner six gold medals at a World Championships. His anchor leg on the 800 freestyle relay enables the Australians to set a world record. In the sprint freestyles, the United States Anthony Ervin is the gold medalist in the 50 and 100 distances. In his first World Championships, 16-year-old Michael Phelps sets a world record in winning the 200 butterfly.

While Thorpe wins three individual events in the men's competition, the Netherlands' Inge DeBruijn pulls off a trifecta in the women's meet, prevailing in the 50 and 100 freestyles, along with the 50 butterfly. Germany's Hannah Stockbauer doubles in the 800 and 1,500 freestyles, and Ukrainian Yana Klochkova is victorious in the 400 freestyle and 400 individual medley. China's Luo Xuejuan (50/100 breaststroke) and Australia's Petria Thomas (100/200 butterfly) are also double winners.

2003 12–27 July: The Fédération International de Natation (FINA) celebrates the 10th anniversary of the World Championships by visiting Barcelona, the city that hosted the 1992 Olympics. For the first time, the athlete count exceeds 2,000, with 2,015 entrants representing 157 nations. There are 14 world records set, a record-breaking 12 in the men's competition. The United States wins each of the medal counts, the men capturing 16 and the women claiming 12 for a total of 28. Australia was second with 22 medals.

Two years after winning his first world title, Michael Phelps makes his biggest international splash by winning four individual gold medals. In addition to repeating as the champion of the 200 butterfly, in which he set a world record, Phelps breaks world standards en route to triumphs in the 200 and 400 medley events. He also breaks a world mark in the semifinals of the 100 butterfly, but wins the silver medal in the event when he places behind United States' teammate Ian Crocker, who sets a global standard in the championship final.

Joining Phelps as a multiple world-record setter is Japan's Kosuke Kitajima, who prevails in the 100 and 200 breaststrokes, events he goes on to win at the 2004 Olympics in Athens. Australians Ian Thorpe and

Grant Hackett repeat as champions, Thorpe going back-to-back in the 200 and 400 freestyles and Hackett winning his third consecutive 1,500 freestyle to go with his first win in the 800 freestyle. Russian sprint great Alexander Popov takes first place in the 50 and 100 freestyles.

Two years after becoming the world champ in the 800 and 1,500 freestyles, Germany's Hannah Stockbauer repeats as the gold medalist in those events, in addition to winning the 400 freestyle. China's Luo Xuejuan doubles for a second consecutive World Championships in the 50 and 100 breaststrokes, and the Netherlands' Inge DeBruijn repeats as the winner of the 50 freestyle and 50 butterfly.

2005 16–31 July: The 11th World Championships is held in North America for the first time, Montreal serving as the host city. There are nine world records set, four by the women and five by the men, with 144 nations represented and 1,784 athletes taking part. The United States dominates the competition with 32 medals, 10 more than the total accumulated by Australia. The United States men capture 18 medals, with the Aussie women leading with 15.

Coming off an eight-medal performance at the 2004 Olympics in Athens, Michael Phelps wins six medals in Montreal, but calls the performance a disappointment. Although he wins the 200 freestyle and 200 individual medley, he fails to advance out of the preliminaries of the 400 freestyle, a new event on his program, and is seventh in the 100 freestyle.

Australian Grant Hackett stars in the distance freestyle events, winning the 400, 800, and 1,500 freestyles, the latter for the fourth consecutive time. Hackett becomes the first man to win a world title in the same event at four straight World Championships. He is joined as a double winner by the United States Brendan Hansen, who wins the 100 and 200 breaststrokes, and South Africa's Roland Schoeman, who wins the 50 freestyle and 50 butterfly. American Aaron Peirsol defends his championships in the 100 and 200 backstrokes.

Australia's Leisel Jones wins the 100 and 200 breaststrokes, setting a world record in the longer distance, and Zimbabwe's Kirsty Coventry is the victor in the 100 and 200 backstrokes. United States' teenager Katie Hoff earns her first international championships by winning the 200 and 400 medley events, and teammate Kate Ziegler, another teen, wins the 800 and 1,500 freestyles.

2007   18 March–1 April: The 12th World Championships, held in Melbourne, marks the third time Australia is the home country to the event. The competition is the final major tune-up for the next year's Olympic Games in Beijing and features 2,158 athletes representing 167 nations. There are 15 world records set, the second-highest total in meet history, and the medal count is won by the United States with 36, 19 from the American men.

Michael Phelps sets a record by winning seven gold medals and establishes four individual world records en route to triumphs in the 200 freestyle, 200 butterfly, 200 individual medley, and 400 individual medley. Phelps also wins the 100 butterfly and would have been in position to win an eighth gold medal, but the United States is disqualified in the preliminaries of the 400 medley relay.

The United States' Aaron Peirsol wins his third consecutive championship in the 100 backstroke, but has his seven-year unbeaten streak in the 200 backstroke snapped when teammate Ryan Lochte sets a world record in winning the 200 backstroke. The United States' Brendan Hansen (100 breaststroke) and South Africa's Roland Schoeman (50 butterfly) are the other repeat champions for the men.

Australia's Libby Lenton is the star of the women's competition, prevailing in the 50 and 100 freestyles, along with the 100 butterfly. She also anchors the Australians to gold medals in the 400 medley and 400 freestyle relays. France's Laure Manaudou doubles in the 200 and 400 freestyles, setting a world record in the shorter event, and the United States' Kate Ziegler and Katie Hoff double for the second straight World Championships. Ziegler wins the 800 and 1,500 freestyles, and Hoff wins the 200 and 400 medley events, setting a world record in the 400 individual medley. Australian Leisel Jones is the other double winner, repeating her performance from the 2005 World Championships by claiming the 100 and 200 breaststrokes.

Outside of the competition pool, one of the major storylines to arise in Melbourne is the report by the French newspaper *L'Equipe* that Australian Olympic legend Ian Thorpe had tested positive for high levels of banned substances during an out-of-competition drug test. Thorpe, after providing information to the Australian Sport Anti-Doping Authority (ASADA), is later exonerated of any charges and faced no disciplinary action by the Fédération Internationale de Natation (FINA) or the World Anti-Doping Agency (WADA).

2009   18 July–2 August: The 13th World Championships is held in Rome, Italy, also the site of the 1994 competition. Rome earns the bid in competition with Athens and Moscow. Only Rome and Perth, Australia, have been the host to the World Championships on more than one occasion. Several top athletes decide to skip the event, opting to take the year off from training following the 2008 Olympics. Among the notable names absent from Rome are the United States' Natalie Coughlin, the 2004 and 2008 Olympic champion in the 100 backstroke, and Japan's Kosuke Kitajima, who swept the breaststroke events at the 2004 and 2008 Games.

The events at the Foro Italico are highlighted by the impact of the high-tech suits that swept the sport. Most athletes don either the Arena X-Glide or Jaked 01, Italian suits made of polyurethane that provide buoyancy and allow athletes to remain stronger through the end of races, rather than slow down the stretch. There are 43 world records established, more than twice the previous mark set at a World Championships.

There are a record 2,556 athletes competing for 185 countries, and the United States wins the overall medal count, totaling 22. The American men capture 14 medals, including eight gold and set world records in all three relays. Australia tops the women's competition with 11 medals, including two gold.

Michael Phelps is the star of the men's competition, winning five gold medals and a silver. The silver is a surprise, as Phelps loses to Germany's Paul Biedermann in the 200 freestyle. Biedermann's victory is largely due to his wearing one of the high-tech suits, while Phelps stays loyal to his sponsor, Speedo, and wears one of the earlier high-tech suits, inferior compared to the new generation.

In addition to helping the United States to three gold medals in the relays, Phelps wins the 100 and 200 butterfly events in world-record time. In his 100 butterfly triumph, he overcomes his nemesis from the Beijing Olympics, Serbia's Milorad Cavic. Prior to the final at the World Championships, Cavic makes several comments to the media that serve as motivation for Phelps. Among the comments is Cavic's assertion that he won the Olympic final, despite what the scoreboard and photos show.

For the women, Italy's Federica Pellegrini and Germany's Britta Steffen are the standout performers. Pellegrini wins the 200 and 400 freestyles in her home nation, setting world records in both events and becoming the first woman to break the four-minute barrier in the 400 freestyle. Steffen, the Olympic champion in the 50 and 100 freestyle, repeats her sprint crowns and sets world records in each discipline.

CHRONOLOGY OF MICHAEL PHELPS' CAREER

1985   30 June: Michael Phelps is born in Baltimore, Maryland. He is the third child of Debbie and Fred Phelps, who have two older daughters, Hilary and Whitney.

1996   1 July: Bob Bowman joins the staff at the North Baltimore Aquatic Club and shortly thereafter becomes Phelps' coach, working with the 11-year-old prodigy and turning him into a National Age Group record holder. By the end of 1997, Bowman has a meeting with Phelps' parents, outlining a future the coach says can be filled with vast accomplishments on the international stage, including the Olympic Games.

2000   12 August: Punching his ticket to the Olympics in Sydney, Michael Phelps finishes second in the 200 butterfly at the United States Olympic Trials in Indianapolis. The 15-year-old Phelps places behind world-record holder Tom Malchow and becomes the youngest American male swimmer to qualify for the Olympics in 68 years. **19 September:** Phelps finishes fifth in the Olympic 200 butterfly final in Sydney, 33 hundredths of a second shy of the bronze medal.

2001   30 March: Michael Phelps becomes the youngest male world-record holder in history when he swims the 200 butterfly in 1:54.92 during the United States National Championships. Phelps is only 15 years, nine months at the time of the record. **24 July:** Phelps captures his first world title, setting a world record of 1:54.58 in claiming victory in the 200 butterfly in Fukuoka, Japan. In the process, the torch in the event is passed, as Phelps defeats Olympic champion Tom Malchow. **4 October:** Phelps signs a contract with Speedo, officially turning professional and ending any possibility of competing at the collegiate level, where pro-athletes are ineligible.

2002   15 August: In a head-to-head duel that ranks among the toughest races of his career, Phelps sets his first world record in the 400 individual medley. Squaring off with Erik Vendt at the United States Nationals, Phelps and Vendt both break the world record in the event, but it's Phelps who gets to the wall slightly quicker, registering a time of 4:11.09. Vendt is just behind in 4:11.27. Two summers later, Phelps and Vendt captured gold and silver, respectively, in the 400 individual medley at the Athens Olympics.

2003   25 July: Phelps is the first man to set world records in different individual events on the same day. He establishes a world standard in the semifinals of the 100 butterfly at the World Championships, a mark that is broken by American Ian Crocker the next day. Phelps also sets a world record in the 200 individual medley. **9 August:** For the fourth time in 42 days, Phelps breaks the world record in the 200 individual medley, clocking 1:55.94 at the United States Nationals in College Park, Maryland. In a little more than a month, Phelps takes more than two seconds off the 1994 standard of Finland's Jani Sievinen, who went 1:58.14. Sievinen's record was no pushover, either, as it lasted a shade under nine years.

2004   14 August: Phelps wins his first Olympic gold medal, setting a world record and defeating American teammate Erik Vendt in the final of the 400 individual medley in Athens. **20 August:** In his tightest race of the Athens Olympics, Phelps pulls off the greatest comeback of his career to date in the final of the 100 butterfly. Trailing United States teammate Ian Crocker heading into the final 10 meters, Phelps pulls ahead right before the wall, edging Crocker, 51.25 to 51.29. The victory entitles Phelps to swim the butterfly leg on the United States' 400 medley relay. Phelps, though, decides to yield his place to Crocker, who goes on to help the United States to a world record and the gold medal. Phelps still receives a gold medal for his butterfly leg during the preliminaries of the medley relay and finishes with six gold medals and two bronze medals, making him the first swimmer to win eight medals in one Olympics. **4 November:** Phelps is charged with driving under the influence after a Maryland state trooper pulls him over for failing to observe a stop sign. Phelps, who is also cited for underage drinking, initially tells the trooper he was not drinking, but later admits his mistake after being put through a number of field sobriety tests. He is eventually sentenced to 18 months probation and speaks at several Mothers Against Drunk Driving functions.

2005   24–31 July: Competing at the World Championships in Montreal, Phelps wins a meet-high six medals, including victories in the 200 freestyle and 200 individual medley. He also helps the United States to gold in three relays and takes silver in the 100 butterfly. Phelps, though, fails to medal in the 100 and 400 freestyles, and at his final press conference of the meet, he discusses how his sponsorship obligations following the 2004 Olympics cut into his training regimen. Going forward, Phelps vows not to allow outside influences to affect his swimming.

2006   17 August: Racing at the Pan Pacific Championships in Victoria, British Columbia, Phelps breaks out of a slump—at least by his standards. Producing a time of 1:53.80 in the 200 butterfly, Phelps sets his first world record in more than two years. His last global standard was in his first event of the 2004 Olympics, when he captured the gold medal in the 400 individual medley.

2007   27 March: As part of his seven gold medals at the World Championships in Melbourne, Phelps takes down Ian Thorpe's world record in the 200 freestyle. Although Phelps was beaten by the Australian great in the event at the 2004 Olympics, Phelps catches Thorpe in the record book. Not only does Phelps break Thorpe's record of 1:44.08, he becomes the first man under 1:44 with a clocking of 1:43.86. Phelps' seven gold medals account for a record at the World Championships, and although he is denied an eighth gold when the United States is disqualified from the 400 medley relay in the preliminary heats, Phelps' performance triggers talk that he'll match or surpass Mark Spitz's seven gold medals from the 1972 Games in Munich.

2008   10 August: Phelps captures his first gold medal of the 2008 Beijing Olympics, setting a world record of 4:03.84 in the 400 individual medley. The race was viewed as one of Phelps' toughest hurdles, but he easily defeats Hungary's Laszlo Cseh and United States teammate Ryan Lochte. **11 August:** Leading off the United States' 400 freestyle relay, Phelps establishes an American record in the 100 freestyle with a time of 47.51. Phelps, though, needs help to win the gold medal. After Garrett Weber-Gale and Cullen Jones swim the second and third legs of the relay, the United States trails France. Over the final leg, however, U.S. anchor Jason Lezak tracks down Frenchman Alain Bernard and the United States wins the event by eight hundredths, keeping alive Phelps' pursuit of eight gold medals. **12 August:** Phelps wins the 200 freestyle by nearly two seconds, becoming the first man to break 1:43 when he stops the clock in 1:42.96. The finish is a two-place improvement over the bronze medal he won in the 200 freestyle at the 2004 Games, where he placed behind Australian Ian Thorpe and Dutchman Pieter van den Hoogenband. **13 August:** Despite his goggles filling up with water, consequently hindering his vision, Phelps repeats as Olympic champion in the 200 butterfly, setting a world record of 1:52.03. It is his record 10th Olympic gold medal, breaking the record of nine held by track stars Carl Lewis and Paavo Nurmi, swimmer Mark Spitz, and gymnast Larissa Latynina. Later in the night, Phelps leads off the United States' 800 freestyle relay, which sets a world record of 6:58.56 to become the first relay quartet to break seven minutes. **15 August:** Again squaring off with U.S. teammate Ryan Lochte and Hungary's Laszlo Cseh, Phelps defends his Olympic title in the 200 individual medley with a world-record time of 1:54.23, good for a two-plus second victory over Cseh. It is Phelps' eighth world record in the event. **16 August:** Seemingly relegated to the silver medal in the 100 butterfly, Phelps finds a way to win the event by a hundredth of a second, defeating Serbia's Milorad Cavic, 50.58 to 50.59. With just 10 meters remaining in the race, Cavic held a half-body length lead on Phelps. But as Cavic glides into the finish, Phelps takes an extra half stroke, which allows him to stop the clock slightly quicker than Cavic. The victory gives him his seventh gold medal, tying the Olympic record set by fellow swimmer Mark Spitz at the 1972 Games in Munich. **17 August:** Following the backstroke leg of Aaron Peirsol and the breaststroke leg of Brendan Hansen, Phelps swims the butterfly leg of the United States' 400 medley relay. He posts the fastest split for his leg and then watches Jason Lezak finish off the American victory, which arrives in world-record time and hands Phelps his record-setting eighth gold medal of the Beijing Games. It is Phelps' 14th overall gold medal and his 16th medal.

2009   31 January: The British tabloid, *News of the World*, publishes a photo of Phelps inhaling from a marijuana pipe during a November 2008 party at the University of South Carolina, a picture captured with a cell phone by a fellow partygoer. Phelps admits to the authenticity of the photo, which touches off a furor of negative publicity. Although Phelps apologizes for his behavior, but because it does not align with his role-model status, he is suspended by USA Swimming for three months. All of his sponsors support him, with the exception of Kellogg's, which ends its relationship with the Olympic champion. Phelps admits that due to the intense media scrutiny, he contemplated retiring from the sport, only to decide against that route. During his suspension, he continues to train under coach Bob Bowman at the North Baltimore Aquatic Club. Phelps returned to competition on May 15, winning the 200 freestyle and 100 butterfly at the Charlotte UltraSwim. **9 July:** Phelps breaks the world record in the 100 butterfly, swimming 50.22 to lower the previous mark of 50.40, set in 2005 by Ian Crocker. It is the 27th individual world record for Phelps, one more than the total accumulated by Mark Spitz and the highest total in history. **26 July–2 August:** Phelps wins five gold medals and a silver medal at the World Championships in Rome. He wins the 100 butterfly and 200 butterfly, along with contributing to three winning U.S. relays. His lone loss is to Germany's Paul Biedermann in the 200 freestyle, where Biedermann breaks Phelps' world record.

Introduction

Competitive swimming as we know it today is not dramatically different from the casual, recreational days at the local pool, which many of us remember from childhood. As children splash around the water, the inevitable urge arises to challenge one another to a race. The first one to the other end of the pool is the winner.

While the spirit of the sport remains the same, the technology and the competitive formats have advanced tremendously through the years. The number of events contested in competition has increased, to the point where the program for a typical international meet, such as the World Championships or Olympics, produces a true reflection of the best swimmers over various distances and in different strokes.

Over time, advances have been made in training techniques, how the four strokes contested—freestyle, backstroke, breaststroke, and butterfly—are performed, and in the types of suits worn by the athletes. Moreover, regular tools of the sport, such as starting blocks and lane lines, have been re-engineered, geared toward making the swimmer faster.

What has not been altered is the way the best athletes in the sport are measured. Unlike diving, where there is a subjective scoring system, swimming is measured in inarguable fashion. There are no points awarded for style or the best-looking stroke. Simply, the individual who swims the fastest time is the winner, no questions asked.

Diving, on the other hand, is not nearly as black and white. As is the case in swimming, the basic premise of the sport has not shifted since its inception. Divers still seek to perform the most difficult dives in the most flawless way, in hopes of receiving the highest scores from the judges, who measure both execution and style. However, unlike swimming, a clock cannot be used to determine an undisputed winner.

Rather, the judging process in diving is arbitrary, there being the distinct possibility of each judge gauging a dive in a vastly different way from the next. Where a swimmer cannot argue against being second in a race, diving contains an artistic component in which the second-place finisher can second-guess the results.

THE TYPES OF COMPETITION

The competition levels offered in swimming are wide-ranging. Most competitive swimmers get their start at a local pool, often joining the community team and beginning to race against other swimmers as young as six years old. This level of the sport, known as age-group swimming, allows individuals to compete against others their age and either develop an interest in the sport or determine that swimming is not something they want to pursue. It is at this age, in which swimmers are taught the various strokes and their technique is developed, providing a solid base with which to work in the years ahead. Although not a rule, it is not uncommon for a top age-group swimmer to continue to improve and develop into one of his or her country's world-class performers. Michael Phelps, who has won 14 Olympic gold medals, is an example of an age-group standout who reached the pinnacle of swimming.

Beyond age-group swimming, opportunities to compete are available in high school and college, at the club and Masters level, and, of course, in the national and international ranks. Where swimmers fit relates to their talent and times. Only elite swimmers receive the opportunity to compete at Division I colleges, the highest level of collegiate athletics, and get the chance to race in national championships or in international competition.

In the United States, the college system, under the jurisdiction of the National Collegiate Athletic Association, features some of the best swimmers in the world. Because the coaching in the United States is among the finest in the world, numerous international swimmers will come to the United States to benefit from the high-level competition and first-rate training programs. At the Division I Championships each year, many of the athletes who compete have Olympic experience or will be future Olympians.

There are two primary types of competitive swimming: long-course competition and short-course competition. The long-course format is contested in a 50-meter pool and is considered the greatest test of an athlete's skill, due to fewer turns and a greater emphasis on stroke technique. The Olympics utilize this format. However, there are far more short-course, 25-meter pools in the world, and far more races occur in this format. The majority of age-group, club, and Masters meets are conducted in a short-course format, and in the U.S. college system, all meets are held in the short-course format.

Because of the different measurement scales used around the world, there are two common measures of distance in short-course swimming. In the United States, where short-course competitions are held in both meters and yards, the National Collegiate Athletic Association (NCAA) uses a yards format for its championship meets. Across Europe, Asia, and other geographies where the metric system dominates, short-course meters' racing is the norm.

Although frequently overshadowed by swimming, diving is a related and often popular sport. Diving is held in two formats: platform and springboard. Platform competition is contested on a 10-meter high tower, while springboard competition is held on a three-meter high board in international competition, although one-meter competition is common in U.S. collegiate and high school meets.

While diving is primarily an individual sport, synchronized diving has grown in popularity in recent years. It is a form of competition in which teammates compete simultaneously, diving next to each other. They are judged not only on technique, but on their ability to perform the dives in harmony.

Water polo also has a growing profile and is a team sport in which swimming plays a key role. The sport is highly popular in Eastern Europe, although the United States has a strong history in international competition. In the United States, the sport is played nationwide, but it is much more popular on the West Coast, with the best college teams based in California.

THE INTERNATIONAL SCENE

The ultimate goal in competitive swimming is to race at the Olympic Games, the quadrennial event that is widely considered the greatest sporting spectacle in the world. The opportunity for an athlete to represent his or her home nation at the Olympics is the fulfillment of years of hard work, and to win a medal in Olympic competition serves as proof that an athlete is one of the best in the world.

Swimming was first held at the Olympics during the first Modern Games in Athens in 1896. Only men competed in the initial Olympiad, and the schedule was limited, including only freestyle events over 100, 400, and 1,500 meters. By the second Olympics in 1900, the backstroke was added to the program, along with a pair of nonroutine disciplines: an obstacle race and an underwater swimming competition.

Olympic swimming continued to grow through 1908, when men contested races in the freestyle, backstroke, and breaststroke. Four years later, women were finally allowed to compete, but only in the 100 freestyle. When the Olympics returned in 1920, following the cancellation of the 1916 Games due to World War I, the women's program had added the 400 freestyle. It was not until 1924, however, that female swimmers began contesting each of the strokes.

At the 1968 Olympics in Mexico City, the competitive swimming schedule took a major step forward, growing close to what it resembles today. Previously, not every stroke was contested over multiple distances. While the freestyle was raced at various lengths for years and the backstroke was contested over 100 and 200 meters starting in 1964, the breaststroke and butterfly were limited to one distance each. That changed in 1968, as a more complete program was adopted, and the results of the Games painted a better picture as to which athletes were the best in a variety of events and over a variety of distances.

Today, the Olympic program features 32 events—16 for men and 16 for women, with only one difference: men compete in the 1,500 freestyle, but not the 800, and vice versa for the women. A push is being made for the International Olympic Committee (IOC) to expand the program to 40 events, perhaps as early as the 2016 Games. If the Fédération Internationale de Natation (FINA), swimming's world governing body, can convince the IOC to expand the program, men's and women's events will be added in the 50-meter distances of the backstroke, breaststroke, and butterfly. Also, the 800 freestyle would be added to the men's program and the 1,500 freestyle would be added for women.

The 40-event schedule is one already used by FINA at its World Championships, considered the second-most prestigious swimming competition in the world. In 1973, as a way to break up the four-year gap between Olympiads, FINA invested in the development of the World Championships. It has been highly successful since its inception, and typically boasts fields as rich in talent as the Olympics.

The first World Championships, held in a long-course pool, was hosted by Belgrade, Yugoslavia. Initially, there was no set timeline in terms of the frequency of the meet, as it was held at two-, three-, and four-year intervals. Since 2001, however, the World Championships has been held on a biennial basis.

The World Championships of 2001 marked the first time sprint specialists were given a major international stage on which to perform their craft. Although the 50 freestyle was part of the competition program, athletes adept at sprinting in the backstroke, breaststroke, and butterfly were not afforded an opportunity to showcase their talents. While some were capable of challenging in the 100-meter distances of their respective strokes, others found themselves at a disadvantage.

Since 2001, these specialists have received equal billing. Because the Olympics does not include these events on the program, though, the winners of the sprint events in the specialty strokes are not as respected for their accomplishments. In some eyes, they are seen as nothing more than one-event wonders who do not possess the ability to measure up in the true Olympic events.

Continuing its development, 20 years after FINA developed the World Championships in long-course swimming, the organization initiated a World Short Course Championships. The first competition was held in 1993 in Palma de Mallorca, Spain, and has been held on a biennial schedule, with the exception of 1999 and 2000, featuring back-to-back meets.

By creating these two versions of the World Championships, FINA has attempted to keep the spotlight on swimming during non-Olympic years.

SWIMMING'S DARK CLOUDS

Founded in 1908, FINA has not avoided controversy. The two main issues it has struggled to address have been performance-enhancing drug use and, most recently, the innovation of high-tech swimsuits that altered the sport's record book in 2008 and 2009.

Individuals across various athletic spectrums have long looked for a competitive advantage, whether or not that edge was sought within the rules. From football to baseball, there have been plenty of incidents of doping violations. Yet, there likely have been many cases in which athletes were not caught while aiding their efforts with performance-enhancing drugs.

Probably the darkest cloud in swimming's history hovered over the sport during the 1970s and early 1980s, a period in which the German Democratic Republic (GDR), most prominently its women, dominated the sport. Between the Olympics and World Championships, the East German women captured the lion's share of the medals available and rewrote the record books.

During this era, there was wide-ranging speculation that foul play was afoot within the GDR, and not limited to only East Germany's swimmers. There was also speculation that sports such as track and field had widespread doping taking place. Not only did the athletes' performances raise questions, the appearance of the athletes was alarming: broad shoulders and acne-covered backs, accompanied by deep voices.

So dominant were the East German women that they won 11 of the 13 gold medals at the 1976 Olympics in Montreal and 10 of the 14 events at the 1982 World Championships. But with no positive drug tests, any athlete or coach who accused the East Germans of doping was labeled as a sore loser and charged with making excuses for her inability to defeat the East German women. This was the fate realized by the United States' Shirley Babashoff, one of the world's elite swimmers, who earned three silver medals at the 1976 Olympics, all behind East German athletes. Babashoff's public declarations that she believed steroid use was rampant in the sport triggered the media to dub her "Surly Shirley."

With the labs reporting continuously negative drug tests among the East German women, FINA did not pursue the possibility that systematic doping was taking place. However, after the fall of the Berlin Wall in 1989, documents of the Ministry for State Security (Stasi), the East German secret police, revealed that a systematic program was indeed in place in which the country's sports officials and coaches provided athletes, many teenage girls, with steroids, administered either orally or through injections.

Some East German swimmers have since admitted to knowingly taking performance-enhancing drugs, while others steadfastly deny taking drugs or knowingly having been part of a doping program.

For swimmers like Babashoff, whose assessments have been proven correct, there will always be the what-if factor of competing in a drug-free atmosphere. Babashoff and others beaten by doped East German women have never had their results upgraded nor were any East German medals or world records erased.

The practices of East Germany during the 1970s and 1980s clearly stand out as the peak of drug use in swimming, but the 1994 World Championships accounts for a second era in which FINA did not control cheating. At this World Championships, Chinese women arrived in Rome surrounded by modest expectations. They had won only nine medals at the 1992 Olympics and a similar medal count was anticipated.

The Chinese, however, won 19 medals in Rome, including 12 gold, in a striking surge. Like the East German women before them, China's athletes had deep voices and abnormally broad backs. Yet, they slipped through the drug-testing process, which at the time was not advanced enough to detect all formulations of performance-enhancing drugs. In the years that followed, though, numerous Chinese swimmers tested positive for drug use, confirming what many suspected in Rome.

While doping has been a national issue, as seen in East Germany and China, individual cases of drug use have also existed. Perhaps the most notable instance is Ireland's Michelle Smith, who won three gold medals at the 1996 Olympics in Atlanta. Far from a medal contender at the previous Olympiad, Smith's performances skyrocketed after her marriage to former Dutch discus thrower and shot putter Erik de Bruin in 1993. De Bruin was banned from track and field for drug use and his wife would realize the same outcome in 1998 when she was found to have tampered with a urine sample during drug testing. The four-year ban handed to Smith ultimately marked the end of her career.

It is almost a guarantee that performance-enhancing drug use will continue in the years to come. While some athletes will be caught, others will avoid detection, largely due to innovations that keep the drug users a step ahead of those testing. Still, the World Anti-Doping Agency (WADA) has played a key role in deterring performance-enhancing drug use and the stiff penalties handed out to athletes who have tested positive for illegal substances should serve as a deterrent to those who contemplate cheating.

Few will argue that FINA's blind eye to the obvious doping violations of the German Democratic Republic and China compares to what it ignored in 2008 and 2009, but the organization's failure to control the high-tech suit craze of those two years surely occupies the No. 2 position in FINA's list of major strategic errors.

In February 2008, Speedo, the premier swimsuit manufacturer in swimming's history, unveiled a new-age suit known as the LZR Racer. Created in conjunction with engineers from the United States National Aeronautics and Space Administration (NASA), the LZR Racer contained polyurethane panels and was designed to aid swimmers' buoyancy and body position while in the water.

The release of the suit, used by the majority of the medal winners at the 2008 Olympics, accounted for most of the 100-plus world records set during 2008. It also opened the door to swimsuit competitors taking the use of polyurethane to a new level, namely the Italian companies Arena and Jaked creating suit models made almost entirely of the material.

As much as the LZR Racer helped swimmers to record-breaking swims and times never before seen, that suit model was outdated by 2009 in comparison to the Italian products. Suddenly, midlevel swimmers, who never before challenged for international medals, were in contention, aided by a suit that neutralized the playing field. Before the high-tech suit craze, the best swimmers achieved that status because they were able to maintain their form and endurance through the end of their race. With the high-tech suits helping swimmers into perfect form, any advantage gained through pure talent and dedicated training was erased.

There were multiple calls for the elimination of the high-tech suit fad, but FINA did not act to remove them, largely because of its affiliations with the swimwear companies and the fear of angering companies that feed money to the highest levels of the sport. As a result, the 2009 World Championships in Rome was considered a mockery of the sport, as 43 world records were set, nearly three times the previous mark for world records at a World Championships.

Finally realizing the sport was out of control and as much about technology as talent, FINA announced during the 2009 World Championships that it was banning the high-tech suits effective 1 January 2010, but not before more than 200 world records were set.

The ban on high-tech suits will require men to wear suits known as jammers, which only stretch from the hip to the knee. As for women, their suits will be cut around the shoulders and thighs. Most athletes and coaches are pleased with FINA's ban, anxious to see the sport return to one based on skill. However, there is a chance that many of the world records set during the high-tech suit craze will endure for many years to come.

THE BEST: PHELPS AND SPITZ

Throughout swimming history, the likes of Johnny Weissmuller, Dawn Fraser, Shane Gould, and Tracy Caulkins have been mentioned as some of the best swimmers in history. But two men have stood out as the undisputed greatest in history: the United States' Mark Spitz and Michael Phelps.

A star at Indiana University and a four-time medalist at the 1968 Olympics, Spitz delivered the finest Olympic exhibition at the 1972 Games in Munich. It was in Germany where Spitz became the first Olympian to capture seven gold medals at a single Olympics. While winning four individual events and contributing to three triumphant United States relays, Spitz set seven world records for a perfect Olympiad.

For Spitz, though, that was the end of the road. At the time, swimmers were forced into retirement after college because of the lack of available funding. Unlike professional sports such as baseball and basketball, swimmers could not earn a living and simultaneously train at the level needed for sustained success.

As a result, Spitz was forced to walk away from the pool instead of chasing additional medals at the 1976 Olympics, where he would have remained a top contender. Still, his efforts from Munich stood the test of time, going unmatched until 2008, when a 23-year-old American named Michael Phelps appeared at his third Olympics.

As a 15-year-old at the 2000 Games in Sydney, Phelps just missed a medal in his lone event, finishing fifth in the 200 butterfly. By the next Olympiad, Phelps was considered a contender to match, or possibly surpass, Spitz's 1972 feat. Although Phelps became the first swimmer to win eight medals in an Olympiad, only six were gold, and his Olympic performance was viewed as slightly inferior to that of Spitz.

It was at the 2008 Games in Beijing where Spitz's record was finally caught, Phelps prevailing in all five of his individual events and as a member of all three U.S. relays that struck gold. After 36 years, the Olympics had its match to Spitz, and swimming had an athlete who managed to break into the athletic mainstream.

While swimming has always been one of the glamour sports at the Olympic Games, battling track and field and gymnastics for top billing, it typically fell off the radar in non-Olympic years. Because the sport received minimal television coverage, the athletes were primarily unknown personalities to the sporting public. What Phelps has done for the sport in the United States is elevate its popularity.

No one will argue that swimming could eventually catch up to the likes of football, basketball, and baseball, the leading sports in the United States and around the world. Nor will swimming ever achieve the popularity of golf, hockey, tennis, and auto racing, other sports with consistent fan bases. Still, Phelps' accomplishments, particularly those at the Olympics, are not lost on general sports fans and have triggered an interest level in the sport among children.

As Phelps chased Spitz's record of seven gold medals from one Olympiad, his pursuit became the lead story on all nightly newscasts, including ESPN's *SportsCenter*. The nation and the world were captivated by his ability to track down a record that had stood for almost four decades. The public was equally enamored by Phelps' elevation to the greatest Olympian in history, his 14 gold medals providing that distinction.

Never before had a swimmer been so talked up. Phelps became central in the conversation of most dominant athlete in the world. At one point, Tiger Woods was tabbed as the most overwhelming force in an individual sport, his prowess on the golf course unmatched. Tournaments featuring Woods usually had him challenging for the championship Sunday afternoon, often hoisting the trophy. Meanwhile, Roger Federer was viewed in a similar way on the tennis court, his game so polished that he racked up major crown after major crown. Eventually, Phelps started to gain inclusion in conversations that once were limited to Woods and Federer.

With Phelps, his losses were far more infrequent. When contesting his premier events, there was never a doubt he would be upset. The only times Phelps failed to better his opposition was in minor competitions, often when Phelps was venturing into events that were not his specialty, or when he was wearing inferior swimwear, as was the case when he was beat in the 200 freestyle by Germany's Paul Biedermann at the 2009 World Championships.

Children who watched Phelps at the Beijing Games developed an interest in swimming and asked their parents to enroll them in swimming lessons. Down the line, this increased participation in the sport, United States Swimming (USS) hopes, will develop a deeper talent pool from which the country will be able to select future teams for the Olympics and World Championships.

Moreover, Phelps' accomplishments were so highly watched in Beijing that the National Broadcasting Company (NBC), which has rights to the Olympics, opted to obtain broadcast rights to the 2009 World Championships in Rome. Previously, the World Championships had never been shown on network television in the United States, with any coverage of the event limited to cable television or, as was more frequent, no television at all.

SWIMMING'S APPEAL

Although swimming in the United States continues to fight for greater coverage and a deeper niche with sports fans, it is making strides. The same does not have to be said for Australia, which has long treated swimming as one of its top sports. Broadcast of the Australian Olympic Trials and other major meets has been routine, and the country's top swimmers, like Ian Thorpe and Grant Hackett, are among Australia's most recognized celebrities.

There is little argument that the United States is the most dominant swimming nation in history. The United States holds significant advantages in the most Olympic medals and World Championships medals won, with Australia ranking second in the Olympic count and the second-most successful nation at the World Championships, once the German Democratic Republic's performances, most aided by drug use, are removed from competition.

In terms of swimming passion and per capita production, however, it can be argued that the United States does not measure up to its counterpart from down under. Historical figures show that the United States (489) has won nearly 500 Olympic swimming medals, almost three times the number won by Australia (168). Yet, to look at those totals through a wider lens illustrates how successful Australia has been on the international stage. With a population of approximately 21 million, Australia is about 1/15th the size of the United States. Yet, it has far exceeded that ratio on the medal charts. While swimming ranks down the list of the most-followed sports in the United States, despite its increasing popularity, swimming rates as one of Australia's most popular athletic activities, alongside cricket, tennis, and rugby.

Australia is far from being the only smaller country to have had significant international success in the pool. Hungary, with a population of about nine million, is fifth on the all-time Olympic medal list with 63. The total may not seem like much in comparison to the medals won by the United States and Australia, but the small population of Hungary and its success clearly prove that there is a great interest in the sport.

Nor should one overlook the long, if not as noticeable, string of success of Great Britain. Over the years, it has accumulated 64 Olympic swimming medals, ranking fourth all-time. It has had a recent upturn in performance after several years of mediocrity, a rise that is expected to continue as London prepares to be the host of the 2012 Olympic Games.

The exploits, too, of the People's Republic of China (CHN) and the former states of the Union of Soviet Socialist Republics (URS) are worth noting. China, with its population of 1.3 billion, has a large pool from which to draw in producing a powerhouse swimming program. Yet, because of its history with performance-enhancing drugs, there is generally suspicion over performances when a Chinese swimmer first arises on the international scene.

Russia and the Ukraine, too, have routinely developed world-class swimmers, and there is no sign of a drop off in the near future. What there are signs of is the continued production of singular athletes from nations without widespread swimming success. In this category are Zimbabwe's Kirsty Coventry and Tunisia's Ous Mellouli, both Olympic champions who developed into world-class athletes while competing collegiately in the United States.

Additionally, there is greater longevity in swimming today than even 15 years ago. The growing popularity of the sport and the increased endorsement opportunities have combined to enable swimmers to compete into their late 20s or early 30s, or in the case of U.S. sprinter Dara Torres, into her 40s.

As recently as the mid- to late 1990s, swimmers continued to encounter the dilemma Spitz faced after the 1972 Olympics. There were limited endorsement opportunities available that would allow swimmers to train and live comfortably by making a living through swimming. But in the past decade, swimwear companies such as Speedo, Arena, and TYR have signed swimmers to endorsement contracts that pay enough money to sustain the swimmers, who have also been supported through paid speaking engagements and other sponsors from such areas as watch manufacturers, insurance companies, and energy drink producers. For a time, Nike, the most prominent sports apparel company in the United States, also sponsored swimmers, but it removed itself from the sport amid the high-tech suit controversy of 2008.

The path swimming travels in the years ahead will be interesting to watch. Never has the sport enjoyed greater popularity than at present, a surge that can be attributed to the accomplishments of Phelps and the way he has redefined the sport through his multievent and never-before-seen excellence. It is likely, especially in the United States, that there will be a spike in swimming participation because of Phelps' influence, eventually providing a greater talent pool from which to select future Olympic and World Championships rosters. Given his revered status in other countries, such as Japan and China, the possibility also exists that swimming will grow on a global scale.

As has been the case over the past 100-plus years, since swimming made its debut as an Olympic sport, there will also be developments in training methods and stroke technique, advancements that will almost guarantee faster times. After all, the goal of swimming will always be getting from point A to point B in the fastest way possible. It's been that way forever, since the first child challenged a friend to a race.

Grant Hackett

Brendan Hansen (diving) and Aaron Peirsol (in water)

Ian Thorpe

Michael Phelps

The Dictionary

– A –

ADLINGTON, REBECCA (GBR). B. 17 February 1989, Nottinghamshire, England. Rebecca Adlington put her name on the international map with a breakout performance in 2008. She started the year by winning the gold medal in the 800 **freestyle** at the **World Short Course Championships**, then excelled at the **Olympic Games** in Beijing, collecting a pair of victories. Adlington first won the 400 freestyle at the Olympics, becoming the first British swimmer to capture a gold medal since **Adrian Moorhouse** prevailed in the 100 **breaststroke** in 1988. She was the first British woman to win Olympic gold since **Anita Lonsbrough** won the 200 breaststroke at the 1960 Games. Adlington followed her 400 freestyle triumph by winning the 800 freestyle, accomplishing the double by erasing **Janet Evans'** 19-year-old world record, the longest-standing record in the sport. *See also* GREAT BRITAIN.

AGE-GROUP SWIMMING. Age-group swimming is the term used for youth competition and is generally broken into five categories: 18 and under, 14 and under, 12 and under, 10 and under, and 8 and under. **United States Swimming (USS)** maintains National Age-Group (NAG) records in each of the classifications. Such Olympic stars as **Michael Phelps** and **Tracy Caulkins** have set NAG standards.

ALSHAMMAR, THERESE (SWE). B. 26 August 1977, Solna Municipality, Sweden. Therese Alshammar won silver medals in the 50 and 100 **freestyles** at the 2000 **Olympics** in Sydney. She has won six medals at the **World Championships**, including gold in the 50 **butterfly** at the 2007 World Champs.

1

ALTITUDE TRAINING. Altitude training is a method used by swimmers several times per year in which they train in locales that are situated well above sea level. Training in this atmosphere is difficult because there is less oxygen available at high altitude, making it harder to progress through training sets. **United States Swimming (USS)**, which has its headquarters in Colorado Springs, Colorado, is a frequent destination for U.S. athletes seeking this type of training. Another familiar locale for altitude training is in Flagstaff, Arizona, where members of **Japan**'s and **Australia**'s national teams have trained.

ANDERSEN, GRETA MARIE (DEN). B. 1 May 1927, Copenhagen, Denmark. Greta Andersen was a two-time Olympian for Denmark who won the 100 **freestyle** at the 1948 **Olympics**, where she added a silver medal in the 400 freestyle **relay**. She failed to defend her title at the 1952 Games after not advancing out of the semifinal round.

ANDREWS, THERESA (USA). B. 25 August 1962, New London, Connecticut. Theresa Andrews is one of several **Olympic** gold medalists produced by the **North Baltimore Aquatic Club (NBAC)**, the training ground for 16-time Olympic medalist **Michael Phelps**. At the 1984 Olympics in Los Angeles, Andrews narrowly beat out U.S. teammate **Betsy Mitchell** for the gold medal and also helped the **United States** to gold in the 400 medley **relay**.

ANKE, HANNELORE (GDR). B. 8 December 1957, Sachsen, Germany. Hannelore Anke won the 100 **breaststroke** and helped the **German Democratic Republic (GDR)** to the gold medal in the 400 medley **relay** at the 1976 **Olympics** in Montreal. She was the silver medalist in the 200 breaststroke at the 1973 **World Championships** and won the 100 and 200 breaststrokes at the 1975 World Championships. Anke's achievements, however, were aided by **performance-enhancing drugs**, administered by her **coaches** as part of East Germany's systematic doping program.

AOKI, MAYUMI (JPN). B. 1 May 1953, Kumamoto, Japan. Mayumi Aoki twice set world records in the 100 **butterfly** and was the gold medalist in that event at the 1972 **Olympics**. At the 1973 **World Championships**, Aoki was the bronze medalist in the 100 butterfly.

ARENA. Arena is an Italian swimwear company that found itself in the middle of the **high-tech suit controversy** that was a major storyline in the sport in 2008 and 2009. Although Arena was part of the international scene for years, its profile was elevated in 2009 when it unveiled a model known as the Arena X-Glide, a polyurethane suit considered one of the fastest in the world. The original version of the suit was not ratified by the **Fédération Internationale de Natation (FINA)**, the sport's world governing body, but a resubmitted model was allowed for use and was worn by numerous athletes at the 2009 **World Championships** in **Rome**. Among the athletes wearing the X-Glide suit was the **United States' Aaron Peirsol**, considered the greatest **backstroker** in history who set world records in the new line of equipment at the United States Nationals and World Championships. *See also* JAKED; SPEEDO; TYR SPORT.

ARMSTRONG, DUNCAN (AUS). B. 7 April 1968, Queensland, Australia. Duncan Armstrong was a middle-distance **freestyler** who trained under legendary **Australian coach Laurie Lawrence**. Not considered a favorite for victory, Armstrong won the gold medal in the 200-meter freestyle at the 1988 **Olympics** in Seoul, breaking the world record with a time of 1:47.25 and upsetting the **United States' Matt Biondi** and the **Federal Republic of Germany**'s (FRG) **Michael Gross**. After the race, Lawrence was so wild in his celebration that officials inside the swimming venue approached him and threatened to escort him out of the facility if he did not calm down. The footage is shown in the documentary *Bud Greenspan's Favorite Stories of Olympic Glory*. Armstrong added a silver medal at those Games in the 400 freestyle and won gold medals in the 200 and 400 freestyle events at the 1986 **Commonwealth Games**. He retired from competitive swimming in 1993.

ARVIDSSON, PAR JOHAN (SWE). B. 27 February 1960, Risinge, Sweden. Par Arvidsson competed for **Sweden** at two **Olympics**. After not medaling at the 1976 Olympic Games in Montreal, he captured the gold medal in the 100 **butterfly** at the 1980 Olympics in Moscow. Arvidsson was also seventh in the 200 butterfly and was the bronze medalist in the 100 butterfly at the 1978 **World Championships**.

He set his sole world record in April 1980 in the 100 butterfly and won four career medals at the European Championships.

AUBURN UNIVERSITY. Located in Alabama, Auburn University features one of the dominant collegiate swimming programs in the **United States** for both men and **women**. Since 1997, the Auburn men have won eight **National Collegiate Athletic Association (NCAA)** championships while the women have won five national championships. The men's program, now under the direction of former **Australian** Olympian Brett Hawke, is best known for its development of world-class **sprint freestylers**, including 2008 50-meter freestyle **Olympic** champion **Cesar Cielo**. *See also* BOUSQUET, FREDERICK.

AUSTRALIA (AUS). Australia has a rich tradition in swimming, ranking second in the all-time swimming medal count from the **Olympics**, having won 168, including 58 gold. Although the nation does not compare to the 489 medals won by the **United States**, it is regarded as equally successful because its population pales in comparison, which is only about 1/15th that of the United States. Among the finest swimmers from the country are **Ian Thorpe**, considered the best middle-distance **freestyler** in history, and **Shane Gould**, who won five medals at the 1972 Olympics in Munich. In men's swimming, there is a long-standing tradition of producing some of the world's premier 1,500 freestylers, including two-time Olympic champions **Grant Hackett** and **Kieren Perkins**. Australia has twice been the site of the Summer Olympics, hosting the 1956 Games in Melbourne and the 2000 Games in Sydney. In 2000, Australia registered one of the biggest victories in its history when the 400 freestyle **relay**, anchored by Thorpe, handed the United States its first loss in Olympic competition. **Swimming Australia** is the governing body in the country and Australia is the only country to have hosted three **World Championships**, two in **Perth** (1991/1998) and one in Melbourne (2007). *See also* ARMSTRONG, DUNCAN; AUSTRALIAN INSTITUTE OF SPORT; BEAUREPAIRE, FRANCIS; BERRY, KEVIN; CAMPBELL, CATE; CARLILE, FORBES; CHARLTON, ANDREW; COOPER, BRADFORD; CRAPP, LORRAINE; DAVIES, JOHN; DENNIS, CLARA; DEVITT, JOHN; DURACK, SARAH;

FORD, MICHELLE; FRASER, DAWN; HANSON, BROOKE; HENRICKS, JOHN; HENRY, JODIE; HOLLAND, STEPHEN; JONES, LEISEL; KLIM, MICHAEL; KONRADS, JANIS; KOW-ALSKI, DANIEL; LANE, FREDERICK; LAWRENCE, LAURIE; LEWIS, HAYLEY; McCLEMENTS, LYNNETTE; NEALL, GAIL; O'BRIEN, LOVETT; O'NEILL, SUSAN; RICE, STEPHANIE; RICKARD, BRENTON; ROSE, IAIN; SCHIPPER, JESSICAH; SIEBEN, JONATHAN; STOCKWELL, MARCUS; SULLIVAN, EAMON; THEILE, DAVID; TRICKETT, LISBETH; WELSH, MATTHEW; WENDEN, MICHAEL; WHITFIELD, BEVERLEY; WINDLE, ROBERT.

AUSTRALIAN INSTITUTE OF SPORT (AIS). The Australian Institute of Sport was opened in 1981 as an elite training center for Australian athletes. While the facility, located in Canberra, also caters to basketball, track and field, and gymnastics, it is best known for producing world-class swimmers, including Olympic champions Petria Thomas and **Michael Klim**.

– B –

BABASHOFF, JACK (USA). B. 13 July 1955, Whittier, California. The oldest of two highly successful swimming siblings from the **United States**, Jack Babashoff was the silver medalist in the 100 **freestyle** at the 1976 **Olympics**. He finished behind U.S. teammate **Jim Montgomery**, who became the first swimmer to break the 50-second barrier in the event when he was timed in 49.99. Babashoff's sister, **Shirley**, is one of the most decorated female swimmers in U.S. history.

BABASHOFF, SHIRLEY FRANCES (USA). B. 31 January 1957, Whittier, California. Shirley Babashoff is one of the **United States'** greatest female swimmers in history, and equally known for her willingness to speak out publicly against **doping** problems in the sport. At the 1972 **Olympics** in Munich, Babashoff won a gold medal on the United States' 400 medley **relay** and picked up silver medals in the 100 and 200 **freestyles**. Four years later, at the Montreal Games,

Babashoff won silver medals in the 200, 400, and 800 freestyles, finishing behind **German Democratic Republic (GDR)** swimmers in each event. She publicly stated her belief that the East German swimmers were using **performance-enhancing drugs**, and these accusations hurt Babashoff's image. She was dubbed "Surly Shirley" and was accused of making up excuses for her inability to win a gold medal. It was later revealed that the East German **women** were part of a systematic doping system, proving Babashoff correct. At the 1972 Games, she also won a silver medal in the medley relay, but helped the United States upset East Germany in the 400 freestyle relay. At the **World Championships**, she won eight medals, including four in 1975 in the 100, 200, 400, and 800 freestyles. She took gold in the 200 and 400 distances.

BACKSTROKE. As its name indicates, the backstroke is performed with the athlete swimming on his or her back, using alternating strokes with the arms and a flutter kick to move through the water. The stroke was first contested in Olympic competition at the 1900 **Olympic Games**, when the men participated in the 200 backstroke. Swimmers formerly had to touch the wall while on their back before starting their next lap, but a rule change in the 1980s allowed swimmers to turn onto their stomachs and use a flip turn to move into their next lap. The backstroke is the only stroke in which the swimmer starts a race in the water and swimmers must break the surface of the water by the 15-meter mark of each lap. This ruling came as a result of athletes, notably the **United States' David Berkoff**, swimming underwater for nearly the entire length of a lap, believing the use of a dolphin kick was faster. In the medley **relay**, the backstroke is the first leg, while the backstroke is the second leg of the **individual medley (IM)**. The best-known men's backstrokers in history are **Roland Matthes** of the **German Democratic Republic (GDR)**, who won gold medals in the 100 and 200 backstrokes at the 1968 and 1972 Olympics and the United States' **Aaron Peirsol**, who was Olympic champion in the 100 and 200 backstroke at the 2004 Olympics in Athens and repeated his 100 backstroke title in 2008 in Beijing. For the women, the United States' **Natalie Coughlin** was the first **woman** to break one minute in the 100 backstroke and **Hungary's Krisztina**

Egerszegi won the 200 backstroke at the 1988, 1992, and 1996 Olympics, making her one of only two individuals to ever win an Olympic title in three consecutive Games. *See also* COVENTRY, KIRSTY; KIEFER, ADOLPH; LOCHTE, RYAN.

BARKMAN, JANE LOUISE (USA). B. 20 September 1951, Bryn Mawr, Pennsylvania. Jane Barkman was a **freestyle** star for the **United States** who competed at the 1968 and 1972 **Olympics**, her second appearance following a brief retirement. At the 1968 Games, Barkman helped the United States to gold in the 400 freestyle **relay** and was the bronze medalist in the 200 freestyle, finishing behind U.S. teammates **Debbie Meyer** and **Jan Henne**. At the 1972 Olympics, she added another gold medal in the 400 freestyle relay as the only holdover from the squad that won four years before.

BARON, BENGT (SWE). B. 6 March 1962, Stockholm, Sweden. Bengt Baron competed at two **Olympics** for **Sweden**, winning the gold medal in the 100 **backstroke** at the 1980 Games in Moscow. At the 1984 Games, Baron won a bronze medal as a member of Sweden's 400 **freestyle** relay and reached the final of the 100 backstroke and 100 **butterfly**. At the 1982 **World Championships**, Baron was the bronze medalist in the 100 butterfly.

BARROWMAN, MICHAEL RAY (USA). B. 4 December 1968, Asuncion, Paraguay. Mike Barrowman was a specialist in the 200 **breaststroke**, winning a gold medal in the event at the 1992 **Olympics** in Barcelona. Barrowman was not known for his 100 breaststroke skill, but his ability to maintain his pace without slowing down made him a standout in the four-lap event. The fourth-place finisher at the 1988 Olympics in the 200 breaststroke, Barrowman was the 1991 world champion. He set six world records from 1989 to 1992, and his winning time from the Barcelona Olympics, 2:10.16, stood as the world record for a little more than 10 years.

BATHE, WALTER (GER). B. 1 December 1892, Dolnoslaskie, Poland. D. 21 September 1959, Casenico, Italy. Walter Bathe was the dominant **breaststroker** at the 1912 **Olympics**, winning gold in the 200 distance and the 400 distance.

BATTISTELLI, STEFANO (ITA). B. 6 March 1970, Rome, Italy. A versatile swimmer who earned international laurels in the **backstroke, freestyle,** and **individual medley (IM),** Stefano Battistelli was the bronze medalist in the 400 individual medley at the 1988 **Olympics** and earned a bronze medal at the 1992 Olympics in the 200 backstroke. At the **World Championships,** Battistelli was the silver medalist in the 1,500 freestyle in 1986 and in the 200 backstroke in 1991, when he also won bronze in the 400 medley and as a member of the Italian 800 freestyle **relay.**

BAUER, SYBIL (USA). B. 18 September 1903, Chicago, Illinois. D. 31 January 1927, Chicago, Illinois. Sybil Bauer was among the first great female **backstrokers,** winning the 1924 **Olympic** title in the 100 backstroke by more than four seconds. She was engaged to future television personality Ed Sullivan, but died from cancer before they were married.

BAUMANN, ALEXANDER SASHA (CAN). B. 21 April 1964, Prague, Czechoslovakia. Alex Baumann is one of the most accomplished swimmers in **Canadian** history. At the 1984 **Olympics** in Los Angeles, he captured gold medals in the 200 and 400 **individual medley (IM)** events, setting world records in both races. They were the last of five career world records and put to rest any doubt that his titles were hollow amid the boycott of many Eastern Bloc nations. At the 1986 **World Championships,** he was the silver medalist in the 200 individual medley and the bronze medalist in the 400 individual medley. Baumann was a double gold medalist in the medley events at the 1982 and 1986 **Commonwealth Games.**

BEARD, AMANDA RAY (USA). B. 29 October 1981, Newport Beach, California. Amanda Beard is one of the most successful **Olympic** swimmers in **United States** history, appearing in four Olympics and totaling seven medals. Beard first appeared in the Olympics as a 14-year-old at the 1996 Games, often toting her teddy bear around the deck. She won silver medals in the 100 and 200 **breaststroke** and gold as a member of the United States' 400 medley **relay.** She returned four years later in Sydney and captured a surprising bronze medal in the 200 breaststroke. At the Athens

Games in 2004, Beard won gold in the 200 breaststroke and silver medals in the 200 **individual medley (IM)** and on the United States' 400 medley relay. Beard did not begin training seriously for the 2008 Olympic Trials until a year before the event, but still managed to secure a berth to Beijing in the 200 breaststroke. At the Olympics, however, she failed to advance out of the preliminary round. At the 2003 **World Championships**, she was the gold medalist in the 200 breaststroke and silver medalist in the 100 breaststroke and 400 medley relay. Beard is equally known for her modeling career and posed nude for the July 2007 issue of *Playboy*. Beard's decision to pose for the magazine drew mixed opinions, some applauding her decision to show off an athletic body and others vilifying her as a poor role model for young female swimmers.

BEAUREPAIRE, FRANCIS JOSEPH EDMUND (AUS). B. 13 May 1891, Melbourne, Australia. **D.** 29 May 1956, Melbourne, Australia. Frank Beaurepaire had a lengthy career as one of the world's best **distance freestylers**, competing in the **Olympics** over a 16-year period for **Australia**. At his first Olympics in 1908, Beaurepaire was the silver medalist in the 400 freestyle and the bronze medalist in the 1,500 freestyle. Because he was giving swimming lessons in the lead up to the 1912 Olympics, Beaurepaire was deemed a professional and banned from competing. He returned to the Olympics in 1920, four years after the Games were postponed by World War I, and added another bronze medal in the 1,500 freestyle, a feat he would again duplicate in 1924. The 1920 and 1924 Olympics also brought Beaurepaire silver medals in the 800 freestyle relay. Following his swimming career, Beaurepaire was knighted and spent time in Australian politics.

BELOTE, MELISSA LOUISE (USA). B. 16 October 1956, Washington, D.C. Only a 15-year-old at the 1972 **Olympics** in Munich, Melissa Belote won three gold medals. In addition to sweeping the 100 and 200 **backstrokes**, the longer distance in world-record time, she led off the winning medley **relay**. Heading into the Games, Belote was considered the second gold-medal option for the **United States**, behind Susie Atwood. Belote also won the 200 backstroke at the first **World Championships** in 1973 and placed second in the 100 backstroke and as a member of the medley relay.

BENNETT, BROOKE MARIE (USA). B. 6 May 1980, Tampa, Florida. Brooke Bennett was a **distance freestyle** specialist who won three gold medals at the **Olympic Games**, one in 1996 in Atlanta and two at the Sydney Games in 2000. She won the 800 freestyle as a 16-year-old for her first Olympic title and, four years later, she doubled in the 400 and 800 freestyles. At the 1994 **World Championships** in **Rome**, she took the bronze medal in the 800 freestyle. At the 1998 World Championships, she was the champion in the 800 and took silver in the 400 freestyle and as a member of the **United States** 800 freestyle **relay**.

BERKOFF, DAVID CHARLES (USA). B. 30 November 1966, Philadelphia, Pennsylvania. Dave Berkoff is a former world-record holder in the **backstroke** events who changed the stroke due to his underwater prowess. He was the silver medalist in the 100 backstroke at the 1988 **Olympics** and took bronze four years later in Barcelona. At each of those Games, Berkoff helped the **United States** win gold in the 400 medley **relay**. Possessing one of the strongest underwater kicks in history, Berkoff would often nearly complete his laps while underwater, taking only a few strokes before turning at the wall. As a result of his tactics, and to place more emphasis on the stroke and not underwater kicking, the **Fédération Internationale de Natation (FINA)**, just after the 1988 Olympics, instituted a rule that forces swimmers to surface by the 15-meter mark of each lap. Berkoff set three world records in the 100 backstroke and became the first man to break the 55-second barrier when he went 54.95 at the 1988 United States Olympic Trials.

BERNARD, ALAIN (FRA). B. 1 May 1983, Aubagne, France. Alain Bernard is a **sprint freestyler** from **France** who enjoyed a rapid ascension in the sport, culminating in three medals at the 2008 **Olympics** in Beijing. Although Bernard was the gold medalist in the 100 freestyle and the bronze medalist in the 50 freestyle from the 2008 Olympics, Bernard is best remembered for being chased down by the **United States'** **Jason Lezak** in the 400 freestyle **relay**. Bernard entered his anchor leg with a considerable lead on Lezak and was still in front by nearly a body length heading into the final lap. Lezak, though, gradually closed the gap, with Bernard making a tactical error by swimming close to the **lane line** and allowing Lezak to draft off him over the last 50 meters. At the 2009 **World Championships**, Bernard was the silver medalist in the 100 freestyle and contributed to France's bronze medal-winning 400 freestyle relay. He was the 2008 European titlist in the 50 and 100 freestyles and has set world records in both the 50 and 100 freestyles.

BERRY, KEVIN JOHN (AUS). B. 10 April 1945, Sydney, Australia. D. 7 December 2006, Sydney, Australia. Kevin Berry was one of the best 200 **butterfly** swimmers of all time, setting five world records during a career that was highlighted by a rivalry with the **United States' Carl Robie**. After finishing sixth in the 200 butterfly at the 1960 **Olympics**, Berry won the gold medal in 1964, setting a world record and defeating Robie. He also helped **Australia** to the bronze medal in the 400 medley **relay**.

BIEBERSTEIN, ARNO (GER). B. 17 October 1886, Sachsen-Anhalt, Germany. D. 4 October 1918, Sachsen-Anhalt, Germany. Arno Bieberstein set a world record for **Germany** in the 100 **backstroke** en route to the gold medal at the 1908 **Olympics**.

BIEDERMANN, PAUL (GER). B. 7 August 1986, Sachsen-Anhalt, Germany. Paul Biedermann rose to stardom at the 2009 **World Championships**, where he took down a pair of world records held by iconic figures in the sport. Only sixth in the 200 **freestyle** and 18th in the 400 freestyle at the 2008 **Olympics**, Biedermann won titles in those events at the World Championships, his improvements partly due to hard work and partly aided by the **high-tech suits** that changed the sport in 2009. Biedermann won his first world championship in the 400 freestyle, taking down **Ian** Thorpe's global standard in the process. He then defeated **Michael Phelps** in the 200 freestyle, while simultaneously bettering Phelps' world record. From the 2008 Olympics to the 2009 World Championships, Biedermann lowered his best time in the 200 freestyle by four seconds, a drop the swimmer attributed to his swimwear, which allows swimmers to possess perfect body position and expend less energy, thus enabling them to be more fresh in the final stages of a race.

BIONDI, MATTHEW NICHOLAS (USA). B. 8 October 1965, Moraga, California. An 11-time **Olympic** medalist, Matt Biondi is one of the most decorated swimmers in history, best known for his **freestyle** prowess. At the 1988 Olympics in Seoul, he was expected to challenge the seven gold medals won by **Mark Spitz** at the 1972 Olympics in Munich. Biondi won seven medals at those Games— five gold, one silver, and one bronze. He earned his gold medals in the 50 and 100 freestyle events and as a member of three **United States relays**. Biondi was also an 11-time medalist at the **World Championships**, winning six gold medals between 1986 and 1991. At both of his World Championships, Biondi won gold in the 100 freestyle. During his career, which ended in 1993, Biondi set 12 world records.

BJEDOV, DURDICA (YUG). B. 5 April 1947, Split, Croatia. Durdica Bjedov won a pair of medals in the **breaststroke** events at the 1968 **Olympics** in Mexico City. In addition to garnering the gold medal in the 100 breaststroke, Bjedov was the silver medalist in the 200 breaststroke.

BLEIBTREY, ETHELDA M. (USA). B. 27 February 1902, Waterford, New York. D. 6 May 1978, West Palm Beach, Florida. Ethelda Bleibtrey was the first **United States woman** to win an **Olympic** gold medal in swimming and was the first woman to win three Olympic gold medals in the sport. At the 1920 Games, she was the champion of the 100 and 300 **freestyles** and helped the United States win the 400 freestyle **relay**.

BOITEUX, JEAN (FRA). B. 20 June 1933, Marseilles, France. Jean Boiteux was the first Frenchman to win an **Olympic** gold medal in swimming, winning the 400 **freestyle** at the 1952 Games. Boiteux added a bronze medal as a member of **France**'s 800 freestyle **relay**. He also competed at the 1956 and 1960 Olympics, but failed to win a medal.

BORG, CLAES ARNE (SWE). B. 18 August 1901, Stockholm, Sweden. D. 6 November 1987, Stockholm, Sweden. Arne Borg was a five-time **Olympic** medalist for **Sweden** who won the gold medal in the 1,500 **freestyle** at the 1928 Olympic Games. He also won the bronze medal in the 400 freestyle at the Amsterdam Games and four years earlier in Paris captured silver medals in the 400 and 1,500 freestyles and a bronze medal for his part in the 800 freestyle **relay**. Borg was the first man to swim the 1,500 freestyle in under 20 minutes and is recognized as being the first person to set a world record while wearing a suit of the **Speedo** brand, doing so in 1929.

BORGES, GUSTAVO FRANCA (BRA). B. 2 December 1972, Sao Paulo, Brazil. Gustavo Borges was a **Brazilian freestyle** specialist who medaled in three **Olympics**. At the 1992 Games in Barcelona, he won the silver medal in the 100 freestyle. He added a silver medal in the 200 freestyle and a bronze in the 100 freestyle at the 1996 Olympics in Atlanta and helped Brazil win a bronze medal in the 400 freestyle **relay** in 2000 in Sydney. Borges won two bronze medals at the 1994 **World Championships**, but had greater success at the **World Short Course Championships**, where he totaled 10 career medals, including four gold medals. Over the course of four Pan American Games, Borges collected 17 medals, including eight gold. Competing collegiately for the University of Michigan, Borges won the 100 freestyle from 1992 to 1995, the 200 freestyle on three occasions, and the 50 freestyle in 1995. Borges is the only male to win the 100 freestyle four times, and his 1995 Michigan team won the **National Collegiate Athletic Association (NCAA)** title.

BOTSFORD, ELIZABETH ANNE (USA). B. 21 May 1981, Baltimore, Maryland. Beth Botsford is one of several teenage **Olympic** medalists produced by the **North Baltimore Aquatic Club (NBAC)**. At the 1996 Olympics, Botsford won the gold medal in the 100 **backstroke** and led off the **United States'** gold-medal winning 400 medley **relay**. At the 1999 Pan American Games, she won a silver medal in the 200 backstroke and a bronze medal in the 100 backstroke.

BOTTOM, JOSEPH STUART (USA). B. 18 April 1955, Santa Clara, California. Joe Bottom was a top **sprinter** and **butterflyer** for the **United States**. At the 1976 **Olympics**, Bottom captured the silver medal in the 100 butterfly when he touched the wall 15 hundredths of a second behind **Australian Matt Vogel**. Bottom won the 1978 world title in the 100 butterfly, five years after taking the silver medal. He picked up three **relay** gold medals at the **World Championships** and was preparing for the 1980 Olympics in Moscow when the United States announced it would boycott the Games. Bottom set a pair of world records in the 50 **freestyle** in 1980.

BOUSQUET, FREDERICK (FRA). B. 8 June 1981, Perpignan, France. Fred Bousquet is a French **sprint freestyler** and **butterflyer** who competed collegiately in the **United States** at **Auburn University**, where he became a **National Collegiate Athletic Association (NCAA)** champion and the first man in history to break the 19-second barrier in the 50-yard freestyle. Bousquet has competed in three **Olympics**, but has never medaled in an individual event. He was a member of **France**'s silver-medal winning 400 freestyle **relay** at the 2008 Games in Beijing. At the 2009 **World Championships**, Bousquet was the bronze medalist in the 100 freestyle and took silver in the 50 freestyle.

BOVELL, GEORGE RICHARD LYCOTT (TRI). B. 18 July 1983, Trinidad, Trinidad and Tobago. George Bovell is the best swimmer in the history of Trinidad and Tobago, having represented his country at three **Olympics**. In 2004, Bovell won the bronze medal in the 200 **individual medley (IM)**, finishing behind Americans **Michael Phelps** and **Ryan Lochte**. Bovell, who was a star of **National Collegiate Athletic Association (NCAA)** championship teams at **Auburn University**, did not compete in the 200 individual medley at the 2008 Olympics, due to knee injuries that hampered his **breaststroke**. He did swim the 50 and 100 **freestyles**, finishing 11th in the 50 distance.

BOWMAN, ROBERT (USA). B. 6 April 1965, Columbia, South Carolina. Bob Bowman is an American swimming **coach** who has overseen the development of 16-time **Olympic** medalist **Michael Phelps**. Bowman competed collegiately for Florida State University and coached at various club programs in the **United States** before coming to the **North Baltimore Aquatic Club (NBAC)** in 1996 and remaining there until 2004. During that time, Bowman began to work with an 11-year-old Phelps, helping him set National Age Group (NAG) records. Under Bowman's watch, Phelps qualified for the 2000 Olympic Games in the 200 **butterfly**, finishing fifth in the final as a 15-year-old. In early 2001, Bowman helped Phelps become the youngest world-record holder in history when he set a global mark in the 200 butterfly. Bowman has guided Phelps to 20 medals, including 17 gold, over four **World Championships** and watched his pupil win six gold medals and two bronze medals at the 2004 Olympics in Athens. After those Games, Bowman left North Baltimore and became the head coach at the University of Michigan and its club program, Club Wolverine. Phelps made the move with Bowman, who also coached Olympians **Peter Vanderkaay, Erik Vendt, Klete Keller,** and Allison Schmitt. Bowman spent four years in Michigan, leading the college program to a Big Ten Conference championship in his final season, then chose to return to the North Baltimore Aquatic Club as its chief executive officer in 2008. At the Beijing Olympics, Bowman led Phelps to eight gold medals, a record for one Olympics that broke the mark of swimmer **Mark Spitz** at the 1972 Games in Munich. Bowman is known as a demanding taskmaster and has twice been a U.S. assistant coach at the Olympics and the head coach of the American team at the 2007 and 2009 World Championships. His interests include horse racing, as he owns Bowman Thoroughbreds, LLC, and classical music.

BRACK, WALTER (GER). B. 20 December 1880, Berlin, Germany. D. 19 July 1919, Berlin, Germany. Walter Brack was a double medalist for **Germany** at the 1904 **Olympics.** He was the gold medalist in the 100 **backstroke** and won the silver medal in the 400 **breaststroke,** an event that was contested just three times in Olympic competition.

BRAUN, MARIA JOHANNA (NED). B. 22 June 1911, Rotterdam, Netherlands. D. 23 June 1982, Gouda, Netherlands. Maria Braun was a world-class **freestyler** and **backstroker** who set world records in the 100 and 200 backstroke events. She was the first Dutch **Olympic** swimming champion, winning the 100 backstroke at the 1928 Olympics, where she added a silver medal in the 400 freestyle.

BRAZIL (BRA). Brazil ranks 20th for most **Olympic** swimming medals with 11, but its first gold medal was not won until the 2008 Games in Beijing, where **Cesar Cielo** beat the field in the 50 **freestyle**. In addition to Cielo's gold medal, Brazil has won three silver medals and seven bronze medals. **Gustavo Borges** is the most decorated Brazilian swimmer. He medaled in three Olympiads, claiming the silver medal in the 100 freestyle at the 1992 Barcelona Games, the silver medal in the 200 freestyle and the bronze in the 100 freestyle at the 1996 Atlanta Olympics, and a bronze in the 400 freestyle **relay** at the 2000 Games in Sydney.

BREASTSTROKE. The breaststroke is considered the most difficult of the four competitive **strokes** and is easily the slowest. The breaststroke requires the synchronization of arm and leg movements to maximize speed. The stroke's upper-body movement entails the swimmer pushing the arms forward, straight in front of the body, and then pulling them through the water in a sweeping motion. That movement is followed by the recovery phase, in which the swimmer brings the arms under the torso until they are extended forward once again. The elbows can never break the surface of the water. The lower-body movement, timed with the sweeping of the arms, requires the swimmer to perform a frog kick, in which the legs are flexed at the knees and thrust in an outward motion. At the start of the race and off each turn, swimmers perform a pullout, a movement in which they pull their arms to their sides to create momentum. The pullout also allows for the use of one **dolphin kick**, a rule change that was implemented in September 2005. At one time, the breaststroke and **butterfly** were synonymous, with athletes using the kick of the breaststroke, but utilizing the butterfly's upper-body movement, in which the elbows come out of the water and allow for greater power.

The 1956 **Olympics** marked the first time the butterfly was contested as a separate event. **Japan's Kosuke Kitajima** is considered the greatest male breaststroker in history, as he is the only man to win both the 100 and 200 breaststroke events at consecutive Olympics, a feat he accomplished in 2004 and 2008. The only **woman** to win both breaststroke events at the Olympics is **South African Penny Heyns**, who doubled at the 1996 Games in Atlanta. *See also* BEARD,

AMANDA; FIORAVANTI, DOMENICO; HANSEN, BRENDAN; HENCKEN, JOHN; WILKIE, DAVID.

BREEN, GEORGE THOMAS (USA). B. 19 July 1935, Buffalo, New York. George Breen flourished in the **distance freestyle** for the **United States** in the middle of the 20th century. He won bronze medals in the 1,500 freestyle at the 1956 and 1960 **Olympics** and was also the bronze medalist in 1956 in the 400 freestyle. He earned a silver medal in the 800 freestyle **relay** in 1956 and set two world records in the 1,500 freestyle during his career. One of his world records was in the preliminaries of his best event at the 1956 Games, a swim he couldn't duplicate during the championship final.

BRIGITHA, ENITH SIJTJE MARIA (NED). B. 15 April 1955, Willemstad, Curacao. Enith Brigitha was the first black swimmer to win an **Olympic** medal. At her first Olympics in 1972, Brigitha advanced to three individual finals for the **Netherlands**, but did not medal. At the 1976 Games, she won bronze medals in the 100 and 200 **freestyles**, beaten in the shorter distance by two **German Democratic Republic (GDR) women** suspected of **doping**. At the 1973 **World Championships**, she won the silver medal in the 200 **backstroke** and the bronze medal in the 100 freestyle. She added a silver medal in the 100 freestyle at the 1977 European Championships.

BRUNER, MICHAEL LEE (USA). B. 23 July 1956, Omaha, Nebraska. Mike Bruner was a **United States** standout in the middle-distance **freestyle** events and the 200 **butterfly**. A member of the dominating U.S. squad at the 1976 **Olympics** in Montreal, Bruner won the gold medal in the 200 butterfly, setting a world record in the process. He won his other gold medal as a member of the triumphant 800 freestyle **relay**. Two years after the Olympics, Bruner won the gold medal in the 200 butterfly at the **World Championships** in Berlin.

BURGESS, GREGORY STEWART (USA). B. 11 January 1972, Baltimore, Maryland. Greg Burgess was a two-time **Olympian** for the **United States** who starred collegiately for the University of Florida. At the 1992 Olympics, Burgess was the silver medalist in the 200 **individual medley (IM)**, finishing just behind individual medley legend **Tamas Darnyi** of **Hungary**. Burgess returned to the Olympics in 1996 and was sixth in the 200 individual medley.

BURKE, LYNN EDYTHE (USA). B. 22 March 1943, New York, New York. Lynn Burke dominated the 100 **backstroke** in 1960, setting four world records and winning the gold medal at the **Rome Olympics**. She also set a world record that year in the 200 backstroke and helped the **United States** to the gold medal in the 400 medley **relay** in Rome.

BURTON, MICHAEL JAY (USA). B. 3 July 1947, Des Moines, Iowa. Mike Burton was a **distance** great for the **United States** who posted back-to-back **Olympic** titles in the 1,500 **freestyle** at the 1968 Olympics in Mexico City and the 1972 Games in Munich. Burton also won gold in the 400 freestyle in Mexico City. In his first 1,500 freestyle championship, Burton recorded an 18-plus-second victory, the largest winning margin in Olympic history by either a male or female swimmer. When he won his second straight crown in the event, he was more than 46 seconds faster, proof of how far the event had developed in just four years. Burton set five world records in the 1,500 freestyle.

BUTTERFLY. The butterfly is one of the most difficult **strokes** in swimming, in which the arms move simultaneously in an arcing motion around the head. In international competition, it is contested over 50, 100, and 200 meters, although only the 100 and 200 distances are part of the **Olympic** program. Until 1952, the butterfly was part of the **breaststroke**, swimmers taking advantage of the upper-body movement of the butterfly while using the breaststroke kick. In 1952, however, the butterfly became a separate event and then became part of the Olympic schedule in 1956. The butterfly kick, known as the **dolphin kick**, features a swimmer keeping his or her legs together and moving them rapidly the way a dolphin does with its tail. The dolphin kick has also been successfully used by top **freestylers** and **backstrokers**.

Michael Phelps is considered the greatest butterfly swimmer in history, the 200 butterfly being the event that put him on the international map. Phelps won Olympic titles in 2004 and 2008 in the 100 and 200 butterfly events. Among **women**, the **United States' Mary T. Meagher** is viewed as the best butterflyer ever, having set world records in the 100 and 200 distances, which lasted nearly a decade each. *See also* BERRY, KEVIN; CROCKER, IAN; ENDER, KORNELIA; SPITZ, MARK.

– C –

CAMPBELL, CATE (AUS). B. 20 May 1992, Blantyre, Malawi. Cate Campbell emerged as a rising **sprint** star in **Australia** just before the Beijing **Olympics**. At the 2008 Games, she won a pair of bronze medals, one as a member of the 400 **freestyle relay** and one in the 50 freestyle. At her first **World Championships** in 2009, Campbell took the bronze medal in the 50 freestyle.

CANADA (CAN). Canada ranks 10th on the all-time list of **Olympic** swimming medals with 40, although only seven are gold. **Alexander Baumann** is considered one of Canada's greatest swimmers, having won gold medals in the 200 and 400 **individual medley (IM)** events at the 1984 Olympics. In 2005, as a way to enhance the country's performances on the international stage, Pierre LaFontaine was made the chief executive officer of **Swimming Canada.** Under his watch, Canadian swimming has improved, highlighted by Brent Hayden winning the world title in the 100 freestyle in 2007 and **Ryan Cochrane** winning the bronze medal in the 1,500 freestyle at the 2008 Olympics. *See also* DAVIS, VICTOR; HODGSON, GEORGE; LIMPERT, MARIANNE; MYDEN, CURTIS; OTTENBRITE, ANNE; TEWKSBURY, MARK.

CAREY, RICHARD JOHN (USA). B. 13 March 1963, Mount Kisco, New York. Rick Carey was an American backstroke specialist who won three gold medals at the 1984 **Olympics** in Los Angeles. Carey was denied the chance to race at the 1980 Games due to the **United States'** boycott. At the Los Angeles Games, Carey won the 100 and 200 **backstrokes** and swam the leadoff leg of the American-winning 400 medley **relay**. Carey was a three-time **National Collegiate**

Athletic Association (NCAA) champion at the University of Texas in the 200 backstroke and was a two-time NCAA champ in the 100 backstroke. At the 1982 World Championships, he took gold in the 200 backstroke and on the medley relay and was the silver medalist in the 100 backstroke. He set three world records in the 100 backstroke and two in the 200 backstroke.

CARLILE, FORBES (AUS). B. 3 June 1921, Armadale, Australia. Forbes Carlile is an Australian swimming coach who introduced several innovative ideas to the sport, including measuring heart rates to gauge an athlete's effort, using a pace clock, and utilizing interval training. A member of the International Swimming Hall of Fame (ISHOF), Carlile was the Australian Olympic coach in 1948 and 1956. In between, he competed in the modern pentathlon at the 1952 Olympics. Carlile's most prized pupil was Shane Gould, who won five medals at the 1972 Olympics, including three gold, and once held every freestyle record from the 100 distance through the 1,500. Carlile has also written books on the sport and opened a swim school in Sydney.

CARR, CATHERINE L. (USA). B. 27 May 1954, Albuquerque, New Mexico. Cathy Carr starred at the 1972 Olympics, winning the gold medal in the 100 breaststroke with a world-record time. She also handled the breaststroke leg on the winning 400 medley relay.

CASLARU, BEATRICE NICOLETA (ROU). B. 20 August 1975, Braila, Romania. Beatrice Caslaru was a multievent star for Romania who excelled greatest in the individual medley (IM) disciplines, but also was an international medalist in freestyle and breaststroke events. A four-time Olympian, she made her biggest imprint at the 2000 Olympics, where she was the silver medalist in the 200 individual medley and the bronze medalist in the 400 individual medley. Caslaru won her only medal at the World Championships when she took bronze in the 400 medley in 2001. Caslaru's best performances were at the European Championships, where she won 15 medals, including four gold. She was a medalist in four different individual events—the 200 and 400 medley races, the 200 breaststroke, and 400 freestyle.

CAULKINS, TRACY ANN (USA). B. 11 January 1963, Winona, Minnesota. Tracy Caulkins is one of the best all-around swimmers the sport has seen, her talent ranging to each of the **strokes** and varied distances. Caulkins was an international star in her early teens and, en route to the 1978 **Sullivan Award** as the top amateur athlete in the **United States**, won six medals at the 1978 **World Championships** in Berlin, including five gold. Her individual victories in the 200 **butterfly** and 200 and 400 **individual medley (IM)** events established high expectations for the 1980 **Olympics** in Moscow. However, due to the U.S. boycott, Caulkins was forced to wait until the 1984 Games in Los Angeles for her chance at Olympic glory. At the 1982 World Championships, she won bronze medals in both medley events, but she then took gold in the 200 and 400 individual medley disciplines in Los Angeles and was part of the gold-medal winning 400 medley **relay**. During her career, Caulkins set five world records, one each in the 200 butterfly and 400 individual medley and three in the 200 individual medley. She set 63 American records and won 48 national titles, split between **long course** and **short course**. Inducted into the **International Swimming Hall of Fame (ISHOF)** in 1990, Caulkins married Australian Olympic **Mark Stockwell**, the silver medalist in the 100 **freestyle** in 1984.

CHARLTON, ANDREW MURRAY (AUS). B. 12 August 1907, Crows Nest, Australia. D. 10 December 1975, Avalon, Australia. Andrew Charlton was among the first **distance** stars from **Australia**, participating in three **Olympics**. At the 1924 Games, Charlton won the gold medal in the 1,500 **freestyle** and added a bronze medal in the 400 freestyle to go with his silver as a member of the Australian 800 freestyle **relay**. Four years later, he was the silver medalist in the 400 and 1,500 freestyles. In his final Olympics, Charlton failed to earn a medal. He was once the world-record holder in the 1,500 freestyle.

CHINA, PEOPLE'S REPUBLIC OF (CHN). The People's Republic of China has had a checkered history in international swimming. While the nation has won 27 medals in **Olympic** competition, the use of **performance-enhancing drugs** by Chinese athletes tarnished the country's reputation in the 1990s. Several Chinese swimmers have failed **doping** tests, including **Wu Yanyan**, a former world-record holder in the 200 **individual medley (IM)**. At the 1994 **World Championships** in **Rome**, Chinese athletes won 12 of the 16 events on the **women**'s program, leading to speculation that performance-enhancing drug use was at work. The women's program has always been much more successful than the country's male swimming program. In the 2000s, there was less belief that a doping program was at work in China. With the nation hosting the 2008 Olympics in Beijing, a highlight of those Games was a gold-silver finish by **Liu Zige** and **Jiao Liuyang**. For the men, **Zhang Lin** won the silver medal in the **400 freestyle** and won the 800 freestyle at the 2009 World Championships, making him one of the most successful male swimmers in China's history. The country has a long-standing tradition in **diving** and ranks second in Olympic history with 48 medals, trailing only the **United States**. Fu Mingxia is one of the most successful divers in the country's history, having won four individual Olympic gold medals from 1992 to 2000. The Republic of China, commonly known as Taiwan, competes separately from the People's Republic of China. Its success in aquatic sports is not noteworthy. *See also* LE JINGYI; LIN LI; LUO XUEJUAN; PANG JIAYING; QIAN HONG; YANG WENYI; ZHUANG YONG.

CIELO, CESAR AUGUSTO (BRA). B. 10 January 1987, Sao Paulo, Brazil. Cesar Cielo became the first **Brazilian** swimmer to win an **Olympic** gold medal when he won the 50 **freestyle** at the 2008 Games. Cielo's award ceremony was among the most dramatic of the Olympics as he continually wiped away tears while sobbing at the playing of the Brazilian national anthem. He also shared the bronze medal with the **United States' Jason Lezak** in the 100 freestyle. Cielo won multiple **National Collegiate Athletic Association (NCAA)** championships at **Auburn University** and is considered the finest **sprinter** in collegiate history. At the 2009 **World Championships**, he affirmed his status as the best sprinter in the world, setting a world record en route to victory in the 100 freestyle, and also prevailing in the 50 freestyle.

COACHES. Coaches are the individuals responsible for preparing swimmers for competition by organizing practices and the training programs to which the swimmers abide. In addition to designing training sets for swimmers, coaches also oversee the **dryland training** of the athletes and frequently decide on the competition schedule of their swimmers. Probably the most important aspect of coaching is the creation of a **taper** that will allow the swimmer to perform at his best during major competitions. The taper process entails lowering a swimmer's training workload to the point where he is rested enough to swim his fastest times. Among the most decorated coaches in history are **Australia**'s **Forbes Carlile** and the **United States' Robert Kiphuth**, among the first men to emphasize interval training. Other famed coaches include the **United States' Mark Schubert, Eddie Reese**, and **Richard Quick**, each a multiple-time **Olympic** coach and mentor to college teams that won **National Collegiate Athletic Association (NCAA)** championships. Due to the pressure to produce champion swimmers, some coaches have used illegal methods to get more from their athletes. The most notable method of cheating is **doping**, in which coaches have their athletes take steroids or other **performance-enhancing drugs**. The **German Democratic Republic (GDR)** is best known for these violations, as many of its coaches in the 1970s and 1980s took part in a systematic doping program. In the late 1990s, two prominent East German coaches, Wolfgang Richter and Jurgen Tanneberger, were found guilty in German court of being part of the systematic doping program. *See also* BOWMAN, ROBERT; COUNSILMAN, JAMES; LAWRENCE, LAURIE; McKEEVER, TERI.

COCHRANE, RYAN (CAN). B. 29 October 1988, Victoria, British Columbia. Ryan Cochrane emerged in 2008 and 2009 as a world-class **distance freestyler**. He won the bronze medal in the 1,500 freestyle at the 2008 **Olympics** in Beijing and followed a year later by winning silver in the 1,500 freestyle and bronze in the 800 freestyle at the **World Championships**.

COHEN, TIFFANY LISA (USA). B. 11 June 1966, Culver City, California. Tiffany Cohen emerged as a top **distance freestyler** in the early 1980s, peaking for the 1984 **Olympics** in Los Angeles for the **United States**. At those Games, Cohen won gold medals in the 400 and 800 freestyles, winning by more than three seconds in the shorter event and by nearly six seconds in the longer discipline. As a prelude to Los Angeles, Cohen was the bronze medalist in the 400 freestyle at the 1982 **World Championships** and won the 400 and 800 freestyles at the 1983 Pan American Games. While competing for the **University of Texas**, she won two **National Collegiate Athletic Association (NCAA)** titles.

COMMONWEALTH GAMES. The Commonwealth Games is an Olympic-style competition held every four years between countries that are part of the Commonwealth of Nations, including **Australia, Great Britain, South Africa**, and **Canada**. Those nations have excelled the most in the swimming competition. The finest performance in Commonwealth Games swimming history was produced by Australian **Ian Thorpe** at the 2002 edition in Manchester, England. Thorpe won six gold medals and a silver medal and established a world record in the 400 **freestyle**.

COOPER, BRADFORD PAUL (AUS). B. 19 July 1954, Singapore. Brad Cooper was a **distance freestyler** from **Australia** who was involved in a controversial decision at the 1972 **Olympics**. After placing one hundredth of a second behind the **United States' Rick DeMont** in the 400 freestyle, Cooper was elevated to the gold medal after DeMont tested positive for a banned substance contained in his asthma medication. He was also fourth in the 200 **backstroke** and seventh in the 1,500 freestyle. A year later, at the first **World Championships**, Cooper placed behind DeMont in the 400 freestyle and was the bronze medalist in the 1,500 freestyle. He also enabled Australia to win the silver medal in the 800 freestyle **relay**. Cooper set one world record in the 400 freestyle and one in the 800 freestyle.

COUGHLIN, NATALIE ANNE (USA). B. 23 August 1982, Vallejo, California. Natalie Coughlin is considered one of the greatest swimmers in **United States** history. Although her best event is the 100 **backstroke**, she has demonstrated impressive versatility. Coughlin made her first international impact when she won the gold medal in the 100 backstroke at the 2001 **World Championships**. A year later, she became the first **woman** to break one minute in the event, and remained the only female to accomplish the feat for six years. Coughlin's efforts at the 2004 **Olympics** in Athens included an individual gold in the 100 backstroke, bronze in the 100 **freestyle**, and three medals in **relay** competition, including gold in the 800 freestyle relay. Leading into the 2008 Olympics in Beijing, she became the first woman to break 59 seconds in the backstroke and parlayed that performance into six medals at the Games. Individually, she repeated in the 100 backstroke and won bronze medals in the 100 freestyle and 200 **individual medley (IM)**. Coughlin has won 15 medals at the World Championships, five of each color, and has set American records in six events in the **long-course** format. As an athlete at the University of California–Berkeley, Coughlin won 11 of a possible 12 individual **National Collegiate Athletic Association (NCAA)** championships. Coughlin is coached by **Teri McKeever**, the first female to be named an assistant coach for a **United States Swimming** Olympic Team, earning that distinction in 2004 and 2008.

COUNSILMAN, JAMES EDWARD (USA). B. 28 December 1920, Birmingham, Alabama. D. 4 January 2004, Bloomington, Indiana. Doc Counsilman is considered one of the greatest **coaches** in the sport's history, his impact felt at the collegiate, national, and international levels. Counsilman was the 1964 and 1976 **United States Olympic Men's Swimming Team** coach, guiding the squad to 21 gold medals. He was the longtime coach at Indiana University and led the Hoosiers to six consecutive **National Collegiate Athletic Association (NCAA)** championships from 1968 to 1973. Counsilman was the founding president of the **International Swimming Hall of Fame (ISHOF)**, a past president of the American Swimming Coaches Association of America, and author of *The Science of Swimming*, a definitive book in the sport. Counsilman's coaching style included the study of film to analyze his swimmers' **strokes** and the use of **interval training**. Among his finest pupils were **Mark Spitz**, **Gary Hall Sr.**, and **Jim Montgomery**.

COVENTRY, KIRSTY LEIGH (ZIM). B. 16 September 1983, Harare, Zimbabwe. Kirsty Coventry is the most decorated athlete in Zimbabwe's history and considered one of the most versatile swimmers of her era. Coventry, a **National Collegiate Athletic Association (NCAA)** champion in the **United States** for **Auburn University**, has accounted for all seven medals won by Zimbabwe in Olympic swimming competition. Coventry won her first three Olympic medals at the 2004 Games, capturing gold in the 200 **backstroke**, silver in the 100 backstroke, and bronze in the 200 **individual medley (IM)**. At the 2008 Games, Coventry won silver medals in her first three events, the 100 backstroke and the 200 and 400 individual medley events, before repeating her title in the 200 backstroke. Coventry is an eight-time medalist at the **World Championships** and has set world records in the 100 and 200 backstrokes.

CRABBE, CLARENCE LINDEN "BUSTER" (USA). B. 7 February 1908, Oakland, California. D. 23 April 1983, Scottsdale, Arizona. Buster Crabbe was a **United States** swimming star in the first half of the 20th century. At the 1928 **Olympics** in Antwerp, Crabbe won a bronze medal in the 1,500 **freestyle** and just missed a medal in the 400 freestyle, placing fourth. Four years later in Los Angeles, Crabbe captured the United States only swimming gold medal, winning the 400 freestyle. He added a fifth-place finish in the 1,500 freestyle. After his swimming career, Crabbe made more than 100 movies, at one point following in the footsteps of fellow Olympic champion **Johnny Weissmuller** by playing the role of Tarzan.

CRAPP, LORRAINE JOYCE (USA). B. 17 October 1938, Sydney, Australia. Lorraine Crapp excelled in the **freestyle**, rating among the elite swimmers during the middle of the 20th century. At the 1956 **Olympics** in Melbourne, Crapp had a superb showing in her home nation. She won the 400 freestyle by nearly eight seconds over countrywoman and close friend **Dawn Fraser**. In the 100 freestyle, Fraser won the gold medal, with Crapp taking the silver medal. Together, Crapp and Fraser helped **Australia** win the 400 freestyle **relay**. At the 1960 Olympics in Rome, Crapp was on the Australian silver-medal winning 400 freestyle relay. Between the 100, 200, 400, and 800 freestyles, Crapp set seven world records.

CROCKER, IAN LOWELL (USA). B. 31 August 1982, Portland, Maine. Ian Crocker is a three-time Olympian who made his biggest mark in the 100-meter **butterfly**. He won gold medals as a member of the **United States'** 400 medley **relay** at the 2000, 2004, and 2008 **Olympic Games** and was the silver medalist in the 100 butterfly at the 2004 Games in Athens, losing to U.S. teammate **Michael Phelps** by four hundredths of a second. He placed fourth in that event at the 2000 and 2008 Games. Crocker won the 100 butterfly at the 2003 and 2005 **World Championships**, setting world records each time, and was the silver medalist in 2001 and 2007. At the **University of Texas**, Crocker won the 100 butterfly in each of his four years and won the 100 **freestyle** as a senior, setting a world record in the process. *See also* REESE, EDWIN.

CSEH, LASZLO (HUN). B. 3 December 1985, Budapest, Hungary. Laszlo Cseh is one of the most accomplished swimmers in the rich history of **Hungarian** swimming. Although Cseh has made his biggest impressions in the **individual medley (IM)** events, he is also an internationally acclaimed **backstroker** and **butterflyer**. At the 2008 **Olympics** in Beijing, Cseh was the silver medalist in three events, finishing behind the **United States'** **Michael Phelps** in the 200 and 400 individual medley events, along with the 200 butterfly. At the 2004 Games in Athens, Cseh won bronze in the 400 individual medley, fourth in the 200 medley, and sixth in the 100 backstroke. Cseh was the 2005 world champion in the 400 individual medley and owns seven medals from the **World Championships**. At the European Championships, he has been a gold medalist in the 200 and 400 medley disciplines and the 100 backstroke and has been a silver medalist in the 200 backstroke.

CSIK, FERENC (HUN). B. 12 December 1913, Kaposvar, Hungary. D. 29 March 1945, Sopron, Hungary. Ferenc Csik was one of the early **Hungarian** standouts, emerging as a world-class swimmer when he won the 1934 European title in the 100 **freestyle**. He followed two years later by becoming the **Olympic** champion in the event and helping Hungary to the bronze medal in the 800 freestyle **relay**.

CURTIS, ANN ELISABETH (USA). B. 6 March 1926, San Francisco, California. Ann Curtis was one of the stars of the 1948 **Olympics**, the first Games since 1936 due to the cancellation of the 1940 and 1944 Olympics during World War II. Curtis was the gold medalist in the 400 **freestyle** and helped the **United States** to the gold medal in the 400 freestyle **relay**. She added a silver medal in the 100 freestyle.

CZENE, ATTILA (HUN). B. 20 June 1974, Csongrad, Hungary. Atilla Czene was a **Hungarian individual medley (IM)** standout who peaked at the right time to achieve the biggest accomplishment of his career. After earning the bronze medal in the 200 individual medley at the 1992 **Olympics** in Barcelona, Czene moved up to the gold medal in Atlanta four years later, swimming the only time under two minutes. En route to the gold medal, Czene defeated Finland's **Jani Sievinen**, the favorite for the title and reigning world-record holder. Czene never won gold in another major international race, but took a pair of silver medals at the 1993 and 1995 European Championships, placing behind Sievinen on both occasions.

– D –

DANGALAKOVA, TANYA (BUL). B. 30 June 1964, Sofia, Bulgaria. At the 1988 **Olympics**, Bulgaria's Tanya Dangalakova was the surprise winner of the 100 **breaststroke**, beating world-record holder **Silke Horner**. Dangalakova was fourth in the 200 breaststroke, an event she won at the 1985 European Championships. On four occasions, Dangalakova was an individual bronze medalist at the European Championships.

DANIEL, ELEANOR SUZANNE (USA). B. 11 June 1950, Philadelphia, Pennsylvania. Ellie Daniel excelled in the butterfly events in two Olympiads for the **United States**. At the 1968 **Olympics** in Mexico City, Daniel helped the United States to the gold medal in the 400 medley **relay**, in addition to claiming the silver medal in the 100 **butterfly** and bronze medal in the 200 butterfly. Four years later, she repeated her bronze medal in the 200 butterfly and was the sixth-place finisher in the 100 butterfly. Daniel set three world records in the 200 butterfly during her career.

DANIELS, CHARLES MULDRUM (USA). B. 21 March 1885, Dayton, Ohio. D. 9 August 1973, Carmel Valley, California. Charles Daniels was one of the first elite **freestyler** swimmers for the **United States**, flourishing at the 1904 and 1908 **Olympics**. At the 1904 Games in St. Louis, Daniels won gold medals in the 200 and 400 freestyles, along with helping the United States to victory in the 200 freestyle **relay**. He added a silver medal in the 100 freestyle and a bronze medal in the 50 freestyle. At the 1908 Games, he prevailed in the 100 freestyle and was a member of the United States' bronze-medal winning 800 freestyle relay. In 1906, he won the gold medal in the 100 freestyle at the Intercalated Games in Athens.

DARNYI, TAMAS (HUN). B. 3 June 1967, Budapest, Hungary. Tamas Darnyi is considered one of the finest **individual medley (IM)** swimmers of all time, having won gold medals in the 200 and 400 medley events for **Hungary** at the 1988 and 1992 **Olympics**. Darnyi set six world records during his career, three in each medley distance, and won the 200 individual medley and 400 individual medley at both the 1986 and 1991 **World Championships**. At the 1991 World Championships, he added a bronze medal in the 200 **butterfly**. The Hungarian was the first man to break two minutes in the 200 individual medley, swimming 1:59.36 in 1991. Darnyi won eight gold medals during his career at the European Championships, four in the 400 individual medley, three in the 200 individual medley, and one in the 200 butterfly.

DASSLER, UWE (GDR). B. 11 February 1967, Ebersbach, Germany. Uwe Dassler is a former **distance** great for the **German Democratic Republic (GDR)** who captured the gold medal in the 400 **freestyle** at the 1988 **Olympics** with a world-record time that lasted almost four years. Dassler added a bronze medal in the 1,500 freestyle and earned a silver medal in the 800 freestyle **relay**. Dassler was a three-time European champion, twice in the 400 freestyle.

DAVIES, DAVID MICHAEL RHYS (GBR). B. 3 March 1985, Cardiff, Wales. David Davies is a British distance **freestyler** who has enjoyed equal success in the pool and **open-water swimming**. For three consecutive major international competitions, Davies was the bronze medalist in the 1,500 freestyle, taking third place at the 2004 **Olympics** and at the 2005 and 2007 **World Championships**. At the 2008 Olympics, Davies took sixth in the 1,500 freestyle, but a few days later earned the silver medal in the inaugural 10-kilometer open-water race. Davies has been a four-time silver medalist in the 1,500 freestyle at the European Championships, three times in **short course**, and once in the **long-course** pool. *See also* GREAT BRITAIN.

DAVIES, JOHN GRIFFITH (AUS). B. 17 May 1929, Willoughby, New South Wales. After placing fourth in the 200 **breaststroke** at the 1948 **Olympics**, Davies improved to win the gold medal in the event at the 1952 Games. *See also* AUSTRALIA.

DAVIS, VICTOR (CAN). B. 10 February 1964, Guelph, Ontario. D. 13 November 1989, Montreal, Quebec. Victor Davis was a **Canadian breaststroke** specialist who won a gold medal in the 200 breaststroke and a silver medal in the 100 breaststroke at the 1984 **Olympics** in Los Angeles. He also won four medals at the **World Championships**, two gold and two silver between 1982 and 1986. Davis, who set three world records in the 200 distance, retired from competition in 1989 and died that year after being struck by a hit-and-run driver.

DE BRUIJN, INGE (NED). B. 24 August 1973, Barendrecht, Netherlands. Inge de Bruijn, often referred to as Inky, was a dominant **sprint freestyler** and **butterflyer**. At the 2000 **Olympics**, de Bruijn captured gold medals in the 50 and 100 freestyles and the 100 butterfly, setting world records in the semifinals of the freestyle events and a world record in the butterfly final. She also helped the **Netherlands** to silver in the 400 freestyle **relay**. In Athens four years later, she repeated her Olympic crown in the 50 freestyle, won silver in the 100 freestyle, and earned bronze medals in the butterfly and as a member of the 400 freestyle relay. De Bruijn won five gold medals at the **World Championships**, along with a bronze medal. During her career, she established nine world records between the 50 and 100 freestyles and the 100 butterfly.

DEBURGHGRAEVE, FREDERIK EDOUARD ROBERT (BEL). B. 6 January 1973, Roeselaere, Belgium. Fred Deburghgraeve became the first Belgian swimmer to win an **Olympic** gold medal when he won the 100 **breaststroke** at the 1996 Olympics, setting a world record during qualifying. Deburghgraeve was the bronze medalist in the 100 breaststroke at the 1994 **World Championships** and won the world title in 1998.

DEMONT, RICHARD JAMES (USA). B. 21 April 1956, San Francisco, California. Rick DeMont was a premier **distance freestyler** in the 1970s who was stripped of a gold medal at the 1972 **Olympics** due to circumstances beyond his control. After winning the 400 freestyle at the Munich Games, DeMont's **doping** test revealed a banned substance that was contained in the medication he was taking for asthma. DeMont had indicated on his paperwork with the United States Olympic Committee (USOC) that he was taking the medication, but the USOC did not properly submit the information. Not only was DeMont stripped of his gold medal in the 400 freestyle, he was suspended for the rest of the meet and denied the chance to race the 1,500 freestyle, in which he was the world-record holder. In 2001, the USOC appealed to the International Olympic Committee (IOC) to have DeMont's gold medal reinstated, but the IOC turned down the request. A year after his Olympic disappointment, DeMont won the gold medal in the 400 freestyle at the first **World Championships**, becoming the first man to break four minutes in the event. He also won the silver medal in the 1,500 freestyle. DeMont set three world records during his career.

DENNIS, CLARA (AUS). B. 7 March 1916, Burwood, Australia. D. 5 June 1971, Manly, Australia. Clare Dennis' only **Olympic** title for **Australia** was in the 200 **breaststroke** at the 1932 Olympics in Los Angeles.

DE ROVER, JOLANDA (NED). B. 10 October 1963, Amstelveen, Netherlands. Jolanda de Rover is a former **backstroke** swimmer for the **Netherlands** who won two medals at the 1984 **Olympics** in Los Angeles, the second of her three Olympiads. Although de Rover never won a gold medal at the **World Championships** or European Championships, she claimed gold in the 200 backstroke at the 1984 Games. That performance was complemented by a bronze medal in the 100 backstroke, her only international medal in the shorter backstroke discipline. At the 1988 Games, de Rover returned to the final of the 200 backstroke, finishing seventh.

DE VARONA, DONNA ELIZABETH (USA). B. 26 April 1947, San Diego, California. Donna de Varona was an **individual medley (IM)** specialist for the **United States** who went on to a career in sports broadcasting. De Varona competed in her first **Olympics** in 1960 in **Rome** as a 13-year-old, then won Olympic gold in the 400 individual medley at the 1964 Games in Tokyo. De Varona also helped the United States to a gold medal in the 400 freestyle **relay** at her second Olympics. She set six world records in the 400 individual medley during her career and then started a career in sports broadcasting, which included coverage of the Olympics and an Emmy Award.

DEVITT, JOHN THOMAS (AUS). B. 4 February 1937, Granville, Australia. John Devitt was an **Australian freestyler** who earned four **Olympic** medals between the 1956 and 1960 Games. After winning the silver medal in the 100 freestyle in 1956, Devitt won the gold medal in the event in 1960 in a close finish with the **United States'** Lance Larson. Devitt was awarded the victory by the chief official after the judges of the race were split on who touched the wall first. Devitt added a gold medal in the 800 freestyle **relay** in 1956 and was a member of the bronze-medal winning 800 freestyle relay four years later.

DIBIASI, KLAUS (ITA). B. 6 October 1947, Tirol, Austria. Klaus Dibiasi is considered one of the best **divers** in history. After winning the silver medal in the **platform** competition at the 1964 **Olympics** in Tokyo, Dibiasi embarked on an unprecedented run by winning the gold medal in the platform event at the 1968, 1972, and 1976 Olympics, the last title a victory over **Greg Louganis**, at the time a rising star from the **United States**. Dibiasi's other Olympic medal was a silver in the three-meter **springboard** at the 1968 Games. At the 1973 **World Championships**, Dibiasi won gold in the platform and silver in the springboard, a feat he repeated at the 1975 World Championships. After his competitive career, Dibiasi served as the **Italian** diving **coach**.

DICARLO, GEORGE THOMAS (USA). B. 13 July 1963, St. Petersburg, Florida. George DiCarlo starred in the **distance freestyle** events for the **United States**. At the 1984 **Olympics**, DiCarlo was the gold medalist in the 400 freestyle and the silver medalist in the 1,500 freestyle. However, those Games featured the Soviet-led boycott, in retaliation for the U.S. boycott of the 1980 Olympics, and the defending champion in each of DiCarlo's events, the Soviet Union's **Vladimir Salnikov**, was absent from the competition.

DIEBEL, NELSON (USA). B. 9 December 1970, Chicago, Illinois. Nelson Diebel was a **United States breaststroker** who had best performances at the 1992 **Olympics** in Barcelona. In the final of the 100 breaststroke, Diebel won the gold medal by defeating **Hungarian Norbert Rozsa**, the world-record holder and favorite for the title. Diebel also swam the breaststroke leg on the United States' gold-medal winning 400 medley **relay**. Diebel was also a superb 200 breaststroker, capturing silver medals in the event at the 1989 **Pan Pacific Championships** and the 1991 Pan American Games.

DIERS, INES (GDR). B. 2 November 1963, Rochlitz, Germany. Ines Diers is one of only a handful of **women** to win five medals in swimming at a single **Olympics**, doing so for the **German Democratic Republic (GDR)**. She accomplished this feat at the 1980 Games in Moscow, winning gold in the 400 **freestyle** and 400 freestyle **relay**, silver in the 200 and 800 freestyles and bronze in the 100 freestyle. All but the 800 freestyle resulted in East German sweeps of the three medals. Her records are tainted, however, by the revelation of the systematic **doping** program used by East Germany during her career.

DISTANCE EVENTS. Swimming's distance events are generally regarded as the 800- and 1,500-meter events, lengths contested only in the **freestyle**. The 400 freestyle is occasionally regarded as a distance event, but fits better in the **middle-distance** classification. The **United States' Janet Evans** is considered the greatest female distance swimmer in history, while **Australian Grant Hackett** is regarded as the elite male distance swimmer in history. In Olympic competition, the 1,500 freestyle is only contested on the men's program, while the 800 freestyle is only contested on the **women**'s program. Since this is the only difference between the men's and women's Olympic schedules, arguments have been made for the 800 freestyle to be replaced by the 1,500 freestyle on the women's program. *See also* BENNETT, BROOKE; BURTON, MICHAEL; PERKINS, KIEREN; SALNIKOV, VLADIMIR; TAYLOR, HENRY.

DIVING. Although it is one of the five aquatic sports recognized by the **Fédération Internationale de Natation (FINA)**, diving enjoys little crossover with swimming. Athletes typically contest one of the sports, with the rare exception existing at the lower levels, such as high school competition.

Diving first debuted at the 1904 **Olympics** with a **platform** competition, while **springboard** diving was added at the 1908 Olympics. Scoring is conducted by a panel of judges, who rate the divers based on technique and difficulty of the dive. Platform diving takes place off a 10-meter high tower, while springboard diving is contested from a three-meter high distance in international competition. However, a one-meter competition on the springboard is a regular event in U.S. college competition and in high school competition. In 2000, the Olympics added **synchronized diving** competitions on the platform and springboard, disciplines in which teammates dive simultaneously and are judged on their technique and synchronization during the dive.

The **United States** (131) and the **People's Republic of China** (48) have won the most diving medals in Olympic competition. The United States' **Greg Louganis** is widely considered the greatest diver in history, repeating as Olympic champion in both disciplines at the 1984 and 1988 Olympics. *See also* DIBIASI, KLAUS; LEE, SAMUEL.

DOLAN, THOMAS FITZGERALD (USA). B. 15 September 1975, Arlington, Virginia. Tom Dolan distinguished himself by winning back-to-back **Olympic** championships in the 400 **individual medley (IM)** in 1996 and 2000, his second title in world-record time. At the 2000 Games in Sydney, Dolan also won a silver medal in the 200 individual medley, placing behind **Italian Massi Rosolino**. Dolan won world championships in the 400 medley in 1994 and 1998 and was a **National Collegiate Athletic Association (NCAA)** champion for the University of Michigan, winning the 500 and 1,650 **freestyles**

and the 400 individual medley twice each. Dolan's achievements are magnified by the fact that he overcame severe asthma that sometimes halted his training sessions.

DOLPHIN KICK. The dolphin kick is a maneuver used off the start and turn in which the swimmer, with legs together, flutters rapidly. It is primarily used during the underwater portion of the race in order to generate speed and momentum. In recent years, it has been referred to as the fifth **stroke**, and **Michael Phelps'** mastery of the dolphin kick has been a major key in his march to being the best swimmer in history. In the **breaststroke**, swimmers are allowed to use only one dolphin kick off the start and each turn. Any additional use of the dolphin kick in the breaststroke results in disqualification.

DOPING. Doping is an illegal practice in which athletes use **performance-enhancing drugs**, such as steroids, thus allowing them to better their times. Not only does doping enable athletes to swim faster, it allows them to handle heavier training regimens. Athletes who test positive for doping are usually subjected to two-year or four-year suspensions from competition.

While athletes have partaken in doping on an individual basis, the best-known form of the practice was the systematic program implemented by the **German Democratic Republic (GDR)** during the 1970s and early 1980s. During this era, **coaches** and doctors from East Germany either injected or orally provided anabolic agents to their athletes, the majority of which were teenage **women** who did not know what the practice entailed. During this era, the women from East Germany were largely unequaled, winning the majority of the medals at the **Olympics** and **World Championships**. Among the athletes who had admitted to being part of the program include **Petra Schneider**, an individual medley great. However, other athletes, such as **Kristin Otto**, have firmly denied being given drugs or taking part in a doping program. Paperwork released by the Stasi, the German secret police, support the systematic program that was used. Another country with a history of systematic doping is **China**, which dominated the 1994 World Championships and has had several athletes, including **Wu Yanyan**, banned for positive drug tests.

The **World Anti-Doping Agency (WADA)** is the group that oversees drug testing within the sport. *See also* ENDER, KORNELIA; MINISTRY FOR STATE SECURITY; TECHNOLOGICAL DOPING.

DOUBLE. A double is the casual term for two practice sessions in one day, a routine followed by the majority of world-class swimmers. Most elite-level performers take part in three doubles each week, with the other days featuring one practice in the water and a **dryland** workout. The term also refers to an athlete winning a pair of events in one session of competition.

DRUGS. *See* DOPING.

DRYLAND TRAINING. Dryland training, as its name indicates, defines exercises and training methods that occur outside of the pool. The use of dryland training was popularized in the 1940s by **Robert J. Kiphuth**, the longtime **coach** at Yale University. In this form of training, performed several times per week, swimmers take part in weight-training programs, running, biking, yoga, and stretching. The primary idea behind dryland training is to build muscle and core strength to enhance the stamina of a swimmer while in the water. All world-class swimmers partake in some form of dryland training, the most popular form being some type of weightlifting.

DUBOSCQ, HUGUES (FRA). B. 29 August 1981, Saint Lo, France. Hugues Duboscq is the best **breaststroker** in **France**'s history, but has mostly been a runner-up during his career. Duboscq won the bronze medal in the 100 breaststroke at the 2004 **Olympics** in Athens and followed with another bronze in the event in 2008, where he was also the bronze medalist in the 200 breaststroke. Duboscq was the bronze medalist in the 100 breaststroke at the 2005 **World Championships** and won the silver medal in the 100 breaststroke at the 2009 World Championships. He has won three individual silver medals and two bronze medals at the European Championships. His only gold medal in major international competition was in the 200 breaststroke at the 2008 European Short Course Championships, where he added a silver medal in the 100 breaststroke.

DUENKEL, VIRGINIA RUTH (USA). B. 7 March 1947, Orange, New Jersey. Virginia Duenkel entered the 1964 **Olympics** as the world-record holder in the 100 **backstroke**, but settled for the bronze medal in that event. However, Duenkel captured a gold medal in the 400 **freestyle**, an event in which she was the third-rated **United States** performer heading into the event.

DURACK, SARAH FRANCES (AUS). B. 27 October 1891, Bronte, New South Wales. D. 21 March 1956, Stanmore, New South Wales. Fanny Durack was the first **woman** to win an **Olympic** gold medal in swimming. At the 1912 Olympics, Durack won the 100 **freestyle** for **Australia** by more than three seconds.

– E –

EDERLE, GERTRUDE CAROLINE (USA). B. 23 October 1906, New York, New York. D. 30 November 2003, Wyckoff, New Jersey. Gertrude Ederle is one of the most accomplished **women**'s swimmers in history, her talents not limited to the pool. Although she won three medals at the 1924 **Olympics**, her greatest accomplishment was becoming the first woman to cross the **English Channel**, making the trek in 1926 and in a faster time that the five men who had previously crossed the English Channel. *See also* UNITED STATES.

EGERSZEGI, KRISZTINA (HUN). B. 16 August 1974, Budapest, Hungary. Krisztina Egerszegi is one of only two swimmers to win **Olympic** gold in the same event at three consecutive Games. **Australia**'s **Dawn Fraser** is the other, doing so in the 100 **freestyle**. Egerszegi accomplished this feat for **Hungary** in the 200 **backstroke** at the 1988, 1992, and 1996 Olympics. At the 1992 Olympics, Egerszegi also won gold medals in the 100 backstroke and 400 **individual medley (IM)**. She was the silver medalist in the 100 backstroke in 1988 and the bronze medalist in the 400 individual medley in 1996. Egerszegi won the 100 and 200 backstroke events at the 1991 **World Championships** and held the 200 backstroke world record from 1991 to 2008, when Zimbabwe's **Kirsty Coventry** went faster. She is a 12-time medalist at the European Championships, including nine gold medals.

ENDER, KORNELIA (GDR). B. 25 October 1958, Plauen, Germany. Kornelia Ender of the **German Democratic Republic (GDR)** finished her career with eight **Olympic** medals, including four gold at the 1976 Olympics in Montreal. Her gold medals came in the 100 and 200 **freestyles**, the 100 **butterfly**, and in the 400 medley **relay**, and all were recorded in world-record time. As a 13-year-old in 1972, she won three Olympic medals in relay duty and was the silver medalist in the 200 **individual medley (IM)**. A four-time gold medalist at the first **World Championships** (1973), she set 10 world records in the 100 freestyle and also set world marks in the 200 freestyle, 100 butterfly, and 200 individual medley. Ender is one of many East German female swimmers who was involved in the systematic **doping** program that spanned the 1970s and early 1980s. Ender, though, denies knowingly taking part in a doping program.

ENGLISH CHANNEL. The English Channel is part of the Atlantic Ocean that separates England and **France** and has become a major part of **open-water swimming.** The Strait of Dover, a 21-mile stretch of the Channel, has been regularly swam across and is considered one of the great feats by open-water enthusiasts. Matthew Webb is recorded as the first individual to swim across the English Channel, doing so in a little more than 21 hours in 1875. In 1926, **Gertrude Ederle** became the first **woman** to complete the crossing. The Channel Swimming Association serves as the official record-keeper of crossings and tracks records for age and time, among other categories.

ERVIN, ANTHONY LEE (USA). B. 26 May 1981, Burbank, California. Anthony Ervin had a highly successful career as a **sprint freestyler,** only to retire from the sport at the peak of his talent. At the 2000 **Olympics,** as a 19-year-old, Ervin tied for the gold medal in the 50 freestyle with **Gary Hall Jr.** While most sprinters enjoyed their greatest success in their mid-20s, Ervin was a prodigy and the first African American to medal in a swimming event at the Olympics. He also helped the **United States** to a silver medal in the 400 freestyle **relay** and was a four-time individual **National Collegiate Athletic Association (NCAA)** champion for the University of California–Berkeley. At the 2001 **World Championships,** Ervin doubled in the 50 and 100 freestyle events. However, after the 2003 NCAA season, Ervin faded away from the competitive swimming scene, not concerned with remaining an international standout.

ESPOSITO, FRANCK (FRA). B. 13 April 1971, Bouches-du-Rhone, France. Franck Esposito was one of the world's best 200 **butterfly** specialists throughout the 1990s and into the first few years of the new millennium. His biggest achievement arrived at the 1992 **Olympics** in Barcelona where Esposito won the bronze medal in his prime event. He was the silver medalist in the event at the 1998 **World Championships** and won four European titles, along with a silver medal in the 200 butterfly. At the 1993 **World Short Course Championships**, he was the gold medalist. Esposito set four world short-course records in the event.

EVANS, JANET ELIZABETH (USA). B. 28 August 1971, Fullerton, California. Considered the finest **distance** swimmer in female swimming history, Evans was a three-time Olympian who won five **Olympic** medals, including four gold, at the 1988 Games in Seoul and the 1992 Games in Barcelona. Evans won the 400 and 800 **freestyle** events and the 400 **individual medley (IM)** at the Seoul Olympics and repeated her title in the 800 freestyle in 1992, when she also took silver in the 400 freestyle. Her world record in the 800 freestyle of 8:16.22, which she set at the 1989 **Pan Pacific Championships** in Tokyo lasted until 2008, when **Great Britain's Rebecca Adlington** broke the record en route to the gold medal at the Beijing Olympics. Evans' 400 freestyle world record, which she **negative split** with a faster back half of the race, endured from 1988 through 2006. At the 1996 Olympics in Atlanta, Evans took part in the torch-lighting ceremony, handing the torch to boxing legend Muhammad Ali. *See also* WOMEN IN SWIMMING.

– F –

FALSE START. A false start is called when a swimmer leaves the **starting block** before the **official** signifies the start of the race. In international competition, one false start leads to disqualification. There was a time when swimmers were allowed one false start without disqualification, but that rule was changed to prevent swimmers from trying to get a flying start by guessing when the referee would begin the race. One of the most notable false starts in swimming history occurred at the 2004 **Australian Olympic** Trials when **Ian Thorpe** lost his balance on the starting block and fell into the water before the 400 **freestyle** started. It initially appeared Thorpe would not get the chance to defend his Olympic title in the event. However, Craig Stevens eventually conceded his place in the race to Thorpe, who went on to win his second consecutive gold medal.

FÉDÉRATION INTERNATIONALE DE NATATION. The Fédération Internationale de Natation (FINA) is the world governing body of aquatic sports, overseeing the disciplines of swimming, **diving**, **water polo**, **synchronized swimming**, and **open-water swimming**. The organization was founded in 1908 by a group of eight European countries and has been primarily based out of Lausanne, Switzerland, since 1986. From 1989 to 1992, FINA was based in Barcelona, Spain. It is responsible for setting the rules of the sport, including making any technical changes to the sport. FINA's two most prominent competitions are the **World Championships**, held every two years and including competition in all five of its governed disciplines, and the **World Short Course Championships**, a swimming-only event also held every two years. *See also* LARFAOUI, MUSTAPHA.

FERGUSON, KATHLEEN JANE (USA). B. 17 July 1948, Stockton, California. Cathy Ferguson captured two gold medals at the 1964 **Olympics** in Tokyo, including a victory in the 100 **backstroke**. Ferguson also guided the **United States** to gold in the 400 medley **relay** and set world records during her career in the 100 and 200 backstrokes.

FESENKO, SERGEY LEONIDOVICH (URS). B. 29 January 1959, Kryvyi Rih, Ukraine. Sergey Fesenko was a **butterfly** and **individual medley (IM)** specialist for the **Union of Soviet Socialist Republics (URS)**, his best success coming at the 1980 boycotted **Olympics** in Moscow. Fesenko was the gold medalist in the 200 butterfly and added a silver medal in the 400 individual medley. Fesenko's son, of the same name, competed collegiately for Indiana University and raced at the Olympics, but not with the same success as his father.

FILIPPI, ALESSIA (ITA). B. 23 June 1987, Rome, Italy. Alessia Filippi is an **Italian distance freestyle** star who also excels in the **individual medley (IM)** events. Filippi was the silver medalist in the 800 freestyle at the 2008 **Olympics** and won gold in the 1,500 freestyle and bronze in the 800 freestyle at the 2009 **World Championships**. Filippi has twice been the European champion in the 400 individual medley and won the silver medal in that event at the 2006 **World Short Course Championships**.

FIORAVANTI, DOMENICO (ITA). B. 31 May 1977, Novara, Italy. The first **Italian** to win an **Olympic** gold medal in swimming, Domenico Fioravanti captured first place in the 100 **breaststroke** and 200 breaststroke at the 2000 Olympics in Sydney. Fioravanti became the first man to win both breaststroke races at the same Olympics, although **Japan**'s **Kosuke Kitajima** repeated the feat in 2004 and 2008. A year after his Olympic victories, Fioravanti won a silver medal in the 100 breaststroke at the **World Championships**. He retired from the sport in 2004 due to a heart condition.

FLIP TURN. The flip turn is a routine maneuver used by swimmers in the **freestyle** and **backstroke** that allows them to push off the wall with their feet when beginning the next lap of a race. As swimmers approach the wall, they perform a somersault in the water, timed so that the feet are able to push off the wall with force. The flip turn is not used in the **butterfly** or **breaststroke** because swimmers are required to touch the wall with both hands simultaneously before starting their next lap.

FORD, MICHELLE JAN (AUS). B. 15 July 1962, Sydney, Australia. Michelle Ford excelled for **Australia** in the **distance freestyles** and the 200 **butterfly**. At the 1980 **Olympics**, she was the gold medalist in the 800 freestyle and added a bronze medal in the 200 butterfly. She narrowly missed out on a third medal, placing fourth in the 400 freestyle. She set two world records in the 800 freestyle.

FORO ITALICO. The Foro Italico is a sports complex in **Rome** that was the primary location of the 1960 **Olympics** and also served as the host of the 1994 and 2009 **World Championships.** The outdoor venue was the site of 43 world records at the 2009 World Championships, a total that was aided by the use of **high-tech suits** that have since been banned from the sport.

FOSTER, MARK ANDREW (GBR). B. 12 May 1970, Essex, England. Mark Foster is a five-time **Olympian** as a British sprinter, but has made his biggest marks in the sport in the **short-course** pool. Foster never won an Olympic medal, his highest finish being a sixth-place effort in the 50 **freestyle** at the 1992 Barcelona Olympics. Although he won a silver medal in the 50 freestyle at the 2003 **World Championships** and a bronze medal in the 50 **butterfly** at the 2001 World Championships, he is best known for his talent in the 25-meter pool. Foster is a 13-time medalist at the **World Short Course Championships,** including four victories in the 50 freestyle and two wins in the 50 butterfly. At the European Short Course Championships, Foster collected 24 medals, including 11 gold for triumphs in the 50 freestyle (six) and 50 butterfly (five). *See also* GREAT BRITAIN.

FRANCE (FRA). France sits 12th for most **Olympic** swimming medals with 33, but only four of the gold variety. The French have won 11 silver medals and 18 bronze medals. France, which has gotten stronger in recent years at the international level, nearly won its first **relay** gold medal at the 2008 Olympic Games, only to be caught at the finish by the **United States** in the 400 freestyle relay. **Laure Manaudou** is considered the top French swimmer in history, having once held the world record in the 200 and 400 **freestyles.** At the 2004 Olympics, she was the gold medalist in the 400 freestyle, the silver medalist in the 800 freestyle, and the bronze medalist in the 100 **backstroke.** *See also* BERNARD, ALAIN; BOITEUX, JEAN; BOUSQUET, FREDERICK; DUBOSCQ, HUGUES; ESPOSITO, FRANCK; LEVEAUX, AMAURY.

FRASER, DAWN LORRAINE (AUS). B. 4 September 1937, Balmain, Australia. The greatest 100 **freestyler** in **Olympic** history, **Australia**'s Dawn Fraser won her specialty event at three consecu-

FRIEDRICH, HEIKE • 43

tive Olympics, in 1956, 1960, and 1964. The only other swimmer to win the same event in three straight Olympiads is **Hungary**'s **Krisztina Egerszegi** in the 200 backstroke. Fraser added a silver medal in the 400 freestyle in 1956 and won four **relay** medals during her Olympic career. She set 11 world records in the 100 freestyle and held the world mark from 1956 to 1972, lowering the standard on nine occasions during that period, and is the first **woman** to break one minute in the event.

FREESTYLE. The freestyle is the most commonly used **stroke** in swimming, whether in a competitive atmosphere or in a recreational setting. It is the fastest of the four strokes, performed while on the stomach and features the arms alternating, one pulling through the water and the other out of the water. Breathing is typically done to the side, and the legs kick in alternating fashion. In competition, the freestyle is contested over distances of 50, 100, 200, 400, 800, and 1,500 meters.

Russian **Alexander Popov** is widely considered the best **sprint** freestyler in history among men, with **Australia**'s **Ian Thorpe** (**middle distance**) and **Grant Hackett** (**distance**) viewed as the best in their disciplines. Australian **Shane Gould** is considered the most versatile freestyler in **women**'s history, having once held the world record simultaneously from the 100 distance through the 1,500 distance. The **United States' Janet Evans** is unarguably the best female distance performer the sport has seen, and the **Netherlands' Inge de Bruijn** is considered one of the finest in the sprint races. *See also* BACKSTROKE; BREASTSTROKE; BUTTERFLY; FRASER, DAWN; VAN DEN HOOGENBAND, PIETER.

FRIEDRICH, HEIKE (GDR). B. 18 April 1970, Chemnitz, Germany. Heike Friedrich represented the **German Democratic Republic (GDR)** at the 1988 **Olympics**, the tail end of the systematic **doping** era that haunted swimmers from East Germany. Friedrich won the 200 and 400 **freestyles**, along with earning a pair of **relay** gold medals, at the 1986 **World Championships**. Two years later, at the Seoul Olympics, Friedrich was the gold medalist in the 200 freestyle, earned a gold medal in the 400 freestyle relay, and was the silver medalist in the 400 freestyle. She held the world record in the 200 freestyle from 1986 to 1994.

FRIIS, LOTTE (DEN). B. 9 February 1988, Horsholm, Denmark. Lotte Friis is a Danish **distance freestyler** who won the bronze medal in the 800 freestyle at the 2008 **Olympics**. At the **World Championships** the following year, Friis won the gold medal in the 800 freestyle and added a silver medal in the 1,500 freestyle.

FROLANDER, LARS ARNE (SWE). B. 26 May 1974, Boden, Sweden. Lars Frolander's ability in the pool spanned the **butterfly** and **freestyle**, but his greatest exploits were in the 100 butterfly. At the 2000 **Olympics** in Sydney, Frolander won the gold medal in the 100 butterfly, defeating world-record holder **Michael Klim** of **Australia**. At the two previous Olympics, Frolander helped **Sweden** win silver medals in the 800 freestyle **relay**. After winning Olympic gold, Frolander won the world championship in 2001 in his specialty event and was twice a silver medalist in the 100 butterfly and once in the 50 butterfly at the **World Championships**. He added two bronze medals in the 100 freestyle. Frolander was actually a better **short-course** swimmer, evident in his 14 medals, including seven gold, at the **World Short Course Championships**.

FURNISS, BRUCE MACFARLANE (USA). B. 27 May 1957, Fresno, California. Bruce Furniss was a multievent star for the **United States** in the 1970s, enjoying his biggest accomplishments at the 1976 **Olympics** in Montreal. Furniss set a world record on the way to a gold medal in the 200 **freestyle** and also helped the United States to gold in the 800 freestyle **relay**. Furniss was the world-record holder in the 200 **individual medley (IM)** at the time, but that event was stricken from the Olympic program for the 1976 and 1980 Games, preventing Furniss from adding to his medal count. Furniss was the silver medalist in the 200 and 400 freestyles at the 1975 **World Championships** and a member of the gold-medal winning 800 freestyle relay, which he also helped the United States win at the 1978 World Championships. He set four world records in the 200 freestyle.

FURNISS, STEVEN CHARLES (USA). B. 21 December 1952, Madison, Wisconsin. Steve Furniss was a top **United States** swimmer in the **individual medley (IM)** events and was followed as a star by his brother, **Bruce**. Furniss won the bronze medal in the 200 individual medley at the 1972 **Olympics** in Munich, where he just missed another medal by placing fourth in the 400 individual medley. Furniss was sixth in the 400 individual medley at the 1976 Olympics, where his brother was the gold medalist in the 200 freestyle. Furniss set the world record in the 200 individual medley in 1974, but had his sibling lower the mark nearly a year later.

FURUKAWA, MASARU (JPN). B. 6 January 1936, Hashimoto, Japan. D. 21 November 1993. Masaru Furukawa was the top **breaststroker** of the 1950s, setting one world record in the 100 distance and four in the 200 breaststroke. He won his sole **Olympic** gold medal for **Japan** in the 200 breaststroke at the 1956 Olympics.

– G –

GAINES, AMBROSE "ROWDY" (USA). B. 17 February 1959, Winter Haven, Florida. Rowdy Gaines is equally known for his talent in the pool and for his voice as a swimming commentator. As an athlete, Gaines was a top **United States freestyler** and expected to challenge for multiple medals at the 1980 **Olympics** in Moscow, only to be denied that opportunity due to the U.S. boycott, ordered by President Jimmy Carter. Four years later, Gaines received his Olympic chance in Los Angeles, but expectations were not high for his individual event, the 100 freestyle. Gaines, however, won gold after getting a great start, prompted by his coach, **Richard Quick**, noticing that the official starter was not holding athletes for a long time on the blocks. Gaines led from wire-to-wire, placing ahead of Australian **Mark Stockwell**, who was angered by the way the race started. Video footage shows Stockwell was not set before the **official** started the race. Gaines, a world-record holder in the 100 and 200 freestyle events, also helped the United States to gold medals in the 400 freestyle **relay** and 400 medley relay. At two **World Championships**, he earned five gold medals in relay events and three silver medals in individual competition. In his second career, Gaines has been an analyst for several networks, including the **National Broadcasting Company (NBC)** and ESPN, working meets such as the Olympic

Games, United States Olympic Trials, and **National Collegiate Athletic Association (NCAA)** Championships. His announcing style is known for being exuberant, with Gaines' voice frequently rising as races near their finish. He has continued to compete in United States **Masters Swimming** competitions, setting several national records. Gaines is also active on the motivational speaking circuit and regularly conducts swimming clinics for youths, combining instruction with his motivational speaking.

GEISSLER, INES (GDR). B. 16 February 1963, Sachsen, Germany. Ines Geissler was the **Olympic** gold medalist in the 200 **butterfly** in 1980, where she also placed seventh in the 800 **freestyle** for the **German Democratic Republic (GDR)**. At the 1982 **World Championships**, she won the 200 butterfly and was part of the triumphant 400 medley **relay**, along with taking silver in the 100 butterfly. Geissler is suspected of using **performance-enhancing drugs** as part of the systematic **doping** program of East Germany during the 1970s and 1980s.

GENTER, ROBERT STEVEN (USA). B. 4 January 1951, Artesia, California. Steve Genter was a **middle-distance freestyler** for the **United States** who overcame a medical issue to win three medals at the 1972 **Olympics** in Munich. Despite suffering a collapsed lung a week before the Games and not receiving approval from doctors to swim, Genter competed anyway. He helped the United States to a gold medal in the 800 freestyle **relay** and won silver medals in the 200 and 400 freestyles. Genter placed behind **Mark Spitz** in the 200 freestyle and was initially third in the 400 freestyle, but was bumped to the silver medal when apparent gold medalist **Rick DeMont** was disqualified for testing positive for a banned substance in his asthma medication.

GERMAN DEMOCRATIC REPUBLIC (GDR). The German Democratic Republic, commonly known as East Germany, was a superpower in swimming until the fall of the Berlin Wall, at which time it was reunited with the **Federal Republic of Germany (FRG)** to form **Germany**. The German Democratic Republic was its own nation from 1949 to 1990. While there were several male swimming stars for East Germany, its greatest medal hauls were provided by the **women**, many of whom were part of a systematic **doping** program implemented by the government in the 1970s and 1980s. Oftentimes, teenage swimmers were given oral steroids by their coaches to enhance performance. Among the women who admitted to steroid use were Olympic champions **Petra Schneider** and **Ute Geweniger**. Some athletes, such as **Kristin Otto**, have maintained they did not take **performance-enhancing drugs**. Although East Germany last competed at the **Olympics** as the GDR in 1988, it remains third on the all-time swimming medal list with 98, including 38 gold. The East German women enjoyed their best Olympic showing at the 1980 Games in Moscow, winning 24 medals. They won 18 medals in 1976 and 22 in 1988. The best-known male swimmer from East Germany was **Roland Matthes**, the 100 and 200 **backstroke** champion at the 1968 and 1972 Olympics. *See also* ANKE, HANNELORE; DASSLER, UWE; DIERS, INES; ENDER, KORNELIA; FRIEDRICH, HEIKE; GEISSLER, INES; HORNER, SILKE; KOTHER, ROSEMARIE; KRAUSE, BARBARA; METSCHUCK, CAREN; MINISTRY FOR STATE SECURITY; NORD, KATHLEEN; PFEIFFER, STEFAN; POLLACK, ANDREA; REINISCH, RICA; RICHTER, ULRIKE; TAUBER, ULRIKE; THUMER, PETRA; WOITHE, JORG.

GERMANY (GER). Germany has a storied swimming history, albeit one that is complicated by its separation during the Cold War. During the first half of the 20th century, German athletes competed under one flag, including during the rule of Adolf Hitler. However, with split of the country into the **German Democratic Republic (GDR)** and the **Federal Republic of Germany (FRG)** in 1949, the nations eventually competed separately in international competition. From 1956 through 1988, East Germany and West Germany fielded their own swimming teams, East Germany being more dominant. After the fall of the Berlin Wall in 1989, East Germany and West Germany reunited as Germany, which has competed as one nation since the 1992 **Olympics** and the 1991 **World Championships**. *See also* BATHE, WALTER; BIEBERSTEIN, ARNO; BIEDERMANN, PAUL; BRACK, WALTER; HAPPE, URSULA; HASE, DAGMAR; HOPPENBERG, ERNST; HUNGER, DANIELA; LURZ,

THOMAS; POLESKA, ANNE; RAUSCH, EMIL; SCHRADER, HILDEGARD; STEFFEN, BRITTA; VOLKER, SANDRA.

GERMANY, FEDERAL REPUBLIC (FRG). The Federal Republic of Germany, commonly referred to as West Germany, was its own nation from 1949 to 1990, until it was reunited with the **German Democratic Republic (GDR)** after the fall of the Berlin Wall. West Germany did not have the same success as East Germany in the pool, largely because East Germany was fueled by a systematic **doping** system in which steroids were fed to its athletes. West Germany collected 22 medals in **Olympic** competition, with all three of its gold medals captured by **Michael Gross**. Nicknamed the Albatross, Gross won the 200 **freestyle** and 100 **butterfly** at the 1984 Olympics and the 200 butterfly at the 1988 Games.

GEWENIGER, UTE (GDR). B. 24 February 1964, Chemnitz, Germany. Ute Geweniger was a member of the elite **German Democratic Republic (GDR)** swim team that dominated the sport in the 1970s and 1980s. She was the gold medalist in the 100 **breaststroke** at the 1980 **Olympics** in Moscow and also picked up a gold medal for her part in the winning 400 medley **relay**. Geweniger did not get the chance to defend her title in Los Angeles in 1984 because of the Soviet-led boycott of the Games, a retaliation for the **United States'** boycott of four years earlier. Geweniger, who admitted to being **doped** by her **coaches**, was the 1982 world champion in the 100 breaststroke and the silver medalist in the 200 breaststroke and 200 **individual medley (IM)**. She set six world records in the 100 breaststroke and one in the 200 individual medley, her record lasting from 1981 to 1992.

GILLINGHAM, NICHOLAS (GBR). B. 22 January 1967, Walsall, England. Nick Gillingham was a **breaststroke** specialist for **Great Britain**, earning a podium position at consecutive **Olympic Games**. At the 1988 Games in Seoul, Gillingham was the silver medalist in the 200 breaststroke. He earned another medal in the event at the 1992 Olympics, winning the bronze with a time that would have won every previous title. Gillingham was the bronze medalist in the 200 breaststroke at the 1991 **World Championships**, won the gold medal in the event at the 1993 **World Short Course Championships**, and twice won gold in the 200 breaststroke at the European Championships. He once shared the world record with the **United States' Mike Barrowman**.

GOODELL, BRIAN STUART (USA). B. 2 April 1959, Stockton, California. Brian Goodell was a **distance** specialist who was a member of the 1976 **United States Olympic Swimming Team** that won gold in 12 of the 13 swimming events and 27 medals overall. Goodell won gold medals in the 400 and 1,500 **freestyles**, events in which he totaled five world records during his career. Goodell earned a silver medal in the 1,500 freestyle at the 1975 **World Championships** and won nine individual **National Collegiate Athletic Association (NCAA)** titles while representing the University of California–Los Angeles (UCLA), three in the 500 freestyle, three in the 1,650 freestyle, and three in the 400 **individual medley (IM)**.

GOODHEW, DUNCAN ALEXANDER (GBR). B. 27 May 1957, London, England. Duncan Goodhew contributed to **Great Britain's** strong history in the **breaststroke** by winning the gold medal in the 100 breaststroke at the 1980 **Olympics** in Moscow. It was the only major title of his career, obtained at a Games boycotted by the **United States**, which would have had numerous medal contenders. Goodhew swam the breaststroke leg on the British medley **relay** that took bronze in Moscow, and he won silver medals in the 100 and 200 breaststrokes at the 1978 **Commonwealth Games**.

GOULD, SHANE ELIZABETH (AUS). B. 23 November 1956, Brisbane, Australia. Shane Gould was a young **Australian** prodigy who accomplished a great deal in the sport, but whose early retirement precluded her from achieving greater heights. As a 15-year-old at the 1972 **Olympics**, Gould won gold medals, all in world-record time, in the 200 and 400 **freestyles** and the 200 **individual medley (IM)**. She added a silver medal in the 800 freestyle, a bronze medal in the 100 freestyle, and was the first female swimmer to win five medals in one Olympiad. Munich was her only Olympic foray, as Gould retired from swimming as a 16-year-old, uncomfortable with the intense media attention cast upon her. Gould remains the only swimmer, male or female, to simultaneously hold world records in every freestyle distance—the 100, 200, 400, 800, and 1,500. She accomplished this feat in 1971 and managed to set 11 world records during her brief, but sensational, career.

GRAEF, JEDWARD RICHARD (USA). B. 1 May 1942, Montclair, New Jersey. Jed Graef's only major international victory arrived at the 1964 **Olympics.** Graef set a world record in the 200 **backstroke** to win the gold medal. His other significant triumph was a **National Collegiate Athletic Association (NCAA)** title for Princeton University in the 200 backstroke. *See also* UNITED STATES.

GREAT BRITAIN (GBR). Swimming has a rich history in Great Britain, which ranks fourth on the list of most **Olympic** swimming medals. Great Britain has won 64 medals in Olympic competition: 15 gold, 21 silver, and 28 bronze. It had its most success during the first half of the 20th century, but has continued to be a prominent nation in international competition. **Henry Taylor** is considered the most successful male swimmer in Great Britain's history, having won gold medals in the 400 and 1,500 **freestyles** at the 1908 Olympics. British **women** have not matched the success of their male counterparts, although **Rebecca Adlington** has contributed to a recent surge. Adlington won gold medals at the 2008 Olympics in the 400 and 800 freestyles, becoming Great Britain's first female Olympic swimming champion since **Anita Lonsbrough** won the 200 **breaststroke** at the 1960 Olympics. Great Britain will host the Olympic Games in 2012 when they are held in London. *See also* DAVIES, DAVID; FOSTER, MARK; GILLINGHAM, NICHOLAS; GOODHEW, DUNCAN; GRINHAM, JUDITH; HARDCASTLE, SARAH; HOLMAN, FREDERICK; JARVIS, JOHN; MOORHOUSE, ADRIAN; MORTON, LUCILLE; WILKIE, DAVID.

GRINHAM, JUDITH BRENDA (GBR). B. 5 March 1939, London, England. Judith Grinham was the first British **woman** in 32 years to win an **Olympic** gold medal in swimming when she won the 100 **backstroke** title at the 1956 Games. Also a standout in the **freestyle** events, Grinham remains the only British woman to win Olympic gold in the event. *See also* GREAT BRITAIN.

GROSS, MICHAEL (FRG). B. 17 June 1964, Frankfurt, Germany. A versatile **freestyler** and **butterflyer** from the **Federal Republic of Germany (FRG)**, Michael Gross was nicknamed "The Albatross" for his wingspan that stretches more than seven feet. Gross won six medals between the 1984 and 1988 **Olympics**, winning gold in the 200 freestyle and 100 butterfly at Los Angeles Games and the gold medal in the 200 butterfly at the Seoul Games. Gross won 13 medals at the **World Championships**, five gold, five silver, and three bronze. At the European Championships, he was an 18-time medalist, with 13 being gold. Gross set 10 individual world records during his career, spanning the 200 freestyle, 400 freestyle, 100 butterfly, and 200 butterfly.

GUTTLER, KAROLY (HUN). B. 15 June 1968, Budapest, Hungary. Part of a long line of world-class **breaststrokers** from **Hungary**, Karoly Guttler was the silver medalist in the 100 breaststroke at the 1988 **Olympics** and was the silver medalist in the 200 breaststroke in 1996. He was fifth in the 200 breaststroke at the 1992 Games and fourth in the 100 breaststroke in 1996. Guttler had difficulty rising to the top of his discipline at the international level, as his only gold medal was in the 100 breaststroke at the 1993 European Championships. Guttler won a silver medal in the 100 breaststroke and a bronze in the 200 breaststroke at the 1994 **World Championships** and was a nine-time medalist at the European Championships.

GYENGE, VALERIA (HUN). B. 3 April 1933, Budapest, Hungary. Valeria Gyenge accounted for one of several highlights for **Hungary** at the 1952 **Olympics**. Gyenge was the winner of the 400 **freestyle**, one of three triumphs for her country in the **women's** swimming competition.

GYURTA, DANIEL (HUN). B. 4 May 1989, Szombathely, Hungary. Before he was a teenager, Daniel Gyurta was identified as one of the next great 200 **breaststrokers** in **Hungary** and the world. He posted several world-class times as young as 12 years old and won the silver medal in the 200 breaststroke as a 15-year-old at the 2004 **Olympics** in Athens. Gyurta was fifth in that event at the 2008 Olympics, although he set an Olympic record in the preliminary round. Gyurta is known for his strong finishes, often trailing the competition in the first 100 meters, but surging past his rivals over the final two laps of the 200 breaststroke. He used this technique to win the 2009 world championship in the 200 breaststroke, moving from eighth at the midway point to beat the United States' Eric Shanteau by one hundredth of a second.

– H –

HACKETT, GRANT GEORGE (AUS). B. 9 May 1980, Southport, Australia. Sometimes overshadowed by his **Australian** counterpart **Ian Thorpe**, Grant Hackett is recognized as one of the best **distance freestylers** in history, the finest over 1,500 meters. Hackett won seven **Olympic** medals, including championships in the 1,500 freestyle at the 2000 and 2004 Games. He made a push for a third consecutive title at the 2008 Games, but took the silver medal behind Tunisia's **Ous Mellouli**. The runner-up finish was Hackett's final race. He also won a silver medal in the 400 freestyle, finishing behind Thorpe at the 2004 Olympics. Hackett is the only swimmer to win four straight world championships in an event, prevailing in the 1,500 freestyle at the 1998, 2001, 2003, and 2005 **World Championships**. He owns 18 medals from the World Championships, the second-highest total in history, trailing only **Michael Phelps**. In addition to setting a world record in the 1,500 freestyle, he briefly held the world record in the 200 freestyle.

HAINES, GEORGE FREDERICK (USA). B. 9 March 1924, Huntington, Indiana. D. 1 May 2006, Carmichael, California. In some circles, George Haines is regarded as the best **coach** in **United States** history. Haines founded the highly successful **Santa Clara Swim Club (SCSC)** in 1951 and turned the team into the top club program in the world. From 1960 to 1988, Haines guided 53 **Olympic** swimmers who combined to win 68 medals at the Games. Haines was a three-time head coach of the United States Olympic Team and served as an assistant coach at four Olympics. He was the head coach of the U.S. Team at the 1978 **World Championships** and had college coaching tenures with the University of California–Los Angeles

(UCLA) men's squad and **Stanford University**'s women's team, which he led to a **National Collegiate Athletic Association (NCAA)** championship during the 1983 season. Among the athletes coached by Haines were Olympic champions **Mark Spitz, Don Schollander,** and **Claudia Kolb.** To commemorate Haines' contributions to the sport, a bronze statue of Haines stands at the Santa Clara Swim Center.

HAISLETT, NICOLE LEA (USA). B. 16 December 1972, St. Petersburg, Florida. Nicole Haislett was a **United States freestyler** who won the **Olympic** gold medal in the 200 freestyle at the 1992 Olympics in Barcelona. She is the last U.S. female to win that event. At those Olympics, Haislett also guided the United States to gold medals in the 400 freestyle and 400 medley **relays.** She was the 1991 world champion in the 100 freestyle and was on two winning American relays. At the University of Florida, she won the 200 freestyle at all four of her **National Collegiate Athletic Association (NCAA)** Championships and took first in the 500 freestyle once. Haislett held the American record in the 200 freestyle for nearly 11 years.

HAJOS, ALFRED (HUN). B. 21 February 1878, Budapest, Hungary. D. 12 November 1955, Budapest, Hungary. Alfred Hajos was among the first swimming stars, competing at the inaugural modern **Olympics** in Athens, where he was the gold medalist in the 100 and 1,200 **freestyles** for **Hungary.** Hajos was also an Olympian in 1924, 1928, and 1932, competing in the artistic competitions that were held at the time. He won a silver medal in art in 1924. Hajos became known for his architecture skills and designed several sports complexes, including the swimming venue in Budapest, which hosted the 2006 European Championships.

HALL, GARY SR. (USA). B. 7 August 1951, Fayetteville, North Carolina. Gary Hall competed in three **Olympics,** medaling in three events, one at each Games. At the 1968 Games in Mexico City, he earned a silver medal in the 400 **individual medley (IM),** then followed with a silver in 1972 in Munich in the 200 **butterfly.** He closed out his Olympic career in Montreal in 1976 with a bronze medal in the 100 butterfly. Versatility was a hallmark of Hall's career, evident in his world records in the 200 and 400 individual medley, the 200 **backstroke**, and the 200 butterfly. Hall's son, sharing the same name, was a 10-time Olympic medalist who repeated as champion in the 50 freestyle in 2000 and 2004. *See also* UNITED STATES.

HALL, GARY WAYNE JR. (USA). B. 26 September 1974, Cincinnati, Ohio. Gary Hall is a 10-time **Olympic** medalist who has overcome a medical condition to become one of the most decorated Olympians in **United States** history. A **sprint-freestyle** specialist, Hall won back-to-back titles in the 50 freestyle at the 2000 and 2004 Olympics, the first of those championships a tie with countryman **Anthony Ervin**. Hall also won silver medals in the 50 and 100 freestyles at the 1996 Olympics, finishing behind rival **Alexander Popov** in both races. At the 2000 Games, he added a bronze medal in the 100 freestyle. Hall has helped the United States to five **relay** medals, including three gold. Between the 2000 and 2004 Olympics, Hall rarely raced competitively, choosing to bypass two **World Championships**. The lack of racing, however, did not affect him once it was time to compete in Athens.

Diagnosed with type 1 diabetes, Hall has had to manage his medical condition and has been a spokesman for overcoming the disease and motivating younger athletes with the affliction. He has also been outspoken about the use of **performance-enhancing drugs** and in 2003 developed **The Race Club**, a professional team that trains in Florida and features some of the best sprinters in the world. Hall's flamboyant personality has been embraced by many and criticized by others. He has often worn boxing robes and red, white, and blue shorts to the starting block and played to the fans when being introduced. At the 2000 Olympics, he boldly predicted the United States would "smash" the Australians in the 400 freestyle relay, only to have the Aussies win, with Hall touching for the silver medal while handling the anchor leg. His father, of the same name, was a three-time Olympian who won a medal each at the 1968, 1972, and 1976 Games.

HALL, KAYE MARIE (USA). B. 15 May 1951, Tacoma, Washington. Kaye Hall left the 1968 **Olympics** in Mexico City with three medals. She was the champion of the 100 **backstroke**, setting a world record on the way to victory. She earned a second gold medal as a member of the **United States'** winning 400 medley **relay** and was the bronze medalist in the 200 backstroke.

HALL OF FAME. *See* INTERNATIONAL SWIMMING HALL OF FAME.

HAMURO, TETSUO (JPN). B. 7 September 1917, Fukuoka, Japan. D. 30 October 2005, Osaka, Japan. Tetsuo Hamuro continued **Japan's breaststroke** dominance at the 1936 **Olympics.** Hamuro won the 200 breaststroke, the third straight year a Japanese swimmer won the event.

HANSEN, BRENDAN JOSEPH (USA). B. 15 August 1981, Havertown, Pennsylvania. Brendan Hansen is regarded as the best **breaststroker** in **United States** history, having set five individual world records. He won four **Olympic** medals, including a pair of gold medals as a member of the United States' 400 medley **relay** in 2004 and 2008. At the 2004 Olympics in Athens, Hansen was the silver medalist in the 100 breaststroke and the bronze medalist in the 200 breaststroke. He was the world champion in the 100 breaststroke in 2005 and 2007 and the world champion in the 200 breaststroke in 2001 and 2005. At the **University of Texas**, Hansen was the **National Collegiate Athletic Association (NCAA)** champion in the 100 and 200 breaststroke for four consecutive years, becoming the first man to sweep those events during his collegiate career. *See also* REESE, EDWIN.

HANSON, BROOKE LOUISE (AUS). B. 18 March 1978, Manly, Australia. Brooke Hanson was a **breaststroke** specialist for **Australia** who occasionally excelled in the **individual medley (IM)**. At the 2004 Olympics, she was the silver medalist in the 100 breaststroke and helped Australia to a gold medal in the 400 medley **relay**. She twice medaled at the **World Championships** in the 50 breaststroke, winning silver in 2003 and bronze in 2005. Hanson's biggest international success came at the 2004 **World Short Course Championships** in Indianapolis when she won five individual gold medals, sweeping the 50, 100, and 200 breaststroke events and prevailing in the 100 and 200 individual medley.

HAPPE, URSULA (GER). B. 20 October 1926, Gdansk, Poland. After failing to qualify for the final of the 200 **breaststroke** at the 1952 **Olympics**, Ursula Happe captured the gold medal in the event at the 1956 Games. *See also* GERMANY.

HARDCASTLE, SARAH LUCY (GBR). B. 9 April 1969, Essex, England. Until the emergence of **Rebecca Adlington**, who won two gold medals and set a world record at the 2008 **Olympics**, Sarah Hardcastle was arguably the best **distance freestyler** in British history. At the 1984 Olympics, Hardcastle won a silver medal in the 400 freestyle and a bronze medal in the 800 freestyle. She was the bronze medalist in the 400 freestyle at the 1986 **World Championships** and was the gold medalist in the 800 freestyle at the 1995 **World Short Course Championships**, where she added a bronze medal in the 400 freestyle. Hardcastle did not compete at the 1988 and 1992 Olympics, but returned to that stage in 1996, when she placed eighth in the 800 freestyle and ninth in the 400 freestyle at the Atlanta Games. *See also* GREAT BRITAIN.

HARDY, JESSICA (USA). B. 12 March 1987, Long Beach, California. Jessica Hardy is one of the **United States'** top **breaststrokers** and **sprint freestylers**, but is best known for her positive test for **performance-enhancing drugs** that led to her withdrawal from the 2008 U.S. **Olympic** Team. At the 2008 Olympic Trials, Hardy qualified to represent the United States at the Beijing Games in the 100 breaststroke, 50 freestyle, and as a member of the 400 freestyle **relay**. However, a few weeks after the Trials, one of Hardy's **doping** tests was revealed to have tested positive for the banned substance clenbuterol, a stimulant that aids aerobic capacity and is often given to asthma patients. She did, however, also have negative tests at other points during the Trials. Hardy claimed the clenbuterol found in her system was the result of using supplements by the company AdvoCare, of which she had an endorsement contract. At the time of her positive test, Hardy admitted to using the AdvoCare products Arginine Extreme and Nighttime Recovery. Because of her positive test, Hardy withdrew from the Olympic Team and was given a two-year ban from competition, a suspension that eventually was reduced to one year by the American Arbitration Association.

Just days after Hardy's suspension ended on 31 July 2009, she made a triumphant return to competition by setting two world records in the 50 breaststroke and a world record in the 100 breaststroke at the U.S. Open in Federal Way, Washington. Before her positive doping tests, Hardy was an elite international performer, winning **short-course** world titles in the 50 and 100 breaststrokes in 2008 and winning the world title in the 50 breaststroke at the 2007 **World Championships**. At the 2005 World Championships, Hardy was the silver medalist in the 50 and 100 breaststrokes and set a world record in the 100 distance during the semifinal round.

HARRISON, JOAN CYNTHIA (RSA). B. 29 November 1935, East London, South Africa. Joan Harrison won her sole **Olympic** gold medal in the 100 **backstroke** at the 1952 Olympics. The **South African** nearly won another medal, but placed fourth in the 100 **freestyle**.

HARUP, KAREN MARGRETHE (DEN). B. 20 November 1924, Hovedstaden, Denmark. Karen Harup had one of the strongest performances at the 1948 **Olympics**, highlighted by a gold medal in the 100 **backstroke**. The Danish swimmer added silver medals in the 400 **freestyle** and 400 freestyle **relay** and was the fourth-place finisher in the 100 freestyle.

HASE, DAGMAR (GER). B. 22 December 1969, Quedlinburg, Germany. Dagmar Hase was one of the first **German** swimmers to emerge as a star following the fall of the Berlin Wall and after the **German Democratic Republic (GDR) doping** program was seemingly ended. Her greatest achievement was at the 1992 Barcelona **Olympics**, where she beat out **United States** world-record holder **Janet Evans**, the defending champion, for the gold medal in the 400 **freestyle**. Hase added a silver medal in the 200 **backstroke** and on the German 400 medley **relay**. At the 1996 Olympics, Hase won four medals, silvers in the 400 and 800 freestyles and in the 800 freestyle relay and a bronze medal in the 200 freestyle. She was a six-time medalist at the **World Championships** and twice won European championships in the 400 freestyle.

HEBNER, HARRY J. (USA). B. 15 June 1891, Chicago, Illinois. D. 12 October 1968, Lake Worth, Florida. Harry Hebner starred in the **backstroke** and **freestyle** for the **United States** in the early 1900s, capturing the **Olympic** gold medal in the 100 backstroke in 1912, when he also won the silver medal in the 800 freestyle **relay**. At the 1908 Games, he helped the United States to bronze in the 800 freestyle relay and competed in the 100 freestyle. Hebner's third Olympics, in 1920, saw him as a member of the United States' sixth-place **water polo** team.

HENCKEN, JOHN FREDERICK (USA). B. 29 May 1954, Culver City, California. John Hencken is one of the best **breaststrokers** in **United States** history. He won five Olympic medals during his career and enjoyed a back-and-forth rivalry with **Great Britain**'s **David Wilkie** in the 100 and 200 breaststroke events. At the 1972 **Olympics** in Munich, Hencken won the 200 breaststroke, defeating Wilkie. He also picked up the bronze medal in the 100 breaststroke. At the 1976 Games in Montreal, Hencken defeated Wilkie in the 100 breaststroke, but settled for the silver medal behind the British swimmer in the 200 breaststroke. Hencken also won gold on the United States' 400 medley **relay**. At the first **World Championships**, he claimed gold medals in the 100 breaststroke and 400 medley relay and took silver in the 200 breaststroke, behind Wilkie. For his career, Hencken set 12 individual world records, seven in the 100 breaststroke and five in the 200 breaststroke.

HENNE, JAN MARGO (USA). B. 11 August 1947, Oakland, California. Jan Henne excelled in several events for the **United States** in the 1960s. Although she initially made her mark as a **breaststroke** swimmer, she achieved the majority of her international success in the **freestyle**. At the 1968 **Olympics**, Henne was the gold medalist in the 100 freestyle and the silver medalist in the 200 freestyle. She added a bronze medal in the 200 **individual medley (IM)** and helped the United States win the gold medal in the 400 freestyle **relay**.

HENRICKS, JOHN MALCOLM (AUS). B. 6 June 1935, Sydney, New South Wales. Jon Henricks competed in two **Olympics** for **Australia**, capturing the gold medal in the 100 **freestyle** at the 1956

Games in world-record time. He also helped Australia win the 800 freestyle **relay** with a world record. Henricks returned to defend his Olympic title in 1960, but failed to advance out of the preliminary heats.

HENRY, JODIE CLARE (AUS). B. 17 November 1983, Brisbane, Queensland. For a two-year period in 2004 and 2005, Jodie Henry was the premier female 100 **freestyler** in the world, winning gold at the 2004 Athens **Olympics** and gold at the 2005 **World Championships** in Montreal. Her semifinal swim in 2004 was a world record and she anchored **Australia** to gold in the 400 freestyle **relay** and 400 medley relay. Henry owns a bronze medal in the 100 freestyle from the 2003 World Championships and is a seven-time medalist at the **Commonwealth Games**. Injuries hampered Henry in her attempts to qualify for the 2008 Olympics.

HEYNS, PENELOPE "PENNY" (RSA). B. 8 November 1974, Springs, South Africa. Penny Heyns was the dominant female **breaststroker** of her era, sweeping the 100 and 200 breaststroke events at the 1996 **Olympics** in Atlanta. Four years later, she won the bronze medal in the 100 breaststroke at the Sydney Games. Her gold medals in Atlanta were the first for **South Africa** since it was readmitted to the Olympics in 1992, following its ban by the International Olympic Committee (IOC) for Apartheid issues. She set nine world records during her career.

HICKCOX, CHARLES BUCHANAN (USA). B. 6 February 1947, Phoenix, Arizona. D. 15 June 2010, San Diego, California. Charles Hickcox was one of the most successful **United States** athletes at the 1968 **Olympics** in Mexico City, claiming individual titles in the 200 and 400 **individual medley (IM)** events and as a member of the American 400 medley **relay**. He also captured a silver medal in the 100 backstroke. Hickcox set one world record in the 200 individual medley and twice broke the world record in the 400 individual medley.

HIGH-TECH SUIT CONTROVERSY. The high-tech suit controversy was a dilemma in swimming from February 2008 through 2009. In February 2008, **Speedo** unveiled its newest suit called the

LZR Racer. Made with polyurethane panels, it enabled swimmers to maintain their body position better through the end of races and added an element of buoyancy. Due to these advantages, it was the most-used suit at the 2008 **Olympics** in Beijing and accounted for the majority of the medals won and world records set. The LZR Racer was also the impetus for the **Italian** companies, **Arena** and **Jaked**, to develop their own high-tech suits, their products made wholly of polyurethane. Due to the full-rubber construction of these Italian suits, they became the prominent suits worn at the 2009 **World Championships**, with the LZR Racer falling off the pace. From the unveiling of the LZR through the end of the World Championships, more than 170 world records were set and thousands of national records were established.

The release of the suits led to a controversy over whether they were good for the sport. The argument against the suits was that they neutralized pure talent, allowing athletes who were good to compete with the best in the world due to the way the suits helped maintain technique in the later portions of races. Prior to the high-tech suit craze, elite athletes had the advantage of relying on their talent to stay strong at the end of races. During the World Championships, the **Fédération Internationale de Natation (FINA)** announced it was banning the high-tech suits effective 1 January 2010, a decision that was largely met with approval by athletes who wanted to see the sport return to a battle between skill and not technology. However, athletes, **coaches**, and journalists have stated that due to a return to textile-made suits, the world records set in high-tech suits must either be eliminated or placed on a separate list. Otherwise, many believe it could be years, even decades, before the records set in the high-tech era will be broken. *See also* JAMMER; TECHNOLOGICAL DOPING; TYR SPORT.

HODGSON, GEORGE RITCHIE (CAN). B. 12 October 1893, Montreal, Quebec. D. 1 May 1983, Montreal, Quebec. George Hodgson was the first **Canadian** swimming star. At the 1912 **Olympics**, he won the 400 **freestyle** in Olympic-record time and followed by winning the gold medal in the 1,500 freestyle with a world-record performance. He also competed in those events at the 1920 Games, but did not advance beyond the preliminary heats.

HOELZER, MARGARET (USA). B. 30 March 1983, Huntsville, Alabama. Margaret Hoelzer is a **backstroke** standout from the **United States** who won three medals at the 2008 **Olympic** Games. In addition to winning silver medals in the 200 backstroke and 400 medley **relay**, Hoelzer earned a bronze medal in the 100 backstroke. She is a former world-record holder in the 200 backstroke and was the 2007 world champion in the event, after finishing second at the 2003 and 2005 **World Championships.** Hoelzer, however, did not have the chance to defend her title as she failed to qualify for the U.S. team that competed at the 2009 World Championships in **Rome.** Hoelzer is also a two-time **short-course** world champion in the 200 backstroke.

HOFF, KATHRYN ELISE (USA). B. 3 June 1989, Palo Alto, California. Katie Hoff is a multievent talent who rose to stardom out of the **North Baltimore Aquatic Club (NBAC)**, known for its development of teenage swimmers into world-class performers. Hoff burst onto the international scene as a 15-year-old, qualifying for the 2004 **Olympics** in the 200 and 400 **individual medley (IM)** events. She was hampered by a case of nerves during the preliminaries of the 400 individual medley at the Athens Games and failed to advance to the finals. However, she rebounded to finish sixth in the 200 individual medley. A year later, Hoff was the gold medalist in the 200 and 400 medleys at the **World Championships** in Montreal and repeated those performances at the 2007 World Championships, where she set a world record in the 400 medley. Hoff was considered a contender for as many as six medals at the 2008 Olympics, but settled for silver in the 400 **freestyle** and bronze medals in the 400 individual medley and 800 freestyle **relay.** She was fourth in both the 200 freestyle and 200 individual medley and did not qualify for the final in the 800 freestyle, a sign that her ambitious schedule had taken a toll. Before the **United States** Trials for the 2009 World Championships, Hoff battled a virus that cut into her training time and she failed to qualify for the World Championships in **Rome.** *See also* BOWMAN, ROBERT.

HOGSHEAD, NANCY LYNN (USA). B. 17 April 1962, Iowa City, Iowa. Nancy Hogshead was a **United States** multi-event talent who had her best showings at the 1984 **Olympics** in Los Angeles. Hogshead left those Games with four medals, and just missed winning a fifth. In the 100 **freestyle**, she tied with American teammate **Carrie Steinseifer** and the two helped the United States to gold in the 400 freestyle relay. Hogshead also anchored the United States' triumphant 400 medley **relay** and garnered a silver medal in the 200 **individual medley (IM)**. In the 200 **butterfly**, she was the fourth-place finish, seven hundredths shy of the bronze-medal time. Hogshead likely would have added to her Olympic medal haul, but the American boycott of the 1980 Games prevented her from competing in Moscow.

HOLLAND, STEPHEN (AUS). B. 31 May 1958, New South Wales, Australia. Stephen Holland ranks among the many internationally renowned **distance freestylers** produced by **Australia**. Holland earned his only Olympic medal at the 1976 Montreal **Olympics**, earning the bronze in the 1,500 freestyle. It was a disappointing finish for Holland, who once held the world record in the event. He was also fifth in the 400 freestyle. Holland was the gold medalist in the 1,500 freestyle at the 1973 **World Championships** and set four world records in the event. His best race was the 800 freestyle, an event not on the Olympic program but in which Holland set seven world records.

HOLM, ELEANOR G. (USA). B. 6 December 1913, Brooklyn, New York. D. 31 January 2004, Miami, Florida. Eleanor Holm was a multiple-time national champion in the **backstroke** and **individual medley (IM)**. After placing fifth in the 100 backstroke at the 1928 **Olympics**, Holm won the gold medal in the event at the 1932 Games. *See also* UNITED STATES.

HOLMAN, FREDERICK (GBR). B. March 1885, Devon, England. D. 23 January 1913, Devon, England. In his only **Olympic** appearance, Fred Holman was the gold medalist in the 200 **breaststroke** at the 1908 Olympics. *See also* GREAT BRITAIN.

HOLMERTZ, ANDERS SOREN (SWE). B. 1 December 1968, Motala, Sweden. Anders Holmertz rated as one of the elite **middle-distance freestylers** of his era, totaling five **Olympic** medals. At the

1988 Seoul Olympics, he claimed the silver medal in the 200 free-style, a race won in upset form by **Australia's Duncan Armstrong**. Holmertz returned for the 1992 Games in Barcelona and won another silver medal in the 200 freestyle, 16 hundredths of a second behind **Evgeny Sadovyi** of the **Unified Team**. Holmertz added a bronze medal in the 400 freestyle and helped **Sweden** to the silver medal in the 800 freestyle **relay**, a feat the country repeated with Holmertz in 1996 at the Atlanta Olympics. Holmertz won a silver medal in the 200 freestyle at the 1994 **World Championships**.

HOPPENBERG, ERNST (GER). B. 26 July 1878, Rheinland-Pfalz, Germany. D. 29 September 1937, Rheinland-Pfalz, Germany. Ernst Hoppenberg represented **Germany** at the second Modern **Olympics** in 1900, winning the 200 **backstroke** and helping his country win the team swimming competition, which was discontinued after the 1900 Games.

HORNER, SILKE (GDR). B. 12 September 1965, Leipzig, Germany. Silke Horner's talent in the **breaststroke** events made her an **Olympic** and world champion, although her achievements are clouded by the systematic **doping** system used by the **German Democratic Republic (GDR)** at the time of her career. At the 1988 Olympics in Seoul, she won the gold medal in the 200 breaststroke with a world-record time that lasted for four years. She added a bronze medal in the 100 breaststroke and helped East Germany to gold in the 400 medley **relay**. Horner was the world champion in 1986 in the 200 breaststroke and the silver medalist in the 100 breaststroke. At the 1987 European Championships, she claimed both breaststroke races. Horner set three world records in the 200 breaststroke.

HOSSZU, KATINKA (HUN). B. 3 May 1989, Baranya, Hungary. Katinka Hosszu is a **Hungarian** swimmer who excels in several events. A two-time Olympian, Hosszu has not won a medal at the **Olympic** Games, but was a three-time medalist at the 2009 **World Championships**. She was victorious in the 400 **individual medley (IM)** and won bronze medals in the 200 individual medley and 200 **butterfly**.

HUNGARY (HUN). An argument can be made that **Hungary's** strongest sport is swimming, as the country ranks fifth in overall medals won through the 2008 **Olympics** in Beijing. **Krisztina Egerszegi** is the most famous female swimmer to be produced by the Eastern European country. She was the gold medalist in the 200 **backstroke** at the 1988, 1992, and 1996 Olympics and added additional gold in 1992 in the 100 backstroke and 400 **individual medley (IM)**. Egerszegi and **Australian Dawn Fraser** are the only swimmers in history to win an event at three consecutive Olympic Games. In men's swimming, Hungary is known for developing world-class **breaststrokers** and individual medley standouts. Among the top male swimmers are Olympic champions **Tamas Darnyi** (medley) and **Norbert Rozsa** (breaststroke), and three-time silver medalist at the 2008 Games, **Laszlo Cseh**. See also CSIK, FERENC; CZENE, ATTILA; GUTTLER, KAROLY; GYENGE, VALERIA; GYURTA, DANIEL; HAJOS, ALFRED; HOSSZU, KATINKA; KOVACS, AGNES; SZABO, JOZSEF; SZEKELY, EVA; SZOKE, KATALIN; VON HALMAY, ZOLTAN; WLADAR, SANDOR.

HUNGER, DANIELA (GER). B. 20 March 1972, Berlin, Germany. Daniela Hunger's career was spent competing for the **German Democratic Republic (GDR)** and, after the fall of the Berlin Wall, unified **Germany**. Racing for East Germany at the 1988 **Olympics**, Hunger was the gold medalist in the 200 **individual medley (IM)** and as a member of the 400 **freestyle relay**. She added a bronze medal in the 400 individual medley. Four years later, competing for Germany, Hunger added three more medals, bronze in the 200 individual medley, silver in the 400 medley relay, and bronze in the 400 freestyle relay. At the 1991 **World Championships**, Hunger was the bronze medalist in the 200 individual medley. She is one of several former East German swimmers to admit publicly she was part of the systematic **doping** program utilized by the country.

HVEGER, RAGNHILD TOVE (DEN). B. 10 December 1920, Nyborg, Denmark. Despite a career that did not include overwhelming **Olympic** success, Ragnhild Heveger is considered one of the greatest female swimmers in history. Her only Olympic medal was a silver in the 400 **freestyle** at the 1936 Games in Berlin, when she was just beginning to peak. Because of World War II, the Games were canceled in 1940 and 1944, thus ending Hveger's best chances at Olympic gold. During her career, she set world records in the 200, 400, and 800 freestyles and the 200 **backstroke**. Her last world record in the 400 freestyle stood from 1940 until 1956.

HYMAN, MISTY DAWN (USA). B. 23 March 1979, Mesa, Arizona. Misty Hyman registered one of the biggest upsets in **Olympic** swimming history when she won the gold medal in the 200 **butterfly** at the 2000 Olympics in Sydney, beating world-record holder and defending champion **Susie O'Neill** in her home country. Hyman took the lead from the start and won with an Olympic-record time of 2:05.88, with O'Neill following in second place. Hyman was also an accomplished **backstroker**, winning gold at the **World Short Course Championships** in the 100 distance in 1995. At **Stanford University**, Hyman won three individual **National Collegiate Athletic Association (NCAA)** championships, two in the 100 butterfly and one in the 200 butterfly.

– I –

ILCHENKO, LARISSA DMITRYEVNA (RUS). B. 18 November 1988, Volgograd, Russia. Larissa Ilchenko is considered the greatest female **open-water** swimmer in history. Ilchenko won the inaugural 10-kilometer race at the 2008 **Olympics**. Previously, she won the 5-kilometer and 10-kilometer races at the 2006, 2007, and 2008 **World Championships** and was also the 5-kilometer world champion in 2004 and 2005. At the 2009 World Championships, however, she was defeated for the first time in major international competition, claiming the silver medal in the 5-kilometer race before having to withdraw in the middle of the 10-kilometer race.

INDIANA UNIVERSITY NATATORIUM. The Indiana University Natatorium was completed in 1982 and is considered the most famous pool in the United States, having hosted the Olympic Trials in 1984, 1992, 1996, and 2000. It has also hosted numerous United States National Championships, the Duel in the Pool between the United

States and Australia, and the U.S. Open, among other smaller meets. Situated on the campus of Indiana University–Purdue University, in Indianapolis, the facility is unlikely to host any Olympic Trials in the future, due to **United States Swimming**'s desire to hold Trials in a larger venue. However, it continues to be a regular site of the U.S. Nationals and served as the host of the 2009 United States **World Championships** Trials. The Indiana University Natatorium has been the site of several world records. *See also* QWEST CENTER; WATER CUBE.

INDIVIDUAL MEDLEY (IM). The individual medley (IM) measures a swimmer's prowess in all four strokes and provides a glimpse as to which swimmers are the most well rounded. In **long-course** swimming, the individual medley is contested over 200 and 400 meters, with the longer distance considered the decathlon of the sport and the truest test of the best all-around swimmer. In **short-course** swimming, the individual medley is contested over 100, 200, and 400 meters. When the individual medley is contested, each stroke is swum for the same length. The **butterfly** is the first stroke, followed by the **backstroke**, **breaststroke**, and **freestyle**.

The **United States' Tracy Caulkins** and **Michael Phelps** are considered two of the best medley swimmers in history, each setting world records in the 200 and 400 distances. **Hungarian Tamas Darnyi** is also regarded as one of the finest medley swimmers, having won the 200 and 400 medley events at both the 1988 and 1992 **Olympic** Games.

INTERNATIONAL SWIMMING HALL OF FAME (ISHOF). The International Swimming Hall of Fame, which was dedicated in 1965, is recognized by the **Fédération Internationale de Natation (FINA)** as the official Hall of Fame of aquatic sports. Located in Fort Lauderdale, Florida, the Hall of Fame features memorabilia commemorating the history of the sport. Among the artifacts found in the exhibition building are **Olympic** gold medals won by **Johnny Weissmuller,** who went on to star as Tarzan in the film industry, and the **starting block** used by **Mark Spitz** in several of his gold-medal winning performances at the 1972 Olympics in Munich. The Hall of Fame also has an aquatic complex with two 50-meter pools and regularly holds competitions, including the YMCA National Championships. Bruce Wigo is the current president and chief executive officer of the Hall of Fame, assuming that role in 2005.

INTERVAL TRAINING. Interval training is a practice style in which swimmers take rests in between workouts sets. An example would be a swimmer performing 10 consecutive 100-meter **freestyles** with 10 seconds of rest between each 100 freestyle. Athletes usually swim these sets at a percentage of their fastest capability. Interval training is a way to build aerobic endurance.

ITALY (ITA). Italy does not have a celebrated swimming history, ranking 15th on the all-time Olympic medals list with 17—four gold, four silver, and nine bronze. All of Italy's **Olympic** gold medals in swimming have been won since 2000, with **Domenico Fioravanti** the only double gold medalist. Fioravanti won the 100 and 200 **breaststrokes** at the 2000 Games, where **Massimiliano Rosolino** won the 200 **individual medley (IM)**. **Federica Pellegrini**, the 2008 Olympic champion in the 200 **freestyle**, is the only Italian woman to win an Olympic gold medal and has been a world-record holder in the 200 and 400 freestyles. *See also* BATTISTELLI, STEFANO; DIBIASI, KLAUS; FILIPPI, ALESSIA; FORO ITALICO.

IVEY, MITCHELL (USA). B. 2 February 1949, San Jose, California. Mitch Ivey was one of the top **backstrokers** during the peak of his career, representing the **United States** at the 1968 and 1972 Olympics. He was the silver medalist in the 200 backstroke in 1968, placing behind legendary **Roland Matthes**. Four years later, Ivey claimed the bronze medal in the 200 backstroke and just missed another medal in the 100 backstroke with a fourth-place finish.

IWASAKI, KYOKO (JPN). B. 21 July 1978, Shizuoka, Japan. Kyoko Iwasaki became just the second **Japanese woman** to win the 200 **breaststroke** when she took the gold medal in the event at the 1992 **Olympics** as a 14-year-old. She failed to defend her title four years later when she placed 10th and did not make the championship final.

– J –

JAGER, THOMAS MICHAEL (USA). B. 6 October 1964, East St. Louis, Illinois. Tom Jager was one of the world's elite **sprint free-stylers**, his best event the 50 freestyle. Jager won seven **Olympic** medals. Jager was the silver medalist in the 50 freestyle at the 1988 Olympics in Seoul, finishing behind **United States** teammate **Matt Biondi**. At the 1992 Games in Barcelona, Jager was the bronze medalist in the 50 freestyle. He was a two-time world champion in the 50 freestyle, winning that event in 1986 and 1991.

JAKED. Jaked is an **Italian** swimwear manufacturer that burst onto the global stage in late 2008 with a suit considered the fastest in history. Made of 100 percent polyurethane, the Jaked 01 is a nonpermeable suit that helped several athletes break records and was one of the most worn suits at the 2009 **World Championships** in **Rome**. The suit provided such an advantage to athletes that many competitors sponsored by other companies opted away from their contracted brand to wear the Jaked product. It was initially banned by the **Fédération Internationale de Natation (FINA)**, but later reinstated after objections were raised by the company. *See also* ARENA; SPEEDO; TECHNOLOGICAL DOPING; TYR SPORT.

JAMMER. A jammer is a type of suit worn by male swimmers that begins at the hips and ends at the knees. It had a rise in popularity when the sport transitioned from the familiar briefs to the waist-to-knee approach, but it experienced a dip in popularity during the era of **high-tech suits** because its minimal coverage lessened the advantage of a swimmer wearing a suit that covered the majority of the body. Beginning on 1 January 2010, the **Fédération Internationale de Natation (FINA)** banned bodysuits and the jammer became the universal suit in male swimming.

JAPAN (JPN). Japan ranks sixth on the all-time medals list in **Olympic** swimming, its best days during the first half of the 20th century. Like **Hungary**, the Japanese men have a long-standing tradition of excellence in the 200 **breaststroke**, an event won by **Yoshiyuki Tsuruta**. Although the Japanese had some lean years during the last half of the century, **Kosuke Kitajima** brought the country back to relevance in the event during the beginning of the 21st century. After winning gold medals in the 100 and 200 breaststrokes at the 2004 Olympics, he repeated that feat at the 2008 Olympics in Beijing. *See also* AOKI, MAYUMI; FURUKAWA, MASARU; HAMURO, TETSUO; IWASAKI, KYOKO; KITAMURA, KUZUO; KIYO-KAWA, MASAJI; MAEHATA, HIDEKO; MIYAZAKI, YASUJI; NAKAMURA, REIKO; NAKANISHI, YUKO; SHIBATA, AI; SU-ZUKI, DAICHI; TAGUCHI, NOBUTAKA; TANAKA, SATOKO; TERADA, NOBORU.

JARVIS, JOHN ARTHUR (GBR). B. 24 February 1872, Leicester, England. D. 9 May 1933, London, England. John Jarvis was the first **Olympic** swimming champion from **Great Britain** and remains the most decorated Olympic swimmer in British history with five medals. At the 1900 Games, Jarvis won gold medals in the now-defunct 1,000 and 4,000-meter **freestyles**. He also won a gold medal in **water polo** playing for the Osborne Swimming Club of Manchester. At the 1906 Intercalated Games, Jarvis was the silver medalist in the one-mile swim and claimed bronze medals in the 400 freestyle and 1,000-meter **relay**. He made a final Olympic appearance in 1908, but did not medal in the 1,500 freestyle.

JEDRZEJCZAK, OTYLIA (POL). B. 13 December 1983, Slaskie, Poland. Recognized as one of the best 200 **butterfly** swimmers in history, Otylia Jedrzejczak also excelled as a **middle-distance free-styler**. She was one of the most decorated swimmers at the 2004 **Olympics**, winning the gold medal in the 200 butterfly and silver medals in the 100 butterfly and 400 freestyle. She has won seven individual medals at the **World Championships**, including back-to-back titles in the 200 butterfly in 2003 and 2005. After her Olympic victory, she auctioned off her gold medal for a little more than $80,000, the money going to a children's hospital in Poland. In October 2005, Jedrzejczak was driving a car at high speeds and crashed into a tree, causing the death of her 19-year-old brother Szymon.

JENDRICK, MEGAN QUANN (USA). B. 15 January 1984, Tacoma, Washington. Megan Jendrick, formerly Megan Quann, rose to swimming stardom when she won the gold medal in the 100 **breast-stroke** as a 16-year-old at the 2000 **Olympics** in Sydney. She added a second gold medal in the 400 medley **relay**, but did not get the chance to defend either title as she failed to qualify for the **United States** squad that competed at the 2004 Games in Athens. Jendrick returned to major international competition at the 2007 **World Championships**, where she shared the silver medal in the 200 breaststroke. She then qualified for the 2008 Olympics in Beijing. Although she did not medal individually, she earned a silver medal in the 400 medley relay by swimming in the preliminaries of the event.

JENSEN, LARSEN ALAN (USA). B. 1 September 1985, Bakersfield, California. Larsen Jensen was one of the world's elite **distance freestylers**, competing at two **Olympics**. At the 2004 Games in Athens, he pushed defending champion **Grant Hackett** of **Australia** to the wire before settling for the silver medal. Four years later, he took the bronze medal at the 2008 Games in Beijing and placed fifth in the 1,500 freestyle, the final race of his career. At the 2005 **World Championships**, Jensen was the silver medalist behind Hackett in the 800 and 1,500 freestyles. Jensen won three individual **National Collegiate Athletic Association (NCAA)** championships swimming for the University of Southern California.

JIAO LIUYANG (CHN). B. 7 March 1990, Harbin, China. Jiao Liuyang is a **butterfly** specialist for **China** who won the silver medal in the 200 butterfly at the 2008 **Olympics** in Beijing, finishing behind teammate **Liu Zige**. The gold-silver sweep by the home nation set off a major celebration inside the **Water Cube**. At the 2009 **World Championships**, Jiao was the bronze medalist in the 100 butterfly and was fifth in the 200 butterfly.

JOHNSON, JENNA LEIGH (USA). B. 11 September 1967, Santa Rosa, California. Jenna Johnson won the silver medal in the 100 **butterfly** at the 1984 **Olympics**, placing behind **United States** teammate **Mary T. Meagher**. Johnson also contributed to the United States capturing gold medals in the 400 **freestyle** and 400 medley **relays**. Johnson earned silver medals in the 100 freestyle, 400 freestyle relay, and 400 medley relay at the 1986 **World Championships** and was the gold medalist in the 100 freestyle at the 1985 **Pan Pacific Championships.**

JONES, CULLEN (USA). B. 29 February 1984, New York, New York. Cullen Jones is a **sprinter** of African American descent who has stressed, through appearances and clinics, the importance of learning to swim to the black population, which has a high rate of drowning among children. Jones has set a **United States** record in the 50 **freestyle** and was a member of the United States' gold-medal winning 400 freestyle **relay** at the 2008 Olympics in Beijing. At the 2007 **World Championships,** Jones was the silver medalist in the 50 freestyle.

JONES, LEISEL MARIE (AUS). B. 30 August 1985, Katherine, Northern Territory. Leisel Jones is a world-record setting **Australian breaststroker.** Jones broke onto the international scene as a 15-year-old at the Sydney **Olympics,** where she won silver medals in the 100 breaststroke and as a member of the Australian 400 medley **relay.** At the next year's **World Championships,** she again won a silver medal in the 100 breaststroke and helped Australia to gold in the 400 medley relay. At the 2003 World Championships, Jones set the world record in the 100 breaststroke in the semifinals, but managed only the bronze medal in the final, to go with a silver in the 200 breaststroke. Despite being the world-record holder in both breaststroke events entering the 2004 Olympics in Athens, Jones settled for bronze in the 100 breaststroke and silver in the 200 breaststroke. After the Athens Games, and due to her inability to capture an individual gold medal in major international competition, Jones was labeled as an athlete who did not handle the pressure at big meets, instead struggling under the spotlight. She finally shed that label at the 2005 World Championships in Montreal, where she won gold in both breaststroke events, a feat she repeated at the 2007 World Championships in Melbourne. At her third Olympics, Jones won the gold medal in the 100 breaststroke in Beijing, to go with a silver medal in the 200 breaststroke and a gold medal in the 400 medley relay. Jones opted to not defend her world titles in 2009, choosing to compete in several smaller meets while taking the year easy following the Olympiad. She has set five world records in **long-course** competition.

JUKIC, MIRNA (AUT). B. 9 April 1986, Novi Sad, Serbia. Mirna Jukic is an Austrian **breaststroker** who was the bronze medalist in the 100 distance at the 2008 **Olympics** in Beijing, where she added a fourth-place finish in the 200 breaststroke. She also won bronze medals in the 200 breaststroke at the 2005 and 2009 **World Championships** and is a three-time gold medalist at the European Championships.

– K –

KACIUSYTE, LINA (URS). B. 1 January 1963, Vilnius, Lithuania. Lina Kaciusyte claimed her lone **Olympic** gold medal in the 200 **breaststroke** at the 1980 Olympics in Moscow. She was also the 1978 world champion in the 200 breaststroke.

KAHANAMOKU, DUKE PAOA KAHINO MAKOE HULIKO-HOA (USA). B. 24 August 1890, Honolulu, Hawaii. D. 22 January 1968, Honolulu, Hawaii. Duke Kahanamoku was an early **United States** swimming star who is better known for heightening the popularity of surfing. Kahanamoku won the gold medal in the 100 **freestyle** at the 1912 and 1920 **Olympics**, his chance at three consecutive victories thwarted twice. The 1916 Olympics were canceled due to World War I and Kahanamoku was the silver medalist at the 1924 Games, finishing behind **Johnny Weissmuller**. In that race, Kahanamoku's brother, Sam, was the bronze medalist. Kahanamoku added a gold medal in the 800 freestyle **relay** in 1920, eight years after helping the United States to silver in the event. He also appeared in several film roles.

KEALOHA, WARREN PAOA (USA). B. 3 March 1904, Honolulu, Hawaii. D. 8 September 1972, Honolulu, Hawaii. Warren Kealoha captured back-to-back gold medals in the 100 **backstroke** at the 1920 and 1924 **Olympics**, becoming the first man to repeat in the event. He set four world records in the event from 1920 to 1926. *See also* UNITED STATES.

KELLER, KLETE (USA). B. 21 March 1982, Las Vegas, Nevada. Klete Keller was one of the **United States'** top **middle-distance**

freestylers, competing in three **Olympics**. Keller qualified for his first Games as an 18-year-old in 2000 and won a bronze medal in the 400 freestyle at the Sydney Olympics to go with a silver medal in the 800 freestyle **relay**. Four years later in Athens, Keller earned another bronze in the 400 freestyle, but made his biggest mark as the anchor of the American 800 freestyle relay. With the United States in the lead going into the final leg and trying to dethrone reigning champion **Australia**, Keller held off **Ian Thorpe** for the gold medal. Keller was joined on that relay by **Michael Phelps, Peter Vanderkaay**, and **Ryan Lochte**. At the 2008 Olympics, Keller again won gold in the 800 freestyle relay. He won four medals at the **World Championships**, including a bronze in the 200 freestyle in 2001, and was a three-time individual **National Collegiate Athletic Association (NCAA)** champion for the University of Southern California before leaving school after two years. Keller's sister, Kalyn, just missed claiming an Olympic medal at the 2004 Games, placing fourth in the 800 freestyle. She finished 36 hundredths of a second behind American teammate **Diana Munz**. *See also* BOWMAN, ROBERT.

KIEFER, ADOLPH GUSTAV (USA). B. 27 June 1918, Chicago, Illinois. Adolph Kiefer is one of the greatest **backstrokers** in history, excelling over both the 100 and 200 distances. Kiefer won his only **Olympic** gold medal at the 1936 Olympics, prevailing in the 100 backstroke. He likely would have won gold medals in 1940 and 1944, but those Games were canceled as a result of World War II. Kiefer set numerous world records in the 100 and 200 backstrokes and was the first man to break a minute in the 100-yard backstroke. Kiefer continues to appear at the **United States** National Championships, often presenting the swimmers with their medals. *See also* PEIRSOL, AARON.

KIPHUTH, ROBERT J. H. (USA). B. 17 November 1890, Tonawanda, New York. D. 7 January 1967, New Haven, Connecticut. Robert Kiphuth was an innovative **United States coach** who oversaw the Yale University program when it was at the height of its existence. Kiphuth led Yale to four **National Collegiate Athletic Association (NCAA)** titles during his 42-year career that ended in 1959 and won 512 of 540 dual meets, including a 165-meet winning streak.

Among the contributions he made to the sport were the introduction of **dryland training** and the use of **interval training** during practice. He is a former publisher of *Swimming World Magazine* and **United States Swimming** has named an award after Kiphuth, one which honors the top point scorer at the National Championships.

KITAJIMA, KOSUKE (JPN). B. 22 September 1982, Tokyo, Japan. Kosuke Kitajima established himself as the best male **breaststroke** swimmer in history, winning gold medals for **Japan** in the 100 and 200 breaststroke events at the 2004 **Olympics** in Athens and the 2008 Olympics in Beijing. He is the only man to sweep the breaststroke events at consecutive Olympics. His victory in the final of the 100 breaststroke at the 2004 Games was clouded in controversy. Video footage showed Kitajima using a **dolphin kick** off the start and turn, an illegal maneuver at the time. Many, including **United States** athlete **Aaron Peirsol**, argued that the tactics of Kitajima provided the winning margin over the United States' **Brendan Hansen**. Kitajima is a 10-time medalist at the **World Championships**, winning gold in the 100 breaststroke in 2003 and taking gold in the 200 breaststroke in 2003 and 2007. Kitajima has broken five world records and was the first man to break the 59-second barrier in the 100 breaststroke and the 2:08 barrier in the 200 breaststroke.

KITAMURA, KUZUO (JPN). B. 9 October 1917, Kochi, Japan. **D.** 6 June 1996. Kuzuo Kitamura was a member of the 1932 **Japanese Olympic** swimming team, perhaps the strongest the country has produced. Kitamura won the gold medal in the 1,500 **freestyle**, setting an Olympic record in the process.

KIYOKAWA, MASAJI (JPN). B. 11 February 1913, Aichi, Japan. D. 13 April 1999, Tokyo, Japan. Masaji Kiyokawa was a member of **Japan**'s powerful 1932 **Olympic** Team, for which he won the gold medal in the 100 **backstroke**. Kiyokawa returned to the Olympics in 1936 and won the bronze medal in the 100 backstroke.

KLIM, MICHAEL (AUS). B. 13 August 1977, Gdynia, Poland. Michael Klim was a three-time Olympian for **Australia**, at one time holding world records in the 100 **butterfly** and 100 **freestyle**. Klim made his biggest mark at the 2000 **Olympics** in Sydney, where he won four medals. He helped Australian win gold and set world records in the 400 and 800 freestyle **relays** and won silver medals in the 100 butterfly and as a member of the Australian 400 medley relay. He led off Australia's 400 freestyle relay with a world-record time of 48.18 for his 100 freestyle leg and celebrated the win by strumming an air guitar, a response to American **Gary Hall Jr.** stating that the **United States** would "smash the Australians like guitars." Klim is an 11-time medalist at the **World Championships**, seven of those medals coming in 1998. He retired in 2007.

KLOCHKOVA, YANA OLEKSANDRIVNA (UKR). B. 7 August 1982, Simferopol, Ukraine. Yana Klockkova is the only **woman** in history to sweep the **individual medley (IM)** events at two Olympiads, accomplishing the feat at the 2000 **Olympics** in Sydney and the 2004 Games in Athens. **Australia's Stephanie Rice** also doubled in the medley disciplines at the 2008 Olympics in Beijing. Klochkova set only one **long-course** world record during her career, but her performance of 4:33.59 from the Sydney Games lasted nearly seven years, until it was broken by the **United States' Katie Hoff.** At the 2000 Olympics, Klochkova added a silver medal in the 800 **freestyle**. At the 2001 **World Championships**, Klochkova won gold in the 400 individual medley and 400 freestyle and silver in the 200 individual medley. At the 2003 World Championships, she was the champion of both individual medley events.

KOJAC, GEORGE HAROLD (USA). B. 2 March 1910, New York, New York. D. 28 May 1996, Fairfax, Virginia. George Kojac was the dominant **backstroker** of his era, setting a world record on the way to the gold medal in the 100 backstroke at the 1928 **Olympics**, where he also won gold on the **United States' 800 freestyle relay.** Kojac did not get the chance to defend his Olympic titles due to his schooling at Columbia University.

KOK, AAGJE (NED). B. 6 June 1947, Amstelveen, Netherlands. Ada Kok was a dominant **butterfly** swimmer for the **Netherlands** in the 1960s. She captured silver medals in the 100 butterfly and 400 medley **relay** at the 1964 **Olympics** and was the gold medalist in the 200 butterfly at the 1968 Games, where she was fourth in the 100 butterfly. Kok set seven world records during her career—three in the 100 butterfly and four in the 200 butterfly.

KOLB, CLAUDIA ANN (USA). B. 19 December 1949, Hayward, California. Claudia Kolb broke onto the international swimming scene as a 14-year-old, capturing a silver medal in the 200 **breaststroke** at the 1964 **Olympics** in Tokyo. Her best performances arrived four years later when Kolb won double gold in the 200 and 400 **individual medley (IM)** events at the Mexico City Games. Her victories were among the most dominant in Olympic history as she won the 200 individual medley by more than four seconds and defeated **United States** teammate Lynn Vidali by almost 14 seconds. Kolb won gold medals in the 200 and 400 medley races and 200 **butterfly** at the 1967 Pan American Games, where she also won the silver medal in the 200 breaststroke. She set five world records in the 200 individual medley and four world records in the 400 individual medley.

KONNO, FORD HIROSHI (USA). B. 1 January 1933, Honolulu, Hawaii. Ford Konno starred in the **distance** events for the **United States** at two **Olympics**. At the 1952 Games, he won gold medals in the 1,500 **freestyle** and as a member of the United States' 800 freestyle **relay**. He also won the silver medal in the 400 freestyle. At the 1956 Games, Konno added a silver medal in the 800 freestyle relay. He was a world-record holder in the 400 and 800 freestyles, although the longer event is not on the men's Olympic program.

KONRADS, JANIS (AUS). B. 21 May 1942, Riga, Latvia. John Konrads was a Latvian born **distance freestyler** who competed for **Australia**, becoming an **Olympic** champion. At the 1960 Olympics in **Rome**, Konrads earned the gold medal in the 1,500 freestyle and won bronze medals in the 400 freestyle and as a member of the Australian 800 freestyle **relay**. Konrads also competed at the 1964 Olympics, but did not medal. Konrads set world records in the 400, 800, and 1,500 freestyle events. Konrads' sister Ilsa won a silver medal in the 400 freestyle relay at the 1960 Olympics and set four world records in the 800 freestyle, an event that was not added to the Olympics' program until 1968.

KOPLYAKOV, SERGEY VIKTOROVICH (URS). B. 23 January 1959, Orsha, Belarus. Sergey Koplyakov earned four **Olympic** medals during his career for the **Union of Soviet Socialist Republics (URS)**, the highlight being a gold medal in the 200 **freestyle** at the 1980 Games in Moscow. The **middle-distance** swimmer also won gold in the 800 freestyle **relay** in 1980 and was a member of the silver-medal winning 400 medley relay. At his first Olympics in 1976, he was part of Soviet Union's silver-medal winning 800 freestyle relay.

KOSHEVAYA, MARINA VLADIMIROVNA (URS). B. 1 April 1960, Moscow, Russia. Representing the **Union of Soviet Socialist Republics (URS)** at the 1976 **Olympics**, Marina Koshevaya was the gold medalist in the 200 **breaststroke**, setting a world record, and added a bronze medal in the 100 breaststroke.

KOTHER, ROSEMARIE (GDR). B. 27 February 1956, Brandenburg, Germany. Rosemarie Kother ranked among the world's top **butterflyers** during the peak of her career for the **German Democratic Republic (GDR)**. She was the bronze medalist in the 200 butterfly at the 1976 **Olympics**, improving one spot from her finish in the event at the 1972 Games. She was also fifth in the 100 butterfly in 1976. Kother's greatest achievements in the sport came at the **World Championships**. She was the gold medalist in the 200 butterfly at the 1973 and 1975 World Championships and was the silver medalist behind **Kornelia Ender** both years in the 100 butterfly.

KOVACS, AGNES (HUN). B. 13 July 1981, Budapest, Hungary. Agnes Kovacs was a **Hungarian breaststroke** specialist who secured medals at two **Olympics**. After claiming the bronze medal in the 1996 Games, Kovacs improved to the gold medal in Sydney in 2000, narrowly beating out the **United States' Kristy Kowal**. Kovacs captured world championships in the 200 breaststroke in 1998 and 2001 and was the bronze medalist at the 2001 **World Championships** in the 100 breaststroke. The seven-time European Championships gold medalist competed collegiately in the United States for Arizona State University.

KOWAL, KRISTY ANN (USA). B. 9 October 1978, Reading, Pennsylvania. Kristy Kowal is a former **breaststroke** swimmer, one of a number of Pennsylvania natives to medal at the **Olympics** in the stroke. After just missing qualifying for the Olympics in 1996, Kowal earned a bid to the 2000 Games in Sydney and claimed a silver medal in the 200 breaststroke, placing just behind **Hungarian Agnes Kovacs**. At the 1998 **World Championships**, Kowal won gold in the 100 breaststroke and silver in the 200 breaststroke while helping the **United States** to gold in the medley **relay**. At the 2001 World Championships, Kowal picked up a silver medal in the 50 breaststroke. At the University of Georgia, she won three **National Collegiate Athletic Association (NCAA)** championships in the 100 breaststroke and three in the 200 breaststroke.

KOWALSKI, DANIEL STEVEN (AUS). B. 2 July 1975, Singapore. Daniel Kowalski was a much-adored **distance freestyler** from **Australia** whose talent and accomplishments were largely disguised by the countrymen with whom he was competing against. Kowalski first competed in the shadow of **Kieren Perkins**, earning the silver medal behind his teammate in the 1,500 freestyle at the 1996 **Olympics** in Atlanta. At those Games, Kowalski added bronze medals in the 200 and 400 freestylers, events won by New Zealand's **Danyon Loader**. At the 2000 Games in Sydney, Kowalski won a gold medal for swimming the preliminary round of the 800 freestyle **relay**. Kowalski was the silver medalist behind Perkins at the 1994 **World Championships** and won bronze in the event at the 1998 World Championships, when Australian **Grant Hackett** was the gold medalist and started his reign as the world's top distance freestyler. Although he never broke through for individual gold at the two biggest meets in the sport, Kowalski won four world **short-course** titles—two in the 400 freestyle and two in the 1,500 freestyle.

KRAUSE, BARBARA (GDR). B. 7 July 1959, Berlin, Germany. Barbara Krause was a **freestyle** specialist for the **German Democratic Republic (GDR)**, winning three gold medals at the 1980 **Olympics** in Moscow. Krause won individual titles in the 100 and 200 freestyles, setting a world record in the 100 distance, and won another gold as a member of East Germany's 400 freestyle **relay**.

She was part of the systematic **doping** program implemented by East Germany in the 1970s and 1980s and was inducted into the **International Swimming Hall of Fame (ISHOF)** before documentation was provided about her involvement in doping. A disclaimer now runs along with her Hall of Fame biography. At the 1978 **World Championships**, Krause was the gold medalist in the 100 freestyle and won silver medals in the 200 freestyle and on two relays. She set three world records in the 100 freestyle.

KRAYZELBURG, LEONID "LENNY" (USA). B. 28 September 1975, Odessa, Ukraine. Lenny Krayzelburg is a Ukrainian-born **backstroker** who, after gaining his **United States** citizenship, became one of the most respected members of the American Olympic swimming team. Krayzelburg showed tremendous range during his career, setting world records in the 50, 100, and 200 distances. At the Sydney Olympics in 2000, Krayzelburg won gold medals in the 100 and 200 backstrokes and led off the United States' gold-medal winning 400 medley **relay**. Krayzelburg was the 1998 world champion in the 100 and 200 backstrokes and served as a mentor to American **Aaron Peirsol** at the 2000 Olympics. Peirsol was the silver medalist in the 200 backstroke in Sydney, then won both backstroke races at the 2004 Games and gold in the 100 backstroke and silver in the 200 backstroke at the 2008 Beijing Games. Although he was a favorite to win his specialty events at the 2001 **World Championships**, Krayzelburg, of Jewish descent, skipped the World Championships and competed at the **Maccabiah Games**, a competition for Jewish athletes.

– L –

LACKIE, ETHEL MINNIE (USA). B. 10 February 1907, Chicago, Illinois. D. 15 December 1979, Newbury Park, California. The first **woman** to break one minute in the 100-yard **freestyle**, Ethel Lackie won two gold medals at the 1924 **Olympics**. She was the champion of the 100 freestyle and a member of the **United States'** winning 400 freestyle **relay**.

LANE, FREDERICK CLAUDE VIVIAN (AUS). B. 2 February 1880, Millers Point, New South Wales. D. 14 May 1969, Avalon, New South Wales. Fred Lane was an early **Olympic** swimming star for **Australia**, winning two gold medals at the 1900 Olympics. Lane was the winner of the 200 freestyle and also won the 200 obstacle course, an event that was discontinued after the 1900 Olympics.

LANE LINES. Lane lines are the coiled ropes, usually made of plastic, that stretch from wall to wall and separate the lanes in which swimmers compete. Swimmers can come in contact with the lane lines during a race, but may not grab on to them and use the lane lines for propulsion. Swimmers will sometimes swim close to the lane lines, hoping to draft off the competitor in the adjacent lane. Oftentimes, swimmers will celebrate significant victories by sitting atop the lane lines.

LARFAOUI, MUSTAPHA (ALG). B. 27 November 1932, Algiers, Algeria. Mustapha Larfaoui was the longest-tenured president of the **Fédération Internationale de Natation (FINA),** the world governing body of aquatic sports. He began serving as president in 1988 and remained active in that role through the 2009 **World Championships.** Larfaoui, a former basketball and **water polo** player, founded the Algerian Swimming Federation in 1962, serving as the organization's president until 1983, and again from 1985 to 1989. He was a founding member of the Algerian Olympic Committee in 1962 and has served as a member of the International Olympic Committee (IOC) and **World Anti-Doping Agency (WADA).**

Under Larfaoui's watch, FINA expanded dramatically. When Larfaoui took office, there were 109 member federations, a number that has nearly doubled in his two decades as president. Larfaoui oversaw the introduction of the **World Short Course Championships** in 1993 and the introduction of 50-meter events in backstroke, breaststroke, and butterfly at the World Championships in 2001. Among the lowlights of his tenure was the dominance of the Chinese women at the 1994 World Championships, where they were suspected of heavy **doping** that led to victories in 12 of the 16 events. Another negative was the controversy that surrounded the **high-tech suits** that were introduced in February 2008. Due to these suits, more than 100 world records were set in a little more than a year, and the sport became more about the technology on the swimmers' bodies than skill. FINA tried to dispel specific suits that were deemed unapproved by FINA's rules, but it was not until January 2010 that the sport was able to rid itself of the nonpermeable swimwear that served as buoyancy aids.

During the end of his tenure, Larfaoui was often cited as a man who lost control of the sport he governed, and FINA came under heavy criticism from several national federations, including those of the **United States** and **Australia**, the world's swimming superpowers.

LARSSON, KARL GUNNAR (SWE). B. 12 May 1951, Skane, Sweden. Gunnar Larsson is considered by many to be the greatest **Swedish** swimmer in history, having won both **individual medley (IM)** events at the 1972 **Olympics** in Munich. Larsson won the 200 medley by more than a second over the **United States' Tim McKee**, setting a world record in the process. In the 400 individual medley, Larsson and McKee went head-to-head a second time and raced stroke for stroke to the wall for the closest finish in Olympic history. Larsson was awarded the gold medal when he touched in 4:31.981, two thousandths of a second ahead of the 4:31.983 posted by McKee. Because of this race, the rules were changed where times are only carried out to the hundredth of a second, with dual medals provided in case of a tie. At the first **World Championships** in 1973, Larsson was the gold medalist in the 200 individual medley. He set a pair of world records in the 200 individual medley.

LAWRENCE, LAURIE JOSEPH (AUS). B. 14 October 1941, Townsville, Queensland. Laurie Lawrence is a former **Australian Olympic coach** who is known for his high energy. He guided his swimmers to numerous Olympic medals, including **Duncan Armstrong** and **Jon Sieben**. At the 1988 Games in Seoul, Lawrence watched from the stands as Armstrong won gold in the 200 **freestyle**, upsetting the likes of the **United States' Matt Biondi** and **Germany's Michael Gross**. Lawrence, who is portrayed in the documentary *Bud Greenspan's Favorite Stories of Olympic Glory*, was so animated during and after the race that security had to calm him down. He developed the Laurie Lawrence Swim School.

LE JINGYI (CHN). B. 19 March 1975, Shanghai, China. Le Jingyi, although she never tested positive for **performance-enhancing drugs,** is one of several **Chinese** swimmers believed to be part of a systematic **doping** program in the 1990s. A number of her Chinese teammates eventually tested positive for steroids. Le burst onto the scene at the 1994 **World Championships,** winning the gold medal and setting world records in the 50 and 100 **freestyles.** She was a silver medalist in the 400 freestyle **relay** at the 1992 **Olympics,** and at the 1996 Games she was the champion of the 100 freestyle and silver medalist in the 50 freestyle and 400 freestyle relay. She won 12 career medals at the **World Short Course Championships,** including 10 gold medals.

LEE, SAMUEL (USA). B. 1 August 1920, Fresno, California. Sammy Lee was the first man to repeat as the 10-meter **platform diving** competition at the **Olympic** Games, claiming back-to-back gold medals at the 1948 Games in London and the 1952 Games in Helsinki. He was also the bronze medalist in the three-meter **springboard** in 1948 and later went on to a successful **coaching** career in the sport.

LEVEAUX, AMAURY (FRA). B. 2 Dec. 1985, Belfort, France. Amaury Leveaux is a French sprinter who was the runner-up in the 50 **freestyle** at the 2008 **Olympics.** Leveaux earned a second silver medal as a member of **France's** 400 freestyle **relay,** which lost to the **United States.** Leveaux was the star of the 2008 European Short Course Championships, setting world records on the way to victory in the 50 freestyle, 100 freestyle, and 50 **butterfly.** At the 2009 **World Championships,** Leveaux was the bronze medalist in the 50 freestyle and was a member of France's 400 freestyle relay.

LEWIS, HAYLEY JANE (AUS). B. 2 March 1974, Brisbane, Australia. Hayley Lewis packaged a distinguished career in the **distance-freestyle** events, but also showed prowess in the 200 **butterfly,** 400 **individual medley (IM),** and in **open-water** swimming. At the 1992 **Olympics,** Lewis was the silver medalist in the 800 freestyle, added a bronze medal in the 400 freestyle, and just missed a third medal by placing fourth in the 200 butterfly. She also competed at the 1996 and 2000 Olympics, but failed to advance to a championship final.

At the **World Championships**, she was the 1991 world champion in the 200 freestyle, and picked up silver medals in the 400 freestyle and 400 individual medley to go with a bronze medal in the 200 butterfly. She was the silver medalist in the 800 freestyle at the 1994 World Championships and, as part of a career rebirth, was the bronze medalist in the 5-kilometer open-water swimming event at the 2001 World Championships.

LEZAK, JASON EDWARD (USA). B. 12 November 1975, Irvine, California. Jason Lezak is a **United States sprint freestyler** who became a household name at the 2008 **Olympics** when he saved **Michael Phelps'** chase for eight gold medals. The anchor of the United States' 400 freestyle **relay**, Lezak entered the water 59 hundredths of a second behind **France's Alain Bernard**, the world-record holder in the 100 freestyle. At the turn, Lezak remained nearly a body length behind the Frenchman. However, on the final lap, Lezak continually cut into Bernard's lead and touched eight hundredths of a second ahead of his rival at the finish. The victory was the United States first in the event since the 1996 Olympics and was a key part of Phelps eventually winning eight gold medals. Lezak's anchor split of 46.06 is the fastest in history. Lezak also won a gold medal as the anchor of the American 400 medley relay in Beijing, and won the first individual medal of his Olympic career when he tied for the bronze in the 100 freestyle with **Brazil's Cesar Cielo**. Between the 2000, 2004, and 2008 Olympics, Lezak won seven medals, four being gold. Lezak has won three gold medals in relays at the **World Championships** but has never medaled individually. At the **World Short Course Championships**, he has won seven medals, including a gold in the 100 freestyle in 2004. Lezak decided to skip the 2009 World Championships and competed at the **Maccabiah Games**, known as the Jewish Olympics. Although his presence at the Maccabiah Games was more about being an ambassador for the sport, Lezak won the 50 and 100 freestyle events, along with helping the United States to gold in the 400 freestyle relay.

LIGUE EUROPÉENE DE NATATION (LEN). The Ligue Européene de Natation (LEN) is the European governing body of swimming, consisting of 17 countries. LEN hosts the European Championships and the European Short Course Championships. The headquarters of LEN is in Geneva, Switzerland.

LIMPERT, MARIANNE LOUISE (CAN). B. 10 October 1972, Matagami, Quebec. Marianne Limpert focused on the **individual medley (IM)** for **Canada**, qualifying for the final of the 200 individual medley at the 1992, 1996, and 2000 Olympics. Limpert won the silver medal in the 200 individual medley at the 1996 Games, placing behind Ireland's **Michelle Smith**, who was later banned from the sport for four years after tampering with a urine sample during a **doping** test. At the 2000 Sydney Games, Limpert nearly earned another medal in the 200 individual medley, but was fourth, 12 hundredths of a second slower than the bronze-medal time. In her first Olympics in 1992, Limpert was sixth in her prime event. At the 2000 **World Short Course Championships**, she was second in the 100 individual medley and third in the 200 individual medley.

LIN LI (CHN). B. 4 May 1970, Nantong, China. Lin Li was a three-time Olympian for **China** who won four **Olympic** medals, three at the 1992 Games. She was the champion in the 200 **individual medley (IM)** and took silver medals in the 200 **breaststroke** and 400 medley. She also raced the 200 backstroke, finishing 12th, and helped the 400 medley **relay** to fourth place. At the 1996 Olympics, she earned a bronze medal in the 200 individual medley. At the 1991 **World Championships**, Lin swept the 200 and 400 medley events. Although she never tested positive for a banned substance, there are questions as to whether Lin used **performance-enhancing drugs** because of the rampant usage by several Chinese swimmers of her era.

LIU ZIGE (CHN). B. 31 March 1989, Shanghai, China. Liu Zige provided one of the highlights of the 2008 **Olympics** when she won the 200 **butterfly** to the delight of a capacity crowd at the **Water Cube**. On her way to the gold medal, Liu set a world record and led a gold-silver finish for her home nation, placing ahead of **Chinese** countrywoman **Jiao Liuyang**. At the 2009 **World Championships**, Liu earned the silver medal in the 200 butterfly.

LOADER, DANYON JOSEPH (NZE). B. 21 April 1975, Timaru, New Zealand. Danyon Loader was a medalist at two Olympiads, his greatest achievements produced at the 1996 **Olympics** in Atlanta. Loader won the 200 and 400 **freestyles**, four years after he was the silver medalist in the 200 **butterfly** at the Barcelona Games. At the 1994 **World Championships** in Rome, Loader captured a silver medal in the 200 butterfly and bronze medals in the 200 and 400 freestyles.

LOCHTE, RYAN STEVEN (USA). B. 3 August 1984, Canandaigua, New York. If not for the presence of **Michael Phelps**, Ryan Lochte might be considered the best swimmer of his era, his talent ranging over multiple events. Lochte made his first **Olympic** appearance at the 2004 Games in Athens, where he won a gold medal as a member of the **United States'** 800 **freestyle relay** and a silver medal behind Phelps in the 200 **individual medley (IM)**. Lochte won four medals at the 2008 Beijing Games, capturing gold in the 200 **backstroke** and again in the 800 freestyle relay. He added bronze medals in the 200 and 400 medley events. A multiple-time **National Collegiate Athletic Association (NCAA)** champion at the University of Florida, Lochte has won 13 medals at the **World Championships**, including eight gold. His best showing was at the 2009 World Championships, where Lochte was the champion of the 200 and 400 individual medley events, breaking Phelps' world record in the 200 distance, and as a member of the American 400 and 800 freestyle relays. In defense of his 2007 world title in the 200 backstroke, Lochte was the bronze medalist. Although Lochte is among the premier swimmers in the world, he is actually more gifted in the **short-course** pool. Lochte has won 15 medals at the **World Short Course Championships**, including a sweep of the 100, 200, and 400 individual medley disciplines at the 2008 event in Manchester, England.

LONG-COURSE SWIMMING. This version of the sport is contested in a 50-meter pool and is the format that is used in **Olympic** competition. Long-course swimming is considered the greatest test of an athlete's endurance and talent, largely due to the requirement of fewer turns. The first **World Championships** in this format debuted in 1973 in Belgrade, Yugoslavia. *See also* SHORT-COURSE SWIMMING.

LONSBROUGH, ANITA (GBR). B. 10 August 1941, Huddersfield, England. Anita Lonsbrough was a **breaststroke** and **individual medley (IM)** star for **Great Britain** who won the **Olympic** gold medal in the 200 breaststroke at the 1960 Olympics in **Rome**. Following Lonsbrough's victory, no British **woman** won a gold medal in swimming at the Games until **Rebecca Adlington** won the 400 and 800 **freestyles** at the 2008 Games in Beijing. Lonsbrough twice set world records, including one en route to her Olympic gold. At the 1964 Games, she was seventh in the 400 individual medley. At the European Championships, Lonsbrough won gold in the 200 breaststroke in 1962, four years after winning a silver medal in the event. She also won silver in the 400 individual medley at the 1962 European Championships. Following her swimming career, she went on to a career as a journalist.

LOPEZ, SERGIO (ESP). B. 15 August 1968, Barcelona, Spain. Sergio Lopez was an international standout in the **breaststroke**. He won the bronze medal in the 200 breaststroke at the 1988 **Olympics** in Seoul. He was the bronze medalist in the 200 breaststroke at the 1991 European Championships and was formerly the **coach** at West Virginia University. Lopez is the coach at the Bolles School in Florida, which features one of the top preparatory programs in the country.

LORD, CRAIG (GBR). B. 23 June 1962, Manchester, England. Craig Lord is a journalist for *The Times of London* and *Swim News*, a **Canadian**-based swimming magazine. Lord is well known for his investigative work into **performance-enhancing drugs** in the sport, most notably the **doping** practices of Chinese swimmers in the 1990s and the case of Ireland's **Michelle Smith**. At the height of the doping allegations launched against **China**, Lord traveled to China and revealed how readily available anabolic steroids are in local marketplaces. Thereafter, several top Chinese swimmers received bans from the sport for testing positive for the use of performance-enhancing drugs. Lord also broke the story of Smith tampering with a urine sample that led to her four-year ban from the sport two years after she won three gold medals at the 1996 **Olympics**, amid speculation she was doping. Lord has also been the world's leading opponent of the **high-tech swimsuits** that emerged in February 2008 and led to more than 100 world records being set, changing the landscape of the sport. While remaining a staunch opponent of the high-tech suits, Lord has come under severe criticism by swimmers, **coaches**, and fans for overlooking the work put in by the athletes producing world records. Others have lauded Lord for his willingness to loudly protest a development in the sport that affected performance at a higher level than at any time in history. Lord was the 2007 recipient of the Al Schoenfield Media Award, presented by the **International Swimming Hall of Fame (ISHOF)** for contributions to the sport of swimming.

LOUGANIS, GREGORY EFTHIMIOS (USA). B. 29 January 1960, El Cajon, California. Greg Louganis is arguably the greatest **diver** in history, equally successful on the three-meter **springboard** as on the 10-meter **platform**. Louganis made his first international mark at the 1976 **Olympics** in Montreal, winning the silver medal in the 10-meter competition. He followed that performance by winning the platform event at the 1978 **World Championships** and was considered the heavy favorite for gold in both diving events at the 1980 Olympics in Moscow. However, because of President Jimmy Carter's boycott of those Games, Louganis was forced to wait until 1984 in Los Angeles to capture Olympic gold, doing so in the three-meter springboard discipline and in the platform event. Louganis was the double world champion in both 1982 and 1986 and again won both events at the 1988 Olympics, but not without difficulty. During the preliminaries of the springboard competition, Louganis hit his head on the board, opening a gash that required medical attention and stitches. He was able to recover, however, and excelled in the final. Louganis is openly gay and was diagnosed with HIV in 1988, declaring in a 1995 interview that the virus had morphed into AIDS. Louganis did not publicly reveal his disease at the time of his competitive career, a decision that was criticized by some when a doctor stitched his wound at the 1988 Olympics without wearing protective gloves.

LOVELESS, LEA (USA). B. 1 April 1971, Yonkers, New York. Lea Loveless was a top **backstroker** in the **United States** in the 1990s, the highlight of her career her performances at the 1992 **Olympics** in Barcelona. Loveless won the bronze medal in the 100 backstroke, beaten by **Hungarians Krisztina Egerszegi** and Tunde Szabo, and handled the backstroke leg on the United States' gold-medal winning 400 medley **relay**. She was the gold medalist in the 100 backstroke at the 1998 **World Championships** and won another gold medal in the medley relay. She won seven medals at the **Pan Pacific Championships**, including five gold medals.

LUNDQUIST, STEPHEN (USA). B. 20 February 1961, Atlanta, Georgia. Steve Lundquist was the premier **United States breaststroker** during the 1980s. Although he once held the American record in the 200-meter distance, Lundquist was best known for his ability in the 100 breaststroke. Like many of his American teammates, he did not get the chance to race at the 1980 Olympics in Moscow due to the U.S. boycott. At the 1984 Olympics, he won the gold medal in the 100 breaststroke with a world-record performance and helped the United States capture gold in the 400 medley **relay**. At the 1982 **World Championships**, Lundquist earned two gold medals—in the 100 breaststroke and medley **relay**. Representing Southern Methodist University, Lundquist won four **National Collegiate Athletic Association (NCAA)** championships in the 100 breaststroke (1980 to 1983) and two titles in the 200 breaststroke. Only **Brendan Hansen** has won four 100 breaststroke titles since, with Hansen also winning four 200 breaststroke crowns. Lundquist set five world records during his career.

LUO XUEJUAN (CHN). B. 26 January 1984, Hangzhou, China. Luo Xuejuan is the best **breaststroker** in **Chinese** history, the world's dominant performer in the 100 breaststroke from 2001 to 2004. During that timeframe, Luo won the 2004 **Olympic** title in Athens and repeated as world champion in 2001 and 2003. She was also the gold medalist in the 50 breaststroke in 2001 and 2003 and, despite being better suited to the shorter distances, won a bronze medal in the 200 breaststroke at the 2001 **World Championships**. Because of a heart condition, Luo was forced to retire before having the opportunity to compete at the 2008 Olympics in Beijing.

LURZ, THOMAS (GER). B. 28 November 1979, Bayern, Germany. Thomas Lurz initially emerged as a world-class performer in swimming's **distance** events, competing at the 2004 **Olympics** in the 1,500 freestyle. It was **open-water swimming**, however, where Lurz made his biggest mark. He won the gold medal in the 5-kilometer event at the 2005, 2007, and 2009 **World Championships** and was the world champ in the 10-kilometer distance at the 2009 World Championships after earning silver medals in the discipline in 2005 and 2007. At the 2008 Olympics, Lurz earned the bronze medal in the 10-kilometer event.

LZR RACER. The LZR Racer swimsuit, a product developed by **Speedo** with the assistance of engineers from the National Aeronautics and Space Administration (NASA), was unveiled in February 2008 during a worldwide launch that featured parties in New York, Sydney, Tokyo, and London. Upon its release, Speedo officials claimed it would significantly aid in the lowering of times, a claim that was proven accurate during the 2008 season. Of the 108 world records set during the year, the majority were posted by athletes wearing the LZR Racer, whose construction helps swimmers maintain proper form in the water. Because of the success of the suit, Speedo's rival companies quickly worked on developing their version of the suit. By 2009, following the development of 100 percent polyurethane suits by Italian companies **Jaked** and **Arena**, the LZR Racer was no longer considered the fastest suit available. Due to this development, the majority of the athletes who wore the LZR Racer at the 2008 Olympics had switched to one of the Italian suits for the 2009 World Championships in **Rome**. However, some swimmers under contract with Speedo, such as **Michael Phelps**, remained loyal to the brand despite it not being the top suit on the market. The excessive number of world and national records set in the new suits has caused considerable controversy in the sport, some claiming that swimming is merely undergoing a technological development. Others have said the suits take away from technique and help middle-of-the-road swimmers compete at the same level as athletes with better form. *See also* TECHNOLOGICAL DOPING; TYR SPORT.

– M –

MACCABIAH GAMES. The Maccabiah Games are regarded as the Jewish Olympics, held every four years in Israel and open to only athletes of Jewish heritage. Through the years, several prominent swimmers have made the trip to Israel for the Games, often citing the opportunity to compete internationally and also have the opportunity to explore their Jewish roots. Among the top names to have competed in the Maccabiah Games are Olympic champions **Mark Spitz, Lenny Krayzelburg,** and **Jason Lezak,** who decided to bypass the 2009 **World Championships** in order to race in the Maccabiah Games.

MADISON, HELENE E. (USA). B. 19 June 1913, Madison, Wisconsin. D. 25 November 1970, Seattle, Washington. Helene Madison was one of the first dominant **freestylers,** setting world records in the 100-, 200-, 400-, and 800-meter distances. At the 1932 **Olympics,** she was the gold medalist in the 100 and 400 freestyles and helped the **United States** to victory in the 400 freestyle **relay.**

MAEHATA, HIDEKO (JPN). B. 20 May 1914, Hashimoto, Japan. D. 24 February 1995. Hideko Maehata was a two-time **Olympic** medalist for **Japan** in the 200 **breaststroke.** After claiming the silver medal in the event at the 1932 Games, Maehata won the gold medal at the 1936 Olympics, becoming the first Japanese **woman** to win the event.

MALCHOW, THOMAS ANDREW (USA). B. 18 August 1976, St. Paul, Minnesota. Tom Malchow was a top 200 **butterflyer** from the mid-1990s through the early 2000s. A product of the University of Michigan, Malchow started his **Olympic** career by swimming to a silver medal behind **Russian Denis Pankratov** in 1996. Four years later, Malchow became Olympic champion in Sydney, winning a championship race that saw 15-year-old **Michael Phelps** finish fifth in the first final of what would be the most accomplished Olympic career in history. At three **World Championships,** Malchow won a silver medal and two bronze medals in the 200 butterfly. He set one world record in his specialty event.

MALMROT, HAKAN (SWE). B. 29 November 1900, Orebro, Sweden. D. 10 January 1987, Blekinge, Sweden. Hakan Malmrot won the first gold medals for **Sweden** in **Olympic** competition, prevailing in the 200 and 400 **breaststrokes** at the 1920 Olympics.

MANAUDOU, LAURE (FRA). B. 9 October 1986, Villeurbanne, France. Laure Manaudou is equally known in the swimming world for her talent as she is for her penchant for switching **coaches** and not fulfilling expectations. At the 2004 **Olympics**, Manaudou won a gold medal in the 400 **freestyle**, silver in the 800 freestyle, and bronze in the 100 **backstroke**. It started a period in which Manaudou was the world's premier 200 and 400 freestyler, setting world records in both events and capturing world championships in 2005 (400 freestyle) and 2007 (200 freestyle/400 freestyle). A little more than a year after the 2007 **World Championships**, Manaudou was shut out of the medals at the 2008 Olympics. She was ill-prepared for the meet in comparison to her past performances, likely due to her split from coach Philippe Lucas and her decision to leave her **Italian** club after just a few months.

MANN, SHELLEY ISABEL (USA). B. 15 October 1937, New York, New York. Shelley Mann produced her biggest achievements at the 1956 **Olympics**, winning the gold medal in the 100 **butterfly** and a silver medal in the 400 **freestyle relay**. She was also sixth in the 100 freestyle. Mann won national titles during her career in freestyle, **breaststroke**, butterfly, and **individual medley (IM)**. *See also* UNITED STATES.

MARE NOSTRUM SERIES. The Mare Nostrum Series is a collection of swim meets held in Europe each summer, usually in June. The series features stops in Barcelona, Spain; Canet, **France**; and Monte Carlo, Monaco. The series, which debuted in 2000, formerly had a fourth segment in **Rome**, but that stop was discontinued after the 2005 tour. Each year an athlete is financially rewarded for having the best combined performance from the series' meets. In many years, the meet serves as a tuneup for a major international competition, such as the **Olympic Games** or **World Championships**.

MARTINO, ANGEL (USA). B. 25 April 1967, Tuscaloosa, Alabama. Angel Martino was a **sprint freestyle** and **butterfly** standout for the **United States**. At the 1992 **Olympics**, she won a bronze medal in the 50 freestyle and helped the United States to gold in the 400 freestyle **relay**. At the 1996 Games in Atlanta, Martino was the bronze medalist in the 100 freestyle and 100 butterfly and earned gold medals with the American 400 freestyle relay and 400 medley relay. Martino was suspended in 1988 when a **doping** test revealed traces of nandrolone, an anabolic steroid, but the suspension lasted only two years and did not interfere with the Olympiads of 1992 and 1996.

MASTENBROEK, HENDRIKA WILHELMINA (NED). B. 26 February 1919, Rotterdam, Netherlands. D. 6 November 2003, Rotterdam, Netherlands. Rie Mastenbroek was a versatile star for the **Netherlands** whose greatest accomplishments were at the 1936 **Olympics**. Mastenbroek won the gold medal in the 100 and 400 **freestyles**, along with the 400 freestyle **relay**, and added a silver medal in the 100 **backstroke**. Her efforts made her the first woman to win four swimming medals in one Olympiad.

MASTERS SWIMMING. Masters Swimming is a competitive form of the sport that is broken down by age groups, allowing athletes to compete against those of the same age. Masters Swimming is generally broken into five-year increments, such as 30–34, 35–39, 40–44, etc. In the **United States**, the United States Masters Swimming (USMS) national championships are held in **long course** and **short course**.

MATTHES, ROLAND (GDR). B. 17 November 1950, Possneck, Germany. Roland Matthes is the only man in history to win the 100 and 200 **backstroke** events at back-to-back **Olympics**, accomplishing that feat at the 1968 and 1972 Games while representing the **German Democratic Republic (GDR)**. The **United States' Aaron Peirsol** had the chance to match the achievement in 2008, but he followed his 2004 victories with gold in the 100 backstroke and silver in the 200 distance. Matthes, who won three relay medals at the Olympics, almost won three consecutive 100 backstrokes, but settled for the bronze medal at the 1976 Games. At the first **World Championships** in 1973, Matthews won both backstroke races. He defended his 100 backstroke title two years later. His career featured 16 world records, and he held the world standard in the 100 backstroke from 1967 to 1976.

McBREEN, THOMAS SEAN (USA). B. 31 August 1952, Spokane, Washington. Tom McBreen was a **United States distance freestyler** who was the beneficiary of misfortune by a U.S. teammate at the 1972 Olympics in Munich. McBreen originally finished fourth in the 400 freestyle, but after **Rick DeMont** tested positive for a banned substance contained in his asthma medication and was disqualified, McBreen was awarded the bronze medal. He set a world record in the 400 freestyle in 1971.

McCLEMENTS, LYNNETTE VELMA (AUS). B. 11 May 1951, Nedlands, Australia. Lyn McClements broke a three-year **United States** stranglehold on the 100 **butterfly** when she won the event at the 1968 **Olympics** for the **Netherlands**. She added a silver medal as a member of the 400 medley **relay**.

McKEE, ALEXANDER TIMOTHY (USA). B. 14 March 1953, Ardmore, Pennsylvania. Tim McKee has the dubious distinction of losing the closest race in **Olympic** swimming history, the **400 individual medley (IM)** at the 1972 Olympics in Munich. At the finish, **Sweden's Gunnar Larsson** and McKee appeared to touch in identical times. **Officials**, however, consulted the timing system and determined that Larsson touched the wall in 4:31.981 to the 4:31.983 of McKee, thus handing the Swede victory by two thousandths of a second. In today's competition, finishes are only measured to the hundredth of a second, with ties being rewarded with identical medals. At the 2000 Olympics in Sydney, Americans **Gary Hall Jr.** and **Anthony Ervin** shared the gold medal in the 50 freestyle after posting identical times. In addition to that silver medal in the 400 individual medley, McKee won silver in the 200 individual medley in Munich and silver again in the 400 individual medley at the 1976 Games in Montreal.

McKEEVER, TERI (USA). Teri McKeever is the head coach of the **women**'s swim team at the University of California–Berkeley. She led the Golden Bears to the 2009 **National Collegiate Athletic Association (NCAA)** championship, becoming the first woman to capture an NCAA title in her sport. She was also the first female to be named an assistant swimming coach for a **United States Olympic** swim team, accomplishing that feat in 2004 and 2008. McKeever is best known for her work with **Natalie Coughlin,** who attended UC–Berkeley and totaled 11 medals between the 2004 and 2008 Olympic Games, including back-to-back gold medals in the 100 backstroke.

McKENZIE, DONALD WARD (USA). B. 11 May 1947, Los Angeles, California. D. 3 December 2008, Reno, Nevada. Although Don McKenzie never won a national championship, he captured the gold medal in the 100 **breaststroke** at the 1968 **Olympics** in Mexico City. McKenzie, whose biggest previous victory was a **National Collegiate Athletic Association (NCAA)** title for Indiana University, also helped the **United States** win gold in the 400 medley **relay.**

McLANE, JAMES PRICE (USA). B. 13 September 1930, Pittsburgh, Pennsylvania. As a 17-year-old at the 1948 **Olympics,** Jimmy McLane captured three medals, including the gold in the 1,500 **freestyle,** making him just the second **United States** swimmer to win that event. He added another gold in the 800 freestyle relay and was the silver medalist in the 400 freestyle. At the 1952 Games, McLane again helped the United States win the 800 freestyle **relay,** but finished fourth in the 1,500 freestyle and seventh in the 400 freestyle.

MEAGHER, MARY TERSTEGGE (USA). B. 27 October 1964, Louisville, Kentucky. Mary T. Meagher, known as "Madame Butterfly" during her career, was the dominant **butterflyer** in the world from the late 1970s into the 1980s. Although the **United States'** boycott of the 1980 **Olympics** in Moscow cost her the chance at three gold medals, Meagher achieved her Olympic glory in Los Angeles four years later, winning the 100 and 200 butterfly events and swimming on the United States' triumphant 400 medley **relay.** At the 1988 Games, she took bronze in the 200 butterfly. She set seven individual world records during her career, and her ability was years ahead of the time. The world record of 2:05.96 that she set in 1981 lasted until 2000, when **Australian Susie O'Neill** was timed in 2:05.81. In the 100 butterfly, her world record of 57.93, also set in 1981, endured until **Jenny Thompson** clocked a time of 57.88 in 1999. A nine-time medalist at the **World Championships**, Meagher was also an accomplished 200 **freestyler**, winning a bronze medal at the 1986 World Championships. In 2009, Meagher was inducted into the United States Olympic Hall of Fame.

MEDALS STAND. The medals stand is the area where the gold, silver, and bronze medals are presented to the top-three finishers in an event. The gold medal platform is generally higher than the silver medal platform, which is usually higher than the bronze medal stage. In major international competitions, the national anthem of the winning athlete's country is played after medals have been awarded.

MEDICA, JACK CHAPMAN (USA). B. 5 October 1914, Seattle, Washington. D. 15 April 1985, Carson City, Nevada. Jack Medica was an elite **freestyler** in the 200- through 1,500-meter distances. He was the gold medalist in the 400 freestyle at the 1936 **Olympics**, where he added a silver medal in the 1,500 freestyle and as a member of the **United States'** 800 freestyle **relay**. Medica once held the world record in the 200 freestyle for nearly nine years and was the world-record holder in the 400 freestyle for almost seven years.

MELLOULI, OUSSAMA (TUN). B. 16 February 1984, Tunis, Tunisia. Ous Mellouli is the only **Olympic** medal winner in swimming from Tunisia. At the 2008 Olympics in Beijing, Mellouli captured the gold medal in the 1,500 **freestyle**, defeating two-time defending champion **Grant Hackett** of **Australia**. Hackett was attempting to become the first man to win gold medals in the same event at three consecutive Olympiads. Mellouli, who competed at the University of Southern California and trains with the Trojan Swim Club, was fortunate to even compete at the Beijing Games. After winning the gold medal in the 800 freestyle and a silver medal in the 400 freestyle at the 2007 **World Championships**, it was revealed Mellouli tested positive for Adderall, an amphetamine on the banned substance list. Although Adderall is not considered a **performance-enhancing**

drug, its presence on the banned list produced by the **Fédération Internationale de Natation (FINA)** led to a retroactive suspension that erased his results from November 2006 through the next 18 months. As a result, Mellouli's accomplishments at the World Championships were stricken. Although his results from the 2007 World Championships have been wiped out, he still holds bronze medals in the 400 **individual medley (IM)** from the 2003 and 2005 World Championships and a bronze medal in the 400 freestyle from 2005. At the 2009 World Championships, Mellouli was the silver medalist in the 400 and 800 freestyles, but won gold in the 1,500 freestyle.

METSCHUCK, CAREN (GDR). B. 27 September 1963, Greifswald, Germany. Caren Metschuck was a four-time medalist at the 1980 **Olympics**, winning the gold medal in the 100 **butterfly** and as a member of the **German Democratic Republic (GDR) 400 freestyle relay** and 400 medley relay. She added a silver medal in the 100 freestyle. Metschuck's accomplishments, however, are tainted due to her involvement with **performance-enhancing drug** use, directed by her **coaches** as part of a systematic **doping** program in East Germany.

MEYER, DEBORAH ELIZABETH (USA). B. 14 August 1952, Annapolis, Maryland. Debbie Meyer was the premier female **freestyler** of her era. At the 1968 **Olympics** in Mexico City, Meyer won the 200, 400, and 800 freestyles for the **United States**. It was the first year the 200 and 800 freestyles were contested in female competition at the Olympics, with Meyer winning the gold in the longer distance by more than 11 seconds. She set five world records each in the 400 and 800 freestyle events and four in the 1,500 freestyle.

MIDDLE DISTANCE EVENTS. Swimming's **middle-distance** events are generally considered to be those contested over 200 and 400 meters. While all **strokes** are raced over 200 meters, only the freestyle and **individual medley (IM)** are contested over 400 meters, and the 400 freestyle is sometimes considered to be a **distance** event. The greatest middle-distance swimmer in history is considered to be **Australian Ian Thorpe**, twice the **Olympic** champion in the 400 freestyle and also an Olympic titlist in the 200 freestyle. Thorpe set world records in both events. **Janet Evans**, also considered the greatest distance swimmer in female history, is also revered as one of the finest in the middle-distance disciplines. *See also* GOULD, SHANE.

MINISTRY FOR STATE SECURITY (GDR). The Ministry for State Security, commonly known as the Stasi, was the secret police of the **German Democratic Republic (GDR)**. After the fall of the Berlin Wall and the unification of **Germany**, Stasi files were made open to the public and many revealed what was long suspected in East German swimming: In the 1970s and 1980s, many athletes, mostly teenage females, were placed on a systematic **doping** program in which they were given steroids either orally or through injections, and without the athletes' knowledge of what was being conducted. Among the athletes revealed to be involved were **Olympic** champions **Petra Schneider** and Jorg Hoffmann, both of whom have admitted to being doped by their **coaches**.

MITCHELL, ELIZABETH "BETSY" (USA). B. 15 January 1966, Cincinnati, Ohio. Betsy Mitchell was a **backstroker** who helped the **United States** win gold in the 400 medley **relay** at the 1984 **Olympics** in Los Angeles. Mitchell also won the silver medal in the 100 backstroke, placing eight hundredths of a second behind teammate **Theresa Andrews**. At the 1988 Olympics, Mitchell collected a silver medal in the medley relay. At the 1986 **World Championships**, Mitchell was the gold medalist in the 100 backstroke and the silver medalist in the 200 backstroke. She also earned silver medals in three relays.

MIYAZAKI, YASUJI (JPN). B. 15 October 1916, Kosai, Japan. D. 30 December 1989. Yasuji Miyazaki is the only **Japanese** swimmer, male or female, to win an **Olympic** gold medal in the 100 **freestyle**, accomplishing the feat at the 1932 Olympics. Miyazaki also helped Japan to victory in the 800 freestyle **relay**, one of only two relay titles for Japan in Olympic swimming competition.

MOCANU, DIANA IULIANA (ROU). B. 19 July 1984, Braila, Romania. Diana Mocanu starred in the **backstroke** events for Romania, enjoying her most success at the 2000 **Olympics** in Sydney. Mocanu won both the 100 and 200 backstrokes, her victory in the longer distance by more than two seconds. A year later, Mocanu won a world championship in the 200 backstroke and claimed a silver medal in the 100 backstroke.

MOE, KAREN PATRICIA (USA). B. 22 January 1953, Del Monte, Philippines. Karen Moe competed at two **Olympics** for the **United States** and also made a mark in postcompetition career as a collegiate **coach.** At the 1972 Olympics, Moe was the gold medalist in the 200 **butterfly** and just missed a medal in the 100 **backstroke,** finishing fourth. Although Moe retired after the Munich Olympics, she made a comeback for the 1976 Games in Montreal and finished fourth in the 200 butterfly, four hundredths of a second shy of the bronze medal. Following her competitive career, she was the head women's coach at University of California–Berkeley, where she developed numerous All-Americans and several Olympians.

MONTGOMERY, JAMES PAUL (USA). B. 24 January 1955, Madison, Wisconsin. Jim Montgomery is a former **United States freestyler** who became the first man in history to break 50 seconds in the 100 freestyle. At the 1976 Olympics in Montreal, Montgomery won the gold medal in the 100 freestyle with a time of 49.99. Montgomery added a bronze medal in the 200 freestyle and helped the United States win gold medals in the 400 medley **relay** and 800 medley relay. At the first **World Championships,** held in Belgrade, Yugoslavia, in 1973, Montgomery was the champion of the 100 and 200 freestyles and took gold in three relay races. Montgomery was the bronze medalist in the 100 freestyle at the 1975 World Championships and the silver medalist in the event at the 1978 World Championships.

MOORHOUSE, ADRIAN DAVID (GBR). B. 24 May 1964, West Yorkshire, England. Adrian Moorhouse was a leading **breaststroker** for **Great Britain** in the 1980s and early 1990s, competing in three **Olympics.** After finishing fourth in the 100 breaststroke at the 1984 Games, Moorhouse came back four years later and won the gold medal over **Hungary**'s **Karoly Guttler** by one hundredth of a second. Moorhouse's last Olympics featured an eighth-place showing in the 100 breaststroke. A former world-record holder in the 100 breaststroke, Moorhouse was the silver medalist in the 100 breaststroke at the 1991 **World Championships** and won five gold medals at the European Championships, three in the 100 breaststroke and two in the 200 breaststroke.

MORALES, PEDRO PABLO (USA). B. 5 December 1964, Chicago, Illinois. Pablo Morales is a former **butterflyer** whose career was defined by a major comeback. After winning silver medals in the 100 butterfly and 200 **individual medley (IM)** at the 1984 **Olympics** in Los Angeles, Morales was expected to win gold in the 100 butterfly at the 1988 Games. Although he was the world-record holder in the event, Morales failed to qualify for the Olympics, the result of a poor showing at the **United States** Trials. He briefly retired afterward, but opted to return to competition and got revenge at the 1992 Olympics in Barcelona. At those Games, Morales won gold in the 100 butterfly and helped the United States prevail in the 400 medley **relay**. Morales won the world title in the 100 butterfly in 1986 and was the world-record holder in the event from 1986 to 1995. While swimming collegiately for **Stanford University**, Morales set a still-standing record for most individual **National Collegiate Athletic Association (NCAA)** titles. He won the 100 and 200 butterfly events in each of his four years and was a three-time champion in the 200 individual medley. **John Naber** (backstroke) and **Brendan Hansen** (breaststroke) are the only other swimmers to have won four NCAA titles in two events. Morales is the coach of the women's team at the University of Nebraska.

MORTON, LUCILLE (GBR). B. 23 February 1898, Blackpool, England. D. 26 August 1980, Blackpool, England. Lucy Morton became **Great Britain**'s first female **Olympic** champion in swimming when she prevailed in the 200 **breaststroke** at the 1924 Olympics.

MOSES, GLENN EDWARD (USA). B. 7 June 1980, Loma Linda, California. Ed Moses burst onto the international scene when he won gold in the 100 **breaststroke** at the 1999 Pan-American Games. Not competing in the sport on a year-round basis until he was 17, Moses made rapid improvements and broke the **United States** record in the 100 breaststroke at the 2000 **Olympic** Trials. He went on to win a silver medal in the 100 breaststroke at the Sydney Olympics and helped the United States to gold in the 400 medley **relay**. Moses set his only **long-course** world record in 2001, swimming the 100 breaststroke in 1:00.29. The mark lasted only three months, when **Russian Roman Sloudnov** went 59.97 to become the first man to break the minute barrier. Although Moses was accomplished in the Olympic-size pool, his tremendous turns and power off the walls enabled him to set numerous world records in the **short-course** pool, including five in the 200 breaststroke. After his swimming career concluded, Moses turned his attention to the golf course and is trying to qualify for the Professional Golfers' Association (PGA) Tour.

MULLIKEN, WILLIAM DANFORTH (USA). B. 27 August 1939, Urbana, Illinois. Despite never winning a national championship in the event, William Mulliken captured the gold medal in the 200 **breaststroke** at the 1960 **Olympics**. His only national title was in the 200 **freestyle**. *See also* UNITED STATES.

MUNOZ, FELIPE (MEX). B. 3 February 1951, Mexico City, Mexico. Felipe Munoz was the first Mexican to win an **Olympic** gold medal in swimming. Competing at the 1968 Olympics in his hometown, Munoz was victorious in the 200 **breaststroke**. He was also the silver medalist in the 200 breaststroke at the 1971 Pan American Games.

MUNZ, DIANA (USA). B. 19 June 1982, Cleveland, Ohio. Diana Munz was one of the world's top **distance freestylers** at the height of her career. At her first **Olympics** in 2000, Munz was the silver medalist in the 400 freestyle, trailing only U.S. teammate **Brooke Bennett**, and helped the **United States** to the gold medal in the 800 freestyle **relay**. At the Athens Games, she added a bronze medal in the 800 freestyle. Munz won three straight silver medals in the 800 freestyle at the **World Championships** (1998, 2001, 2003), took bronze in the 1,500 freestyle in 2001, and won bronze in the 400 freestyle in 2003. At the 2002 **Pan Pacific Championships**, she was the gold medalist in the 400, 800, and 1,500 freestyles and a member of the winning 800 freestyle relay.

MYDEN, CURTIS ALLEN (CAN). B. 31 December 1973, Calgary, Alberta. Curtis Myden was an international medalist for **Canada** in the **individual medley (IM)** disciplines who could not break through for a gold medal on the biggest stages. During the 1996 Olympics in Atlanta, Myden was the bronze medalist in the 200 and 400 individual medley events and repeated that bronze medal four years later in Sydney in the 400 individual medley. He took another bronze at the 1998 **World Championships** in the 400 individual medley and was the silver medalist in both medley races at the 1995 **World Short Course Championships**. He did win four gold medals in the individual medley events at the Pan American Games, but the competition level is considered a step below the Olympics and World Championships.

– N –

NABER, JOHN PHILLIPS (USA). B. 20 January 1956, Evanston, Illinois. John Naber was a **backstroker** and **middle-distance freestyler** for the **United States** who won five medals at the 1976 **Olympics** in Montreal. Naber captured gold in the 100 and 200 backstrokes, setting world records in both events, and collected a silver medal in the 200 freestyle behind American teammate **Bruce Furniss**. Naber also helped the United States to gold medals in the 400 medley **relay** and 800 freestyle relay. As a collegiate swimmer at the University of Southern California, Naber won 10 individual **National Collegiate Athletic Association (NCAA)** championships, two in the 500 freestyle and four-year sweeps of the 100 and 200 backstrokes. Naber is one of three men to have career sweeps in two events, joining **Pablo Morales** (100 butterfly/200 butterfly) and **Brendan Hansen** (100 breaststroke/200 breaststroke). Naber is still involved with the sport, often serving as an on-deck host and interviewer during major competitions in the United States.

NAKAMURA, REIKO (JPN). B. 17 May 1982, Yokohama, Japan. Reiko Nakamura was among the world's finest **backstrokers**, although her career for **Japan** was defined by third-place performances. Nakamura was the bronze medalist in the 200 backstroke at the 2004 and 2008 **Olympics** and was the bronze medalist in the event at the 2005 and 2007 **World Championships**. At the 2007 World Championships, she added another bronze medal in the 100 backstroke.

NAKANISHI, YUKO (JPN). B. 24 April 1981. Yuko Nakanishi was a 200 **butterfly** standout for **Japan**, claiming the bronze medal in the event at the 2004 **Olympics** in Athens. Nakanishi's only world record was in the **short-course** version of the 200 butterfly. At the 2008 Olympics, she advanced to the final of her specialty event, placing fifth.

NALL, NADIA ANITA (USA). B. 21 July 1976, Harrisburg, Pennsylvania. Anita Nall is one of several Pennsylvania-born **breaststrokers** who have medaled at the **Olympics**, along with Jeremy Linn, **Kristy Kowal**, and **Brendan Hansen**. At the 1992 Olympics in Barcelona, the 16-year-old won a silver medal in the 100 breaststroke and a bronze medal in the 200 breaststroke, adding to the legacy of the **North Baltimore Aquatic Club (NBAC)** producing teenage Olympic medalists. She also helped the United States to gold in the 400 medley **relay**. Nall set two world records in the 200 breaststroke.

NAMESNIK, ERIC JOHN (USA). B. 7 August 1970, Butler, Pennsylvania. D. 11 January 2006, Ypsilanti, Michigan. Eric Namesnik was one of the top **individual medley (IM)** swimmers in **United States** history, capturing silver medals in the 400 individual medley at the 1992 and 1996 Olympics. In 1996, he finished just 35 hundredths of a second behind American teammate **Tom Dolan**. He was the silver medalist in the 200 and 400 individual medley events at the 1991 **World Championships** and won a bronze medal in the 400 individual medley at the 1994 World Championships. Namesnik was a **National Collegiate Athletic Association (NCAA)** champion at the University of Michigan and served as an assistant coach at his alma mater under head coach Jon Urbanchek. Namesnik died four days after being involved in a car accident on icy roads.

NATIONAL BROADCASTING COMPANY (NBC). The National Broadcasting Company has broadcast every Summer **Olympics** since

1988, with the swimming competition one of its highlight sports. **Rowdy Gaines**, a three-time gold medalist in swimming at the 1984 Games in Los Angeles, has been part of the swimming broadcasts since the 1992 Olympics in Barcelona. The swimming competition at the 2008 Olympics, in which the **United States' Michael Phelps** won a record eight gold medals, was the most-watched sport of the Games.

NATIONAL COLLEGIATE ATHLETIC ASSOCIATION (NCAA). The National Collegiate Athletic Association (NCAA) is the governing body for college sports in the **United States**. In swimming, the NCAA oversees three levels of competition, Division I, Division II, and Division III. Division I is the top level, the championship meets for men and **women** frequently featuring past and future Olympians, along with world-record holders.

NATIONAL COLLEGIATE ATHLETIC ASSOCIATION (NCAA) SWIMMING. National Collegiate Athletic Association (NCAA) Swimming is what the college programs in the **United States** compete in from November through March, their seasons capped by NCAA Championships at three levels: Division I, Division II, and Division III. The regular season consists of dual-meet competitions and invitational meets, while the postseason consists of conference championships followed by the NCAA Championships. Competition is held in a **short-course** format, using 25-yard pools. In Division I, the highest level, the University of Michigan and Ohio State University have won the most NCAA team titles with 11 each, although Michigan's last title was won in 1995 and Ohio State's last championship in 1962. In recent years, the top programs have been the **University of Texas**, which has won 10 titles, and **Auburn University**, which has won eight, including five in a row from 2003 to 2007. **Coach Eddie Reese** has been at the helm of all 10 Texas championships. At the Division I level in **women**'s swimming, the first NCAA Championships was held in 1982, long after the men began hosting the event in 1937. **Stanford University** has won the most women's titles through 2009, with eight, all but one under the direction of legendary coach **Richard Quick**. Texas ranks second with seven championships, five with Quick as coach. **Pablo Morales**

is the most accomplished men's swimmer in NCAA history with 11 individual titles, while **Tracy Caulkins** (12) and **Natalie Coughlin** (11) have won the most individual crowns among women. Although the majority of athletes hail from the United States, NCAA swimming features numerous international athletes who use the U.S. college system to gain an education and benefit from the top coaching available.

NEALL, GAIL (AUS). B. 2 August 1955, Sydney, New South Wales. Gail Neall was the 1972 **Olympic** champion in the 400 **individual medley (IM)**, setting a world record in the final. She was the only **Australian** to win an Olympic title in the event until **Stephanie Rice** was victorious at the 2008 Olympics in Beijing. Neall was also seventh in the 200 **butterfly** at the 1972 Games.

NEGATIVE SPLITTING. Negative splitting is a term used in swimming to describe a race in which the last half was swum faster than the first half. Negative splitting is a difficult strategy to employ, primarily for two reasons. Not only does the body tire from the exertion put forth during the early stages of the race, but the athlete risks falling too far behind the competition to catch up. The most famous race that was negative split was the 1988 **Olympic** final in the **women**'s 400 **freestyle**, in which the **United States**' **Janet Evans** won the gold medal and set a world record. On her way to a time of 4:03.85, Evans covered the first 200 meters in 2:02.14, but was timed in 2:01.71 during the second half of the race, where she overtook her rivals and won comfortably.

NEILSON, ALEXANDRA LYNN (USA). B. 20 March 1956, Burbank, California. Sandy Neilson was one of the surprise performers at the 1972 **Olympics**. In the 100 **freestyle**, she defeated **United States** teammate **Shirley Babashoff** and **Australian** great **Shane Gould** for the gold medal. She added two more gold medals as a member of the United States' 400 freestyle **relay** and 400 medley relay.

NESTY, ANTHONY CONRAD (SUR). B. 25 November 1967, Paramaribo, Suriname. Anthony Nesty was the first black male to win an **Olympic** medal in swimming. At the 1988 Games in Seoul, Nesty narrowly defeated the **United States' Matt Biondi** in the 100 **butterfly**, Nesty finishing one hundredth of a second ahead, 53.00 to 53.01. Four years later, at the Barcelona Games, Nesty won the bronze medal in the 100 butterfly. As a University of Florida athlete, Nesty won three **National Collegiate Athletic Association (NCAA)** titles in the 100 butterfly and one in the 200 butterfly. Nesty is an assistant coach at his alma mater.

NETHERLANDS (NED). The Netherlands has enjoyed steady success in the pool for generations and ranks ninth all-time in Olympic swimming medals with 53 — 17 gold, 17 silver, and 19 bronze. Two of the country's best swimmers are from recent years, **Inge De Bruijn** and **Pieter van den Hoogenband**. De Bruijn once simultaneously held the world record in the 50 and 100 **freestyles** and the 100 **butterfly** and won Olympic gold in each of those events at the 2000 Games in Sydney. Van den Hoogenband was the 2000 Olympic champion in the 100 and 200 freestyles and repeated as the champion in the 100 freestyle in 2004. The Netherlands boasts the first black swimmer to medal in Olympic competition, **Enith Brigitha**, who won bronze medals in the 100 and 200 freestyles at the 1976 Games in Montreal. *See also* BRAUN, MARIA; DE ROVER, JOLANDA; KOK, AAGJE; MASTENBROEK, HENDRIKA; SENFF, DINA; VAN STAVEREN, PETRONELLA; VAN VLIET, PIETJE.

NEUMANN, PAUL (AUT). B. 13 June 1875, Vienna, Austria. D. 9 February 1932, Vienna, Austria. Paul Neumann was the first **Olympic** champion from Austria, winning the now-defunct 500 **freestyle** at the first Modern Olympics in 1896.

NIKE. Nike is the Oregon-based sportswear company founded by Phil Knight. The brand was among the leaders in swimwear until 2008, when it announced it was pulling out of the competitive swimming market rather than compete with other companies, such as **Speedo**, which had developed better-performing suits. Nike formerly had some of the top **United States** swimmers under contract, including **Aaron Peirsol** and **Brendan Hansen**, who set world records in Nike apparel. *See also* ARENA; JAKED; TYR SPORT.

NORD, KATHLEEN (GDR). B. 26 December 1965, Magdeburg, Germany. Racing during a period in which the **German Democratic Republic (GDR)** systematically **doped** its athletes, Kathleen Nord won the gold medal in the 200 **butterfly** at the 1988 **Olympics**, where she also placed fifth in the 400 **individual medley (IM)**. Nord would have been a medal contender four years earlier at the Los Angeles Olympics, but East Germany boycotted the Games. After winning a silver medal in the 400 medley at the 1982 **World Championships,** Nord was the gold medalist in the 400 individual medley at the 1986 World Championships and added a bronze medal in the 200 individual medley.

NORELIUS, MARTHA MARIA (USA). B. 22 January 1909, Stockholm, Sweden. D. 25 September 1955, St. Louis, Missouri. Martha Norelius was a **middle-distance** great for the **United States** who won three **Olympic** gold medals. Norelius won her first Olympic title at the 1924 Olympics, prevailing in the 400 **freestyle**. She repeated that championship at the 1928 Games and remains the only woman to win back-to-back gold medals in the 400 freestyle. Norelius won her third gold medal as a member of the United States' 400 freestyle **relay** at the 1928 Olympics.

NORTH BALTIMORE AQUATIC CLUB (NBAC). The North Baltimore Aquatic Club was founded in 1968 by Murray Stephens and has been one of the **United States'** top club programs for decades, best known for its molding of teenagers into Olympians. Its most famous pupil is **Michael Phelps,** who was coached by **Bob Bowman** and qualified for the 2000 **Olympics** as a 15-year-old, finishing fifth in the 200 **butterfly.** He was the youngest male swimmer to make the United States Olympic Team in 68 years. He won eight medals—six gold and two bronze—four years later in Athens and won eight gold medals at the 2008 Games. Aside from Phelps, NBAC has guided **Theresa Andrews, Anita Nall**, and **Beth Botsford** to Olympic gold medals. Its most recent female star has been **Katie Hoff**, who has won world championships and set world records in the **individual medley (IM)** events. The primary training facility is the Meadowbrook Aquatic and Fitness Club.

– O –

O'BRIEN, LOVETT IAN (AUS). B. 3 March 1947, Wellington, New Zealand. Ian O'Brien was an **Australian breaststroker** who medaled twice at the 1964 **Olympics**. O'Brien set his only world record en route to gold in the 200 breaststroke and helped Australia to the bronze medal in the 400 medley **relay**. He also competed at the 1968 Olympics, but failed to medal in two individual events and a relay.

O'BRIEN, MICHAEL JON (USA). B. 23 October 1965, Skokie, Illinois. Mike O'Brien was a top **distance freestyler** for the **United States** who won the gold medal in the 1,500 freestyle at the 1984 Olympics in Los Angeles. He is the last American swimmer to win Olympic gold in the event. O'Brien was the 1987 Pan American Games champion in the 200 **backstroke**.

OCTAGON. Octagon is an entertainment and sports agency that represents some of the top swimmers in the world, most notably **Michael Phelps**. Peter Carlisle is the agent who primarily directs the careers of swimmers and is the man credited with helping Phelps land the biggest endorsement deals in the sport, including the million-dollar bonus Phelps received from **Speedo** for winning a record eight gold medals at the 2008 **Olympic Games** in Beijing. Phelps is joined as an Octagon client by **United States** teammates **Ryan Lochte** and **Katie Hoff**, both of whom have set world records and won world championships. After the 2004 Olympics, where Phelps won six gold medals and two bronze medals, Octagon organized a national tour in which Phelps, **Ian Crocker**, and **Lenny Krayzelburg** traveled the country putting on swim clinics and exhibitions.

OFFICIALS. Officials are the individuals who oversee competition, led by the meet referee. The referee has the ultimate authority on the meet and the final say on debates, which can arise over violations such as **false starts**, illegal finishes, or illegal turns. Meets also typically feature a starter, who initiates the start of races and is responsible for calling false starts, and stroke and turn judges who assure that the rules are followed in those areas. A finish judge ensures that swimmers complete their races within the rules, and timekeepers are used to determine the times of swimmers when an electronic timing system is not in use. If an official witnesses an infraction, it is his or her responsibility to call a disqualification.

OLYMPIC GAMES. The Olympics, in their modern-day form, were first held in 1896 in Athens and have evolved into one of the most-watched sporting spectacles worldwide. The Olympics, featuring summer and winter versions, are held every four years and are governed by the International Olympic Committee (IOC). Swimmer **Michael Phelps** is the most decorated Olympian in history, having won 14 gold medals.

Swimming has been an Olympic sport since the inception of the Games, with the 100, 400, and 1,500 **freestyles** being the original events, along with the 100 freestyle for sailors. The **backstroke** was added in 1900 while the **breaststroke** was first conducted in 1908. The **butterfly** did not make its first appearance as an Olympic event until 1956 and it was not until 1964 that the **individual medley (IM)** was added to the competition program. The 800 freestyle relay was the first **relay** contested, held in 1906. During the early years of the Olympics, events such as the plunge for distance, an obstacle race, and underwater swimming were contested, but these have since been discontinued.

Women's events were added in 1912 when **Australia**'s **Fanny Durack** won the 100 freestyle. It was the only individual women's event that year, but there was a 400 freestyle relay. By 1924, women were competing in the freestyle, backstroke, and breaststroke. The butterfly was added in 1956 and the individual medley was added in 1964.

Two performances stand out in Olympic lore and both were in swimming. At the 1972 Olympics in Munich, **Mark Spitz** won seven gold medals, setting a world record in each event. That performance stood as the record for most gold medals in a single Olympiad until 2008, when Michael Phelps won eight gold medals at the Beijing Olympics. His eight victories included seven world records. For women, one of the greatest Olympic performances in history was given by the **German Democratic Republic's (GDR) Kristin Otto** at the 1988 Games. Otto won individual gold medals in the 50 and 100 freestyle events, the 100 backstroke, and 100 butterfly, in addition to winning two relay gold medals. Her efforts, however, are tainted by the systematic **doping** program in use by East Germany during the height of her career.

Diving has been an Olympic sport since 1904, when **platform** diving debuted. **Springboard** diving became a sport four years later. For women, platform diving made its first Olympic appearance in 1912 and was followed by springboard diving in 1920. For both men and women, **synchronized diving** became an Olympic sport in 2000.

O'NEILL, SUSAN (AUS). B. 2 August 1973, Mackay, Queensland. Susie O'Neill's international swimming success spanned three **Olympics** for **Australia** and featured eight medals from the Games. O'Neill collected a gold medal in the 200 **butterfly** in 1996 and won the 200 **freestyle** in her home country in 2000. In the 200 butterfly, she also won bronze (1992) and silver medals (2000). O'Neill was a member of three silver-medal winning **relays** and a bronze-medal relay. At the 2000 Olympic Trials in Sydney, she broke the 18-year world record of American **Mary T. Meagher** in the 200 butterfly. O'Neill claimed a world title in the 200 butterfly in 1998 and added two silver medals and four bronze medals at the **World Championships**.

OPEN-WATER SWIMMING. Open-water swimming has been around since the beginning of time, defined as any form of the sport that takes place in the ocean or lake, or a body of water without confines. This discipline, acknowledged by the **Fédération Internationale de Natation (FINA)** as one of the five aquatic sports, has gained popularity in recent years and was first included in the **Olympics** during the 2008 Games in Beijing when 10-kilometer races were contested. The first Open-Water World Championships were held in 2000, with races contested over 5, 10, and 25 kilometers. Open-water swimming can be a physical test beyond the endurance required, due to dozens of swimmers colliding during racing. While there is no man considered the greatest open-water swimmer in history, **Russia's Larissa Ilchenko** is viewed as the finest female swimmer in the sport's history, having won the first Olympic title to go with eight world championships. **Germany's Thomas Lurz** is among the most heralded male open-water swimmers.

OSIPOWICH, ALBINA LUCY CHARLOTTE (USA). B. 26 February 1911, Worcester, Massachusetts. D. 6 June 1964. Despite finishing third at the **United States** Trials, Albina Osipowich went on to win the gold medal and set a world record in the 100 **freestyle** at the 1928 **Olympics**. Osipowich added a second gold medal as part of the United States' 400 freestyle **relay**.

OTTENBRITE, ANNE (CAN). B. 12 May 1966, Ontario, Canada. Anne Ottenbrite represented **Canada** at the 1984 **Olympics** in Los Angeles and won three medals, taking advantage of the weaker fields due to the Eastern Bloc boycott that kept the **Union of Soviet Socialist Republics (URS)** and **German Democratic Republic (GDR)** out of the competition. Ottenbrite was the gold medalist in the 200 **breaststroke** and earned the silver medal in the 100 breaststroke. Ottenbrite picked up her third medal by swimming the breaststroke leg of the Canadian 400 medley **relay**, which finished third. A year before the Olympics, Ottenbrite was the Pan American Games gold medalist in the 100 breaststroke.

OTTO, KRISTIN (GDR). B. 7 February 1966, Leipzig, Germany. Kristin Otto was one of the stars of the 1988 **Olympics** in Seoul, winning six gold medals for the **German Democratic Republic (GDR)**. Otto won individual crowns in the 50 and 100 **freestyles**, along with the 100 **butterfly** and 100 **backstroke**. She is the only **woman** to win Olympic gold in three different 100-meter events. Otto also won nine medals between the 1982 and 1986 **World Championships**, but she was denied the chance to win additional Olympic gold when East Germany boycotted the 1984 Games in Los Angeles. The absence of East Germany was in response to the **United States'** boycotting the Moscow Games four years earlier. Otto, who set world records in the 100 and 200 freestyles, has denied knowingly being part of the systematic **doping** system implemented by Eastern Germany in the 1970s and 1980s, although several of her teammates have admitted to knowledge of the doping system.

OYAKAWA, YOSHINOBU (USA). B. 9 August 1933, Kona, Hawaii. Yoshi Oyakawa was the 1952 **Olympic** champion in the 100 **backstroke**, stretching the **United States'** streak of victories in the event to three. A multiple-time **National Collegiate Athletic Association (NCAA)** champion for Ohio State University, Oyakawa's gold was won in Olympic-record time, beating the 1936 standard of **Adolph Kiefer**.

– **P** –

PANG JIAYING (CHN). B. 6 January 1985, Shanghai, China. Pang Jiaying is a **Chinese freestyler** who has won four **Olympic** medals. She was the bronze medalist in the 200 freestyle at the 2008 Olympics in Beijing and was a member of silver-medal winning 800 freestyle **relay** teams in 2004 and 2008. In 2004, she helped China to a bronze medal in the 400 medley relay. At the 2009 **World Championships**, Pang helped China to a world record and gold medal in the 800 freestyle relay.

PANKRATOV, DENIS (RUS). B. 4 July 1974, Volgograd, Russia. Denis Pankratov was a **Russian butterfly** specialist who enjoyed his finest success at the 1996 **Olympics** in Atlanta, where he won the 100 and 200 butterfly events and handled the butterfly leg on Russia's silver-medal winning 400 medley **relay**. He was known for his strong underwater kick, and his win in the 100 butterfly was one of two world records he set in the event. His first record, set in 1995, erased **Pablo Morales'** nine-year standard. Pankratov also broke the world record in the 200 butterfly once and was the world champion in the 200 butterfly in 1994 in **Rome**, where he also captured bronze in the 100 distance.

PAN PACIFIC CHAMPIONSHIPS. The Pan Pacific Championships, commonly referred to as the Pan Pacs, were started in 1985 by the **United States**, **Australia**, **Canada**, and **Japan**. The meet was intended to provide top international competition in non-**Olympic** and **World Championships** years, although the Pan Pacs and World Championships were both held in 1991 due to the World Championships being held in January. The meet was initially held every other year, but was shifted to every four years beginning in 2002. Japan has been the most common host of the event, holding five editions. *See also* COMMONWEALTH GAMES.

PARALYMPIC SWIMMING. Paralympic swimming is contested by athletes with physical impairments that vary in severity and type. The Paralympics are held every four years in the city that hosts the **Olympics**. They usually take place a couple of weeks after the Olympics conclude.

PARK, TAE HWAN (KOR). B. 27 September 1989, Seoul, South Korea. Tae Hwan Park became the first South Korean **Olympic** swimming champion at the 2008 Beijing Olympics when he won the gold medal in the 400 **freestyle**. Park added a silver medal in the 200 freestyle, finishing behind **Michael Phelps**, and became one of the most hyped athletes in his country. He made his first international impact at the 2007 **World Championships**, winning gold in the 400 freestyle and bronze in the 200 freestyle. He was expected to excel at the 2009 World Championships, but Park surprisingly failed to qualify for the final of the 200 and 400 freestyles.

PARKIN, TERENCE (RSA). B. 12 April 1980, Bulawayo, Zimbabwe. Terence Parkin is a South African **breaststroker** who overcame a disability to medal in **Olympic** competition. Despite being deaf, Parkin won the silver medal in the 200 breaststroke at the 2000 Olympics in Sydney. Because he couldn't hear the starting signal, Parkin relied on a strobe light to indicate the beginning of a race. He was a silver medalist in the 200 breaststroke at the 2000 **World Short Course Championships** and won a bronze medal in the 200 breaststroke at the 1999 **Pan Pacific Championships**. Also a 2004 Olympian, Parkin won 12 gold medals and a silver medal at the 2005 Deaflympics in Melbourne.

PEIRSOL, AARON WELLS (USA). B. 23 July 1983, Irvine, California. Aaron Peirsol is considered the greatest **backstroke** specialist in history, and his easygoing personality has made him one of the most popular athletes in swimming. The Southern California native broke onto the international scene at the 2000 **Olympics** in Sydney, where he won a silver medal in the 200 backstroke behind **United States** teammate **Lenny Krayzelburg**, who Peirsol viewed as an idol. A year later, Peirsol was the world champion in the 200 backstroke and on his way to dominating his prime **stroke**. Peirsol won three gold medals at the 2004 Olympics, sweeping the 100 and 200 backstrokes and leading off the victorious 400 medley **relay**. At the 2008 Games, he repeated as champion of the 100 backstroke, again led off the winning medley relay, and took silver in the 200 backstroke. Peirsol won the 100 backstroke at the 2003, 2005, and 2007 **World Championships**, but surprisingly failed to qualify for the final at the 2009 event, admitting that he miscalculated his semifinal swim. However, Peirsol rebounded at the 2009 World Championships to set a world record in the 200 backstroke, complementing his previous titles from 2001, 2003, and 2005. He was the silver medalist in 2007. Peirsol was the first man to break 53 seconds in the 100 backstroke and the first man to break 52 seconds. He has set six world records in the 100 backstroke and seven in the 200 backstroke. Peirsol competed for the **University of Texas** as a freshman and sophomore, but forfeited his last two years of eligibility in order to turn professional. *See also* REESE, EDWIN.

PELLEGRINI, FEDERICA (ITA). B. 5 August 1988, Mirano, Italy. Federica Pellegrini is an **Italian middle-distance** standout who rebounded from a setback at the 2008 **Olympics** to capture a gold medal. The world-record holder in the 400 **freestyle** heading into the final, Pellegrini finished a surprising fifth, but managed to recover and win the gold medal in the 200 freestyle in world-record time. Pellegrini was the silver medalist in the 200 freestyle at the 2004 Olympics and won silver (2005) and bronze (2007) in the 200 freestyle at the **World Championships**. At the 2009 World Championships, Pellegrini became the first woman to break four minutes in the 400 freestyle when she set a world record of 3:59.15. She added another gold medal and world record in the 200 freestyle.

PERFORMANCE-ENHANCING DRUGS. Performance-enhancing drugs are substances, such as steroids and human growth hormones, that are banned for use. While swimmers such as Ireland's **Michelle Smith** have taken them on an individual basis, performance-enhancing drugs have also been supplied to athletes on a systematic basis, such as the **doping** program run by the **German Democratic Republic (GDR)** in the 1970s and early 1980s. Athletes who test positive for performance-enhancing drugs receive suspensions varying in length, although two and four years are the most common penalties.

PERKINS, KIEREN JOHN (AUS). B. 14 August 1973, Brisbane, Australia. Kieren Perkins is one of the best **distance freestylers** in history. He won the 1,500 freestyle gold medal at the 1992 and 1996 **Olympics** and took the silver medal at the 2000 Games, where he was supplanted by countryman **Grant Hackett**. Perkins also won the silver medal in the 400 freestyle at the 1992 Olympics and was the world champion in the 400 and 1,500 freestyle events in 1994. His other medal was a silver in the 1,500 freestyle at the **World Championships** in 1991. Perkins set one world record in the 400 freestyle and three world marks in the 1,500 freestyle.

PERTH. Perth is an **Australian** city that has twice been the host of the **World Championships**. Perth was the site of the event in 1991 and 1998 and is joined by **Rome** (1994/2009) as the only cities to twice be the host to the World Championships.

PFEIFFER, STEFAN (GDR). B. 15 November 1965, Hamburg, Germany. Stefan Pfeiffer's career was one of runner-up finishes for the **German Democratic Republic (GDR)**. Although he had significant success at the international level, a gold medal in major competition proved elusive. After winning a bronze medal in the 1,500 **freestyle** at the 1984 **Olympics**, Pfeiffer moved up to silver in the event at the 1988 Games, where he also won silver in the 800 freestyle **relay**. Pfeiffer twice just missed picking up additional bronze medals in Olympic competition, as he was fourth in the 400 freestyle in 1988 and fourth in the 1,500 freestyle in 1992. Pfeiffer claimed three silver medals at the **World Championships** and was a six-time medalist at the European Championships, winning three silver medals and three bronze.

PHELPS, MICHAEL FRED (USA). B. 30 June 1985, Baltimore, Maryland. Michael Phelps is considered the greatest swimmer in history and the greatest Olympian of all-time, the winner of a record 14 **Olympic** gold medals. He first emerged as an age-group standout, starring for the **North Baltimore Aquatic Club (NBAC)** under the coaching of **Bob Bowman**.

Phelps first rose to international prominence at the 2000 Olympic Trials in Indianapolis, where he placed second in the 200 **butterfly** to earn a berth to the Sydney Games as a 15-year-old. By qualifying for the Olympics, Phelps became the youngest male Olympic swimmer from the **United States** in 68 years. At the Olympics, Phelps advanced to the finals of the 200 butterfly and placed fifth, 33 hundredths of a second shy of claiming a medal.

At the United States Nationals in March 2001, Phelps set the first world record of his career, clocking 1:54.92 for the 200 butterfly to become the youngest male world-record holder in history. A few months later, Phelps captured his first world championship when he won the 200 butterfly in Fukuoka, Japan, lowering his world record to 1:54.58. It was the last time Phelps contested just one event in international competition.

After setting his first world record in the 400 **individual medley (IM)** at the 2002 United States Nationals, Phelps used 2003 as his major breakthrough as a multievent star. Before the **World Championships** in Barcelona, Phelps set world records in the 200 and 400 individual medley events, then won individual titles at the World Championships in the 200 butterfly and both individual medleys, to go with a silver medal in the 100 butterfly. At the meet, Phelps became the first man to set five world records in one competition. Two weeks later, he set his eighth world record of the year by lowering his standard in the 200 individual medley at the United States Nationals.

Leading into the 2004 Olympics in Athens, **Speedo** offered Phelps a million-dollar bonus if he could match the seven gold medals won by **Mark Spitz** at the 1972 Olympics in Munich. Ultimately, Phelps won six gold medals and two bronze medals and while his showing was short of Spitz's performance, it was still viewed as one of the finest efforts in Olympic history. His gold medals were won in the 100 and 200 butterfly and the 200 and 400 individual medleys, along with the 800 **freestyle relay** and 400 medley relay. Phelps won bronze medals in the 400 freestyle relay and 200 freestyle, where he placed behind fellow Olympic champions **Ian Thorpe (Australia)** and **Pieter van den Hoogenband (Netherlands)** in a matchup billed as the "Race of the Century."

Phelps' gold medal in the medley relay was achieved due to his swimming in the preliminaries of the event. As a goodwill gesture toward U.S. teammate **Ian Crocker**, whom Phelps defeated in the

100 butterfly final, Phelps yielded his position in the final to Crocker, who went on to post the fastest **split** in history on the United States' gold-medal winning swim.

Just after the Athens Games, Phelps relocated his training base from the North Baltimore Aquatic Club to Ann Arbor, Michigan, where Bowman moved to take the head coaching job at the University of Michigan. Because he was a professional athlete under contract with Speedo, Phelps was ineligible to swim collegiately, but began to represent Club Wolverine in national competition.

With much of 2005 spent tending to endorsement deals and appearances around the world, Phelps' training was not what it might have been heading into Athens. Nonetheless, he won six medals at the World Championships in Montreal, claiming individual titles in the 200 freestyle and 200 individual medley and as a member of three relays. His other medal was a silver behind Crocker in the 100 butterfly. In his two other events, which were new to his program, Phelps placed seventh in the 100 freestyle and failed to advance out of the preliminary heats in the 400 freestyle. At his closing press conference, Phelps spoke of his lack of training and vowed to return to his Olympic form.

By the time the 2007 World Championships started in Melbourne, the Olympic hype for the following year was in full force and Phelps did nothing but fuel the expectations for the Games in Beijing. At the World Championships, Phelps raced the program he was planning for 2008 and became the first individual to win seven gold medals, prevailing in two relays along with the 200 freestyle, both butterfly events and both medleys. Individually, Phelps set world records in each of his individual events, except for the 100 butterfly. An expected eighth gold medal was lost when the United States was disqualified in the preliminaries of the 400 medley relay.

Before the 2008 Olympics started, Phelps' second pursuit of Spitz's iconic seven gold medals was the talk of the Games, Phelps appearing on numerous magazine covers, including *Sports Illustrated* and *ESPN The Magazine*. Once again, Speedo offered a million-dollar bonus for the equaling of Spitz's medal haul.

Phelps opened his program impressively, setting a world record in the 400 individual medley. His second event, however, was not nearly as easy and required the finest anchor split in history for the gold medal. Although Phelps led off the 400 freestyle relay in American-record time, by the time **Jason Lezak** entered the water for the final leg, the United States faced a sizable deficit against **France** and its anchor **Alain Bernard**. At the midpoint of the anchor leg, Lezak still trailed Bernard by a half-body length. Gradually, though, Lezak pulled closer to the Frenchman and ultimately caught him, touching the wall eight hundredths of a second ahead at the finish.

After winning that second gold medal, Phelps added victories in the 200 freestyle, 200 butterfly, 200 individual medley, and 800 freestyle relay, all in world-record time. He then won his seventh gold medal by the slimmest of margins, beating Serbia's Milorad Cavic by one hundredth of a second. Phelps appeared beaten at the wall, but instinctively took an extra stroke in the closing meters to prevail. He then closed out his meet with an eighth gold medal as a member of the United States' 400 medley relay.

Following the Beijing Games, Phelps took a five-month break from the sport, but returned to training in early 2009 in preparation for the World Championships in **Rome**. His training base also returned to Baltimore, where he moved after Bowman became chief executive officer of the North Baltimore Aquatic Club. Phelps' comeback was not without its bumps as he was suspended for three months by **United States Swimming** for a photograph that surfaced in a British tabloid showing Phelps using a marijuana pipe at a party at the University of South Carolina. In addition to the suspension, Kellogg's ended its endorsement deal with Phelps, but he was still supported by his other sponsors, including Speedo.

For the 2009 World Championships, Phelps opted for a six-event schedule, a lighter load than what he was familiar with handling. In Rome, Phelps won five gold medals and a silver medal, setting individual world records in the 100 butterfly and 200 butterfly. His only loss was to Germany's **Paul Biedermann** in the 200 freestyle, although that defeat has been considered the result of Biedermann wearing a **high-tech suit**, compared to Phelps wearing an older model without similar benefits.

In addition to the photo of Phelps using a marijuana pipe, Phelps was cited for driving under the influence after the 2004 Olympics. As a result of the transgression, he was required to speak to antidrunk driving groups, such as Mothers Against Drunk Driving (MADD), detailing the dangers of operating a vehicle while under the influence of alcohol.

Not only is Phelps the all-time leader with 14 Olympic gold medals, he is the only athlete to reach double digits. His 16 overall Olympic medals are the most by a male athlete and trail only **Russian** gymnast Larissa Latynina (18) for the most ever. Phelps also holds the record for most gold medals and medals won at the World Championships with 22 and 26, respectively. His 29 individual world records account for another record.

PLATFORM DIVING. Platform diving is one of the four diving events contested in **Olympic** competition, joining the **springboard** event and **synchronized diving** off both the platform and springboards. Platform diving takes place on a 10-meter high tower, which, unlike the springboard, has no bouncing properties. The finest platform divers in history are considered to be the **United States' Greg Louganis** and **Italy's Klaus Dibiasi**.

POLESKA, ANNE (GER). B. 20 February 1980, Krefeld, Germany. Anne Poleska was a **German** 200 **breaststroke** specialist who had her biggest highlight at the 2004 **Olympics** in Athens, where she claimed the bronze medal in her prime event. Poleska also advanced to the semifinals of the 200 breaststroke at the 2000 and 2008 Olympics. Outside of Olympic competition, she had her biggest achievements at the European Short Course Championships, winning three gold medals in the 200 breaststroke and one title in the 100 breaststroke.

POLL, CLAUDIA MARIA (CRC). B. 21 December 1972, Managua, Nicaragua. Claudia Poll was a world-class **middle-distance freestyler** whose career accomplishments came under a cloud of suspicion after she failed an out-of-competition **doping** test in 2002. Poll's biggest achievement was capturing the gold medal in the 200 freestyle at the 1996 **Olympics** in Atlanta, where she finished ahead of world-record holder **Franziska van Almsick** of **Germany**. Poll went on to win bronze medals in the 200 and 400 freestyles at the 2000 Games in Sydney, but in 2002 failed a drug test after her sample was found to include traces of a steroid. She originally received a four-year ban from competition, but that penalty was eventually reduced to two years, allowing her to compete in the 2004 Olympics in Athens, where she failed to reach the finals of the 400 freestyle. Poll has steadfastly maintained that she did not knowingly take **performance-enhancing drugs**. She was the 1994 world champion in the 200 freestyle, won bronze medals in the 200 and 400 freestyles at the 1994 **World Championships**, and was the silver medalist in the 400 freestyle at the 2001 World Championships.

POLLACK, ANDREA (GDR). B. 8 May 1961, Schwerin, Germany. Andrea Pollack's swimming career was as much defined by her six **Olympic** medals as her involvement in the systematic **doping** program used by the **German Democratic Republic (GDR)** on its athletes. At the 1976 Olympics, Pollack won gold medals in the 200 **butterfly** and as a member of the 400 medley **relay**. She added a silver medal in the 100 butterfly and a silver medal in the 400 **freestyle** relay. Four years later, Pollack won another silver in the 100 butterfly and was on the victorious medley relay. At the 1978 **World Championships**, Pollack was second in the 100 butterfly and medley relay and earned bronze in the 200 butterfly. In the late 1990s, Pollack admitted to taking **performance-enhancing drugs** as part of orders from her coaches. Pollack set one world record each in the 100 butterfly and 200 butterfly.

POLYANSKY, IGOR NIKOLAYEVICH (URS). B. 20 March 1967, Novosibirsk, Russia. Igor Polyanksy was one of the world's top **backstrokers** in the late 1980s, starring at the 1988 Olympics in Seoul for the **Union of Soviet Socialist Republics (URS)**. In addition to winning the gold medal in the 200 backstroke, Polyansky added bronze medals in the 100 backstroke and as a member of the Soviet Union's 400 medley **relay**. His bronze medal in the 100 backstroke was a disappointment as Polyansky had set three world records in the event earlier in the year. He set one world record in the 200 backstroke, an effort in 1985 that lasted a little more than six years.

POPOV, ALEXANDER VLADIMIROVICH (RUS). B. 16 November 1971, Volgograd, Russia. Nicknamed the "Tsar," Alex Popov is one of the greatest **sprint freestylers** in swimming history. At the

1992 and 1996 **Olympics,** Popov won gold medals in the 50 and 100 freestyle events, representing the **Unified Team (EUN)** and **Russia,** respectively. Popov's repeat in the 100 freestyle was the first since **Johnny Weissmuller** prevailed at the 1924 and 1928 Olympics. Popov's main rivals were the **United States' Matt Biondi, Tom Jager,** and **Gary Hall Jr.,** each of whom he defeated in Olympic competition. His world record in the 50 freestyle, set in June 2000, lasted until 2008, when **Australian Eamon Sullivan** broke the mark. After the 1996 Olympics, Popov was stabbed by a watermelon vendor during a dispute in Moscow and had to undergo emergency surgery after the knife grazed his lung and extended 15 centimeters into his stomach. He recovered in time to win four gold medals at the 1997 European Championships. Popov was a three-time world champion in the 100 freestyle and a two-time world champion in the 50 freestyle. He won 21 gold medals at the European Championships and 26 overall medals from 1991 to 2004. Popov is a member of the International Olympic Committee (IOC).

POTEC, CAMELIA ALINA (ROU). B. 19 February 1982, Braila, Romania. Camelia Potec is a **middle-distance** swimmer who ranks among the top swimmers produced by Romania. She was the gold medalist in the 200 **freestyle** at the 2004 **Olympics,** holding off **Italian Federica Pellegrini.** Potec claimed a bronze medal in the 200 freestyle at the 2001 **World Championships** and has had considerable success at the European Championships. She has won 17 medals at the European Championships—four gold, four silver, and nine bronze. At the 2008 Olympics, Potec failed to defend her title when she placed fifth in the 200 freestyle. She just missed medals in the 400 and 800 freestyles, too, placing sixth and fourth, respectively.

PREMIER MANAGEMENT GROUP (PMG). The Premier Management Group, casually known as PMG Sports, is one of the larger representative agencies for **Olympic** athletes, a majority of whom are swimmers. The agency was established in 1995 by Evan Morgenstein, who initially took on Olympic gold medal swimmer Josh Davis as a client. It has grown considerably through the years, with the likes of **Janet Evans, Amanda Beard, Mark Spitz,** and **Dara Torres** as swimmers represented by the company. Aside from securing sponsorships and endorsement deals for its athletes, PMG Sports sets up speaking engagements for its athletes. Among the sponsorships it has landed for clients include **Nike**, Coca-Cola, Pepsi, and Verizon. *See also* HANSEN, BRENDAN; PEIRSOL, AARON.

PRIDE. The movie *Pride*, released in 2007, was based on the life of Jim Ellis, an African American who made the Philadelphia Department of Recreation program into a well-respected club. Ellis was played by Terrence Howard and the movie focuses on Ellis improving a dilapidated pool and introducing African American children to swimming, a sport with low representation in that demographic group.

PROZUMENSHCHIKOVA, GALINA NIKOLAYEVNA (URS). B. 26 November 1948, Sevastopol, Ukraine. Galina Prozumenshchikova was an **Olympic** medalist for the **Union of Soviet Socialist Republics (URS)** in the **breaststroke** events at three Olympics, 1964, 1968, and 1972. Her lone gold medal came in the 200 breaststroke in 1964, when she defeated the **United States'** **Claudia Kolb**. She earned silver medals in the 100 breaststroke in 1968 and 1972 and claimed a pair of bronze medals in the 200 breaststroke in 1968 and 1972. Prozumenshchikova set one world record in the 100 breaststroke and four world records in the 200 breaststroke during her career.

– Q –

QIAN HONG (CHN). B. 30 January 1971, Baoding, China. Qian Hong won her first **Olympic** medal for **China** in the 100 **butterfly** as a 17-year-old at the 1988 Olympics. She returned in 1992 and won the gold medal in the 100 butterfly, setting an Olympic record. She was the 1991 world champion in the 100 butterfly.

QUICK, RICHARD (USA). B. 31 January 1943, Akron, Ohio. D. 10 June 2009, Austin, Texas. Richard Quick was the most successful college coach in **United States** history. His **coaching** skills were also among the finest at the international level. Quick's initial head-coaching stints were at Southern Methodist University, Iowa State University, and **Auburn University**, but his first major success came as the head coach of the women's program at the **University of Texas**, which he led to **National Collegiate Athletic Association (NCAA)** championships from 1984 to 1988. Quick left Texas to take the reins at **Stanford University**, which he guided to NCAA titles in 1989, from 1992 to 1996, and in 1998. Quick retired after the 2005 season, but returned to Auburn as the men's and women's coach for the 2007–2008 season. Diagnosed with an inoperable brain tumor, Quick was forced to take a leave of absence during the 2009 season, with former **Australian** Olympian Brett Hawke serving as coach in his absence. Auburn won the NCAA men's title, giving Quick a record 13 college championships. He died a little more than three months later. Quick was an **Olympic** head coach on three occasions (1988, 1996, 2000) and an assistant at the Olympics in 1984, 1992, and 2004. Some of his best swimmers over the years were Olympic gold medalists **Rowdy Gaines, Dara Torres,** and **Jenny Thompson.**

QWEST CENTER. The Qwest Center, a 17,000-seat arena in Omaha, Nebraska, served as the site of the 2008 **United States** Olympic Trials and will again host the event in 2012. Two temporary pools were installed for the 2008 Trials, one for competition and the other for warmup and practice purposes. The Olympic Trials averaged more than 12,000 fans per day at the 2008 Trials and a higher total is expected in 2012. *See also* INDIANA UNIVERSITY NATATORIUM.

– R –

RACE CLUB, THE. The Race Club is a **sprint**-based swimming club founded by 10-time **Olympic** medalist **Gary Hall Jr.** in Islamorada, Florida. Hall designed the club to bring together the top sprinters in the world to work with one another in preparation for qualifying for the Olympic Games and pursuing Olympic medals. In addition to Hall, some of the other members have included Milorad Cavic, the 2008 Olympic silver medalist in the 100 **butterfly,** five-time British Olympian **Mark Foster,** and **Sweden's Therese Alshammar,** one of the premier female sprinters in history.

RAPP, SUSAN GERARD (USA). B. 5 July 1965, Eden Prairie, Minnesota. Susan Rapp was a **breaststroke** swimmer for the **United States** at the 1984 **Olympics** in Los Angeles. She won the silver medal in the 200 breaststroke, finishing behind **Canadian Anne Ottenbrite.** Rapp was also awarded a gold medal in the 400 medley **relay** for swimming the breaststroke leg during the preliminary round. Rapp was seventh in the 100 breaststroke in Los Angeles and competed in the 1988 Games in Seoul, where she placed 13th. She remains active in the sport, having set numerous world records in **Masters** competition and competing at the 2008 United States Olympics Trials at the age of 42.

RAUSCH, EMIL A. (GER). B. 11 September 1882. D. 14 December 1954. Emil Rausch was one of the stars of the 1904 **Olympics.** In addition to winning the 880-yard **freestyle** and the one-mile freestyle, he won a bronze medal in the 220-yard freestyle. At the 1906 Intercalated Games, Rausch earned a silver medal in the 1,000-meter freestyle **relay.** *See also* GERMANY.

READY ROOM. The ready room is the area designated for athletes who are nearing the beginning of their race. During major competitions, the athletes walk out of the room in single file and march to the **starting blocks** to be introduced to the crowd. They are generally arranged in order, from Lane One to Lane Eight, and often are accompanied by music, which adds hype to the atmosphere and generates a spectacle for the fans. Athletes have different approaches in the ready room. While some swimmers remain quiet and do not speak, choosing to focus on their upcoming race, other athletes engage in conversation with one another. Some athletes use the ready room to gain a mental edge on their rivals, directing trash talk toward the opposition. In the summer of 2009, a second ready room was instituted in which swimmers had their suits checked to be sure they were within the guidelines approved by the **Fédération Internationale de Natation (FINA).** Once their suits were verified as legal, they were allowed to move to the ready room set aside for race preparation. *See also* HIGH-TECH SUITS.

REESE, EDWIN C. (USA). B. 23 July 1941, Daytona Beach, Florida. Eddie Reese, the head **coach** at the **University of Texas** since 1978, is considered one of the greatest swimming coaches in history. He has guided Texas to nine **National Collegiate Athletic Association (NCAA)** team championships and has produced numerous **Olympic** medal winners, including **Aaron Peirsol, Brendan Hansen,** and **Ian Crocker.** Reese has been the **United States'** Men's Olympic Coach on three occasions, for the 1992 Games in Barcelona, the 2004 Olympics in Athens, and the 2008 Games in Beijing. Reese has also served as a United States' Olympic assistant in 1988, 1996, and 2000. Under Reese's watch, the U.S. men won 17 medals at the 2008 Olympics, including 10 gold.

REINISCH, RICA (GDR). B. 6 April 1965, Seifhennersdorf, Germany. Rica Reinisch was one of many teenage girls systematically fed anabolic steroids by **German Democratic Republic (GDR)** officials, who were seeking to develop the world-class athletes. At the 1980 **Olympics,** Reinisch won three gold medals, all in world-record time. In addition to winning the 100 and 200 **backstroke** events, she led off the victorious 400 medley **relay.** Reinisch has been outspoken about her disgust for the **doping** program used by East Germany, a stance not all of the athletes have taken.

RELAYS. Relay events are team disciplines in which four swimmers unite, either representing the same country or the same team. At the international level, three relays are held—the 400 **freestyle** relay, 800 freestyle relay, and 400 medley relay. In the freestyle relays, each of the swimmers contest the same distance in freestyle. In the medley relay, the four swimming **strokes** are brought together with an order of **backstroke, breaststroke, butterfly,** and freestyle. A key to relay races is the exchange, the point when one swimmer touches the wall and the other swimmer leaves the **starting blocks** for the next leg. The best relays can time the exchanges to just a few hundredths of a second. If a swimmer leaves the starting block before a teammate finishes his leg, the team suffers a disqualification. In swimming, individual records can be established by the leadoff swimmers for the 100 freestyle in the 400 freestyle relay, the 200 freestyle in the 800 freestyle relay, and the 100 backstroke in the 400 medley relay.

RICE, STEPHANIE LOUISE (AUS). B. 17 June 1988, Queensland, Australia. Stephanie Rice emerged on the international scene as a top-flight **individual medley (IM)** swimmer in 2006 and 2007, but it was her performance at the 2008 **Olympics** that stood out. At the Beijing Games, Rice set world records on the way to gold medals in the 200 and 400 individual medley events, and also contributed a leg to **Australia**'s triumphant 800 freestyle **relay**. Rice was the 2006 **Commonwealth Games** champion in both medley events and followed a year later by winning bronze medals in the disciplines at the **World Championships**. At the 2009 World Championships, Rice was the silver medalist in the 200 individual medley and bronze in the 400 individual medley.

RICHTER, ULRIKE (GDR). B. 17 June 1959, Gorlitz, Germany. Ulrike Richter was one of the finest **backstrokers** in history, setting world records and winning **Olympic** titles in the 100 and 200 backstrokes. However, her accomplishments were tainted by the revelation that she was administered steroids as part of the **German Democratic Republic's (GDR)** systematic **doping** program that was prominent in the 1970s and 1980s. Richter won the 100 backstroke at the 1973 and 1975 **World Championships** and was the bronze medalist in the 200 backstroke in 1975. At the 1976 Olympics, she won gold medals in the 100 and 200 backstrokes and as a member of East Germany's 400 medley **relay**.

RICKARD, BRENTON (AUS). B. 19 October 1983, Brisbane, Australia. Brenton Rickard is the best **breaststroker** in **Australian** history and winner of a pair of silver medals at the 2008 **Olympics**. In addition to placing second in the 200 breaststroke, Rickard was a member of Australia's runner-up 400 medley **relay**. At the 2009 **World Championships**, Rickard set his first world record while claiming the gold medal in the 100 breaststroke. At the 2007 World Championships, Rickard was the bronze medalist in the 100 breaststroke and silver medalist in the 200 breaststroke.

RIS, WALTER STEPHEN (USA). B. 4 January 1924, Chicago, Illinois. D. 25 December 1989, Mission Viejo, California. Walter Ris excelled as one of the **United States'** premier **sprint freestylers** during the first half of the 1900s. He was a **National Collegiate Athletic Association (NCAA)** champion at the University of Iowa and won two gold medals at the 1948 **Olympics.** In addition to capturing the 100 freestyle, Ris helped the United States win the 800 freestyle **relay.**

ROBIE, CARL JOSEPH (USA). B. 12 May 1945, Darby, Pennsylvania. Carl Robie was a two-time Olympian for the **United States** who used his silver medal at the 1964 **Olympics** in Tokyo as his inspiration to win the gold medal in Mexico City four years later. He set four world records in the 200 **butterfly** during his career and had a rivalry with **Australian Kevin Berry,** in which the men exchanged the record five times between 1962 and 1964. It was Berry who defeated Robie in the 200 butterfly in Tokyo.

ROGAN, MARKUS ANTONIUS (AUT). B. 4 May 1982, Vienna, Austria. Markus Rogan was one of the world's best **backstrokers** for much of the 2000s. A **National Collegiate Athletic Association (NCAA)** champion at **Stanford University,** he won silver medals in the 100 and 200 backstrokes at the 2004 **Olympics** in Athens. He was twice the silver medalist in the 200 backstroke at the **World Championships** (2001/2005) and was the bronze medalist in the event at the 2007 World Championships. Rogan was the 2008 world **short-course** gold medalist in the 200 backstroke and has won European titles in the 100 and 200 backstroke, along with the 200 **individual medley (IM).**

ROME. Rome is one of two cities to twice play host to the **World Championships,** having held the event in 1994 and 2009. The other city to hold the distinction is **Perth, Australia,** which was the site of the World Championships in 1991 and 1998. Rome has also been the host of the **Olympic** Games, filling that role in 1960.

ROSE, IAIN MURRAY (AUS). B. 6 January 1939, Nairn, Scotland. Murray Rose was among the first **distance** stars for **Australia,** a country that has become well known for its excellence in the longer **freestyle** events. Rose was the most successful swimmer at the 1956

Olympics in Melbourne, thanks to victories in the 400 and 1,500 freestyles, and as a member of the Australian 800 freestyle **relay.** Rose defended his championship in the 400 freestyle at the 1960 Games, where he took silver in the 1,500 freestyle and bronze in the 800 freestyle relay. Rose swam collegiately in the **United States** for the University of Southern California and set two world records each in the 400 and 1,500 freestyles.

ROSOLINO, MASSIMILIANO (ITA). B. 11 July 1978, Napoli, Italy. Massi Rosolino was a versatile **Italian** swimmer who enjoyed his biggest performances at the 2000 **Olympics** in Sydney. In addition to capturing the gold medal in the 200 **individual medley (IM)**, Rosolino took silver behind **Australian Ian Thorpe** in the 400 **freestyle** and was the bronze medalist in the 200 freestyle. Four years later in Athens, he won a bronze medal by swimming on Italy's 800 freestyle **relay.** Rosolino followed his Olympic title in the 200 individual medley by winning that event at the 2001 **World Championships.** He took bronze in that event at the 2003 World Championships and was the silver medalist in the 200 freestyle at the 1998 World Championships. He was a 21-time medalist at the European Championships, including seven gold medals.

ROSS, NORMAN DEMILLE (USA). B. 2 May 1896, Portland, Oregon. D. 19 June 1953, Evanston, Illinois. Norman Ross was an elite **distance freestyler** in the early part of the 20th century. A world-record holder in the 200 and 400 freestyles, he won the 400 freestyle and 1,500 freestyle at the 1920 **Olympics.** Ross added a third gold medal as a member of the **United States'** 800 freestyle **relay.**

ROTH, RICHARD WILLIAM (USA). B. 26 September 1947, Palo Alto, California. Richard Roth was the first **individual medley (IM)** champion in **Olympic** history, winning the event at the 1964 Olympics with a world-record time. Prior to winning the gold medal in the 400 individual medley, Roth was suffering from appendicitis, but decided to postpone surgery until after his Olympic races.

ROTHHAMMER, KEENA RUTH (USA). B. 26 February 1957, Little Rock, Arkansas. Keena Rothhammer was a versatile **freestyler** for the **United States**. At the 1972 **Olympics**, she was the gold medalist in the 800 freestyle, beating **Australian** star **Shane Gould**, and was the bronze medalist in the 200 freestyle. Rothhammer, though, managed only a sixth-place performance in the 400 freestyle. At the 1973 **World Championships**, she failed to medal in the 800 freestyle, but won gold in the 200 freestyle and silver in the 400 freestyle.

ROUSE, JEFFREY NORMAN (USA). B. 6 December 1970, Fredericksburg, Virginia. Jeff Rouse was the dominant 100 **backstroker** of the 1990s, holding the world record in the event from 1991 to 1999. At the 1992 **Olympics**, Rouse had a bittersweet showing. He was upset in the 100 backstroke final by **Canadian Mark Tewksbury**, but Rouse set a world record during the Games while leading off the **United States'** 400 medley **relay**. Four years later, Rouse found redemption when he won the gold medal in the 100 backstroke and again helped the United States win gold in the 400 medley relay. He was the 1991 world champion in the 100 backstroke and won the silver medal in the event at the 1994 **World Championships**.

RUDKOVSKAYA, YELENA GRIGORYEVNA (EUN). B. 21 April 1973, Belarus. Yelena Rudkovskaya was the 1992 **Olympic** champion in the 100 **breaststroke**, the only female to win a swimming event for the **Unified Team**. She narrowly missed another individual medal, placing fourth in the 200 breaststroke, but was a member of the bronze-medal winning 400 medley **relay**.

RUSSELL, DOUGLAS ALBERT (USA). B. 20 February 1946, New York, New York. Doug Russell was a multievent standout for the **United States** who set world records in the 100 **backstroke** and 100 **butterfly**. At the 1968 **Olympics**, Russell won the gold medal in the 100 butterfly and helped the United States win the gold medal in the 400 medley **relay**.

RUSSIA (RUS). A former state of the **Union of Soviet Socialist Republics (URS)**, Russia gained its independence late in 1991. Its team competed at the **Olympics** as a member of the Soviet Union through the 1988 Games and was part of the **Unified Team** at the 1992 Olympics in Barcelona. Russia has won 15 medals in Olympic swimming competition—five gold, five silver, and five bronze. **Alexander Popov** is the greatest swimmer in Olympic history. He was the champion in the 50 and 100 **freestyles** at the 1996 Games in Atlanta, where countryman **Denis Pankratov** was the winner of the 100 and 200 **butterfly** events. *See also* ILCHENKO, LARISSA; SADOVYI, EVGENY; SAUTIN, DMITRY; SLOUDNOV, ROMAN; VYATCHANIN, ARKADY.

ROZSA, NORBERT (HUN). B. 9 February 1972, Dombovar, Hungary. Norbert Rozsa is one of a number of world-class **breaststrokers** to emerge from **Hungary.** At the 1992 **Olympics** in Barcelona, Rozsa was the runner-up in both breaststroke races, placing behind the **United States' Nelson Diebel** in the 100 distance and American **Mike Barrowman** in the 200 breaststroke. Four years later, however, Rozsa claimed the Olympic gold medal in Atlanta when he bested the field in the 200 breaststroke, edging countryman **Karoly Guttler** for the title. Rozsa won seven medals at the **World Championships**, including three individual titles. He set three world records in the 100 breaststroke.

– S –

SADOVYI, EVGENY VIKTOROVICH (RUS). B. 19 January 1973, Volgograd, Russia. Evgeny Sadovyi was the dominant **middle-distance freestyler** at the 1992 **Olympics** in Barcelona, representing the **Unified Team (EUN).** The **Russian** won the 200 freestyle by just 16 hundredths of a second over **Sweden's Anders Holmertz**, then took gold in the 400 freestyle by defeating **Australia's Kieren Perkins** by the same margin. Sadovyi earned his third gold medal by anchoring the Unified Team to victory in the 800 freestyle **relay**, setting a world record in the process. Sadovyi twice earned individual medals at the European Championships, claiming gold in the 400 freestyle in 1991 and silver in the 200 freestyle in 1993.

SALNIKOV, VLADIMIR VALERYEVICH (URS). B. 21 May 1960, Leningrad, Russia. Vladimir Salnikov is viewed as one of the premier **distance** swimmers of all-time, having won gold medals in the 400 and 1,500 **freestyles** at the 1980 **Olympics** in Moscow for the **Union of Soviet Socialist Republics (URS)**. He also helped the Soviet Union win gold in the 800 freestyle **relay**, and his winning time in the 1,500 freestyle of 14:58.27 was the first sub-15-minute performance. After missing the 1984 Olympics due to the Soviet boycott, Salnikov returned to win gold in the 1,500 freestyle at the 1988 Olympics. He set 13 world records between the 400, 800, and 1,500 freestyles and was the champion in the 400 and 1,500 freestyle events at the 1978 and 1982 **World Championships**. Had the Soviet Union not boycotted the 1984 Games, in retaliation to the American boycott of the 1980 Olympics, Salnikov could have been the first male swimmer to win the same event at three consecutive Olympics.

SANDENO, KAITLIN (USA). B. 13 March 1983, Mission Viejo, California. Kaitlin Sandeno was a multi-event **United States** star who competed in two **Olympics**, achieving her best results at the 2004 Games in Athens. As a 17-year-old at the 2000 Olympics in Sydney, Sandeno won a bronze medal in the 800 **freestyle**, was fourth in the 400 **individual medley (IM)**, and placed sixth in the 200 **butterfly**. Four years later, Sandeno was the silver medalist in the 400 individual medley and bronze medal winner in the 400 freestyle. She also anchored the United States to gold in the 800 freestyle **relay**. Sandeno won three bronze medals in her career at the **World Championships** and was a six-time medalist at the **World Short Course Championships**, winning three individual gold medals at the 2004 event. She retired after not qualifying for the 2008 Olympics.

SANDERS, SUMMER ELISABETH (USA). B. 13 October 1972, Roseville, California. Summer Sanders flourished in multiple events for the **United States**, making her biggest imprints in the 200 **butterfly** at the 1992 **Olympics** in Barcelona. Sanders won the gold medal in the event and also picked up a gold for her contribution to the United States' 400 medley **relay**. Sanders added a silver medal in the 200 **individual medley (IM)** and was the bronze medalist in the 400 individual medley, setting American records in both events that lasted for 12 years each. A year before the Olympics, Sanders had identical finishes at the **World Championships**, winning the 200 butterfly and collecting silver and bronze medals for her medley efforts. She was a triple-gold medalist at the 1991 **Pan Pacific Championships** and starred for **Stanford University**, where she won six individual **National Collegiate Athletic Association (NCAA)** titles.

SANTA CLARA SWIM CLUB (SCSC). The Santa Clara Swim Club is one of the most storied clubs in the United States. Founded in 1951 by legendary coach **George Haines**, the club has produced swimmers totaling 71 **Olympic** medals. Among those competing for the club include **Mark Spitz** and **Don Schollander**. Each summer, the club hosts the Santa Clara International Swim Meet, one of the top summer invitational meets in the United States, annually attracting fields of Olympic athletes and serving as a tuneup competition for major competitions such as the Olympics and **World Championships**.

SAUTIN, DMITRY IVANOVICH (RUS). B. 15 March 1974, Voronezh, Russia. Although **Greg Louganis** is widely considered the best **diver** in history, **Russia**'s Dmitry Sautin has won more **Olympic** medals than any diver ever with eight. Sautin won medals at every Olympics from 1992 to 2008, an unusually long period to remain at the top of a sport. Sautin represented the **Unified Team** at his first Olympics in 1992, winning the bronze medal in the three-meter **springboard**. In 1996, while representing **Russia**, he won the gold medal in the 10-meter **platform** and followed four years later with a gold in the 10-meter **synchronized diving** platform, where he teamed with Igor Lukashin. The 2000 Olympics marked the first time synchronized diving was contested at the Games. Of the nine world championship medals won by Sautin, five are gold. He has also won 12 gold medals at the European Championships and 17 overall.

SCHEFF, OTTO (AUT). B. 12 December 1889, Berlin, Germany. D. 26 October 1956, Niederosterreich, Austria. Otto Scheff was a three-time **Olympic** medalist for Germany, his best achievement a gold medal in the 400 **freestyle** at the Intercalated Games in 1906. He also won a bronze medal in the one-mile freestyle and was the bronze medalist in the 400 freestyle at the 1908 Games. Scheff competed for Austria in **water polo** at the 1912 Olympics.

SCHIPPER, JESSICAH LEE (AUS). B. 19 November 1986, Brisbane, Queensland. Jessicah Schipper is the best all-around **butterfly** swimmer in **Australian** history. At the 2008 **Olympics**, she won her second straight gold medal in the 400 medley **relay** and added bronze medals in the 100 butterfly and 200 butterfly. Schipper was the gold medalist in the 200 butterfly at the 2007 and 2009 **World Championships,** adding silver medals each year in the 100 butterfly. At the 2005 World Championships, she won gold in the 100 butterfly and was second in the 200 butterfly, although video indicated Schipper should have been awarded the gold when Poland's **Otylia Jedrzejczak,** the winner, was shown to touch the wall illegally at the finish.

SCHNEIDER, PETRA (GDR). B. 11 January 1963, Chemnitz, Germany. Petra Schneider is a former **Olympic** champion from the **German Democratic Republic (GDR)** who has admitted to being part of the systematic **doping** program implemented by her nation's government. At the 1980 Olympics in Moscow, Schneider was the gold medalist in the 400 **individual medley (IM)** and took silver in the 400 **freestyle.** She did not get the chance to defend her title four years later due to the Eastern Bloc boycott of the Los Angeles Games. At the 1982 **World Championships,** Schneider was the champion of the 200 and 400 individual medley events and was the silver medalist in the 400 freestyle. At the 1978 World Championships, she was the bronze medalist in the 400 individual medley. Unlike some other East German swimmers, who have denied knowingly being doped with steroids, Schneider came clean about the program. During her career, she set four world records in the 400 individual medley and one in the 200 medley. Her last world mark in the longer medley lasted from 1982 until 1997, when **China**'s Yan Chen broke the record. Ironically, the Chinese swimmer eventually tested positive for **performance-enhancing drugs.**

SCHOEMAN, ROLAND MARK (RSA). B. 3 July 1980, Pretoria, South Africa. Roland Schoeman is a **South African sprint** star who has trained for the majority of his career in the **United States,** where he excelled collegiately for the University of Arizona. Schoeman's greatest achievements arrived at the 2004 **Olympics,** where he led South Africa to the gold medal in the 400 **freestyle relay.** Schoeman also won the silver medal in the 100 freestyle and was the bronze medalist in the 50 freestyle. He also competed at the 2000 and 2008 Olympics, but did not win a medal. Schoeman is a five-time medalist at the **World Championships**, winning the 50 **butterfly** in 2005 and 2007 and the 50 freestyle in 2005.

SCHOLES, CLARKE CURRIE (USA). B. 25 November 1930, Detroit, Michigan. Clarke Scholes was a multiple-time **National Collegiate Athletic Association (NCAA)** champion for Michigan State University who was awarded the gold medal in the 100 **freestyle** at the 1952 **Olympics**, although he and **Japan**'s Hiroshi Suzuki finished in identical times of 57.4.

SCHOLLANDER, DONALD ARTHUR (USA). B. 30 April 1946, Charlotte, North Carolina. Don Schollander was a two-time Olympian who won four gold medals at the 1964 **Olympics** in Tokyo. In addition to winning the 100 and 400 **freestyles**, Schollander helped the **United States** win two **relays**. He would have been the heavy favorite to win gold in the 200 freestyle, but the event did not return to the Olympic program until four years later. At the 1968 Games, Schollander earned a silver medal in the 200 freestyle and took gold on the American 800 freestyle relay. Coached by **George Haines** at the famed **Santa Clara Swim Club (SCSC)**, Schollander set 13 world records, including 10 in the 200 freestyle.

SCHRADER, HILDEGARD (GER). B. 4 January 1910, Strassfurt, Germany. D. 26 March 1966, Magdeburg, Germany. Hilde Schrader is one of only three **German women** to win the 200 **breaststroke** at the **Olympics**, accomplishing the feat with a two-second triumph at the 1928 Olympics.

SCHUBERT, MARK (USA). Mark Schubert is the general manager and national team head **coach** for **United States Swimming (USS)**, having accepted that role in 2006. Prior to joining United States Swimming, Schubert was one of the most successful collegiate coaches in the United States, with his biggest impact at the University of Southern California and the **University of Texas**. Schubert coached the Texas women from 1989 to 1992 and led the Longhorns to **National Collegiate Athletic Association (NCAA)** titles in 1990 and 1991. He then moved to the University of Southern California and led the Trojan women to the 1997 NCAA crown while also guiding the nationally ranked men's program. Schubert was the club coach of the Mission Viejo Nadadores from 1972 to 1985, leading the team to 44 national team titles. Schubert has been a member of every United States' Olympic coaching staff since 1980, serving as head coach of the men in 1992 and 2000 and as the women's head coach in 2004. Among those he has coached are **Cynthia Woodhead** and **Mary T. Meagher.**

SCHULER, CAROLYN JANE (USA). B. 5 January 1943, San Francisco, California. Carolyn Schuler was rated behind **United States** teammate Carolyn Wood in the 100 **butterfly** at the 1960 **Olympics**. Wood, however, did not finish the final and Schuler earned the gold medal by nearly a second. She added a second gold as a member of the United States' 400 medley **relay**.

SCHWENK, WILLIAM DOUGLAS (USA). B. 17 June 1971, Sarasota, Florida. Tripp Schwenk was a **backstroker** for the **United States** who medaled in two events at the 1996 **Olympics**. Schwenk was the runner-up in the 200 backstroke, placing behind countryman Brad Bridgewater. Schwenk earned a gold medal in the 400 medley **relay** and was fifth in the 100 backstroke. At the first **World Short Course Championships** in 1993, Schwenk won the 100 and 200 backstrokes and also prevailed as a member of the United States' 400 medley relay. He was the 200 backstroke champion at the 1995 **Pan Pacific Championships**.

SENFF, DINA WILLEMINA JACOBA (NED). B. 3 April 1920, Rotterdam, Netherlands. D. 27 June 1995, Amstelveen, Netherlands. Nida Senff was the gold medalist in the 100 **backstroke** at the 1936 **Olympics**, the second **Netherlands woman** to win the event.

SHANTEAU, ERIC LEE (USA). B. 1 October 1983, Snellville, Georgia. Eric Shanteau rose to prominence in 2008 when he qualified to represent the **United States** in the 200 **breaststroke** at the Beijing **Olympics** just a week after being informed he had testicular cancer.

Although Shanteau did not medal at the Games, where he was 10th, his story was one of the more inspirational tales from Beijing. After the Olympics, Shanteau underwent surgery to treat his cancer and returned to training, setting an American record in the 200 breaststroke at the 2009 United States Nationals. A few weeks later, Shanteau set United States' records in the 100 and 200 breaststrokes at the **World Championships**, placing fourth in the shorter distance and earning a silver medal in the 200 breaststroke. Shanteau also medaled in the 200 **individual medley (IM)**, claiming bronze in an event won by U.S. teammate **Ryan Lochte**. Before his international success, Shanteau had a heartbreaking performance at the 2004 Olympic Trials, where he placed third in the 200 and 400 medley events, one spot shy of qualifying for the Athens Games.

SHAW, TIMOTHY ANDREW (USA). B. 8 November 1957, Long Beach, California. Tim Shaw was a two-time **Olympic** medalist for the **United States**, winning his medals in different sports. At the 1976 Games in Montreal, he won the silver medal in the 400 **freestyle** behind teammate **Brian Goodell**. Because of the U.S. boycott of the Moscow Games, Shaw did not get the chance to compete in the 1980 Olympics, but he returned to the Olympic stage in Los Angeles in 1984 and helped the United States win the silver medal in **water polo**. At the 1975 **World Championships**, Shaw was the dominant freestyler, winning the 200, 400, and 1,500 events.

SHIBATA, AI (JPN). B. 14 May 1982, Fukuoka, Japan. Ai Shibata is the best female **distance freestyler** in **Japanese** history, the highlight of her career a gold medal in the 800 freestyle at the 2004 **Olympics** in Athens. Shibata continued to excel on the international scene after the Athens Games, capturing a silver medal in the 400 freestyle and a bronze medal in the 800 freestyle at the 2005 **World Championships** in Montreal. At the 2007 World Championships in Melbourne, Shibata added bronze medals in the 400 and 800 freestyles. She was the champion in the 400 freestyle at the 2006 **Pan Pacific Championships**.

SHORT-COURSE SWIMMING. This version of the sport is held in a 25-meter pool and it is not utilized by the International Olympic

Committee (IOC). Because this format features more turns than **long-course** swimming, athletes who have greater mastery of that aspect of racing can gain an advantage. The first **World Championships** in this format debuted in 1993 in Palma de Mallorca, Spain. In the United States, short-course swimming is conducted more often in a 25-yard pool than in a 25-meter pool.

SIDORENKO, ALEKSANDR ALEKSANDROVICH (URS). B. 27 May 1960, Mariupol, Ukraine. Aleksandr Sidorenko was the 1980 **Olympic** gold medalist in the 400 **individual medley (IM)** for the **Union of Soviet Socialist Republics (URS).** He was twice a medalist at the **World Championships**, winning the bronze medal in the 200 individual medley in 1978 and the gold medal in the 200 medley in 1982. Sidorenko would have been the favorite for the gold medal in the 200 individual medley at the Olympics, but the event was not part of the program in 1976 and 1980.

SIEBEN, JONATHAN SCOTT (AUS). B. 24 August 1966, Brisbane, Australia. Jon Sieben was an **Australian butterfly** specialist who registered a big upset at the 1984 **Olympics** in Los Angeles. Facing off with **Germany's Michael Gross**, the world-record holder, Sieben was not expected to contend for the gold medal. Sieben, however, tracked Gross down in the final lap and won with a world-record time of 1:57.04, compared to the 1:57.40 of Gross. Sieben, who also competed at the 1988 and 1992 Olympics, added a bronze medal in the 100 butterfly in 1984.

SIEVINEN, JANI NIKANOR (FIN). B. 31 March 1974, Vihti, Finland. Jani Sievinen was a top **individual medley (IM)** swimmer for Finland, a country not known for routinely producing world-class swimmers. At the 1996 **Olympics** in Atlanta, Sievinen claimed the silver medal, behind **Hungarian Attila Czene**, in the 200 individual medley, a disappointment considering he was the world-record holder. At the 1994 **World Championships**, Sievinen set a world record in the 200 individual medley to win gold and added a silver medal in the 400 medley. His world record in the 200 individual medley lasted from 1994 to 2003, when **Michael Phelps** broke the mark at the Santa Clara International Swim meet. Sievinen won nine medals at the European Championships, all individual, with five being gold. Sievinen was actually a better **short-course** swimmer, winning four gold medals and two silvers at the **World Short Course Championships**.

SJOSTROM, SARAH FREDERICA (SWE). B. 17 August 1993, Stockholm, Sweden. Sarah Sjostrom burst onto the international stage at the 2009 **World Championships**, where she won the gold medal in the 100 **butterfly**. Although Sjostrom competed at the 2008 **Olympics** as a 14-year-old, she did not advance beyond the preliminaries of the 100 **backstroke** or the 100 butterfly. A year later, she broke the oldest record in **women**'s swimming, breaking **Inge de Bruijn**'s eight-year-old 100 butterfly standard during the semifinals of the World Championships. She lowered the mark a second time in the final, winning the gold medal with a time of 56.06.

SKELTON, ROBERT D. (USA). B. 25 June 1903, Wilmette, Illinois. D. 25 June 1977, Houston, Texas. Bob Skelton was the first **breaststroke Olympic** champion for the **United States**, winning the 200 breaststroke at the 1924 Games.

SKINNER, JOHN ALEXANDER (RSA). B. Cape Town, South Africa. Jonty Skinner is a former world-record holder in the 100 **freestyle** who never got his chance to compete in the **Olympic** Games due to the International Olympic Committee (IOC) banning **South Africa** for its Apartheid practices. Skinner would have been among the top contenders for gold at the 1976 Olympics, where **Jim Montgomery** prevailed and became the first man in history to break the 50-second barrier with a time of 49.99. Less than a month after Montgomery won the gold medal, Skinner defeated him and lowered the world record to 49.44. That standard stood as the world mark for nearly five years. Skinner served as a **coach** and technical consultant for **United States Swimming (USS)** for 15 years.

SLOUDNOV, ROMAN ANDREYEVICH (RUS). B. 24 February 1980, Omsk, Russia. Roman Sloudnov became the first man in history to break the one-minute barrier in the 100-meter **breaststroke**, clocking 59.97 at the 2001 **Russian** National Championships. A few weeks later, Sloudnov again dipped under one minute while winning the world championship in Fukuoka, Japan. Sloudnov won a bronze medal in the 100 breaststroke at the 2000 **Olympics** in Sydney.

SMITH, MICHELLE (IRL). B. 16 December 1969, Dublin, Ireland. Michelle Smith was a multievent Irish swimmer who emerged as an international star at the 1996 **Olympics** amid allegations of **performance-enhancing drug** use. Two years after the Olympics, she was banned for four years after tampering with a urine sample during an out-of-competition **doping** test. Smith was a 1988 and 1992 Olympian for Ireland, but her performances left her far from contending for medals. She started to show major improvements in 1994, a year after she began dating Erik de Bruin, her future husband, a weight-event performer for the **Netherlands** in track and field who was suspended from his sport for doping violations. Smith won two gold medals and a silver medal at the 1995 European Championships, then won Olympic gold at the 1996 Games in Atlanta in the 400 **freestyle** and 200 and 400 **individual medley (IM)** events and won a bronze medal in the 200 **butterfly**. During the Olympics, there was considerable speculation that Smith's meteoric rise in the sport was not solely based on enhanced training methods. In addition to reporters suggesting she was using performance-enhancing drugs, athletes publically suspected usage, including U.S. **distance** star **Janet Evans**. She added two gold medals and two silver medals at the 1997 European Championships, but a year later provided a doping sample that was tainted with excessive amounts of alcohol and was also found to include traces of banned substances. The tampering of the sample generated a four-year ban, although Smith denies any use of performance-enhancing drugs.

SMITH, WILLIAM M. (USA). B. 16 May 1924, Puunene, Hawaii. Bill Smith was a world-record setting **middle-distance freestyler** who won the 1948 **Olympic** title in the 400 freestyle. He also helped the **United States** to gold in the 800 freestyle **relay**. Smith also was a nationally ranked wrestler.

SONI, REBECCA (USA). B. 18 March 1987, Freehold, New Jersey. Rebecca Soni is a **United States breaststroker** who registered one of the biggest upset victories of the 2008 **Olympics** in Beijing. After winning the silver medal in the 100 breaststroke behind **Australia**'s **Leisel Jones**, Soni bettered Jones' world record and defeated the Australian star in the 200 breaststroke. She added a third medal in the 400 medley **relay**, helping the United States take silver. At the 2009 **World Championships**, Soni became the world-record holder in the 100 breaststroke and won gold while becoming the first woman to break 1:05 in the event. However, in the final of the 200 breaststroke, where she was heavily favored to win, Soni led for 190 meters before faltering at the finish and placing fourth. She added a silver medal in the 50 breaststroke. At the University of Southern California, Soni became the first **woman** to win four consecutive **National Collegiate Athletic Association (NCAA)** titles in the 200 breaststroke.

SOUTH AFRICA (RSA). South Africa has had a strong swimming tradition for several decades, but its practice of Apartheid led the International Olympic Committee (IOC) to ban the nation from **Olympic** competition in 1970, a banishment that was not lifted until the 1992 Games in Barcelona. Because of this ban, **Jonty Skinner** was denied the chance to contend for Olympic gold in 1976, where the **United States' Jim Montgomery** won gold in the 100 **freestyle**. A few weeks after the Games, Skinner lowered Montgomery's world record, proof that he would have been a contender for the Olympic title. South Africa's biggest swimming achievement was at the 2004 Olympics in Athens, when the foursome of **Roland Schoeman**, Darian Townsend, Lyndon Ferns, and Ryk Neethling combined for the gold medal in the 400 freestyle **relay**, defeating **Australia** and the United States in the championship final. *See also* HARRISON, JOAN; PARKIN, TERENCE.

SPEEDO. Speedo is the most famous swimwear company in the world, founded in 1914 by Alexander McRae in **Australia**. It was originally known as McRae Hosiery Manufacturers, but became known as Speedo in 1928. The company has continually developed through the years, producing nylon and lycra suits and, most recently, a high-tech piece of swimwear known as the **LZR Racer**, which consists of ultrasonically welded panels of nonpermeable material. The majority of the world's top swimmers wear Speedo products, notably **Michael**

Phelps. *See also* ARENA; JAKED; NIKE; TECHNOLOGICAL DOPING; TYR SPORT.

SPITZ, MARK ANDREW (USA). B. 10 February 1950, Modesto, California. Mark Spitz is recognized as one of the greatest Olympians and swimmers of all time, with his performance at the 1972 **Olympics** in Munich viewed as one of the finest sporting achievements in history. In Munich, Spitz won seven gold medals and set seven world records, the gold-medal count a record that stood until **Michael Phelps** won eight gold medals in swimming at the 2008 Olympics in Beijing. Spitz's gold medals were obtained in the 100 and 200 **freestyle** events, the 100 and 200 **butterfly** races, and as a member of the **United States**' 400 and 800 freestyle **relays** and 400 medley relay. Spitz's performance followed a disappointing showing—by his standards—at the 1968 Olympics in Mexico City. Before those Games, Spitz predicted he would win six gold medals, but ended up with only two in relay action. He added a silver medal in the 100 butterfly, in which he was the world-record holder, and a bronze medal in the 100 freestyle.

Because there were no financial opportunities available during his swimming career, Spitz retired after the Munich Olympics. During his career, Spitz established 26 individual world records, spanning the 100, 200, and 400 freestyles and the 100 and 200 butterfly events. Spitz competed collegiately for Indiana University, where he was coached by **Doc Counsilman**. Spitz helped Indiana win **National Collegiate Athletic Association (NCAA)** team championships in each of his four years, and he was an eight-time individual champion. His popularity has led to numerous motivational speaking engagements. Spitz attempted a comeback in the early 1990s with his focus being a spot on the 1992 United States Olympic Team, but Spitz never came close to regaining the form he showed in his prime.

SPLIT TIME. A split time refers to the times clocked by a swimmer at various points during a race. During a 200 **freestyle**, for example, a split time will be recorded at the 50-, 100-, and 150-meter marks. During events with television coverage, the split times for the current race will be shown in the bottom corner of the screen compared to the split times of the existing world record.

SPRINGBOARD DIVING. Springboard diving is one of the four **diving** events contested in **Olympic** competition, joined by **platform** diving and **synchronized** events off both the platform and springboards. In Olympic competition, the springboard event is held on a three-meter high board. Springboard competition is also held on a one-meter board in collegiate and World Cup competition. **Greg Louganis** is considered among the best springboard divers in history, having won Olympic titles in 1984 and 1988.

SPRINT EVENTS. Swimming's sprint events are those contested over 50 and 100 meters, the shortest distances raced in the sport. Many athletes have made careers out of specializing in the 50-meter races, although most of those swimmers are equally accomplished over the 100-meter distance. **Russian Alexander Popov**, who represented the **Union of Soviet Socialist Republics (URS)** and the **Unified Team (EUN)** at the **Olympics**, is considered the best male sprinter in history, with the **Netherlands' Inge de Bruijn** among the premier names on the **women**'s side.

STACK, ALLEN McINTYRE (USA). B. 23 January 1928, New Haven, Connecticut. D. 12 September 1999, Honolulu, Hawaii. Allen Stack was the successor to **Adolph Kiefer** as the premier **backstroker** in the **United States** and the world. He broke world records of Kiefer's in the 100 and 200 backstroke events, erasing a 12-year-old standard in the 100 distance in 1948. Stack won the gold medal in the 100 backstroke at the 1948 **Olympics** and was fourth in the event at the 1952 Games.

STANFORD UNIVERSITY. Stanford University, located in Palo Alto, California, boasts the most successful **women**'s swimming program in **National Collegiate Athletic Association (NCAA)** history, having won eight NCAA championships through 2009. Seven of those championships came under the direction of **coach Richard Quick**. The most successful swimmer in program history is **Jenny Thompson**, a winner of 12 Olympic medals. The men's program at Stanford has also enjoyed high levels of success, evident in eight NCAA team titles. The most decorated men's swimmer in Stanford history is **Pablo Morales**, who won a record 11 individual NCAA championships during his career, including career sweeps of the 100 and 200 **butterfly** events. He added three championships in the 200 **individual medley (IM)**.

STARTING BLOCK. A starting block is the platform, angled slightly downward toward the water, on which swimmers stand before a race begins. The starting block is used for the **freestyle, breaststroke, butterfly,** and **individual medley (IM)** events, along with the free-style **relays**. It is not used in the backstroke, where swimmers start the race in the water, and is not used in the medley relay, in which the first leg is the backstroke. The starting blocks used today have electronic sensors that determine the reaction time of the swimmer to the starting signal and in relays to measure whether the swimmer next in line did not leave the block before his teammate touched the wall, finishing his leg.

STEFFEN, BRITTA (GER). B. 16 November 1983, Schwedt, Germany. Britta Steffen is a **sprint-freestyle** specialist for **Germany**, considered one of the top stars produced by Germany in the past two decades. Entering the 2008 **Olympics**, Steffen was considered a medal contender in the sprints, but her name was frequently mentioned after those of **Australia**'s **Libby Trickett**, the **Netherlands**' Marleen Veldhuis, and the **United States**' **Dara Torres**. In Beijing, however, Steffen won the gold medal in the 50 and 100 freestyles. She actually earned her first Olympic medal at the 2000 Games, when she picked up a bronze while swimming in the preliminaries of the 800 freestyle **relay**. Steffen was the bronze medalist in the 100 freestyle at the 2007 **World Championships** and improved that showing at the 2009 World Championships. She twice set the world record in the 100 freestyle, once leading off the German 400 freestyle relay and again en route to the gold medal in the 100 freestyle. She added another gold in the 50 freestyle, setting another world record. In 2006, her breakout meet as an individual, Steffen won gold in the 50 and 100 freestyles, setting a world record in the longer distance at the European Championships.

STEINSEIFER, CAROLYN LYNNE (USA). B. 12 February 1968, Redwood City, California. Carrie Steinseifer was a **freestyle** swimmer for the **United States** who won a pair of gold medals at the 1984 Olympics in Los Angeles. Steinseifer shared her gold medal in the 100 freestyle with teammate **Nancy Hogshead**, as they touched the wall with identical times of 55.92. She also teamed with Hogshead to help the United States win the gold medal in the 400 freestyle **relay**. Other international highlights for Steinseifer included a gold medal in the 100 freestyle at the 1983 Pan American Games and a gold medal in the 200 freestyle at the 1985 **Pan Pacific Championships**.

STERKEL, JILL ANN (USA). B. 27 May 1961, Los Angeles, California. Jill Sterkel, a **sprint-freestyle** specialist, was the first **United States woman** to qualify for four **Olympic** Games, although she did not compete at the 1980 Olympics due to the American boycott. Sterkel won gold medals in the 400 freestyle **relay** in 1976 and 1984 and won bronze medals in 1988 in the 50 freestyle and 400 freestyle relay. Sterkel set two world records in the 50 freestyle and helped the United States win gold at the 1978 **World Championships** in Berlin. She served as the women's coach at the **University of Texas** from 1992 to 2006. Aside from swimming, Sterkel was a standout in **water polo**, helping the United States win a bronze medal at the 1986 World Championships.

STEWART, MELVIN MONROE (USA). Mel Stewart was once the world's best 200 **butterflyer**, dominating the event in the early 1990s. After finishing fifth in the 200 butterfly at the 1988 **Olympics** in Seoul, Stewart came back to capture the gold medal at the 1992 Barcelona Games, setting an Olympic record. He also earned a gold medal in the 400 medley **relay** and a bronze medal in the 800 freestyle relay. Stewart was the 1991 world champion and won two **National Collegiate Athletic Association (NCAA)** titles while representing the University of Tennessee, his 1991 winning time remaining the collegiate record until 2008. Stewart remains involved in swimming, working as a feature commentator on the Internet. *See also* UNITED STATES.

STOCKWELL, MARCUS WILLIAM (AUS). B. 5 July 1963, Queensland, Australia. Mark Stockwell is a former **Australian** swimmer who won three medals at the 1984 Olympics in Los

Angeles, where he was involved in controversy surrounding the 100 **freestyle**. In the 100 freestyle, Stockwell won the silver medal behind the **United States' Rowdy Gaines**, but video footage shows that the race was started before Stockwell had the chance to get set on the **starting block**. Conversely, Gaines beat the entire field into the water, having been warned by his **coach Richard Quick** that the official had a penchant for starting the race quickly. At the end of the race, Stockwell demonstrated his anger by slamming his fist against the water. He added a silver medal in the 400 freestyle **relay** and won bronze in the 400 medley relay. Stockwell eventually married the United States' **Tracy Caulkins**, considered one of the greatest all-around swimmers in history.

STOUDER, SHARON MARIE (USA). B. 9 November 1948, Altadena, California. Sharon Stouder was one of the stars of the 1964 **Olympics**, winning four medals. She was the gold medalist in the 100 **butterfly**, setting a world record to defeat the former standard-bearer, **Ada Kok** of the **Netherlands**. Stouder also won gold medals in the 400 freestyle **relay** and 400 medley relay and earned silver in the 100 freestyle, nearly upstaging **Australian** great **Dawn Fraser**.

STRACHAN, RODNEY (USA). B. 16 October 1955, Santa Monica, California. Rod Strachan was a member of the 1976 **United States Olympic Men's Swimming Team** that won gold medals in all but one of the events contested. Strachan was the winner of the 400 **individual medley (IM)** in Montreal, defeating teammate **Tim McKee**. Strachan won the silver medal in the 400 individual medley at the first **World Championships** in 1973, and his winning time from the Montreal Olympics was a world record, the only global mark of his career.

STROKES. *See* BACKSTROKE; BREASTSTROKE; BUTTERFLY; FREESTYLE; INDIVIDUAL MEDLEY.

SULLIVAN AWARD. The James E. Sullivan Award is given on a yearly basis by the **United States'** Amateur Athletic Union (AAU) to the top amateur athlete in the United States, although some of its winners, such as **Michael Phelps**, are actually professionals based on their endorsement deals. The award, first presented in 1930, honors athletic achievement, along with acknowledging character and sportsmanship. **Ann Curtis** was the first swimmer to win the award, receiving the honor in 1944. Other swimmers who have won the Sullivan Award are **Don Schollander** (1964), **Debbie Meyer** (1968), John Kinsella (1970), **Mark Spitz** (1971), **Tim Shaw** (1975), **John Naber** (1977), **Tracy Caulkins** (1978), **Janet Evans** (1989), and **Michael Phelps** (2003). **Sammy Lee** (1953) and **Greg Louganis** (1984) are divers who have won the award and Jessica Long (2006) won the Sullivan Award for **Paralympic Swimming**.

SULLIVAN, EAMON (AUS). B. 30 August 1985, Perth, Australia. Eamon Sullivan is a **sprint** star for **Australia** who won three medals at the 2008 **Olympics**. Sullivan made his first major international mark when he won the bronze medal in the 100 **freestyle** at the 2007 **World Championships**. In early 2008, he set world records in the 50 and 100 freestyles and was considered a gold-medal favorite in each event. He ended up winning silver in the 100 freestyle, finishing behind **France's Alain Bernard**, and failed to earn a medal in the 50 freestyle. He added a silver medal in the 400 medley **relay** and a bronze medal in the 400 freestyle relay, both times as the Australian anchor. He was expected to contend for titles at the 2009 World Championships, but illness forced him to withdraw from the meet a little more than a week before its start.

SUZUKI, DAICHI (JPN). B. 10 March 1967, Chiba, Japan. Daichi Suzuki was a **backstroke** standout from **Japan** who helped revolutionize the event. Suzuki was one of the first swimmers to employ the **dolphin kick** at the start of his race, often covering the first 20 to 25 meters underwater. Swimmers are now allowed to stay under water for only 15 meters. At the 1988 **Olympics**, Suzuki captured the gold medal in the 100 backstroke, defeating world-record holder **David Berkoff** and former world-record holder **Igor Polyansky**. Suzuki also competed at the 1984 Olympics, tying for 11th in the 100 backstroke.

SWEDEN (SWE). Sweden ranks just outside the top-10 among countries with the most **Olympic** swimming medals, having won 35—

eight gold, 14 silver, and 13 bronze. **Gunnar Larsson** is among the most celebrated Swedish swimmers, with victories in the 200 and 400 **individual medley (IM)** events at the 1972 Munich Olympics. Men's swimming in the country has been much more successful than **women**'s swimming, with all eight of the country's gold medals won by male athletes. *See also* ALSHAMMAR, THERESE; AR-VIDSSON, PAR; BARON, BENGT; FROLANDER, LARS; HOL-MERTZ, ANDERS; MALMROT, HAKAN; SJOSTROM, SARAH.

SWIM NEWS. *Swim News* is a **Canadian**-based swimming magazine with an international circulation. Although it features a heavy amount of Canadian-related content, it also covers news and provides features on the rest of the world. Its Web site, swimnews.com, is better known than the magazine and is updated daily with content from around the world. The primary writer on the Web site is **Craig Lord**, a European-based journalist who has been recognized for his work by the **International Swimming Hall of Fame (ISHOF)**. *See also* *SWIMMING WORLD MAGAZINE*.

SWIMMING CANADA. Swimming Canada is the governing body of the sport in **Canada** and has made strides in recent years to have the nation rank among the elite in the world. Unhappy with its results at the 2000 and 2004 **Olympics**, which produced just one Olympic medal, Swimming Canada hired Pierre LaFontaine as its chief executive officer in 2005, charging him with the task of rejuvenating the sport in Canada. LaFontaine is regarded as one of the top **coaches** in the world and a master motivator, having served stints as the head coach of the Phoenix Swim Club and the **Australian Institute of Sport (AIS)**. In the first Olympics after LaFontaine's hiring, Canada won just one medal at the Beijing Games, but had several swimmers contend by advancing to various championship finals.

SWIMMING WORLD MAGAZINE. *Swimming World* is an Arizona-based magazine that is considered one of the top publications in the world for aquatic sports. Published monthly, it provides a mixture of event coverage, features, opinion columns, and results for swimming, **diving, water polo**, and **synchronized** swimming. Its first issue was published in January 1960, then under the title of *Junior Swimmer*.

The magazine features correspondents from around the world and also has a Web site, www.swimmingworldmagazine.com, which is updated with daily content, including a Monday through Friday Internet show called the *Morning Swim Show*. *See also SWIM NEWS*.

SYNCHRONIZED DIVING. Synchronized diving is a team sport that began to rise in popularity in the 1990s and is contested on the three-meter **springboard** and 10-meter **platform**. Athletes compete on diving boards that are side-by-side and are judged on their individual execution, along with the synchronization of their dives, which are expected to mirror each other. The scores are combined for a final total. Synchronized diving was added to the program at the **World Championships** in 1998 and became an **Olympic** sport at the 2000 Olympics in Sydney.

SYNCHRONIZED SWIMMING. Synchronized swimming is one of the five aquatic disciplines overseen by the **Fédération Internationale de Natation (FINA)**. It is an acrobatic and artistic form of swimming primarily performed by an individual, in pairs, or as part of a team. The routines performed are evaluated by judges who look for characteristics such as timing, grace, and difficulty of the acrobatic moves. The sport is primarily contested by **women**, especially in international competition, although some nations have men's competitions. Synchronized swimming was officially added to the **Olympic** program in 1984 with solo and duet competition and remained in this form through the 1992 Olympics. In 1996, a team competition was the sole medal event, although the duet competition was restored in 2000 and both team and duet events have been contested since. **Russia** has won the team competition at the 2000, 2004, and 2008 Olympics.

SZABO, JOZSEF (HUN). B. 1 March 1969, Budapest, Hungary. Jozsef Szabo was a **breaststroker** for **Hungary**, a country with a deep tradition of developing world-class swimmers in the **stroke**. In 1988, Szabo left the Seoul **Olympics** with a gold medal in the 200 breaststroke. He's been joined as an Olympic breaststroke medalist by countrymen **Norbert Rozsa**, **Karoly Guttler**, and **Daniel Gyurta**.

He was the 1987 European champion in the 200 breaststroke and won silver in the 400 **individual medley (IM)**. At the 1989 European Championships, he added a silver medal in the 200 breaststroke.

SZEKELY, EVA (HUN). B. 3 April 1927, Budapest, Hungary. Eva Szekely was long one of the best **breaststrokers** in history, competing in the 200 breaststroke at three consecutive **Olympics** for **Hungary**. She was the fourth-place finisher at the 1948 Olympics, then won the gold medal at the 1952 Games. She concluded her Olympic career by winning a silver medal in the 200 breaststroke in 1956.

SZOKE, KATALIN (HUN). B. 17 August 1935, Budapest, Hungary. Katalin Szoke was a member of **Hungary**'s strong 1952 **women**'s swimming team that produced three individual **Olympic** champions and a gold medal in the 400 **freestyle relay**. In addition to helping that relay to victory, Szoke was the winner of the 100 freestyle.

– T –

TAGUCHI, NOBUTAKA (JPN). B. 18 June 1951, Ehime, Japan. Nobutaka Taguchi was a world-record setting **breaststroker** who won the 1972 **Olympic** gold medal in the 100 breaststroke for **Japan**. He added a bronze medal in the 200 breaststroke. At the first **World Championships** in 1973, Taguchi was the bronze medalist in the 100 and 200 breaststrokes.

TANAKA, SATOKO (JPN). B. 3 February 1942, Nagasaki, Japan. Satoko Tanaka is one of the best female **backstrokers** in history, but she never won an **Olympic** title. Tanaka won the bronze medal in the 100 backstroke at the 1960 Olympics and followed with a fourth-place finish in the 1964 Olympics in the same event. Tanaka's best event was the 200 backstroke, in which she set 10 world records for **Japan** from 1959 to 1963, but the event was not added to the Olympic program until 1968, after Tanaka's career had come to a close.

TAPER. A taper is the term used to describe a training regimen a swimmer follows in preparation for a major competition, typically an international meet or national-level event for swimmers of world-class ability. During the taper, swimmers gradually reduce their practice workload over a set timeframe in order to have the body in peak condition for the major meet ahead. Because the body is accustomed to heavier volumes of training, the body's muscles during a taper feel rested and, consequently, swimmers expect to produce their fastest times. Because tapers rely on a heavy training base prior to their implementation, they are only beneficial a few times per year.

TAUBER, ULRIKE (GDR). B. 16 June 1958, Chemnitz, Germany. Ulrike Tauber is suspected to be one of the **German Democratic Republic (GDR)** athletes who was given **performance-enhancing drugs**, most notably steroids, during the systematic **doping** program of the 1970s and 1980s. She was the **Olympic** champion in the 400 **individual medley (IM)** in 1976, where she added a silver medal in the 200 **butterfly.** Tauber won gold in the 400 individual medley and silver in the 200 individual medley at the 1975 **World Championships** and followed at the 1978 World Championships by winning silver in the 400 individual medley and bronze in the 200 individual medley.

TAYLOR, HENRY (GBR). B. 17 March 1885, Greater Manchester, England. D. 28 February 1951, Greater Manchester, England. Henry Taylor is the most decorated **Olympian** in British history, having won eight medals over the course of four Olympiads. Taylor's first three medals came at the 1906 Intercalated Olympics in Athens, an Olympiad that is not recognized as official. At the 1908 Games, Taylor won the 400 and 1,500 **freestyles** and helped **Great Britain** to the gold medal in the 800 freestyle **relay.** His last two medals were of the bronze variety at the 1912 and 1920 Games in the 800 freestyle relay. It was not until 2008, when **Rebecca Adlington** won the 400 and 800 freestyles, that a British swimmer matched Taylor's feat of winning two swimming gold medals at a single Olympics.

TECHNOLOGICAL DOPING. The term technological doping was introduced in 2008 by **Italian** coach Alberto Castagnetti in response to the introduction of **high-tech swimsuits** that led to a rash of world records, including more than 100 during 2008. Because suits such as the **Speedo LZR Racer**, **Jaked** 01, **Arena** X-Glide, and blueseventy aided athletes with buoyancy and featured compression panels that helped keep the swimmers' bodies in perfect position, it was difficult to determine how much of the world records set were due to talent and how much was the result of technological advances in the sport.

TEMPORARY POOLS. The phenomenon of temporary pools took off in the early part of this century. As a way to stage major events in front of larger crowds, temporary pools are set up in existing arenas, then taken apart at the conclusion of the competition and sometimes sent to other facilities for permanent use. The 2007 **World Championships** were held in a temporary pool, set up inside Rod Laver Arena in Melbourne. That facility is best known as the home of the **Australian** Open tennis championships. The **United States** moved toward the use of temporary pools for its Olympic Trials beginning in 2004. That summer, **United States Swimming (USS)** constructed a temporary pool in a parking lot in Long Beach, California, adjacent to the city's aquarium. In 2008, the United States Trials were held indoors, with a temporary pool set up in the **Qwest Center** in Omaha, Nebraska. The 2008 event drew more than 12,000 spectators per session, vastly more than the few thousand fans that can be accommodated by the **Indiana University Natatorium**, which staged the Olympic Trials in 1984, 1992, 1996, and 2000.

TERADA, NOBORU (JPN). B. 25 November 1917, Shizuoka, Japan. D. 26 September 1986. Noboru Terada won the **Olympic** gold medal in 1936 in the 1,500 **freestyle**, an event won by his countryman Kuzuo Kitamura four years earlier. To date, no other **Japanese** man has won the 1,500 freestyle.

TEWKSBURY, MARK (CAN). B. 2 July 1968, Calgary, Alberta. Mark Tewksbury was a **Canadian backstroker** who notched an upset victory at the 1988 **Olympics** in Barcelona. Swimming the only time under 54 seconds, Tewksbury defeated the **United States'** **Jeff Rouse** and **David Berkoff**, along with Spain's **Martin Zubero**. Tewksbury also won silver and bronze medals in the 400 medley **relay** at the 1988 and 1992 Games, respectively. He collected four medals in the backstroke events at three **Pan Pacific Champion-ships**, including a gold medal in the 100 backstroke in 1987.

THEILE, DAVID EGMONT (AUS). B. 17 January 1938, Maryborough, Australia. David Theile was the first **backstroke** star from **Australia** and is still considered one of the best performers in that event from his country. After winning the gold medal in the 100 backstroke at the 1956 **Olympics** in Melbourne, Theile repeated as champion at the 1960 Games in **Rome**, where he also helped Australia to the silver medal in the 400 medley **relay**. Theile set one world record in the 100 backstroke.

THOMPSON, JENNIFER BETH (USA). B. 26 February 1973, Dover, New Hampshire. Jenny Thompson is one of the most decorated **Olympians** in history, ranking in a tie for second all-time for the most medals won by a female athlete with 12. Over four Olympiads spanning 1996 to 2004, Thompson earned eight gold medals, all in **relay** duty. She won two individual medals—silver in the 100 **free-style** in 1992 and bronze in that event in 2000. Thompson excelled in the freestyle and **butterfly** events and won 14 medals in the **World Championships**, including individual titles in the 100 freestyle (1998) and 100 butterfly (1998/2003). During her career, Thompson established world records in the 100 freestyle and 100 butterfly and was a multiple **National Collegiate Athletic Association (NCAA)** champion for **Stanford University**. Following her career, she attended medical school and earned her doctorate in anesthesiology, which she practices today.

THORPE, IAN JAMES (AUS). B. 13 October 1982, Sydney, Australia. Nicknamed "The Thorpedo," Ian Thorpe is regarded as the greatest **middle-distance freestyler** in swimming history, despite retiring from the sport at the age of 24. Thorpe broke onto the international scene as a 14-year-old at the 1998 **World Championships**, winning the 400 freestyle to become the youngest male world titlist. The event became his signature, and he never lost the race in international competition through 2004, his final year of competitive swimming. Competing in front of his home fans at the 2000 **Olympics** in

Sydney, Thorpe won the 400 freestyle and helped **Australia** to gold medals in the 400 and 800 freestyle **relays**. He also won silver medals in the 200 freestyle and 400 medley relay. A year later, he was the dominant performer at the World Championships in Fukuoka, Japan, becoming the first man to win six gold medals. He won his three individual events, the 200, 400, and 800 freestyles, in world-record time. He again won the 200 and 400 freestyles at the 2003 World Championships and added a silver medal in the 200 individual medley and a bronze in the 100 freestyle, proof of his versatility.

At the 2004 Australian Olympic Trials, Thorpe encountered a disaster in the 400 freestyle when he lost his balance on the **starting block** and fell into the water, causing a **false start** and disqualification. With Thorpe out of the race, **Grant Hackett** and Craig Stevens claimed the two Olympic berths in the event. Stevens eventually gave his spot to Thorpe, who went on to repeat his gold medal. Thorpe also avenged his 2000 loss to the **Netherlands' Pieter van den Hoogenband** in the 200 freestyle, beating van den Hoogenband and the **United States' Michael Phelps** to the wall in what is considered one of the greatest races in Olympic history. Thorpe added a bronze medal in the 100 freestyle. Although he had planned on returning to competition after the 2004 Olympics, a one-year hiatus turned into retirement. Thorpe finished his career with nine Olympic medals, 13 medals at the World Championships, and 14 **long-course** world records.

During the 2007 World Championships in Melbourne, in which Thorpe was not competing, the French newspaper *L'Equipe* reported that Thorpe had tested positive for two banned substances during out-of-competition drug testing. The Australian Sports Anti-Doping Agency (ASADA) confirmed the results, but cleared Thorpe of any violations. The **Fédération Internationale de Natation (FINA)**, the swimming world's governing body, agreed with the stance of ASADA and closed the case. On several occasions, primarily before the 2004 and 2008 Olympics, Thorpe stated that he did not believe Phelps could pull off his goal of winning eight gold medals at the Games. Phelps has noted that he used the doubts as motivation. Thorpe was in the stands at the **Water Cube** in Beijing when Phelps won his record-setting eighth gold medal at the 2008 Olympics.

THUMER, PETRA (GDR). B. 29 January 1961, Chemnitz, Germany. Petra Thumer was a **distance freestyle** star at the 1976 **Olympics** while representing the **German Democratic Republic (GDR)**. In Montreal, Thumer won gold medals in the 400 and 800 freestyles, setting world records in both events and defeating the **United States' Shirley Babashoff**, who suggested the East German women were on **performance-enhancing drugs**. It was later revealed that Babashoff's assertions were correct, the result of the German Democratic Republic using a systematic **doping** program.

TORRES, DARA GRACE (USA). B. 15 April 1967, Beverly Hills, California. Dara Torres is widely considered the greatest **sprinter** in **United States** history, her longevity the hallmark of her career. Torres has appeared in five **Olympics** spanning seven Olympiads, participating in the Games in 1984, 1988, 1992, 2000, and 2008. Torres has won 12 Olympic medals—eight in **relay** action and four as an individual. She did not win an individual Olympic medal until her fourth Games, when she came out of her first retirement and was the bronze medalist in Sydney in the 50 and 100 **freestyles**, along with the 100 **butterfly**. Torres retired again after those 2000 Games, but revived her career in time to qualify for the 2008 Olympics. At 41 years old, Torres became the oldest athlete to compete in an Olympic swimming competition. In addition to winning silver medals in the 400 freestyle relay and 400 medley relay, Torres won silver in the 50 freestyle, finishing a hundredth of a second behind champion **Britta Steffen** of Germany. Torres continued to compete after the Beijing Games and qualified for the 2009 **World Championships** in **Rome**. Torres qualified for the final of the 50 freestyle, but a knee injury hampered her on the way to an eighth-place finish.

Because of her success, particularly what she accomplished in her 40s, Torres has often been the target of accusations that suggest she has used **performance-enhancing drugs**. However, she has never tested positive, and leading up to the Olympics in 2008 she was part of a program in which she was tested more frequently than most athletes. Aside from a swimming career, Torres was also a model and was the first athlete to appear in the *Sports Illustrated* swimsuit issue. She has also been a television commentator and was a spokesperson for the infomercial selling the workout video *Tae-Bo*.

TRICKETT, LISBETH CONSTANCE (AUS). B. 28 January 1985, Townsville, Australia. Libby Trickett is one of the premier **sprint freestylers** and **butterfly** performers of her era, having accumulated more than 40 medals in international competition for **Australia**. Trickett is a six-time **Olympic** medalist, having won two medals at the 2004 Games in Athens and four medals, including gold in the 100 butterfly, at the 2008 Games in Beijing. Trickett has won 15 medals at the **World Championships,** highlighted by two individual victories in the 50 freestyle (2005/2007) and individual gold medals in the 100 freestyle and 100 butterfly in 2007. Trickett has also won 12 medals at the **World Short Course Championships.**

TROY, MICHAEL FRANCIS (USA). B. 3 October 1940, Indianapolis, Indiana. Mike Troy set five world records in the 200 **butterfly** during the early 1960s and was the 1960 **Olympic** gold medalist in the event. At those Olympics, Troy was also a member of the **United States'** 800 **freestyle relay** that set a world record.

TSURUTA, YOSHIYUKI (JPN). B. 1 November 1903, Kagoshima, Japan. D. 24 July 1986, Kagoshima, Japan. Yoshiyuki Tsuruta was the first repeat **Olympic** champion in a **breaststroke** event, winning the 200 distance at the 1928 and 1932 Olympics. Tsuruta established a strong tradition in the breaststroke for **Japan**, one that was carried forward by the likes of **Nobutaka Taguchi** and **Kosuke Kitajima.**

TYR SPORT. TYR is a swimwear and aquatic accessories company that was co-founded in 1985 by **Steve Furniss**, the bronze medalist in the 200 **individual medley (IM)** at the 1972 **Olympics** and a former world-record holder in the event. The company is named after the Norse god of warriors. In 2008, the company filed a lawsuit against **United States Swimming (USS)**, its national team head coach **Mark Schubert**, and **Speedo**. The lawsuit alleged violations of antitrust laws, connected with the release of Speedo's **LZR Racer**, and Schubert's public assertions that athletes wearing a product other than the Speedo brand would be at a competitive disadvantage at the 2008 Olympic Games in Beijing. *See also* ARENA; JAKED; NIKE.

– U –

UKRAINE (UKR). The Ukraine is a former state of the **Union of Soviet Socialist Republics (URS)** that received its independence in 1991. Athletes from the Ukraine competed for the Soviet Union through the 1988 Olympics and competed for the **Unified Team (EUN)** at the 1992 **Olympics**. The Ukraine has won 10 medals in Olympic competition—four gold, five silver, and one bronze. All four of the gold medals have been won by **Yana Klochkova**, who was victorious in the 200 and 400 **individual medley (IM)** events at the 2000 and 2004 Olympics.

UNIFIED TEAM (EUN). Due to the breakup of the **Union of Soviet Socialist Republics (URS)**, the 1992 **Olympics** in Barcelona featured the various Soviet states competing under the umbrella of the Unified Team. The squad did well in the swimming competition, winning 10 medals, eight in men's events. The Unified Team especially excelled in the **freestyle** events, where sprinter **Alexander Popov** won the 50 and 100 freestyles, the first of back-to-back titles in each discipline. In the 200 and 400 freestyles, **Evgeny Sadovyi** was the gold medalist, and the Unified Team won silver medals in the 400 freestyle and 400 medley **relays** and gold in the 800 freestyle relay. At future Games, the former Soviet states competed individually, **Russia** and the **Ukraine** having the most success in the pool. *See also* RUDKOVSKAYA, YELENA.

UNION OF SOVIET SOCIALIST REPUBLICS (URS). The Union of Soviet Socialist Republics, despite competing only through the 1988 **Olympics** in Seoul, still ranks ninth on the all-time Olympic swimming medals list with 59—12 gold, 21 silver, and 26 bronze. After the breakup of the Soviet Union in 1991, the nations of the former superpower competed as the **Unified Team (EUN)** at the 1992 Olympics and have competed as separate republics in the years since, **Russia** and the **Ukraine** enjoying the most success. The most famous Soviet swimmer is **Vladimir Salnikov**, the winner of the 1,500 **freestyle** at the 1980 and 1988 Olympics and the 400 freestyle in 1980. His chance to win both events at the 1984 Games was denied because of the Soviet boycott of the Los Angeles Olympics. *See also* FESENKO, SERGEY; KACIUSYTE, LINA; KOPLYAKOV, SERGEY; KOSHEVAYA, MARINA; POLYANSKY, IGOR; PROZUMENSHCHIKOVA, GALINA; SIDORENKO, ALEKSANDR; ZULPA, ROBERTAS.

UNITED STATES (USA). The United States is the most successful swimming country in history, evident in the nearly 500 overall medals and more than 200 gold medals won at the **Olympics** since 1896. **Australia** is widely considered the United States' top rival, but the historical medal count dispels any belief that Australia is on the same level. Since 1960, the United States has won the most medals at every Olympics except for the 1988 Games in Seoul and the 1980 Games in Moscow, which the United States boycotted. The only two individuals to win seven gold medals at a single Olympics, **Michael Phelps** and **Mark Spitz**, are from the United States. Phelps produced what is considered the greatest Olympic performance in history at the 2008 Games in Beijing, where he won eight gold medals and set seven world records. That performance bettered the seven gold medals won by Spitz at the 1972 Olympics in Munich, with each of his victories coming in world-record time.

Tracy Caulkins is considered one of the greatest female swimmers in American history, although her Olympic medal record is not overwhelming. Caulkins was in her prime during the late 1970s and early 1980s, but did not get the chance to compete at the 1980 Olympics in Moscow due to the U.S. boycott of those Games. However, she won the 200 **individual medley (IM)** and 400 individual medley at the 1984 Olympics in Los Angeles. Another great United States female swimmer is **Janet Evans**, widely viewed as the finest female **distance** swimmer in history. Evans won the 400 and 800 freestyles at the 1988 Olympics, along with the 400 individual medley. She also won the 800 free at the 1992 Olympics.

The efforts of the 1976 **United States Olympic Men's Swimming Team** were so overwhelming, the squad winning 12 of the 13 events, that a rule change was implemented that limits each country to two entries per event. The United States has been the host of four Summer

Olympics: the 1904 Games in St. Louis, the 1932 and 1984 Games in Los Angeles, and the 1996 Games in Atlanta.

The United States generally holds two national championships each year, a **long-course** competition during the summer and a **short-course** competition during the winter. The long-course competition oftentimes is used as the selection meet for such major international competitions as the Olympics, **World Championships**, and **Pan Pacific Championships**. The meet's title during Olympic years is known as the United States Olympic Trials.

While **United States Swimming (USS)** oversees the sport in this country, United States **Masters Swimming** (USMS) organizes competition in an **age-group** format. Additionally, the United States relies heavily on its collegiate programs to build future talent. Swimmers competing collegiately in the United States compete under the jurisdiction of the **National Collegiate Athletic Association (NCAA)**, which oversees three classifications of competition: Division I, Division II, and Division III. Division I is the highest level and frequently features swimmers who either have or will compete at the Olympic Games. The **University of Texas** and **Stanford University** are among the top college programs, along with **Auburn University**. In recent years, however, Auburn's success has been the result of contributions by foreign athletes competing for the school. *See also* ANDREWS, THERESA; BABASHOFF, JACK; BABASHOFF, SHIRLEY; BARKMAN, JANE; BARROWMAN, MICHAEL; BAUER, SYBIL; BEARD, AMANDA; BELOTE, MELISSA; BENNETT, BROOKE; BERKOFF, DAVID; BIONDI, MATTHEW; BLEIBTREY, ETHELDA; BOTSFORD, ELIZABETH; BOTTOM, JOSEPH; BOWMAN, ROBERT; BREEN, GEORGE; BRUNER, MICHAEL; BURGESS, GREGORY; BURKE, LYNN; BURTON, MICHAEL; CAREY, RICHARD; CARR, CATHERINE; COHEN, TIFFANY; COUGHLIN, NATALIE; COUNSILMAN, JAMES; CRABBE, CLARENCE; CRAPP, LORRAINE; CROCKER, IAN; CURTIS, ANN; DANIEL, ELEANOR; DANIELS, CHARLES; DEMONT, RICHARD; DE VARONA, DONNA; DICARLO, GEORGE; DIEBEL, NELSON; DOLAN, THOMAS; DUENKEL, VIRGINIA; EDERLE, GERTRUDE; ERVIN, ANTHONY; FERGUSON, KATHLEEN; FURNISS, BRUCE; FURNISS, STEVEN;

GAINES, AMBROSE; GENTER, ROBERT; GOODELL, BRIAN; GRAEF, JEDWARD; HAINES, GEORGE; HAISLETT, NICOLE; HALL, GARY, JR.; HALL, GARY, SR.; HALL, KAYE; HANSEN, BRENDAN; HARDY, JESSICA; HEBNER, HARRY; HENCKEN, JOHN; HENNE, JAN; HICKCOX, CHARLES; HOELZER, MARGARET; HOFF, KATHRYN; HOGSHEAD, NANCY; HOLM, ELEANOR; HYMAN, MISTY; IVEY, MITCHELL; JAGER, THOMAS; JENDRICK, MEGAN; JENSEN, LARSEN; JOHNSON, JENNA; JONES, CULLEN; KAHANAMOKU, DUKE; KEALOHA, WARREN; KELLER, KLETE; KIEFER, ADOLPH; KIPHUTH, ROBERT; KOJAC, GEORGE; KOLB, CLAUDIA; KONNO, FORD; KOWAL, KRISTY; KRAYZELBURG, LEONID; LACKIE, ETHEL; LEE, SAMUEL; LEZAK, JASON; LOCHTE, RYAN; LOUGANIS, GREGORY; LOVELESS, LEA; LUNDQUIST, STEPHEN; MADISON, HELENE; MALCHOW, THOMAS; MANN, SHELLEY; MARTINO, ANGEL; McBREEN, THOMAS; McKEE, ALEXANDER; McKEEVER, TERI; McKENZIE, DONALD; McLANE, JAMES; MEAGHER, MARY; MEDICA, JACK; MEYER, DEBORAH; MITCHELL, ELIZABETH; MOE, KAREN; MONTGOMERY, JAMES; MORALES, PEDRO; MOSES, GLENN; MULLIKEN, WILLIAM; MUNZ, DIANA; NABER, JOHN; NALL, NADIA; NAMESNIK, ERIC; NEILSON, ALEXANDRA; NORELIUS, MARTHA; O'BRIEN, MICHAEL; OSIPOWICH, ALBINA; OYAKAWA, YOSHINOBU; PEIRSOL, AARON; QUICK, RICHARD; RAPP, SUSAN; REESE, EDWIN; RIS, WALTER; ROBIE, CARL; ROSS, NORMAN; ROTH, RICHARD; ROTHHAMMER, KEENA; ROUSE, JEFFREY; RUSSELL, DOUGLAS; SANDENO, KAITLIN; SANDERS, SUMMER; SCHOLES, CLARKE; SCHOLLANDER, DONALD; SCHUBERT, MARK; SCHULER, CAROLYN; SCHWENK, WILLIAM; SHANTEAU, ERIC; SHAW, TIMOTHY; SKELTON, ROBERT; SMITH, WILLIAM; SONI, REBECCA; STACK, ALLEN; STEINSEIFER, CAROLYN; STERKEL, JILL; STEWART, MELVIN; STOUDER, SHARON; STRACHAN, RODNEY; THOMPSON, JENNIFER; TORRES, DARA; TROY, MICHAEL; VANDERKAAY, PETER; VAN DYKEN, AMY; VASSALLO, JESUS; VENDT, ERIK; VERDEUR, JOSEPH; VOGEL, MATTHEW; VON SALTZA, SUSAN; WAGNER, ALLISON; WATSON, LILLIAN; WAYTE, MARY;

WEBSTER, ROBERT; WEISSMULLER, JOHNNY; WHARTON, DAVID; WHITTEN, PHILLIP; WICHMAN, SHARON; WILKENS, THOMAS; WOODHEAD, CYNTHIA; YORZYK, WILLIAM.

UNITED STATES OLYMPIC MEN'S SWIMMING TEAM (1976). The squad the **United States** sent to the 1976 Olympic Games in Montreal is considered the best in history. The U.S. men won 12 of the 13 gold medals, added 10 silver medals, and won five bronze medals. The team was **coached** by the legendary **Doc Counsilman** and all but one of the gold medals was won in world-record time. **Brian Goodell** was a double winner in the 400 and 1,500 **freestyles**, and **John Naber** won the 100 and 200 **backstrokes**, along with contributing to a pair of triumphant **relays** and taking silver in the 200 freestyle. The U.S. dominance at the Games led to changes in participation for future Olympic swimming competitions. Rather than each nation being allowed three swimmers per individual event, countries can now send only two athletes in each event.

UNITED STATES SWIMMING (USS). United States Swimming is the governing body of the sport in the country, overseeing levels ranging from **age-group**, to collegiate, to national. The governing body is based in Colorado Springs, Colorado, where many of the other national bodies for **Olympic** sports are situated. **Mark Schubert**, the former **coach** at the University of Southern California, is the national team head coach and oversees all U.S. teams at international competitions, although those teams have individual head coaches for the men's and **women**'s squads, which are selected on a meet-by-meet basis.

UNIVERSIADE. The World University Games are a global competition in various sports between collegiate athletes. The first version of the Universiade was held in Paris in 1923, but the competition was not officially named the Universiade until 1959. The World University Games are held every two years and are conducted in both the summer and winter. Although some Olympians compete in the event, the World University Games are often a launching pad for swimmers trying to gain experience at the international level.

UNIVERSITY OF TEXAS. The University of Texas is regarded as one of the top programs in the nation; its men's team owns 10 **National Collegiate Athletic Association (NCAA)** championships. That total trails on Ohio State University and the University of Michigan for the most men's championships. **Eddie Reese** has been the coach for all 10 of Texas' NCAA titles and is a three-time head coach of the United States Olympic Team. Texas won its most recent NCAA championship in 2010. Reese has overseen the career of Olympians **Aaron Peirsol, Ian Crocker,** and **Brendan Hansen.** The Texas women's program has won seven NCAA titles, but has not finished first since 1991.

– V –

VAN ALMSICK, FRANZISKA (GER). B. 5 April 1978, Berlin, Germany. Franziska van Almsick was one of her era's top **freestylers,** winning 10 medals in **Olympic** competition for **Germany.** However, none of the medals she won were gold. Van Almsick first competed at the Olympics as a 14-year-old at the 1992 Games in Barcelona, winning four medals. Individually, she took silver in the 200 freestyle and bronze in the 100 freestyle. She added another silver medal in the 200 freestyle at the 1996 Games and totaled seven **relay** medals during her career, spread among the 1992, 1996, 2000, and 2004 Games. Van Almsick won her lone individual world title in 1994, setting a world record in the 200 freestyle. That mark stood for nearly eight years, until van Almsick took it lower in 2002. She added a gold medal in the 800 freestyle relay at the 1998 **World Championships** and won four other medals in World Championships competition. While she struggled to dominate at the Olympics and World Championships, that was not the case at the European Championships, where van Almsick won 21 medals, including 18 gold. She won individual titles in the 50, 100, 200, and 400 freestyles and won a silver medal in the 200 **butterfly.**

VAN DEN HOOGENBAND, PIETER (NED). B. 14 March 1978, Maastricht, Netherlands. Pieter van den Hoogenband was a four-time Olympian for the **Netherlands,** capturing three gold medals. Nicknamed "Hoogie" and "The Flying Dutchman," van den Hoogenband was the **Olympic** champion in the 100 **freestyle** at the 2000 and 2004 Games, claiming those championships after placing fourth in Atlanta in 1996. At the 2008 Games in Beijing, he finished fifth, failing to become the first male swimmer to win an event at three consecutive Olympiads. **Australian Grant Hackett** was trying to accomplish the same feat in the 1,500 freestyle, but took home the silver medal. At the 2000 Games in Sydney, van den Hoogenband also won gold in the 200 freestyle, registering an upset of **Australian Ian Thorpe** in front of Thorpe's home nation. Van den Hoogenband took second to Thorpe in the 200 freestyle in 2004 and was the bronze medalist in the 50 freestyle in 2000. He added silver and bronze medals in **relay** action. Van den Hoogenband never won a gold medal at the **World Championships**, but he collected eight silver medals and two bronze medals and was a 10-time European Championships gold medalist. During his career, van den Hoogenband set three world records, with his 100 freestyle mark from Sydney in 2000 lasting almost eight years.

VANDERKAAY, PETER (USA). B. 12 February 1984, Royal Oak, Michigan. Peter Vanderkaay is a **middle-distance freestyle** star for the **United States** who earned gold medals as a member of the U.S. 800 freestyle **relay** at the 2004 and 2008 **Olympics**. A **National Collegiate Athletic Association (NCAA)** champion for the University of Michigan, Vanderkaay added a bronze medal in the 200 freestyle at the 2008 Olympics and is a two-time gold medalist at the **World Championships** in the 800 freestyle relay. *See also* BOWMAN, ROBERT.

VAN DYKEN, AMY D. (USA). B. 15 February 1973, Englewood, Colorado. Amy Van Dyken is a six-time **Olympic** gold medalist and one of the stars of the 1996 Olympics in Atlanta. At those Olympics, Van Dyken was the gold medalist in the 50 **freestyle** and 100 **butterfly** and as a member of the American 400 freestyle **relay** and 400 medley relay. At the Sydney Games in 2000, she again won gold on two relay squads. Van Dyken has been surrounded by controversy, first for spitting water in the lane of her competition and for being a client of the Bay Area Laboratory Co-Operative (BALCO), the facility that has been linked to the steroid scandals of Olympic sprinter

Marion Jones and baseball player Barry Bonds. Van Dyken, who provided grand jury testimony concerning BALCO in 2003, never tested positive for a banned substance or **performance-enhancing drug.**

VAN STAVEREN, PETRONELLA GRIETJE (NED). B. 2 June 1966, Kampen, Netherlands. At the 1984 **Olympics** in Los Angeles, van Staveren was the gold medalist in the 100 **breaststroke** and finished 10th in the 200 breaststroke for the **Netherlands.**

VAN VLIET, PIETJE (NED). B. 17 January 1926, Hilversum, Netherlands. D. 4 January 2006, Naarden, Netherlands. Nel van Vliet was a late-comer to swimming, not entering the sport until she was 16 years old. Nonetheless, she had a rapid rise and won the gold medal in the 200 **breaststroke** at the 1948 **Olympics** for the **Netherlands.**

VASSALLO, JESUS DAVID (USA). B. 9 August 1961, Ponce, Puerto Rico. Jesse Vassallo was a world-class **individual medley (IM)** performer and backstroker whose career was defined by patience. Born in Puerto Rico, Vassallo moved to the **United States** in 1974. He wanted to qualify for the **Olympics** at the Puerto Rican Trials, but his homeland required that he live in Puerto Rico. As a result, Vassallo tried to qualify for the U.S. squad for the 1976 Games in Moscow, but finished sixth in three events. At the 1978 **World Championships,** Vassallo won gold in the 200 **backstroke** and 400 individual medley, along with silver in the 200 individual medley. That success did not carry over to the 1980 Olympics, however, as President Jimmy Carter chose to boycott the Games. Vassallo earned his lone Olympic opportunity in 1984 in Los Angeles, where he placed fourth in the 400 individual medley. Vassallo set one world record in the 200 individual medley and two in the 400 individual medley, the second lasting nearly four years.

VENDT, ERIK (USA). B. 9 January 1981, North Easton, Massachusetts. Erik Vendt made his mark as an **individual medley (IM)** performer and **distance freestyler,** appearing in three **Olympics.** Vendt competed in his first Olympics in 2000, leaving Sydney with a silver medal in the 400 individual medley behind **United States** teammate **Tom Dolan.** Four years later, Vendt won another silver medal in the

400 individual medley, this time finishing behind **Michael Phelps**. At his final Olympics, Vendt picked up a gold medal by swimming in the preliminaries of the 800 freestyle **relay** at the Beijing Games. He was the silver medalist in the 400 individual medley at the 2001 **World Championships** and won five **National Collegiate Athletic Association (NCAA)** titles for the University of Southern California. Vendt came closest to setting a world record at the 2002 United States National Championships where he went under the existing world mark in the 400 individual medley. However, Phelps was competing in the same race and went slightly quicker, consequently nullifying Vendt's pursuit of a world record. *See also* BOWMAN, ROBERT.

VERDEUR, JOSEPH THOMAS (USA). B. 7 March 1926, Philadelphia, Pennsylvania. D. 6 August 1991, Bryn Mawr, Pennsylvania. Joseph Verdeur captured the 1948 **Olympic** gold medal in the 200 **breaststroke** and was a **National Collegiate Athletic Association (NCAA)** champion for La Salle University in the 200 **butterfly**.

VOGEL, MATTHEW HAYNES (USA). B. 3 June 1957, Fort Wayne, Indiana. Matt Vogel was a surprise gold medalist at the 1976 **Olympics** in Montreal in the 100 **butterfly**. The third-place finisher at the **United States** Olympic Trials, Vogel delivered his best performance at the Olympics, defeating U.S. teammates **Joe Bottom** and **Gary Hall Sr.** for the gold medal. He later added a second gold medal as a member of the U.S. 400 medley **relay**. Vogel was the only male winner at the 1976 Games who did not set a world record, his time of 54.35 missing **Mark Spitz**'s world record by eight hundredths of a second.

VOLKER, SANDRA (GER). B. 1 April 1974, Schleswig-Holstein, Germany. Sandra Volker represented **Germany** in four Olympics, obtaining her three medals at the 1996 Games in Atlanta. Volker was the silver medalist in the 100 **freestyle** and won bronze in the 50 freestyle and in the 400 freestyle **relay**. Volker claimed six medals during her career at the **World Championships**, but her greatest performances were at the World Short Course Championships, where she won 10 medals in four appearances, including three gold medals, one each in the 50 freestyle, 50 **backstroke**, and 100 backstroke.

VON HALMAY, ZOLTAN (HUN). B. 18 June 1881, Bratislava, Slovakia. D. 20 May 1956, Budapest, Hungary. Zoltan Von Halmay is considered one of the first worldwide swimming stars. The **Hungarian** competed in four **Olympics**, winning nine medals, a total that still ranks among the most ever by a swimmer. He won two individual gold medals at the 1904 Games in St. Louis, beating the competition in the 50 and 100 **freestyles**. After 1904, the 50 freestyle did not return to the Olympic schedule until 1988. His other individual medals were in the 200, 1,000, and 4,000 freestyle races, the latter two no longer contested. He is credited with setting the first world record in the 100 freestyle.

VON SALTZA, SUSAN CHRISTINA (USA). B. 13 January 1944, San Francisco, California. Chris Von Saltza was the elite **freestyler** in the **United States** in the late 1950s and early 1960s. At the 1960 **Olympics** in **Rome**, she claimed three gold medals and a silver. Von Saltza won the 400 freestyle and helped the United States to victories in the 400 freestyle **relay** and 400 medley relay. Her silver medal was in the 100 freestyle, where she finished behind **Australian** legend and world-record holder **Dawn Fraser**. Training under legendary **coach George Haines**, she won the 100, 200, and 400 freestyles at the 1959 Pan American Games and once set a world record in the 200 **backstroke**.

VYATCHANIN, ARKADY ARKADYEVICH (RUS). B. 4 April 1984, Vorkuta, Russia. At the 2008 **Olympics**, Arkady Vyatchanin medaled twice in the **backstroke** events, sharing bronze in the 100 distance and taking third in the 200 backstroke. Vyatchanin was the silver medalist in the 100 backstroke at the 2003 **World Championships** and has been the European champion in both backstroke disciplines.

– W –

WAGNER, ALLISON MARIE (USA). B. 21 July 1977, San Francisco, California. Allison Wagner was one of the **United States'** finest **individual medley (IM)** swimmers, capturing the silver medal in the 400 individual medley at the 1996 **Olympics** in Atlanta. Wagner finished behind Ireland's **Michelle Smith**, who was later suspended by the **Fédération Internationale de Natation (FINA)**, the world governing body of the sport, for tampering with a urine sample submitted for drug testing. Wagner was also sixth in the 200 individual medley and won silver medals in the 200 and 400 medley races at the 1994 **World Championships**. At the first **World Short Course Championships**, Wagner was the gold medalist in the 200 individual medley and silver medalist in the 400 individual medley. In winning the shorter individual medley, she set a world record that lasted until 2008, when Zimbabwe's **Kirsty Coventry** went faster.

WATER CUBE. Officially named the Beijing National Aquatic Center, the Water Cube was the site of the swimming, **diving**, and **synchronized swimming** competitions at the 2008 **Olympic** Games. The venue was a centerpiece of the Games, along with the Olympic Stadium, known as the Bird's Nest. The facilities sat across from each other. Ground was broken on the Water Cube in 2003 and completed in 2007, with seating for 17,000 at the Olympics—6,000 permanent and 11,000 temporary. The Water Cube was built at a cost of $140 million and resembled a bubble-wrapped rectangle. It was blue in color for the most part, but with lighting it changed colors during the night.

WATER POLO. Water polo is one of the five aquatic disciplines governed by the **Fédération Internationale de Natation (FINA)**. It is a team sport that includes seven players per side, six in the field and a goalkeeper, and is physically demanding in the way the players are required to swim and tread water for the four quarters of action. Quarters are eight minutes in FINA competition and seven minutes in **Olympic** competition. The sport is played with a ball, with the objective to shoot the ball in the opposition's net. Men's water polo has been played in the Olympics since 1900, making it the longest continuous team sport in the Olympics.

The best teams generally hail from Europe, with **Hungary** holding the Olympic record with nine gold medals. **Women**'s water polo was added to the Olympic program in 2000, the **United States** being the only country to medal in each Olympiad (two silver, one bronze). Water polo is also contested collegiately in the United States, governed by the **National Collegiate Athletic Association (NCAA)**. California universities have been the most dominant, with the University of California–Berkeley, **Stanford University**, and the University of California–Los Angeles (UCLA) winning the most men's championships and UCLA winning the most women's championships.

WATSON, LILLIAN DEBRA (USA). B. 11 July 1950, Mineola, New York. Pokey Watson was a multievent standout for the **United States** who won two **Olympic** gold medals. Her first came at the 1964 Games, where she was a member of the U.S. triumphant 400 **freestyle relay**. Four years later, she won the 200 **backstroke**, her first major title in the event. During her career, she also broke the world record in the 200 freestyle, lowering a six-year mark set by the legendary **Australian Dawn Fraser**.

WAYTE, MARY ALICE (USA). B. 25 March 1965, Mercer Island, Washington. Mary Wayte was a two-time **Olympian** for the **United States**, winning two medals each at the 1984 and 1988 Olympics. At the 1984 Olympics in Los Angeles, Wayte was the gold medalist in the 200 **freestyle** and helped the United States to victory in the 400 freestyle **relay**. At the 1988 Games, she earned a silver medal in the 400 medley relay and a bronze medal in the 400 freestyle relay. She added a fourth-place finish in the 200 freestyle and also competed in the 200 **individual medley (IM)**. After her swimming career, Wayte served as a television commentator, working such competitions as the Olympics and **National Collegiate Athletic Association (NCAA)** Championships.

WEBSTER, ROBERT DAVID (USA). B. 25 October 1938, Berkeley, California. Bob Webster was an **Olympic diving** champion who followed his career by becoming a successful **coach**. Webster won the 1960 Olympic title in the 10-meter **platform**, then repeated for a gold at the 1964 Games, matching a feat first performed by **United States** diver **Sammy Lee** in 1948 and 1952. After his competitive days, Webster became a college diving coach, serving stints at the

University of Minnesota, Princeton University, and the University of Alabama.

WEISSMULLER, JOHNNY (USA). B. 2 June 1904, Freidorf, Hungary. D. 20 January 1984, Acapulco, Mexico. One of the first superstars in the sport, Johnny Weissmuller is still better known for his postathletic career, namely his film career as Tarzan. He played the role 19 times over a 15-year period that ended in 1948. Weissmuller won five gold medals at the **Olympics**, capturing the 100 **freestyle** title in 1924 and 1928 and the 400 freestyle championship in 1924. Both years, he helped the **United States** to victory in the 800 freestyle **relays**. Because the 200 freestyle was discontinued after the 1904 Games and not brought back until 1968, Weissmuller was denied the chance to win further gold in an event he likely would have dominated. Weissmuller set 28 world records during his career.

WELSH, MATTHEW JAMES (AUS). B. 18 November 1976, Victoria, Melbourne. Matt Welsh is regarded as the best **backstroker** in **Australian** history, equally talented as a **long-course** and **short-course** performer. He is also an elite sprint **butterflyer**. At the 2000 **Olympics** in his home country, Welsh won the silver medal in the 100 backstroke and the bronze medal in the 200 backstroke, events that were won by the **United States'** **Lenny Krayzelburg**. Welsh also helped Australia to a silver medal in the 400 medley **relay**. Welsh won nine medals at the **World Championships** during his career, two individual gold and three gold medals in relay competition. He also won 14 medals at the **World Short Course Championships**, half of them gold. Welsh's only long-course world record was in the 50 butterfly.

WENDEN, MICHAEL VINCENT (AUS). B. 17 November 1949, Sydney, Australia. Mike Wenden was a **freestyle** star for **Australia** at the 1968 **Olympics** in Mexico City. In addition to winning gold medals in the 100 and 200 freestyles, the 100 distance in world-record time, Wenden earned a silver medal in the 800 freestyle **relay** and a bronze in the 400 freestyle relay. A fourth-place finish by Australia in the 400 medley relay left him just short of a fifth medal.

Wenden returned to the Olympics in 1972, but had three near-misses on medals, placing fourth in the 200 freestyle and fifth in the 100 freestyle and 800 freestyle relay. He was the bronze medalist at the 1973 **World Championships** in the 100 freestyle.

WHARTON, DAVID LEE (USA). B. 19 May 1969, Warminster, Pennsylvania. Dave Wharton is one of several internationally renowned **individual medley (IM)** swimmers coached by Dick Shoulberg at Germantown Academy. Wharton won the silver medal in the 400 individual medley at the 1988 **Olympics** in Seoul, placing behind Hungarian **Tamas Darnyi**. Wharton set one world record each in the 200 and 400 individual medley events and was an eight-time medalist at the **Pan Pacific Championships**, twice winning the 200 and 400 individual medley disciplines and also earning medals in the 200 **butterfly**. At the University of Southern California, Wharton won the 400 individual medley in each of his four seasons (1988 to 1991) and won the 200 individual medley in his final three years.

WHITFIELD, BEVERLEY JOY (AUS). B. 15 June 1954, Wollongong, New South Wales. D. 20 August 1996, Shellharbour, New South Wales. Beverley Whitfield was a **breaststroke** standout for **Australia** in the early 1970s. She won the gold medal in the 200 breaststroke at the 1972 Munich **Olympics** and added a bronze medal in the 100 breaststroke.

WHITTEN, PHILLIP (USA). B. 19 August 1943, Philadelphia, Pennsylvania. Phil Whitten was the editor-in-chief of *Swimming World Magazine* from 1992 to 2007, best known for his investigative reporting on the systematic **doping** program of the **German Democratic Republic (GDR)** in the 1970s and 1980s and the rampant **performance-enhancing drug** use of **Chinese** swimmers in the 1990s. Whitten's research led *Swimming World Magazine* to publish actual documents from the Stasi, the German **Ministry for State Security**, confirming systematic doping of athletes. Aside from overseeing *Swimming World Magazine*'s editorial content, Whitten was part of the launch of www.swiminfo.com, *Swimming World Magazine*'s Web site of daily news and issues in swimming. The site is now found at www.swimmingworldmagazine.com. Whitten left *Swimming World Magazine* in 2007 to take over as the executive director of the College Swimming Coaches Association of America (CSCAA), a role he held through June 2009. As the head of the CSCAA, Whitten fought against the cuts of collegiate swimming programs from athletic budgets, an increasingly popular decision by athletic directors in order to save money. Whitten was the 2008 recipient of the Al Schoenfield Media Award, presented by the **International Swimming Hall of Fame (ISHOF)** for contributions to the sport of swimming. Whitten was also an elite swimmer, setting a National **Age Group** record in the 15- to 16-year-old category and setting several **Masters** world records during his career.

WICHMAN, SHARON (USA). B. 13 May 1952, Fort Wayne, Indiana. Sharon Wichman was one of the top **breaststroke** swimmers of her era. At the 1968 **Olympics** in Mexico City, she was the gold medalist in the 200 breaststroke and added a bronze medal in the 100 breaststroke. Wichman, although among the world's elite, was not the **United States** breaststroker expected to have the best performances at the meet. Catherine Ball, the world-record holder in the 100 and 200 breaststroke events, was the favorite to win both distances, but illness limited Ball to fifth place in the 100 breaststroke and kept her out of the 200 breaststroke. She did recover in time to help the United States to gold in the 400 medley **relay**.

WILKENS, THOMAS PETER (USA). B. 25 November 1975, Middletown, New Jersey. Tom Wilkens excelled in the **individual medley (IM)** and **breaststroke** for the **United States** during the 1990s and 2000s. At the 2000 **Olympics** in Sydney, he failed to advance to the final of the 200 breaststroke, but captured a bronze medal in the 200 individual medley. At the next year's **World Championships**, Wilkens was the silver medalist in the 200 medley and earned bronze in the 400 medley. His career featured four medals at the **Pan Pacific Championships**.

WILKIE, DAVID ANDREW (GBR). B. 8 March 1954, Colombo, Sri Lanka. David Wilkie was a former British standout in the **breaststroke** events, winning three medals at the **Olympics**. Wilkie earned a silver medal in the 200 breaststroke at the 1972 Olympics, placing behind **United States** rival **John Hencken**. At the 1976 Games in Montreal, Wilkie and Hencken exchanged gold-silver finishes, with Wilkie winning the 200 breaststroke and Hencken taking first place in the 100 breaststroke. The Scotsman was the gold medalist in the 200 breaststroke at the first two **World Championships** (1973/1975) and also took gold in the 100 breaststroke in 1975. At the 1973 World Championships, Wilkie demonstrated his prowess beyond the breaststroke by winning a bronze medal in the 200 **individual medley (IM)**. He set two world records in the 200 breaststroke. *See also* GREAT BRITAIN.

WINDLE, ROBERT GEORGE (AUS). B. 2 November 1944, Sydney, Australia. Robert Windle's versatility in the **freestyle** events was on display in the 1960s when he won the gold medal at the 1964 **Olympics** in the 1,500 freestyle. He had enough sprint speed to help **Australia** win bronze medals in the 400 freestyle **relay** at the 1964 and 1968 Games and added a silver medal in the 800 freestyle relay at the 1968 Olympics.

WLADAR, SANDOR (HUN). B. 19 July 1963, Budapest, Hungary. In the absence of the **United States**, Sandor Wladar won the 200 **backstroke** gold medal at the 1980 **Olympics**. Wladar was the silver medalist in the 200 backstroke at the 1982 **World Championships** and swept the 100 and 200 backstrokes at the 1981 European Championships.

WOITHE, JORG (GDR). B. 11 April 1963, Berlin, Germany. Jorg Woithe was a **freestyle** standout for the **German Democratic Republic (GDR)** in the early 1980s. At the 1980 **Olympics** in Moscow, Woithe won the gold medal in the 100 **freestyle** and helped East Germany to the silver medal in the 800 freestyle **relay**. He just missed another medal by placing fourth in the 200 freestyle. Woithe's title in the 100 freestyle was in the absence of the **United States' Rowdy Gaines**, who did not compete due to the U.S. boycott of the Moscow Games. At the 1982 **World Championships**, Woithe edged Gaines for the gold medal in the 100 freestyle and took bronze in the 200 freestyle.

WOJDAT, ARTUR (POL). B. 20 May 1968, Olsztyn, Poland. Artur Wojdat excelled as a **middle-distance freestyler** for Poland in the late 1980s and early 1990s. Although Wojdat won the bronze medal in the 400 freestyle at the 1988 **Olympics** in Seoul, his career was defined by several heartbreaking finishes in Olympic competition. In 1988, he added a fourth-place finish in the 200 freestyle. At the 1992 Games, he again just missed earning a medal, placing fourth in both the 200 and 400 freestyles. Wojdat won a pair of European titles, taking the 400 freestyle in 1989 and the 200 freestyle in 1991. Wojdat competed for Iowa at the collegiate level, establishing himself as a distance star. He won nine individual **National Collegiate Athletic Association (NCAA)** championships, including winning the 500 freestyle in each of his four seasons.

WOMEN IN SWIMMING. Through the years, women in swimming have gradually seen their profile rise, to the point where it is now on par with men in the sport. The first time women competed at the **Olympics** was in 1912 when the 100 **freestyle** and 400 freestyle **relay** were added to the Olympic program. **Australia**'s **Fanny Durack** became the first women's Olympic champion, winning the 100 freestyle ahead of countrywoman Wilhelmine Wylie. The 400 freestyle was added in 1920, and in 1924, women first competed in the **backstroke** and **breaststroke** events.

Women have competed in the same number of events at the Olympics since 1996, when the 800 freestyle relay was added to the women's program. The only difference between the current Olympic men's schedule and that of the women is that men swim a 1,500 freestyle for their longest race, while women swim the 800 freestyle as their longest event. Discussion has been ongoing for the replacement of the 800 freestyle with the 1,500 freestyle for women, or for the addition of the 1,500 freestyle for women and the 800 freestyle for men. At the **World Championships**, men and women swim both the 800 and 1,500 freestyles.

Although there have been numerous examples of **performance-enhancing drug** use among men's swimmers, women's swimmers have been the subject of two of the most documented **doping** programs in the sport's history. In the 1970s and 1980s, the **German**

Democratic Republic (GDR) implemented a systematic doping program in which coaches either injected or provided oral anabolic steroids to athletes. Many of the swimmers in this program were teenage girls. Among those who have admitted to being systematically doped include **Petra Schneider**, the 1980 Olympic champion in the 400 **individual medley (IM)**. A doping program was also utilized by **China** in the first half of the 1990s, with swimmers such as **Wu Yanyan** testing positive for performance-enhancing drug use.

Among the greatest women's swimmers in history include Australia's **Dawn Fraser** and **Shane Gould**. Fraser was the first woman to win three consecutive Olympic gold medals in the same event when she prevailed at the 1956, 1960, and 1964 Olympics in the 100 freestyle. At the 1972 Olympics, Gould became the first woman to win five Olympic medals at the same Games, winning the 200 and 400 freestyles, along with the 200 individual medley. She added a silver medal in the 800 freestyle and a bronze medal in the 100 freestyle.

Tracy Caulkins is widely considered the greatest **United States** female swimmer in history and one of the most versatile performers in the world. Although Caulkins was denied the chance to compete at the 1980 Olympics due to the U.S. boycott of the Moscow Games, she won the 200 and 400 individual medley events at the 1984 Olympics in Los Angeles.

At the 1988 Olympics, East Germany's **Kristin Otto** won four individual gold medals and two relay gold medals to become the first woman to win six swimming gold medals in an Olympiad. However, Otto is widely suspected of being part of the East German doping program, although she has continually denied any involvement. *See also* ADLINGTON, REBECCA; ANDERSEN, GRETA; ANDREWS, THERESA; ANKE, HANNELORE; AOKI, MAYUMI; BABASHOFF, SHIRLEY; BARKMAN, JANE; BAUER, SYBIL; BEARD, AMANDA; BELOTE, MELISSA; BENNETT, BROOKE; BJEDOV, DURDA; BLEIBTREY, ETHELDA; BOTSFORD, ELIZABETH; BRAUN, MARIA; BRIGITHA, ENITH; BURKE, LYNN; CAMPBELL, CATE; CARR, CATHERINE; CASLARU, BEATRICE; COHEN, TIFFANY; COUGHLIN, NATALIE; COVENTRY, KIRSTY; CRAPP, LORRAINE; CURTIS, ANN; DANGALAKOVA, TANYA; DANIEL, ELEANOR; DE BRUIJN, INGE; DENNIS, CLARA; DE ROVER, JOLANDA;

DE VARONA, DONNA; DIERS, INES; DUENKEL, VIRGINIA; EDERLE, GERTRUDE; EGERSZEGI, KRISZTINA; ENDER, KORNELIA; EVANS, JANET; FERGUSON, KATHLEEN; FILIPPI, ALESSIA; FORD, MICHELLE; FRIEDRICH, HEIKE; FRIIS, LOTTE; GEISSLER, INES; GEWENIGER, UTE; GRIN-HAM, JUDITH; GYENGE, VALERIA; HAISLETT, NICOLE; HALL, KAYE; HANSON, BROOKE; HAPPE, URSULA; HARD-CASTLE, SARAH; HARDY, JESSICA; HARRISON, JOAN; HA-RUP, KAREN; HASE, DAGMAR; HENNE, JAN; HENRY, JODIE; HEYNS, PENELOPE; HOELZER, MARGARET; HOFF, KATH-RYN; HOGSHEAD, NANCY; HOLM, ELEANOR; HORNER, SILKE; HOSSZU, KATINKA; HUNGER, DANIELA; HVEGER, RAGNHILD; HYMAN, MISTY; ILCHENKO, LARISSA; IWA-SAKI, KYOKO; JEDRZEJCZAK, OTYLIA; JENDRICK, MEGAN; JIAO LIUYANG; JOHNSON, JENNA; JONES, LEISEL; JUKIC, MIRNA; KACIUSYTE, LINA; KLOCHKOVA, YANA; KOK, AAGJE; KOLB, CLAUDIA; KOSHEVAYA, MARINA; KOTHER, ROSEMARIE; KOVACS, AGNES; KOWAL, KRISTY; KRAUSE, BARBARA; LACKIE, ETHEL; LE JINGYI; LEWIS, HAYLEY; LIMPERT, MARIANNE; LIN LI; LIU ZIGE; LONSBROUGH, ANITA; LUO XUEJUAN; MADISON, HELENE; MAEHATA, HIDEKO; MANAUDOU, LAURE; MANN, SHELLEY; MAR-TINO, ANGEL; MASTENBROEK, HENDRIKA; McCLE-MENTS, LYNNETTE; McKEEVER, TERI; MEAGHER, MARY; METSCHUCK, CAREN; MEYER, DEBORAH; MITCHELL, ELIZABETH; MOCANU, DIANA; MOE, KAREN; MORTON, LUCILLE; MUNZ, DIANA; NAKAMURA, REIKO; NAKANISHI, YUKO; NALL, NADIA; NEALL, GAIL; NEILSON, ALEXAN-DRA; NORD, KATHLEEN; NORELIUS, MARTHA; O'NEILL, SUSAN; OSIPOWICH, ALBINA; OTTENBRITE, ANNE; PANG JIAYING; PELLEGRINI, FEDERICA; POLESKA, ANNE; POLL, CLAUDIA; POLLACK, ANDREA; POTEC, CAMELIA; PRO-ZUMENSHCHIKOVA, GALINA; QIAN HONG; RAPP, SUSAN; REINISCH, RICA; RICE, STEPHANIE; RICHTER, ULRIKE; ROTHHAMMER, KEENA; RUDKOVSKAYA, YELENA; SAN-DENO, KAITLIN; SANDERS, SUMMER; SCHIPPER, JESSI-CAH; SCHRADER, HILDEGARD; SCHULER, CAROLYN; SENFF, DINA; SHIBATA, AI; SJOSTROM, SARAH; SMITH, MI-

CHELLE; SONI, REBECCA; STEFFEN, BRITTA; STEINSEIFER, CAROLYN; STERKEL, JILL; STOUDER, SHARON; SZEKELY, EVA; SZOKE, KATALIN; TANAKA, SATOKO; TAUBER, ULRIKE; THOMPSON, JENNIFER; THUMER, PETRA; TORRES, DARA; TRICKETT, LISBETH; VAN ALMSICK, FRANZISKA; VAN DYKEN, AMY; VAN STAVEREN, PETRONELLA; VAN VLIET, PIETJE; VOLKER, SANDRA; VON SALTZA, SUSAN; WAGNER, ALLISON; WATSON, LILLIAN; WAYTE, MARY; WHITFIELD, BEVERLEY; WICHMAN, SHARON; WOODHEAD, CYNTHIA; YANG WENYI; ZHUANG YONG.

WOODHEAD, CYNTHIA LEE (USA). B. 7 February 1964, Riverside, California. Sippy Woodhead was one of the premier **freestylers** in the **United States**. At the 1978 **World Championships**, competing as a 14-year-old, Woodhead won five medals, including gold in the 200 freestyle and as a member of the United States 400 freestyle and 400 medley **relays**. She added silver medals in the 400 and 800 freestyles. When President Jimmy Carter announced the United States was going to boycott the 1980 Olympics in Moscow, Woodhead was among the swimmers who lost the most from the decision, as she was a gold-medal contender in four freestyle events. She received her Olympic opportunity in Los Angeles in 1984, winning the silver medal in the 200 freestyle at a point in her career when her best days had past.

WORLD ANTI-DOPING AGENCY (WADA). Founded in November 1999, the World Anti-Doping Agency was formed at the recommendation of the International Olympic Committee (IOC) during the February 1999 World Conference on **Doping** in Sport. WADA is intended to police drug use in sports by overseeing testing procedures and educating athletes about the use of drugs and which drugs and medications are allowable. Because swimming has had a history of **performance-enhancing drug** use, most notably by the **German Democratic Republic (GDR) women** during the 1970s and 1980s and the Chinese women during the 1990s, WADA is a valuable organization in the fight against cheating in competition. *See also* LARFAOUI, MUSTAPHA.

WORLD CHAMPIONSHIPS. The World Championships, held by the **Fédération Internationale de Natation (FINA)**, the world governing body of aquatic sports, are conducted in two formats: **long course** (50-meter pool) and **short course** (25-meter pool). The first long-course championships were held in Belgrade, Yugoslavia, in 1973 and then in 1975, 1978, 1982, 1986, 1991, 1994, and 1998. Since 2001, the meet has been held every two years. The first short-course championships was held in 1993 in Palma de Mallorca, Spain. The short-course meet is also held every two years, although 1999 and 2000 featured back-to-back years of competition. Unlike the **Olympics**, the World Championships conduct championship races in the 50-meter distances of the **backstroke, breaststroke**, and **butterfly**. Additionally, the program includes 800 and 1,500 **freestyle** events for both genders. At the Olympics, the men contest only the 1,500 with the **women** racing only the 800. On several occasions, the competitions have been held in cities that formerly hosted the Olympic Games. For the long-course competition, Summer Olympic cities that have hosted the World Championships are Berlin, Rome, Barcelona, Melbourne, and Montreal. The short-course competition has been held in the Summer Olympic cities of Athens and Moscow.

WORLD SHORT COURSE CHAMPIONSHIPS. The World Short Course Championships debuted in 1993 and is held in a 25-meter pool. It serves as a complement to the **World Championships** held in **long course**. The competition is held every two years.

WU YANYAN (CHN). B. 7 January 1978, Beijing, China. Wu Yanyan was an **individual medley (IM)** swimmer who was a world champion but is best known for receiving a four-year ban from the sport for testing positive for **performance-enhancing drugs**. A medal contender at the 1996 **Olympics** in the 200 and 400 individual medley events, Wu failed to advance to the final of either event. A year later, however, she set a world record in the 200 individual medley, swimming 2:09.72. The record lasted until the **Australian Stephanie Rice** broke it at her Olympic Trials in 2008. Before the 2000 Olympics in Sydney, Wu tested positive for drugs and as a result was dropped from the Olympic Team and received her ban. She was the

1998 world champion in the 200 medley, but that title is considered to be a drug-enhanced result.

– Y –

YANG WENYI (CHN). B. 11 January 1972, Shanghai, China. Yang Wenyi was the first **woman** to break the 25-second barrier in the 50 **freestyle**, clocking 24.98 at the 1988 Asian Games. She was the silver medalist at that year's **Olympics**, but returned four years later to win the gold medal in the 50 freestyle and help **China** to the silver medal in the 400 freestyle **relay**.

YORZYK, WILLIAM ALBERT (USA). B. 29 May 1933, Northampton, Massachusetts. William Yorzyk was the first **Olympic** champion in a **butterfly** event. At the 1956 Games, Yorzyk won the 200 butterfly for the **United States** by more than four seconds over **Japan**'s Takashi Ishimoto.

– Z –

ZHANG LIN (CHN). B. 6 January 1987, Beijing, China. Zhang Lin had a major breakthrough for **Chinese** swimming at the 2008 **Olympics** in his home city, winning the silver medal in the 400 **freestyle**. Although the Chinese **women**, oftentimes under **drug** suspicion, won numerous Olympic medals throughout the years, Zhang's performance was the best for a Chinese male. At the 2009 **World Championships**, he shattered **Australian Grant Hackett**'s world record in the 800 freestyle and won the bronze medal in the 400 freestyle.

ZHUANG YONG (CHN). B. 10 August 1972, Shanghai, China. Zhuang Yong was a **Chinese** swimmer who won four medals over two Olympiads. A sprint-freestyle specialist, she was the silver medalist in the 100 **freestyle** at the 1988 **Olympics** in Seoul, but moved up to take the gold medal in the event at the 1992 Games in Barcelona. Zhuang added silver medals in the 50 freestyle and 400 freestyle **relay** in 1992. Although her talents were best suited to the **sprint** freestyles, Zhuang raced the 200 freestyle at both of her Olympic Games.

ZORRILLA, VICTORIANO ALBERTO (ARG). B. 6 April 1906, Buenos Aires, Argentina. D. 23 April 1986, Miami, Florida. Alberto Zorrilla is the only Argentine swimmer to win an **Olympic** gold medal, winning the 400 **freestyle** at the 1928 Olympics. He also qualified for the finals of the 100 and 1,500 freestyles.

ZUBERO, MARTIN (ESP). B. 23 April 1969, Jacksonville, Florida. Holding dual citizenship between the **United States** and Spain, Martin Zubero represented Spain in international competition. He was the 1992 **Olympic** champion in the 200 **backstroke**, winning that gold medal in front of a crowd that roared approval of a Spaniard prevailing in front of his home nation. He just missed capturing a medal four years later, finishing fourth in the 100 backstroke in Atlanta. Zubero, who competed collegiately at the University of Florida, was the gold medalist in the 100 backstroke at the 1994 **World Championships** and the gold medalist in the 200 backstroke at the 1991 World Championships. Zubero twice set a world record in the 200 backstroke and his brother, David Zubero, was the bronze medalist in the 100 **butterfly** at the 1980 Olympics in Moscow.

ZULPA, ROBERTAS RIMANTOVICH (URS). B. 23 March 1960, Vilnius, Lithuania. Robertas Zulpa was a **breaststroker** for the **Union of Soviet Socialist Republics (URS)** who won the 200 breaststroke at the 1980 **Olympics**. Zulpa was the European champion in the 200 breaststroke in 1981 and won the 100 breaststroke at the European Championships in 1983.

Appendix A
Fédération Internationale
de Natation (FINA) Presidents

Name	Country	Service
Erik Bergvall	Sweden	1924–28
Ernest Georges Drigny	France	1928–32
Walther Binner	Germany	1932–36
Harold E. Fern	Great Britain	1936–48
Rene de Raeve	Belgium	1948–52
Mario L. Negri	Argentina	1952–56
Jan de Vries	Netherlands	1956–60
R. Max Ritter	United States	1960–64
W. Berge Phillips	Australia	1964–68
Javier Ostos	Mexico	1968–72
Harold Henning	United States	1972–76
Javier Ostos	Mexico	1976–78
Ante Lambasa	Yugoslavia	1980–84
Robert H. Helmick	United States	1984–88
Mustapha Larfaoui	Algeria	1988–2009
Julio Maglione	Uruguay	2009–present

Appendix B
The World Championships: Sites, Dates, Nations, Athletes, and Attendance

Year	Site	Dates	Nations	Athletes	Attendance
1973	Belgrade, Yugoslavia	31 Aug.–9 Sept.	47	686	N/A
1975	Cali, Colombia	19–27 July	39	682	N/A
1978	Berlin, Germany	18–23 Aug.	49	828	N/A
1982	Guayaquil, Ecuador	29 July–8 Aug.	52	848	N/A
1986	Madrid, Spain	13–23 Aug.	34	1,119	N/A
1991	Perth, Australia	3–13 Jan.	60	1,142	60,000
1994	Rome, Italy	1–11 Sept.	102	1,400	110,000
1998	Perth, Australia	7–18 Jan.	121	1,371	95,000
2001	Fukuoka, Japan	16–29 July	134	1,498	105,000
2003	Barcelona, Spain	12–27 July	157	2,015	205,563
2005	Montreal, Canada	16–31 July	144	1,784	140,00
2007	Melbourne, Australia	18 March–1 April	167	2,158	215,000
2009	Rome, Italy	19 July–2 Aug.	185	2,556	N/A
2011	Shanghai, China	16–31 July	TBA	TBA	TBA
2013	TBA	TBA	TBA	TBA	TBA

Appendix C
The World Short Course Championships: Sites, Dates, Nations, Athletes, and Attendance

Year	Site	Dates	Nations	Athletes	Attendance
1993	Palma de Mallorca, Spain	31 Aug.–9 Sept.	46	313	20,000
1995	Rio de Janeiro, Brazil	30 Nov.–3 Dec.	57	350	70,000
1997	Gothenburg, Sweden	17–20 April	71	501	45,000
1999	Hong Kong	1–4 April	61	516	15,000
2000	Athens, Greece	16–19 March	78	563	22,000
2002	Moscow, Russia	3–7 April	92	599	25,000
2004	Indianapolis, Indiana	7–10 Oct.	94	502	71,659
2006	Shanghai, China	5–9 April	117	578	42,000
2008	Manchester, England	9–13 April	116	616	50,246
2010	Dubai, UAE	TBA	TBA	TBA	TBA

Appendix D
World Championships:
Most Gold Medals (Career)

Name	Number
Michael Phelps, United States	22
Ian Thorpe, Australia	11
Grant Hackett, Australia	10
Aaron Peirsol, United States	10
Kornelia Ender, East Germany	8
Libby Trickett, Australia	8
Jim Montgomery, United States	7
Ryan Lochte, United States	7
Kristin Otto, East Germany	7
Leisel Jones, Australia	7
Jenny Thompson, United States	7

Appendix E
World Championships: Most Medals (Career)

Name	Number	Gold	Silver	Bronze
Michael Phelps, United States	26	22	4	0
Grant Hackett, Australia	18	10	6	2
Libby Trickett, Australia	15	8	3	4
Natalie Coughlin, United States	15	5	5	5
Jenny Thompson, United States	14	7	5	2
Ian Thorpe, Australia	13	11	1	1
Ryan Lochte, United States	13	7	3	3
Michael Gross, Germany	13	5	5	3
Aaron Peirsol, United States	12	10	2	0
Leisel Jones, Australia	12	7	3	2
Alexander Popov, Russia	11	6	4	1
Matt Biondi, United States	11	6	2	3

Appendix F
World Championships: Men's Medal Winners

Note: If a year is not listed, the event was not contested.

50 FREESTYLE

	Gold	Silver	Bronze
1986	Tom Jager, USA	Dano Haisall, Switzerland	Matt Biondi, USA
1991	Tom Jager, USA	Matt Biondi, USA	Gennadiy Prigoda, Russia
1994	Alexander Popov, Russia	Gary Hall Jr., USA	R. Mazuolis, Lithuania
1998	Bill Pilczuk, USA	Alexander Popov, Russia	Ricardo Busquets, Portugal
2001	Anthony Ervin, USA	P. v.d. Hoogenband, Holland	Roland Schoeman, S. Africa/ Tomohiro Yamanoi, Japan
2003	Alexander Popov, Russia	Mark Foster, G. Britain	P. v.d. Hoogenband, Holland
2005	Roland Schoeman, S. Africa	Duje Draganja, Croatia	Bartosz Kisierowski, Poland
2007	Ben Wildman-Tobriner, USA	Cullen Jones, USA	Stefan Nystrand, Sweden
2009	Cesar Cielo, Brazil	Fred Bousquet, France	Amaury Leveaux, France

100 FREESTYLE

	Gold	Silver	Bronze
1973	Jim Montgomery, USA	Michel Rousseau, France	Michael Wenden, Australia
1975	Andy Coan, USA	Vladimir Bure, S. Union	Jim Montgomery, USA
1978	David McCagg, USA	Jim Montgomery, USA	Klaus Steinbach, Germany

Year	Gold	Silver	Bronze
1982	Jorg Woithe, E. Germany	Rowdy Gaines, USA	Per Johansson, Sweden
1986	Matt Biondi, USA	Stephan Caron, France	Tom Jager, USA
1991	Matt Biondi, USA	Tommy Werner, Sweden	Giorgio Lamberti, Italy
1994	Alexander Popov, Russia	Gary Hall Jr., USA	Gustavo Borges, Brazil
1998	Alexander Popov, Russia	Michael Klim, Australia	Lars Frolander, Sweden
2001	Anthony Ervin, USA	P. v.d. Hoogenband, Holland	Lars Frolander, Sweden
2003	Alexander Popov, Russia	P. v.d. Hoogenband, Holland	Ian Thorpe, Australia
2005	Filippo Magnini, Italy	Roland Schoeman, S. Africa	Ryk Neethling, S. Africa
2007	Filippo Magnini, Italy/ Brent Hayden, Canada	Not Awarded	Eamon Sullivan, Australia
2009	Cesar Cielo, Brazil	Alain Bernard, France	Fred Bousquet, France

200 FREESTYLE

Year	Gold	Silver	Bronze
1973	Jim Montgomery, USA	Kurt Krumpholz, USA	Roger Pyttel, E. Germany
1975	Tim Shaw, USA	Bruce Furniss, USA	Brian Brinkley, G. Britain
1978	Billy Forrester, USA	Rowdy Gaines, USA	Sergey Kopliakov, S. Unio
1982	Michael Gross, W. Germany	Rowdy Gaines, USA	Jorg Woithe, E. Germany
1986	Michael Gross, W. Germany	Sven Lodziewski, E. Germany	Matt Biondi, USA
1991	Giorgio Lamberti, Italy	Steffen Zesner, E. Germany	Artur Wojdat, Poland
1994	Antti Kasvio, Finland	Anders Holmertz, Sweden	Danyon Loader, N. Zealand

Year	Gold	Silver	Bronze
1998	Michael Klim, Australia	Massi Rosolino, Italy	P. v.d. Hoogenband, Holland
2001	Ian Thorpe, Australia	P. v.d. Hoogenband, Holland	Klete Keller, USA
2003	Ian Thorpe, Australia	P. v.d. Hoogenband, Holland	Grant Hackett, Australia
2005	Michael Phelps, USA	Grant Hackett, Australia	Ryk Neethling, S. Africa
2007	Michael Phelps, USA	P. v.d. Hoogenband, Holland	Tae Hwan Park, S. Korea
2009	Paul Biedermann, Germany	Michael Phelps, USA	Danila Izotov, Russia

400 FREESTYLE

Year	Gold	Silver	Bronze
1973	Rick DeMont, USA	Brad Cooper, Australia	Bengt Gingsjoe, Sweden
1975	Tim Shaw, USA	Bruce Furniss, USA	Frank Pfuetze, E. Germany
1978	Vladimir Salnikov, S. Union	Jeff Float, USA	Billy Forrester, USA
1982	Vladimir Salnikov, S. Union	Sviatoslav Semenov, S. Union	Sven Lodziewski, E. Germany
1986	Rainer Henkel, W. Germany	Uwe Dassler, E. Germany	Dan Jorgensen, USA
1991	Joerg Hoffman, Germany	Stefan Pfeiffer, Germany	Artur Wojdat, Poland
1994	Kieren Perkins, Australia	Antti Kasvio, Finland	Danyon Loader, N. Zealand
1998	Ian Thorpe, Australia	Grant Hackett, Australia	Paul Palmer, G. Britain
2001	Ian Thorpe, Australia	Grant Hackett, Australia	Emiliano Brembilla, Italy
2003	Ian Thorpe, Australia	Grant Hackett, Australia	Dragos Coman, Romania
2005	Grant Hackett, Australia	Yuri Prilukov, Russia	Ous Mellouli, Tunisia
2007	Tae Hwan Park, S. Korea	Grant Hackett, Australia	Yuri Prilukov, Russia
2009	Paul Biedermann, Germany	Ous Mellouli, Tunisia	Zhang Lin, China

800 FREESTYLE

	Gold	Silver	Bronze
2001	Ian Thorpe, Australia	Grant Hackett, Australia	Graeme Smith, G. Britain
2003	Grant Hackett, Australia	Larsen Jensen, USA	Igor Chervynskyi, Ukraine
2005	Grant Hackett, Australia	Larsen Jensen, USA	Yuri Prilukov, Russia
2007	Przemyslaw Stanczyk, Poland	Craig Stevens, Australia	Federico Colbertaldo, Italy
2009	Zhang Lin, China	Ous Mellouli, Tunisia	Ryan Cochrane, Canada

1,500 FREESTYLE

	Gold	Silver	Bronze
1973	Stephen Holland, Australia	Rick DeMont, USA	Brad Cooper, Australia
1975	Tim Shaw, USA	Brian Goodell, USA	David Parker, G. Britain
1978	Vladimir Salnikov, S. Union	Borut Petric, Yugoslavia	Bobby Hackett, USA
1982	Vladimir Salnikov, S. Union	Sviatoslav Semenov, S. Union	Darjan Petric, Yugoslavia
1986	Rainer Henkel, W. Germany	Stefano Battistelli, Italy	Dan Jorgensen, USA
1991	Joerg Hoffman, Germany	Kieren Perkins, Australia	Stefan Pfeiffer, Germany
1994	Kieren Perkins, Australia	Daniel Kowalski, Australia	Steffen Zesner, Germany
1998	Grant Hackett, Australia	Emiliano Brembilla, Italy	Daniel Kowalski, Australia
2001	Grant Hackett, Australia	Graeme Smith, G. Britain	Alexei Filipets, Russia
2003	Grant Hackett, Australia	Igor Chervynskyi, Ukraine	Erik Vendt, USA
2005	Grant Hackett, Australia	Larsen Jensen, USA	David Davies, G. Britain

	Gold	Silver	Bronze
2007	M. Sawrymowicz, Poland	Yuri Prilukov, Russia	David Davies, G. Britain
2009	Ous Mellouli, Tunisia	Ryan Cochrane, Canada	Sun Yang, China

50 BACKSTROKE

	Gold	Silver	Bronze
2001	Randall Bal, USA	Thomas Rupprath, Germany	Matt Welsh, Australia
2003	Thomas Rupprath, Germany	Matt Welsh, Australia	Gerhard Zandberg, S. Africa
2005	A. Grigoriadis, Greece	Matt Welsh, Australia	Liam Tancock, G. Britain
2007	Gerhard Zandberg, S. Africa	Thomas Rupprath, Germany	Liam Tancock, G. Britain
2009	Liam Tancock, G. Britain	Junya Koga, Japan	Gerhard Zandberg, S. Africa

100 BACKSTROKE

	Gold	Silver	Bronze
1973	Roland Matthes, E. Germany	Mike Stamm, USA	Lutz Wanja, E. Germany
1975	Roland Matthes, E. Germany	John Murphy, USA	Mel Nash, USA
1978	Bob Jackson, USA	Peter Rocca, USA	Romulo Arantes, Brazi
1982	Dirk Richter, E. Germany	Rick Carey, USA	Vladimir Shemetov, S. Union
1986	Igor Polianskiy, S. Union	Dirk Richter, E. Germany	Sergey Zabolotnov, S. Union
1991	Jeff Rouse, USA	Mark Tewksbury, Canada	Martin Zubero, Spain

Year	Gold	Silver	Bronze
1994	Martin Zubero, Spain	Jeff Rouse, USA	Tamas Deutsch, Hungary
1998	Lenny Krayzelburg, USA	Mark Versfeld, Canada	Stev Theloke, Germany
2001	Matt Welsh, Australia	Orn Arnarson, Iceland	Steffen Driesen, Germany
2003	Aaron Peirsol, USA	Arkady Vyatchanin, Russia/ Matt Welsh, Australia	Not Awarded
2005	Aaron Peirsol, USA	Randall Bal, USA	Laszlo Cseh, Hungary
2007	Aaron Peirsol, USA	Ryan Lochte, USA	Liam Tancock, G. Britain
2009	Junya Koga, Japan	Helge Meeuw, Germany	Aschwin Wildeboer, Spain

200 BACKSTROKE

Year	Gold	Silver	Bronze
1973	Roland Matthes, E. Germany	Zoltan Verraszto, Hungary	John Naber, USA
1975	Zoltan Verraszto, Hungary	Mark Tonelli, Australia	Paul Hove, USA
1978	Jesse Vassallo, USA	Gary Hurring, N. Zealand	Zoltan Verraszto, Hungary
1982	Rick Carey, USA	Sandor Wladar, Hungary	Frank Baltrusch, E. Germany
1986	Igor Polianskiy, S. Union	Frank Baltrusch, E. Germany	Frank Hoffmeister, FRG
1991	Martin Zubero, Spain	Stefano Battistelli, Italy	Vladimir Selkov, S. Union
1994	Vladimir Selkov, S. Union	Martin Zubero, Spain	Royce Sharp, USA
1998	Lenny Krayzelburg, USA	Ralf Braun, Germany	Mark Versfeld, Canada
2001	Aaron Peirsol, USA	Markus Rogan, Austria	Orn Arnarson, Iceland
2003	Aaron Peirsol, USA	Gordan Kozulj, Croatia	Simon Dufour, France

	Gold	Silver	Bronze
2005	Aaron Peirsol, USA	Markus Rogan, Austria	Ryan Lochte, USA
2007	Ryan Lochte, USA	Aaron Peirsol, USA	Markus Rogan, Austria
2009	Aaron Peirsol, USA	Ryosuke Irie, Japan	Ryan Lochte, USA

50 BREASTSTROKE

	Gold	Silver	Bronze
2001	Oleg Lisogor, Ukraine	Roman Sloudnov, Russia	Domenico Fioravanti, Italy
2003	James Gibson, G. Britain	Oleg Lisogor, Ukraine	Mihaly Flaskay, Hungary
2005	Mark Warnecke, Germany	Mark Gangloff, USA	Kosuke Kitajima, Japan
2007	Oleg Lisogor, Ukraine	Brendan Hansen, USA	C. van der Burgh, S. Africa
2009	C. van der Burgh, S. Africa	Felipe Silva, Brazil	Mark Gangloff, USA

100 BREASTSTROKE

	Gold	Silver	Bronze
1973	John Hencken, USA	Mikhail Kriukin, S. Union	Nobutaka Taguchi, Japan
1975	David Wilkie, G. Britain	Nobutaka Taguchi, Japan	David Leigh, G. Britain
1978	Walter Kusch, W. Germany	Graham Smith, Canada	Gerald Moerken, FRG
1982	Steve Lundquist, USA	Victor Davis, Canada	John Moffet, USA
1986	Victor Davis, Canada	Gianni Minervini, Italy	Dmitriy Volkov, S. Union
1991	Norbert Rozsa, Hungary	A. Moorhouse, G. Britain	Gianni Minervini, Italy

1994	Norbert Rozsa, Hungary	Karoly Guttler, Hungary	F. Deburghgraeve, Belgium
1998	F. Deburghgraeve, Belgium	Zeng Qiliang, China	Kurt Grote, USA
2001	Roman Sloudnov, Russia	Domenico Fioravanti, Italy	Ed Moses, USA
2003	Kosuke Kitajima, Japan	Brendan Hansen, USA	Jamie Gibson, G. Britain
2005	Brendan Hansen, USA	Kosuke Kitajima, Japan	Hugues Duboscq, France
2007	Brendan Hansen, USA	Kosuke Kitajima, Japan	Brenton Rickard, Australia
2009	Brenton Rickard, Australia	Hugues Duboscq, France	Cameron v.d. Burgh, RSA

200 BREASTSTROKE

	Gold	Silver	Bronze
1973	David Wilkie, G. Britain	John Hencken, USA	Nobutaka Taguchi, Japan
1975	David Wilkie, G. Britain	Rich Colella, USA	Nikolai Pankin, S. Union
1978	Nick Nevid, USA	Arsen Miskarov, S. Union	Walter Kusch, W. Germany
1982	Victor Davis, Canada	Robertas Zhulpa, S. Union	John Moffet, USA
1986	Jozsef Szabo, Hungary	Victor Davis, Canada	Steven Bentley, USA
1991	Mike Barrowman, USA	Norbert Rozsa, Hungary	Nick Gillingham, G. Britain
1994	Norbert Rozsa, Hungary	Eric Wunderlich, USA	Karoly Guttler, Hungary
1998	Kurt Grote, USA	Jean Sarnin, France	Norbert Rozsa, Hungary
2001	Brendan Hansen, USA	Maxim Podoprigora, Austria	Kosuke Kitajima, Japan
2003	Kosuke Kitajima, Japan	Ian Edmond, G. Britain	Brendan Hansen, USA
2005	Brendan Hansen, USA	Mike Brown, Canada	Genki Imamura, Japan
2007	Kosuke Kitajima, Japan	Brenton Rickard, Australia	Loris Facci, Italy

2009 Daniel Gyurta, Hungary   Eric Shanteau, USA   Giedrius Titenis, Lithuania/ Christian Sprenger, Australia

50 BUTTERFLY

Gold	Silver	Bronze
2001 Geoff Huegill, Australia	Lars Frolander, Sweden	Mark Foster, G. Britain
2003 Matt Welsh, Australia	Ian Crocker, USA	E. Korotychkine, Russia
2005 Roland Schoeman, S. Africa	Ian Crocker, USA	Sergiy Breus, Ukraine
2007 Roland Schoeman, S. Africa	Ian Crocker, USA	Jakob Andjkaer, Denmark
2009 Milorad Cavic, Serbia	Matt Targett, Australia	Rafael Munoz, Spain

100 BUTTERFLY

Gold	Silver	Bronze
1973 Bruce Robertson, Canada	Joe Bottom, USA	Robin Backhaus, USA
1975 Greg Jagenburg, USA	Roger Pyttel, E. Germany	Bill Forrester, USA
1978 Joe Bottom, USA	Greg Jagenburg, USA	Par Arvidsson, Sweden
1982 Matt Gribble, USA	Michael Gross, W. Germany	Bengt Baron, Sweden
1986 Pablo Morales, USA	Matt Biondi, USA	Andrew Jameson, G. Britain
1991 Anthony Nesty, Suriname	Michael Gross, Germany	Viacheslav Kulikov, S. Union

Year	Gold	Silver	Bronze
1994	Rafal Szukala, Poland	Lars Frolander, Sweden	Denis Pankratov, Russia
1998	Michael Klim, Australia	Lars Frolander, Sweden	Geoff Huegill, Australia
2001	Lars Frolander, Sweden	Ian Crocker, USA	Geoff Guegill, Australia
2003	Ian Crocker, USA	Michael Phelps, USA	Andriy Serdinov, Ukraine
2005	Ian Crocker, USA	Michael Phelps, USA	Andriy Serdinov, Ukraine
2007	Michael Phelps, USA	Ian Crocker, USA	Albert Subirats, Venezuela
2009	Michael Phelps, USA	Milorad Cavic, Serbia	Rafael Munoz, Spain

200 BUTTERFLY

Year	Gold	Silver	Bronze
1973	Robin Backhaus, USA	Steve Gregg, USA	H. Floeckner, E. Germany
1975	Bill Forrester, USA	Roger Pyttel, E. Germany	Brian Brinkley, G. Britain
1978	Mike Bruner, USA	Steve Gregg, USA	Roger Pyttel, E. Germany
1982	Michael Gross, W. Germany	Sergey Fesenko, S. Union	Craig Beardsley, USA
1986	Michael Gross, W. Germany	Anthony Mosse, N. Zealand	Benny Nielsen, Denmark
1991	Mel Stewart, USA	Michael Gross, W. Germany	Tamas Darnyi, Hungary
1994	Denis Pankratov, Russia	Danyon Loader, N. Zealand	Chris Bremer, Germany
1998	Denys Sylantyev, Ukraine	Franck Esposito, France	Tom Malchow, USA
2001	Michael Phelps, USA	Tom Malchow, USA	Anatoli Poliakov, Russia
2003	Michael Phelps, USA	Takashi Yamamoto, Japan	Tom Malchow, USA
2005	Pawel Korzeniowski, Poland	Takeshi Matsuda, Japan	Wu Peng, China

| 2007 | Michael Phelps, USA | Wu Peng, China | Nikolay Skvortsov, Russia |
| 2009 | Michael Phelps, USA | Pawel Korzeniowski, Poland | Takeshi Matsuda, Japan |

200 INDIVIDUAL MEDLEY

	Gold	Silver	Bronze
1973	Gunnar Larsson, Sweden	Stan Carper, USA	David Wilkie, G. Britain
1975	Andras Hargitay, Hungary	Steve Furniss, USA	Andrei Smirnov, S. Union
1978	Graham Smith, Canada	Jesse Vassallo, USA	Alexander Sidorenko, S. Union
1982	Alexander Sidorenko, S. Union	Bill Barrett, USA	Giovanni Franceschi, Italy
1986	Tamas Darnyi, Hungary	Alex Baumann, Canada	Vadim Yaroshuk, S. Union
1991	Tamas Darnyi, Hungary	Eric Namesnik, USA	Christian Gessner, Germany
1994	Jani Sievinen, Finland	Greg Burgess, USA	Attila Czene, Hungary
1998	Marcel Wouda, Holland	Xavier Marchand, France	Ron Karnaugh, USA
2001	Massi Rosolino, Italy	Tom Wilken, USA	Justin Norris, Australia
2003	Michael Phelps, USA	Ian Thorpe, Australia	Massi Rosolino, Australia
2005	Michael Phelps, USA	Lszlo Cseh, Hungary	Ryan Lochte, USA
2007	Michael Phelps, USA	Ryan Lochte, USA	Laszlo Cseh, Hungary
2009	Ryan Lochte, USA	Laszlo Cseh, Hungary	Eric Shanteau, USA

400 INDIVIDUAL MEDLEY

	Gold	Silver	Bronze
1973	Andras Hargitay, Hungary	Rod Strachan, USA	Rick Colella, USA
1975	Andras Hargitay, Hungary	Andrei Smirnov, S. Union	Hans Geisler, W. Germany
1978	Jesse Vassallo, USA	Sergey Fesenko, S. Union	Andras Hargitay, Hungary
1982	Ricardo Prado, Brazil	J.-Peter Berndt, E. Germany	Sergey Fesenko, S. Union
1986	Tamas Darnyi, Hungary	Vadim Yaroshuk, S. Union	Alex Baumann, Canada
1991	Tamas Darnyi, Hungary	Eric Namesnik, USA	Stefano Battistelli, Italy
1994	Tom Dolan, USA	Jani Sievinen, Finland	Eric Namesnik, USA
1998	Tom Dolan, USA	Marcel Wouda, Holland	Curtis Myden, Canada
2001	Alessio Boggiatto, Italy	Erik Vendt, USA	Tom Wilken, USA
2003	Michael Phelps, USA	Laszlo Cseh, Hungary	Ous Mellouli, Tunisia
2005	Laszlo Cseh, Hungary	Luca Marin, Italy	Ous Mellouli, Tunisia
2007	Michael Phelps, USA	Ryan Lochte, USA	Luca Marin, Italy
2009	Ryan Lochte, USA	Tyler Clary, USA	Laszlo Cseh, Hungary

400 FREESTYLE RELAY

	Gold	Silver	Bronze
1973	USA	Soviet Union	East Germany
1975	USA	West Germany	Italy

	Gold	Silver	Bronze
1978	USA	West Germany	Sweden
1982	USA	Soviet Union	Sweden
1986	USA	Soviet Union	East Germany
1991	USA	Germany	Soviet Union
1994	USA	Russia	Brazil
1998	USA	Australia	Russia
2001	Australia	Holland	Germany
2003	Russia	USA	France
2005	USA	Canada	Australia
2007	USA	Italy	France
2009	USA	Russia	France

800 FREESTYLE RELAY

	Gold	Silver	Bronze
1973	USA	Australia	West Germany
1975	West Germany	Great Britain	Soviet Union
1978	USA	Soviet Union	West Germany
1982	USA	Soviet Union	West Germany
1986	East Germany	West Germany	USA
1991	Germany	USA	Italy
1994	Sweden	Russia	Germany

Year	Gold	Silver	Bronze
1998	Australia	Holland	Great Britain
2001	Australia	Italy	USA
2003	Australia	USA	Germany
2005	USA	Canada	Australia
2007	USA	Australia	Canada
2009	USA	Russia	Australia

400 MEDLEY RELAY

Year	Gold	Silver	Bronze
1973	USA	East Germany	Canada
1975	USA	West Germany	Great Britain
1978	USA	West Germany	Great Britain
1982	USA	Soviet Union	West Germany
1986	USA	West Germany	Soviet Union
1991	USA	Soviet Union	Germany
1994	USA	Russia	Hungary
1998	Australia	USA	Hungary
2001	Australia	Germany	Russia
2003	USA	Russia	Japan
2005	USA	Russia	Japan
2007	Australia	Japan	Russia
2009	USA	Germany	Australia

Appendix G
World Championships: Women's Medal Winners

Note: If a year is not listed, the event was not contested.

50 FREESTYLE

	Gold	Silver	Bronze
1986	Tamara Costache, Romania	Kristin Otto, E. Germany	M. Armentero, Switzerland
1991	Zhuang Yong, China	Leigh Ann Fetter, USA	Catherine Plewinski, France
1994	Jingyi Le, China	N. Mesheryakova, Russia	Amy Van Dyken, USA
1998	Amy Van Dyken, USA	Sandra Volker, Germany	Ying Shan, China
2001	Inge de Bruijn, Holland	Therese Alshammar, Sweden	Sandra Volker, Germany
2003	Inge de Bruijn, Holland	Alice Mills, Australia	Libby Lenton, Australia
2005	Libby Lenton, Australia	Marleen Veldhuis, Holland	Zhu Yingwen, China
2007	Libby Lenton, Australia	Therese Alshammar, Sweden	Marleen Veldhuis, Holland
2009	Britta Steffen, Germany	Therese Alshammar, Sweden	Marleen Veldhuis, Holland
			Cate Campbell, Australia

100 FREESTYLE

	Gold	Silver	Bronze
1973	Kornelia Ender, E. Germany	Shirley Babashoff, USA	Enith Brigitha, Holland
1975	Kornelia Ender, E. Germany	Shirley Babashoff, USA	Enith Brigitha, Holland
1978	Barbara Krause, E. Germany	Lene Jenssen, Norway	Larisa Tsareva, S. Union

Year	Gold	Silver	Bronze
1982	Birgit Meineke, E. Germany	A. Verstappen, Holland	Jill Sterkel, USA
1986	Kristin Otto, E. Germany	Jenna Johnson, USA	Conny van Bentum, Holland
1991	Nicole Haislett, USA	Catherine Plewinski, France	Zhuang Yong, Chin
1994	Jingyi Le, China	Lu Bin, China	F. van Almsick, Germany
1998	Jenny Thompson, USA	Martina Moravcova, Slovakia	Ying Shan, China
2001	Inge de Bruijn, Holland	Katrin Meissner, Germany	Sandra Volker, Germany
2003	Hanna Seppala, Finland	Jodie Henry, Australia	Jenny Thompson, USA
2005	Jodie Henry, Australia	Malia Metella, France/ Natalie Coughlin, USA	Not Awarded
2007	Libby Lenton, Australian	Marleen Veldhuis, Holland	Britta Steffen, Germany
2009	Britta Steffen, Germany	Fran Halsall, G. Britain	Libby Trickett, Australia

200 FREESTYLE

Year	Gold	Silver	Bronze
1973	Keena Rothhammer, USA	Shirley Babashoff, USA	Andrea Eife, E. Germany
1975	Shirley Babashoff, USA	Kornelia Ender, E. Germany	Enith Brigitha, Holland
1978	Cynthia Woodhead, USA	Barbara Krouse, E. Germany	Larisa Tsareva, S. Union
1982	A. Verstappen, Holland	Birgit Meineke, E. Germany	Annelies Maas, Holland
1986	Heike Friedrich, E. Germany	M. Stellmach, E. Germany	Mary T. Meagher, USA
1991	Hayley Lewis, Australia	Janet Evans, USA	Mette Jacobsen, Denmark
1994	F. van Almsick, Germany	Lu Bin, China	Claudia Poll, Costa Rica
1998	Claudia Poll, Costa Rica	Martina Moravcova, Slovakia	Julia Greville, Australia

Year			
2001	Giaan Rooney, Australia	Yang Yu, China	Camelia Potec, Romania
2003	Alena Popchanka, Belarus	Martina Moravcova, Slovakia	Yang Yu, China
2005	Solenne Figues, France	Federica Pellegrini, Italy	Yang Yu, China
2007	Laure Manaudou, France	Annika Lurz, Germany	Federica Pellegrini, Italy
2009	Federica Pellegrini, Italy	Allison Schmitt, USA	Dana Vollmer, USA

400 FREESTYLE

Year	Gold	Silver	Bronze
1973	Heather Greenwood, USA	Keena Rothhammer, USA	Novella Calligaris, Italy
1975	Shirley Babashoff, USA	Jenny Turrall, Australia	Kathy Heddy, USA
1978	Tracey Wickham, Australia	Cynthia Woodhead, USA	Kim Linehan, USA
1982	Camela Schmidt, E. Germany	Petra Schneider, E. Germany	Tiffany Cohen, USA
1986	Heike Friedrich, E. Germany	Astrid Strauss, E. Germany	Sarah Hardcastle, G. Britain
1991	Janet Evans, USA	Hayley Lewis, Australia	Suzu Chiba, Japan
1994	Yang Aihua, China	Cristina Teuscher, USA	Claudia Poll, Costa Rica
1998	Chen Yan, China	Brooke Bennett, USA	Dagmar Hase, Germany
2001	Yana Klochkova, Ukraine	Claudia Poll, Costa Rica	H. Stockbauer, Germany
2003	H. Stockbauer, Germany	Eva Risztov, Hungary	Diana Munz, USA
2005	Laure Manaudou, France	Ai Shibata, Japan	C. McClatchey, G. Britain
2007	Laure Manaudou, France	Otylia Jedrzejczak, Poland	Ai Shibata, Japan
2009	Federica Pellegrini, Italy	Joanne Jackson, G. Britain	Rebecca Adlington, GBR

800 FREESTYLE

	Gold	Silver	Bronze
1973	Novella Calligaris, Italy	Jo Harshbarger, USA	Gudrun Wegner, E. Germany
1975	Jenny Turrall, Australia	Heather Greenwood, USA	Shirley Babashoff, USA
1978	Tracey Wickham, Australia	Cynthia Woodhead, USA	Kim Linehan, USA
1982	Kim Linehan, USA	Jackie Willmott, G. Britain	C. Schmidt, E. Germany
1986	Astrid Strauss, E. Germany	Katja Hartmann, E. Germany	Debbie Babashoff, USA
1991	Janet Evans, USA	Grit Mueller, Germany	Jana Henke, Germany
1994	Janet Evans, USA	Hayley Lewis, Australia	Brooke Bennett, USA
1998	Brooke Bennett, USA	Diana Munz, USA	Kirsten Vlieghuis, Holland
2001	H. Stockbauer, Germany	Diana Munz, USA	Kaitlin Sandeno, USA
2003	H. Stockbauer, Germany	Diana Munz, USA	Rebecca Cooke, G. Britain
2005	Kate Ziegler, USA	Brittany Reimer, Canada	Ai Shibata, Japan
2007	Kate Ziegler, USA	Laure Manaudou, France	Hayley Peirsol, USA
2009	Lotte Friis, Denmark	Joanne Jackson, G. Britain	Alessia Filippi, Italy

1,500 FREESTYLE

	Gold	Silver	Bronze
2001	H. Stockbauer, Germany	F. Rigamonti, Switzerland	Diana Munz, USA
2003	H. Stockbauer, Germany	Hayley Peirsol, USA	Jana Henke, Germany

	Gold	Bronze
2005	F. Rigamonti, Switzerland	Brittany Reimer, Canada
2007	F. Rigamonti, Switzerland	Ai Shibata, Japan
2009	Lotte Friis, Denmark	Camelia Potec, Romania

50 BACKSTROKE

	Gold	Silver	Bronze
2001	Haley Cope, USA	A. Buschschulte, Germany	Natalie Coughlin, USA
2003	Nina Zhivanevskaya, Spain	I. Hlavackova, Czech Rep.	Noriko Inada, Japan
2005	Giaan Rooney, Australia	Gao Chang, China	A. Buschschulte, Germany
2007	Leila Vaziri, USA	A. Herasimenia, Belarus	Tayliah Zimmer, Australia
2009	Zhao Jing, China	Daniela Samulski, Germany	Gao Chang, China

100 BACKSTROKE

	Gold	Silver	Bronze
1973	Ulrike Richter, E. Germany	Melissa Belote, USA	Wendy Cook, Canada
1975	Ulrike Richter, E. Germany	Birgit Treiber, E. Germany	Nancy Garapick, Canada
1978	Linda Jezek, USA	Birgit Treiber, E. Germany	Cheryl Gibson, Canada
1982	Kristin Otto, E. Germany	Ina Kleber, E. Germany	Sue Walsh, USA
1986	Betsy Mitchell, USA	K. Zimmermann, E. Germany	Natalia Shibaeva, S. Union
1991	Krisztina Egerszegi, Hungary	Tunde Szabo, Hungary	Janie Wagstaff, USA

Year	Gold	Silver	Bronze
1998	Lea Maurer, USA	Mai Nakamura, Japan	Sandra Volker, Germany
2001	Natalie Coughlin, USA	Diana Mocanu, Romania	A. Buschschulte, Germany
2003	A. Buschschulte, Germany	Louise Ornstedt, Denmark	Katy Sexton, G. Britain
2005	Kirsty Coventry, Zimbabwe	A. Buschschulte, Germany	Natalie Coughlin, USA
2007	Natalie Coughlin, USA	Laure Manaudou, France	Reiko Nakamura, Japan
2009	Gemma Spofforth, G. Britain	Anastasia Zueva, Russia	Emily Seebohm, Australia

200 BACKSTROKE

Year	Gold	Silver	Bronze
1973	Melissa Belote, USA	Enith Brigitha, Holland	Andrea Gyarmati, Hungary
1975	Birgit Treiber, E. Germany	Nancy Garapick, Canada	Ulrike Richter, E. Germany
1978	Linda Jezek, USA	Birgit Treiber, E. Germany	Cheryl Gibson, Canada
1982	Cornelia Sirch, E. Germany	Georgina Parkes, Australia	Carmen Bunaciu, Romania
1986	Cornelia Sirch, E. Germany	Betsy Mitchell, USA	K. Zimmermann, E. Germany
1991	Krisztina Egerszegi, Hungary	Dagmar Hase, Germany	Janie Wagstaff, USA
1994	He Cihong, China	Krisztina Egerszegi, Hungary	Lorenza Vigarani, Italy
1998	R. Maracineaunu, France	Dagmar Hase, Germany	Mai Nakamura, Japan
2001	Diana Mocanu, Romania	Stanislava Komarova, Russia	Joanna Fargus, Australia
2003	Katy Sexton, G. Britain	Margaret Hoelzer, USA	Stanislava Komarova, Russia
2005	Kirsty Coventry, Zimbabwe	Margaret Hoelzer, USA	Reiko Nakamura, Japan
2007	Margaret Hoelzer, USA	Kirsty Coventry, Zimbabwe	Reiko Nakamura, Japan

	Gold	Silver	Bronze
1994	He Cihong, China	Nina Zhivanevskaya, Russia	B.J. Beford, USA
2009	Kirsty Coventry, Zimbabwe	Anastasia Zueva, Russia	Elizabeth Beisel, USA

50 BREASTSTROKE

	Gold	Silver	Bronze
2001	Luo Xuejuan, China	Kristy Kowal, USA	Zoe Baker, G. Britain
2003	Luo Xuejuan, China	Brooke Hanson, Australia	Zoe Baker, G. Britain
2005	Jade Edmistone, Australia	Jessica Hardy, USA	Brooke Hanson, Australia
2007	Jessica Hardy, USA	Leisel Jones, Australia	Tara Kirk, USA
2009	Yuliya Efimova, Russia	Rebecca Soni, USA	Sarah Katsoulis, Australia

100 BREASTSTROKE

	Gold	Silver	Bronze
1973	Renate Vogel, E. Germany	Lubov Rusanova, S. Union	B. Schuchardt, E. Germany
1975	Hannelore Anke, E. Germany	Wijda Mazereeuw, Holland	Marcia Morey, USA
1978	Julia Bogdanova, S. Union	Tracy Caulkins, USA	Margaret Kelly, G. Britain
1982	Ute Geweniger, E. Germany	Anne Ottenbrite, Canada	Kim Rhodenbaugh, USA
1986	Sylvia Gerasch, E. Germany	Silke Horner, E. Germany	Tanya Bogomilova, Bulgaria
1991	Linley Frame, Australia	Jana Doerries, Germany	Elena Volkova, S. Union
1994	Samantha Riley, Australia	Dai Guohong, China	Yuan Yuan, China

	Gold	Silver	Bronze
1998	Kristy Kowal, USA	Helen Denman, Australia	Lauren Van Oosten, Canada
2001	Luo Xuejuan, China	Leisel Jones, Australia	Agnes Kovacs, Hungary
2003	Luo Xuejuan, China	Amanda Beard, USA	Leisel Jones, Australia
2005	Leisel Jones, Australia	Jessica Hardy, USA	Tara Kirk, USA
2007	Leisel Jones, Australia	Tara Kirk, USA	Anna Khlistunova, Ukraine
2009	Rebecca Soni, USA	Yuliya Efimova, Russia	Kasey Carlson, USA

200 BREASTSTROKE

	Gold	Silver	Bronze
1973	Renate Vogel, E. Germany	Hannelore Anke, E. Germany	Lynn Colella, USA
1975	Hannelore Anke, E. Germany	Wijda Mazereeuw, Holland	Karla Linke, E. Germany
1978	Lina Kachushite, S. Union	Julia Bogdanova, S. Union	Susanne Nielsson, Denmark
1982	Svetlana Varganova, S. Union	Ute Geweniger, E. Germany	Anne Ottenbrite, Canada
1986	Silke Horner, E. Germany	Tania Bogomilova, Bulgaria	Allison Higson, Canada
1991	Elena Volkova, S. Union	Linley Frame, Australia	Jana Doerries, Germany
1994	Samantha Riley, Australia	Yuan Yuan, China	Brigitte Becue, Belgium
1998	Agnes Kovacs, Hungary	Kristy Kowal, USA	Jenna Street, USA
2001	Agnes Kovacs, Hungary	Qi Hui, China	Luo Xuejuan, China
2003	Amanda Beard, USA	Leisel Jones, Australia	Qi Hui, China
2005	Leisel Jones, Australia	Anne Poleska, Germany	Mirna Jukic, Austria
2007	Leisel Jones, Australia	Kirsty Balfour, G. Britain/ Megan Jendrick, USA	Not Awarded
2009	Nadja Higl, Serbia	Annamay Pierse, Canada	Mirna Jukic, Austria

50 BUTTERFLY

Year	Gold	Silver	Bronze
2001	Inge de Bruijn, Holland	Therese Alshammar, Sweden	Anna Kammerling, Sweden
2003	Inge de Bruijn, Holland	Jenny Thompson, USA	Anna Kammerling, Sweden
2005	Danni Miatke, Australia	Anna Kammerling, Sweden	Therese Alshammar, Sweden
2007	Therese Alshammar, Sweden	Danni Miatke, Australia	Inge Dekker, Holland
2009	Marieke Guehrer, Australia	Zhou Yafei, China	Ingvild Snildal, Norway

100 BUTTERFLY

Year	Gold	Silver	Bronze
1973	Kornelia Ender, E. Germany	R. Kother, E. Germany	Mayumi Aoki, Japan
1975	Kornelia Ender, E. Germany	R. Kother, E. Germany	Camille Wright, USA
1978	Joan Pennington, USA	Andrea Pollack, E. Germany	Wendy Quirk, Canada
1982	Mary T. Meagher, USA	Ines Geissler, E. Germany	Melanie Buddemeyer, USA
1986	K. Gressler, E. Germany	Kristin Otto, E. Germany	Mary T. Meagher, USA
1991	Hong Qian, China	Xiaohong Wang, China	Catherine Plewinski, Canada
1994	Liu Limin, China	Yun Qu, China	Susie O'Neill, Australia
1998	Jenny Thompson, USA	Ayari Aoyama, Japan	Petria Thomas, Australia
2001	Petria Thomas, Australia	Otylia Jedrzejczak, Poland	Junko Onishi, Japan
2003	Jenny Thompson, USA	Otylia Jedrzejczak, Poland	Martina Moravcova, Slovakia
2005	Jessicah Schipper, Australia	Libby Lenton, Australia	Otylia Jedrzejczak, Poland
2007	Libby Lenton, Australia	Jessicah Schipper, Australia	Natalie Coughlin, USA
2009	Sarah Sjostrom, Sweden	Jessicah Schipper, Australia	Jiao Liuyang, China

200 BUTTERFLY

	Gold	Silver	Bronze
1973	R. Köther, E. Germany	Roswitha Beier, E. Germany	Lynn Colella, USA
1975	R. Köther, E. Germany	Valerie Lee, USA	G. Wuschek, E. Germany
1978	Tracy Caulkins, USA	Nancy Hogshead, USA	Andrea Pollack, E. Germany
1982	Ines Geissler, E. Germany	Mary T. Meagher, USA	Heike Dahne, E. Germany
1986	Mary T. Meagher, USA	K. Gressler, E. Germany	Birte Weigang, E. Germany
1991	Summer Sanders, USA	Rie Shito, Japan	Hayley Lewis, Australia
1994	Liu Limin, China	Yun Qu, China	Susie O'Neill, Australia
1998	Susie O'Neill, Australia	Petria Thomas, Australia	Misty Hyman, USA
2001	Petria Thomas, Australia	Annika Mehlhorn, Germany	Kaitlin Sandeno, USA
2003	Otylia Jedrzejczak, Poland	Eva Risztov, Hungary	Yuko Nakanishi, Japan
2005	Otylia Jedrzejczak, Poland	Jessicah Schipper, Australia	Yuko Nakanishi, Japan
2007	Jessicah Schipper, Australia	Kim Vandenberg, USA	Otylia Jedrzejczak, Poland
2009	Jessicah Schipper, Australia	Liu Zige, China	Katinka Hosszu, Hungary

200 INDIVIDUAL MEDLEY

	Gold	Silver	Bronze
1973	Andrea Huebner, E. Germany	Kornelia Ender, E. Germany	Kathy Heddy, USA
1975	Kathy Heddy, USA	Ulrike Tauber, E. Germany	Angela Franke, E. Germany
1978	Tracy Caulkins, USA	Joan Pennington, USA	Ulrike Tauber, E. Germany
1982	Petra Schneider, E. Germany	Ute Geweniger, E. Germany	Tracy Caulkins, USA

1986	Kristin Otto, E. Germany	Elena Denderberova, S. Union	Kathleen Nord, E. Germany
1991	Li Lin, China	Summer Sanders, USA	Daniela Hunger, Germany
1994	Bin Lu, China	Allison Wagner, USA	Elli Overton, Australia
1998	Wu Yanyan, China	Chen Yan, China	Martina Moravcova, Slovakia
2001	Maggie Bowen, USA	Yana Klochkova, Ukraine	Qi Hui, China
2003	Yana Klochkova, Ukraine	Alice Mills, Australia	Zhou Yafei, China
2005	Katie Hoff, USA	Kirsty Coventry, Zimbabwe	Lara Carroll, Australia
2007	Katie Hoff, USA	Kirsty Coventry, Zimbabwe	Stephanie Rice, Australia
2009	Ariana Kukors, USA	Stephanie Rice, Australia	Katinka Hosszu, Hungary

400 INDIVIDUAL MEDLEY

	Gold	**Silver**	**Bronze**
1973	Gugrun Wegner, E. Germany	Angela Franke, E. Germany	Novella Calligaris, Italy
1975	Ulrike Tauber, E. Germany	Karla Linke, E. Germany	Kathy Heddy, USA
1978	Tracy Caulkins, USA	Ulrike Tauber, E. Germany	Petra Schneider, E. Germany
1982	Petra Schneider, E. Germany	Kathleen Nord, E. Germany	Tracy Caulkins, USA
1986	Kathleen Nord, E. Germany	Michelle Griglione, USA	Noemi Lung, Romania
1991	Li Lin, China	Hayley Lewis, Australia	Summer Sanders, USA
1994	Dai Guohong, China	Allison Wagner, USA	Kristine Quance, USA
1998	Chen Yan, China	Yana Klochkova, Ukraine	Yasuko Tajima, Japan
2001	Yana Klochkova, Ukraine	Maggie Bowen, USA	Beatrice Caslaru, Romania
2003	Yana Klochkova, Ukraine	Eva Risztov, Hungary	Beatrice Caslaru, Romania

2005	Katie Hoff, USA	Kirsty Coventry, Zimbabwe	Kaitlin Sandeno, USA
2007	Katie Hoff, USA	Yana Martynova, Russia	Stephanie Rice, Australia
2009	Katinka Hosszu, Hungary	Kirsty Coventry, Zimbabwe	Stephanie Rice, Australia

400 FREESTYLE RELAY

	Gold	**Silver**	**Bronze**
1973	East German	USA	West Germany
1975	East Germany	USA	Canada
1978	USA	East Germany	Canada
1982	East Germany	USA	Holland
1986	East Germany	USA	Holland
1991	USA	Germany	Holland
1994	China	USA	Germany
1998	USA	Germany	Australia
2001	Germany	USA	Great Britain
2003	USA	Germany	Australia
2005	Australia	Germany	USA
2007	Australia	USA	Holland
2009	Holland	Germany	Australia

800 FREESTYLE RELAY

	Gold	Silver	Bronze
1986	East Germany	USA	Holland
1991	Germany	Holland	Denmark
1994	China	Germany	USA
1998	Germany	USA	Australia
2001	USA/ Great Britain	Germany	Japan
2003	USA	Australia	China
2005	USA	Australia	China
2007	USA	Germany	France
2009	China	USA	Great Britain

400 MEDLEY RELAY

	Gold	Silver	Bronze
1973	East Germany	USA	West Germany
1975	East Germany	USA	Holland
1978	USA	East Germany	Soviet Union
1982	East Germany	USA	Soviet Union
1986	East Germany	USA	Holland
1991	USA	Australia	Germany

Year			
1994	China	USA	Russia
1998	USA	Australia	Japan
2001	Australia	USA	China
2003	China	USA	Australia
2005	Australia	USA	Germany
2007	Australia	USA	China
2009	China	Australia	Germany

Appendix H
World Short Course Championships:
Most Gold Medals (Career)

Name	Number
Jingyi Le, China	10
Jenny Thompson, United States	9
Therese Alshammar, Sweden	9
Ryan Lochte, United States	8
Matthew Dunn, Australia	8
Matt Welsh, Australia	7
Lars Frolander, Sweden	7
Grant Hackett, Australia	7
Martina Moravcova, Slovakia	7
Libby Trickett, Australia	7
Brooke Hanson, Australia	7

Appendix I
World Short Course Championships:
Most Medals (Career)

Name	Number	Gold	Silver	Bronze
Jenny Thompson, United States	17	9	6	2
Martina Moravcova, Slovakia	17	7	5	5
Ryan Lochte, United States	15	8	4	3
Therese Alshammar, Sweden	15	9	2	4
Michael Klim, Australia	15	5	5	5
Matt Welsh, Australia	14	7	5	2
Lars Frolander, Sweden	14	7	5	2
James Hickman, Great Britain	14	5	4	5
Johanna Sjoberg, Sweden	14	5	4	5
Mark Foster, Great Britain	14	6	4	3

Appendix J
World Short Course Championships:
Men's Medal Winners

Note: If a year is not listed, the event was not contested.

50 FREESTYLE

	Gold	Silver	Bronze
1993	Mark Foster, G. Britain	Hu Bin, China	Robert Abernethy, Canda
1995	Francisco Sanchez, Venezuela	Fernando Scherer, Brazil	Jiang Changji, China
1997	Francisco Sanchez, Venezuela	Mark Foster, G. Britain	R. Busquets, Puerto Rico
1999	Mark Foster, G. Britain	J. Martin Meolans, Argentina	Mark Veens, Holland
2000	Mark Foster, G. Britain	Brendon Dedekind, S. Africa	Stefan Nystrand, Sweden
2002	J. Martin Meolans, Argentina	Mark Foster, G. Britain	O. Volynets, Ukraine/
			Alexander Popov, Russia
2004	Mark Foster, G. Britain	Stefan Nystrand, Sweden	Nick Brunelli, USA/
			Nicholas Santos, Brazil
2006	Duje Draganja, Croatia	Cullen Jones, USA	O. Volynets, Ukraine/
			Nick Brunelli, USA
2008	Duje Draganja, Croatia	Mark Foster, G. Britain	Gerhard Zandberg, S. Africa

100 FREESTYLE

	Gold	Silver	Bronze
1993	Fernando Scherer, Brazil	Gustavo Borges, Brazil	Jon Olsen, USA
1995	Fernando Scherer, Brazil	Gustavo Borges, Brazil	F. Sanchez, Venezuela
1997	Francisco Sanchez, Venezuela	Gustavo Borges, Brazil	Michael Klim, Australia
1999	Lars Frolander, Sweden	Michael Klim, Australia	Bartosz Kizierowski, Poland
2000	Lars Frolander, Sweden	Stefan Nystrand, Sweden	Scott Tucker, USA
2002	Ashley Callus, Australia	J. Martin Meolans, Argentina	Salim Iles, Algeria
2004	Jason Lezak, USA	Salim Iles, Algeria	Rick Say, Canada
2006	Ryk Neethling, S. Africa	Filippo Magnini, Italy	J. Martin Meolans, Argentin
2008	Nathan Adrian, USA	Filippo Magnini, Italy	Duje Draganja, Croatia

200 FREESTYLE

	Gold	Silver	Bronze
1993	Antti Kasvio, Finland	Trent Bray, N. Zealand/ Artur Wojdat, Poland	Not Awarded
1995	Gustavo Borges, Brazil	Trent Bray, N. Zealand	Michael Klim, Australia
1997	Gustavo Borges, Brazil	Trent Bray, N. Zealand	Lars Conrad, Germany
1999	Ian Thorpe, Australia	Michael Klim, Australia	P. v.d. Hoogenband, Holland
2000	Bela Szabados, Hungary	Massi Rosolino, Italy	Chad Carvin, USA

	Gold	Silver	Bronze
2004	Michael Phelps, USA	Rick Say, Canada	Ryan Lochte, USA
2006	Ryk Neethling, S. Africa	Filippo Magnini, Italy	Massi Rosolino, Italy
2008	Kenrick Monk, Australia	Kirk Palmer, Australia	Massi Rosolino, Italy

400 FREESTYLE

	Gold	Silver	Bronze
1993	Daniel Kowalski, Australia	Antti Kasvio, Finland	Paul Palmer, G. Britain
1995	Daniel Kowalski, Australia	Jorg Hoffmann, Germany	Malcolm Allen, Australia
1997	Jacob Carstensen, Denmark	Chad Carvin, USA	Grant Hackett, Australia
1999	Grant Hackett, Australia	Ian Thorpe, Australia	Massi Rosolino, Italy
2000	Chad Carvin, USA	Paul Palmer, G. Britain	Massi Rosolino, Italy
2002	Grant Hackett, Australia	K. Svoboda, Czech Rep.	Chad Carvin, USA
2004	Yuri Prilukov, Russia	Chad Carvin, USA	Justin Mortimer, USA
2006	Yuri Prilukov, Russia	Tae Hwan Park, S. Korea	Massi Rosolino, Italy
2008	Yuri Prilukov, Russia	Massi Rosolino, Italy	Robert Renwick, G. Britain

1,500 FREESTYLE

	Gold	Silver	Bronze
1993	Daniel Kowalski, Australia	Jorg Hoffman, Germany	Piotr Albinski, Poland
1995	Daniel Kowalski, Australia	Ian Wilson, G. Britain	Jorg Hoffmann, Germany

2002	Klete Keller, USA	Gustavo Borges, Brazil	Mark Johnston, Canada
1997	Grant Hackett, Australia	Jorg Hoffmann, Germany	Graeme Smith, G. Britain
1999	Grant Hackett, Australia	Graeme Smith, G. Britain	Daniel Kowalski, Australia
2000	Jorg Hoffmann, Germany	Igor Chervynskiy, Ukraine	Chad Carvin, USA
2002	Grant Hackett, Australia	Chris Thompson, USA	Christian Minotti, Italy
2004	Yuri Prilukov, Russia	Simone Ercoli, Italy	Dragos Coman, Romania
2006	Yuri Prilukov, Russia	Tae Hwan Park, S. Korea	Zhang Lin, China
2008	Yuri Prilukov, Russia	David Davies, G. Britain	M. Sawrymowicz, Poland

50 BACKSTROKE

	Gold	Silver	Bronze
1999	Rodolfo Falcon, Cuba	Mariusz Siembida, Poland	Matt Welsh, Australia
2000	Neil Walker, USA	Lenny Krayzelburg, USA	Rodolfo Falcon, Cuba
2002	Matt Welsh, Australia	Peter Marshall, USA	Toni Helbig, Germany
2004	Thomas Rupprath, Germany	Matt Welsh, Australia	Peter Marshall, USA
2006	Matt Welsh, Australia	Thomas Rupprath, Germany	Helge Meeuw, Germany
2008	Peter Marshall, USA	Liam Tancock, G. Britain	Ashley Delaney, Australia

100 BACKSTROKE

	Gold	Silver	Bronze
1993	Tripp Schwenk, USA	Martin Harris, G. Britain	Rodolfo Falcon, Cuba
1995	Rodolfo Falcon, Cuba	Neil Willey, G. Britain	Jirka Letzin, Germany
1997	Neisser Bent, Cuba	Brian Retterer, USA	Adrian Radley, Australia
1999	Rodolfo Falcon, Cuba	Matt Welsh, Australia	Mariusz Siembida, Poland
2000	Neil Walker, USA	Rodolfo Falcon, Cuba	Derya Buyukuncu, Turkey
2002	Matt Welsh, Australia	Aaron Peirsol, USA	Peter Marshall, USA
2004	Aaron Peirsol, USA	Matt Welsh, Australia	Thomas Rupprath, Germany
2006	Matt Welsh, Australia	Markus Rogan, Austria	Randall Bal, USA/
2008	Liam Tancock, G. Britain	Randall Bal, USA	Helge Meeuw, Germany
			Stanislav Donets, Russia

200 BACKSTROKE

	Gold	Silver	Bronze
1993	Tripp Schwenk, USA	Luca Bianchin, Italy	Stefaan Maene, Belgium
1995	Rodolfo Falcon, Cuba	Chris Renaud, Canada	Tamas Deutsch, Hungary
1997	Neisser Bent, Cuba	Wang Wei, China	Vladimir Selkov, Russia
1999	Josh Watson, Australia	Mark Versfeld, Canada	Serguei Ostaptchouk, Russia
2000	Gordan Kozulj, Croatia	Brad Bridgewater, USA	V. Nikolaychuk, Ukraine.

Year	Gold	Silver	Bronze
2002	Aaron Peirsol, USA	Marko Strahija, Croatia	Blaz Medvesek, Slovenia
2004	Aaron Peirsol, USA	Matt Welsh, Australia	Arkady Vyatchanin, Russia
2006	Ryan Lochte, USA	Markus Rogan, Austria	Matt Welsh, Australia
2008	Markus Rogan, Austria	Ryan Lochte, USA	Stanislav Donets, Russia

50 BREASTSTROKE

Year	Gold	Silver	Bronze
1999	Dmytro Kraevskyy, Ukraine	Patrick Isaksson, Sweden	Remo Lutolf, Switzerland
2000	Mark Warnecke, Germany	Brendon Dedekind, S. Africa	Oleg Lisogor, Ukraine
2002	Oleg Lisogor, Ukraine	Jose Couto, Portugal	Eduardo Fischer, Brazil
2004	Brendan Hansen, USA	Brenton Rickard, Australia	Stefan Nystrand, Sweden
2006	Oleg Lisogor, Ukraine	Alessandro Terrin, Italy	Chris Cook, G. Britain
2008	Oleg Lisogor, Ukraine	Mark Gangloff, USA	C. van der Burgh, S. Africa

100 BREASTSTROKE

Year	Gold	Silver	Bronze
1993	Philip Rogers, Australia	Ron Decker, Holland	Seth VanNeerden, USA
1995	Mark Warnecke, Germany	Paul Kent, N. Zealand	Stanislav Lopukhov, Russia
1997	Patrick Isaksson, Sweden	Stanislav Lopukhov, Russia	Jens Kruppa, Germany
1999	Patrick Isaksson, Sweden	Domenico Fioravanti, Italy	Morgan Knabe, Canada

2000	Roman Sloudnov, Russia	Zhu Yi, China	Roman Ivanovski, Russia
2002	Oleg Lisogor, Ukraine	Kosuke Kitajima, Japan	Jarno Pihlava, Finland
2004	Brendan Hansen, USA	Brenton Rickard, Australia	Vlad Polyakov, Kazakhstan
2006	Oleg Lisogor, Ukraine	Brenton Rickard, Australia	Alexander Dale Oen, Norway
2008	Igor Borysik, Ukraine	C. van der Burgh, S. Africa	Oleg Lisogor, Ukraine

200 BREASTSTROKE

	Gold	**Silver**	**Bronze**
1993	Nick Gillingham, G. Britain	Philip Rogers, Australia	Eric Wunderlich, USA
1995	Wang Yiwu, China	Ryan Mitchell, Australia	Jean-Lionel Rey, France
1997	Alexandre Goukov, Belarus	Andrei Korneyev, Russia	Jens Kruppa, Germany
1999	Philip Rogers, Australia	Ryan Mitchell, Australia	Dimitri Komornikov, Russia
2000	Roman Sloudnov, Russia	Terence Parkin, S. Africa	Andrei Ivanov, Russia
2002	Jim Piper, Australia	Dave Denniston, USA	Jarno Pihlava, Finland
2004	Brendan Hansen, USA	Brenton Rickard, Australia	Vlad Polyakov, Kazakhstan
2006	Vlad Polyakov, Kazakhstan	Brenton Rickard, Australia	Y. Ryzkkov, Kazakhstan
2008	Kris Gilchrist, G. Britain	Igor Borysik, Ukraine	William Diering, S. Africa

50 BUTTERFLY

	Gold	Silver	Bronze
1999	Mark Foster, G. Britain	Zhang Qiang, China	Joris Keizer, Holland
2000	Mark Foster, G. Britain	Neil Walker, USA	Sabir Muhammad, USA
2002	Geoff Huegill, Australia	Adam Pine, Australia	Mark Foster, G. Britain
2004	Ian Crocker, USA	Mark Foster, G. Britain	Duje Draganja, Croatia
2006	Matt Welsh, Australia	Sergiy Breus, Ukraine	Kaio Almeida, Brazil
2008	Adam Pine, Australia	Sergiy Breus, Ukraine	Evgeni Korotyshkin, Russia

100 BUTTERFLY

	Gold	Silver	Bronze
1993	Milos Milosevic, Croatia	Mark Henderson, USA	Rafal Szukala, Poland
1995	Scott Miller, Australia	Denis Pimankov, Russia	Michael Klim, Australia
1997	Lars Frolander, Sweden	Geoff Huegill, Australia	Michael Klim, Australia
1999	Lars Frolander, Sweden	Michael Klim, Australia	James Hickman, G. Britain
2000	Lars Frolander, Sweden	James Hickman, G. Britain	Denys Sylantyev, Ukraine
2002	Geoff Huegill, Australia	Adam Pine, Australia	Igor Martchenko, Russia
2004	Ian Crocker, USA	James Hickman, G. Britain	Peter Mankoc, Slovenia
2006	Kaio Almeida, Brazil	Albert Subirats, Venezuela	Jayme Cramer, USA
2008	Peter Mankoc, Slovenia	Adam Pine, Australia	Nikolay Skvortsov, Russia

200 BUTTERFLY

	Gold	Silver	Bronze
1993	Franck Esposito, France	Christian Keller, Germany	Chris Bremer, Germany
1995	Scott Goodman, Australia	Scott Miller, Australia	Chris Bremer, Germany
1997	James Hickman, G. Britain	Denys Sylantyev, Ukraine	Scott Goodman, Australia
1999	James Hickman, G. Britain	Takashi Yamamoto, Japan	Denys Sylantyev, Ukraine
2000	James Hickman, G. Britain	Shamek Pietucha, Canada	Anatoli Poliakov, Russia
2002	James Hickman, G. Britain	Justin Norris, Australia	Stefan Gherghel, Romania
2004	James Hickman, G. Britain	Stefan Gherghel, Romania	Wu Peng, China
2006	Wu Peng, China	Moss Burmester, N. Zealand	Nikolay Skvortsov, Russia
2008	Moss Burmester, N. Zealand	Nikolay Skvortsov, Russia	Pawel Korzeniowski, Poland

100 INDIVIDUAL MEDLEY

	Gold	Silver	Bronze
1999	Jani Sievinen, Finland	Matthew Dunn, Australia	Jakob Andersen, Denmark
2000	Neil Walker, USA	Jani Sievinen, Finland	James Hickman, G. Britain
2002	Peter Mankoc, Slovenia	Jani Sievinen, Finland	Jakob Andersen, Denmark
2004	Peter Mankoc, Slovenia	Thomas Rupprath, Germany	Thiago Pereira, Brazil
2006	Ryk Neethling, S. Africa	Peter Mankoc, Slovenia	Stefan Nystrand, Sweden
2008	Ryan Lochte, USA	Peter Mankoc, Slovenia	Liam Tancock, G. Britain

200 INDIVIDUAL MEDLEY

	Gold	Silver	Bronze
1993	Christian Keller, Germany	Fraser Walker, G. Britain	Curtis Myden, Canada
1995	Matthew Dunn, Australia	Curtis Myden, Canada	Marcin Malinski, Poland
1997	Matthew Dunn, Australia	Christian Keller, Germany	Ron Karnaugh, USA
1999	Matthew Dunn, Australia	James Hickman, G. Britain	Marcel Wouda, Holland
2000	Jani Sievinen, Finland	James Hickman, G. Britain	Massi Rosolino, Italy
2002	Jani Sievinen, Finland	Peter Mankoc, Slovenia	Tom Wilkens, USA
2004	Thiago Pereira, Brazil	Ryan Lochte, USA	Ous Mellouli, Tunisia
2006	Ryan Lochte, USA	Markus Rogan, Austria	Igor Berezutskiy, Russia
2008	Ryan Lochte, USA	Liam Tancock, G. Britain	James Goddard, G. Britain

400 INDIVIDUAL MEDLEY

	Gold	Silver	Bronze
1993	Curtis Myden, Canada	Sergei Mariniuk, Moldova	Petteri Lehtinen, Finland
1995	Matthew Dunn, Australia	Curtis Myden, Canada	Marcin Malinski, Poland
1997	Matthew Dunn, Australia	Xie Xufeng, China	Christian Keller, Germany
1999	Matthew Dunn, Australia	Marcel Wouda, Holland	Frederick Hviid, Spain
2000	Jani Sievinen, Finland	Terence Parkin, S. Africa	Michael Halika, Israel
2002	Tom Wilkens, USA	Brian Johns, Canada	Jacob Carstensen, Denmark

2004	Ous Mellouli, Tunisia	Robin Francis, G. Britain	Eric Shanteau, USA
2006	Ryan Lochte, USA	Luca Marin, Italy	Igor Berezutskiy, Russia

400 FREESTYLE RELAY

	Gold	**Silver**	**Bronze**
1993	Brazil	USA	Russia
1995	Brazil	Australia	Romania
1997	Germany	Sweden	Australia
1999	Australia	Holland	Australia
2000	Sweden	USA	Sweden
2002	USA	Sweden	Germany
2004	USA	Brazil	Russia
2006	Italy	Sweden	Canada
2008	USA	Holland	USA
			Sweden

800 FREESTYLE RELAY

	Gold	**Silver**	**Bronze**
1993	Sweden	Germany	Brazil
1995	Australia	Germany	Brazil

	Gold	Silver	Bronze
1997	Australia	Sweden	Great Britain
1999	Holland	Great Britain	Canada
2000	USA	Great Britain	Russia
2002	Australia	Russia	USA
2004	USA	Australia	Brazil
2006	Italy	Australia	USA
2008	Australia	Great Britain	Italy

400 MEDLEY RELAY

	Gold	Silver	Bronze
1993	USA	Spain	Great Britain
1995	New Zealand	Australia	Russia
1997	Australia	Russia	Great Britain
1999	Australia	Sweden	Great Britain
2000	USA	Germany	Great Britain
2002	USA	Australia	Russia
2004	USA	Australia	Russia
2006	Australia	USA	Ukraine
2008	Russia	USA	New Zealand

Appendix K
World Short Course Championships:
Women's Medal Winners

Note: If a year is not listed, the event was not contested.

50 FREESTYLE

	Gold	Silver	Bronze
1993	Le Jingyi, China	Angel Martino, USA	Linda Olofsson, Sweden
1995	Le Jingyi, China	Angela Postma, Holland	Sandra Volker, Germany
1997	Sandra Volker, Germany	Jenny Thompson, USA	Le Jingyi, China
1999	Inge De Bruijn, Holland	Jenny Thompson, USA	Alison Sheppard, G. Britain
2000	Therese Alshammar, Sweden	Sandra Volker, Germany	Alison Sheppard, G. Britain
2002	Therese Alshammar, Sweden	Alison Sheppard, G. Britain	Tammie Spatz-Stone, USA
2004	Marleen Veldhuis, Holland	Libby Lenton, Australia	Therese Alshammar, Sweden
2006	Libby Lenton, Australia	Therese Alshammar, Sweden	Marleen Veldhuis, Holland
2008	Marleen Veldhuis, Holland	Hinkelien Schreuder, Holland	Francesca Halsall, G. Britain

100 FREESTYLE

	Gold	Silver	Bronze
1993	Le Jingyi, China	Angel Martino, USA	Karen Pickering, G. Britain
1995	Le Jingyi, China	Chao Na, China	Sandra Volker, Germany
1997	Jenny Thompson, USA	Sandra Volker, Germany	Le Jingyi, China
1999	Jenny Thompson, USA	Sandra Volker, Germany	Susan Rolph, G. Britain

	Gold	Silver	Bronze
2000	Therese Alshammar, Sweden	Jenny Thompson, USA	Martina Moravcova, Slovakia
2002	Therese Alshammar, Sweden	Martina Moravcova, Slovakia	Xu Yavei, China
2004	Libby Lenton, Australia	Josefin Lillhage, Sweden	Marleen Veldhuis, Holland
2006	Libby Lenton, Australia	Marleen Veldhuis, Holland	Maritza Correia, USA
2008	Marleen Veldhuis, Holland	Francesca Halsall, G. Britain	H.–Maria Seppala, Finland

200 FREESTYLE

	Gold	Silver	Bronze
1993	Karen Pickering, G. Britain	Susie O'Neill, Australia	Lu Bin, China
1995	Claudia Poll, Costa Rica	Susie O'Neill, Australia	Martina Moravcova, Slovakia
1997	Claudia Poll, Costa Rica	Nian Yin, China	Martina Moravcova, Slovakia
1999	Martina Moravcova, Slovakia	Qin Caini, China	Josefin Lillhage, Sweden
2000	Yang Yu, China	Martina Moravcova, Slovakia	N. Baranovskaya, Bulgaria
2002	Lindsay Benko, USA	Yang Yu, China	Xu Yanvei, China
2004	Josefin Lillhage, Sweden	Lindsay Benko, USA	Dana Vollmer, USA
2006	Yang Yu, China	Federica Pellegrini, Italy	Annika Liebs, Germany
2008	Kylie Palmer, Australia	Femke Heemskerk, Holland	C. McClatchey, G. Britain

400 FREESTYLE

	Gold	Silver	Bronze
1993	Janet Evans, USA	Trina Jackson, USA	Julie Majer, Australia
1995	Claudia Poll, Costa Rica	Carla Geurts, Holland	Sarah Hardcastle, G. Britain
1997	Claudia Poll, Costa Rica	Natasha Bowron, Australia	Kerstin Kielgass, Germany
1999	Nadejda Chemezova, Russia	Qin Caini, China	Joanne Malar, Canada
2000	Lindsay Benko, USA	Yana Klochkova, Ukraine	Chen Hua, China
2002	Yana Klochkova, Ukraine	Chen Hua, China	Rachel Komisarz, USA
2004	Kaitlin Sandeno, USA	Sara McLarty, USA	Sachiko Yamada, Japan
2006	Kate Ziegler, USA	Bronte Barratt, Australia	Federica Pellegrini, Italy
2008	Kylie Palmer, Australia	Camelia Potec, Romania	Joanne Jackson, G. Britain

800 FREESTYLE

	Gold	Silver	Bronze
1993	Janet Evans, USA	Julie Majer, Australia	Trina Jackson, USA
1995	Sarah Hardcastle, G. Britain	Carla Geurts, Holland	Luo Ping, China
1997	Natasha Bowron, Australia	Kerstin Kielgass, Germany	Carla Geurts, Holland
1999	Chen Hua, China	Rachel Harris, Australia	F. Rigamonti, Switzerland
2000	Chen Hua, China	Brooke Bennett, USA	F. Rigamonti, Switzerland
2002	Chen Hua, China	Irina Oufimtseva, Russia	F. Rigamonti, Switzerland
2004	Sachiko Yamada, Japan	Kate Ziegler, USA	Melissa Gorman, Australia

	Gold	Silver	Bronze
2006	Anastasia Ivanenko, Russia	Kate Ziegler, USA	Rebecca Cooke, G. Britain
2008	R. Adlington, G. Britain	Kylie Palmer, Australia	Erika Villaecija, Spain

50 BACKSTROKE

	Gold	Silver	Bronze
1999	Sandra Volker, Germany	Mai Nakamura, Japan	Kellie McMillan, Australia
2000	A. Buschschulte, Germany	Marylan Chiang, Canada	Kellie McMillan, Australia
2002	Jennifer Carroll, Canada	Haley Cope, USA	Diana MacManus, USA
2004	Haley Cope, USA	Gao Chang, China	Sophie Edington, Australia
2006	Janine Pietsch, Germany	Tayliah Zimmer, Australia	Gao Chang, China
2008	Sanja Jovanovic, Croatia	Gao Chang, China	Kateryna Zubkova, Ukraine

100 BACKSTROKE

	Gold	Silver	Bronze
1993	Angel Martino, USA	He Cihong, China/ Elli Overton, Australia	Not Awarded
1995	Misty Hyman, USA	Mette Jacobsen, Denmark	B. J. Bedford, USA
1997	Lu Donghua, China	Chen Yan, China	Misty Hyman, USA
1999	Mai Nakamura, Japan	Kelly Stefanyshyn, Canada	Erin Gammel, Canada
2000	Sandra Volker, Germany	Marylyn Chiang, Canada	A. Buschschulte, Germany

Year	Gold	Silver	Bronze
2002	Haley Cope, USA	I. Hlavackova, Czech Rep.	Diana MacManus, USA
2004	Haley Cope, USA	Gao Chang, Canada	Sophie Edington, Australia
2006	Janine Pietsch, Germany	Tayliah Zimmer, Australia	Gao Chang, China
2008	Kirsty Coventry, Zimbabwe	Kateryna Zubkova, Ukraine	Sanja Jovanovic, Croatia

200 BACKSTROKE

Year	Gold	Silver	Bronze
1993	He Cihong, China	Jia Yuan-Yuan, China	Cathleen Rund, Germany
1995	Mette Jacobsen, Denmark	Dagmar Hase, Germany	Leigh Habler, Australia
1997	Chen Yan, China	Misty Hyman, USA	Lia Oberstar, USA
1999	Mai Nakamura, Japan	H. Don-Duncan, G. Britain	Kelly Stefanyshyn, Canada
2000	A. Buschschulte, Germany	Clementine Stoney, Australia	Lindsay Benko, USA
2002	Lindsay Benko, USA	Reiko Nakamura, Japan	Irina Amshennikova, Ukraine
2004	Margaret Hoelzer, USA	Tayliah Zimmer, Australia	Melissa Ingram, N. Zealand
2006	Margaret Hoelzer, USA	Tayliah Zimmer, Australia	Hannah McLean, N. Zealand
2008	Kirsty Coventry, Zimbabwe	E. Simmonds, G. Britain	Margaret Hoelzer, USA

50 BREASTSTROKE

Year	Gold	Silver	Bronze
1999	Masami Tanaka, Japan	Penelope Heyns, S. Africa	Xan Xue, China
2000	Sarah Powe, S. Africa	Pao Ping, China	Tara Kirk, USA

Year	Gold	Silver	Bronze
2002	Emma Igelstrom, Sweden	Luo Xuejuan, China	Zoe Baker, G. Britain
2004	Brooke Hanson, Australia	Jade Edmistone, Australia	Tara Kirk, USA
2006	Jade Edmistone, Australia	Brooke Hanson, Australia	Jessica Hardy, USA
2008	Jessica Hardy, USA	Kate Haywood, G. Britain/ Sarah Katsoulis, Australia	Not Awarded

100 BREASTSTROKE

Year	Gold	Silver	Bronze
1993	Dai Guohong, China	Linley Frame, Australia	Samantha Riley, Australia
1995	Samantha Riley, Australia	S. Bondarenko, Ukraine	Linley Frame, Australia
1997	Kristy Ellem, Australia	Alicja Peczak, Poland	S. Bondarenko, Ukraine
1999	Masami Tanaka, Japan	Penelope Heyns, S. Africa	Samantha Riley, Australia
2000	Sarah Poewe, S. Africa	Alicja Peczak, Poland	Elena Bogomazova, Russia
2002	Emma Igelstrom, Sweden	Sarah Poewe, S. Africa	Luo Xuejuan, China
2004	Brooke Hanson, Australia	Jade Edmistone, Australia	Tara Kirk, USA
2006	Tara Kirk, USA	Suzaan Van Biljon, S. Africa	Jade Edmistone, Australia
2008	Jessica Hardy, USA	Jade Edmistone, Australia	Suzaan Van Biljon, S. Africa

200 BREASTSTROKE

	Gold	Silver	Bronze
1993	Dai Guohong, China	Hitomi Maehara, Japan	Samantha Riley, Australia
1995	Samantha Riley, Australia	S. Bondarenko, Ukraine	Alicja Peczak, Poland
1997	Kristy Ellem, Australia	Larisa Lacusta, Romania	Alicja Peczak, Poland
1999	Masami Tanaka, Japan	Penelope Heyns, S. Africa	Qi Hui, China
2000	Rebecca Brown, Australia	Alicja Peczak, Poland	Brooke Hanson, Australia
2002	Qi Hui, China	Emma Igelstrom, Sweden	Mirna Jukic, Austria
2004	Brooke Hanson, Australia	Amanda Beard, USA	Sarah Katsoulis, Australia
2006	Qi Hui, China	Tara Kirk, USA	Luo Nan, China
2008	Suzaan Van Biljon, S. Africa	Sally Foster, G. Britain	Yuliya Efimova, Russia

50 BUTTERFLY

	Gold	Silver	Bronze
1999	Jenny Thompson, USA	A. K. Kammerling, Sweden	Inge De Bruijn, Holland
2000	Jenny Thompson, USA	A. K. Kammerling, Sweden	Nicola Jackson, G. Britain
2002	A. K. Kammerling, Sweden	Petria Thomas, Australia	Vered Borochovski, Israel
2004	Jenny Thompson, USA	A. K. Kammerling, Sweden	Libby Lenton, Australia
2006	Therese Alshammar, Sweden	Fabienne Nadarajah, Austria	A. K. Kammerling, Sweden
2008	Felicity Galvez, Australia	Hinkelien Schreuder, Holland	Inge Dekker, Holland

100 BUTTERFLY

	Gold	Silver	Bronze
1993	Susie O'Neill, Australia	Liu Limin, China	Kristie Krueger, USA
1995	Liu Limin, China	Susie O'Neill, Australia	Angela Kennedy, Australia
1997	Jenny Thompson, USA	Cai Huijue, China	Misty Hyman, USA
1999	Jenny Thompson, USA	Johanna Sjoberg, Sweden	Ayari Aoyama, Japan
2000	Jenny Thompson, USA	Johanna Sjoberg, Sweden	Karen Campbell, USA
2002	Martina Moravcova, Slovakia	Petria Thomas, Australia	A.K. Kammerling, Sweden
2004	Martina Moravcova, Slovakia	Rachel Komisarz, USA	Jenny Thompson, USA
2006	Libby Lenton, Australia	Rachel Komisarz, USA	Jessicah Schipper, Australia
2008	Felicity Galvez, Australia	Rachel Komisarz, USA	Jemma Lowe, G. Britain

200 BUTTERFLY

	Gold	Silver	Bronze
1993	Liu Limin, China	Susie O'Neill, Australia	Petria Thomas, Australia
1995	Susie O'Neill, Australia	Liu Limin, China	Mette Jacobsen, Denmark
1997	Liu Limin, China	Hitomi Kashima, Japan	Misty Hyman, USA
1999	Mette Jacobsen, Denmark	Petria Thomas, Australia	Sophia Skou, Denmark
2000	Mette Jacobsen, Denmark	Katrin Jaeke, Germany	Otylia Jedrzejczak, Poland
2002	Petria Thomas, Australia	Yang Yu, China	Mary DeScenza, USA
2004	Kaitlin Sandeno, USA	Mary DeScenza, USA	Audrey Lacroix, Canada

Year	Gold	Silver	Bronze
2006	Jessicah Schipper, Australia	Francesca Segat, Italy	Yang Yu, China
2008	Mary DeScenza, USA	Felicity Galvez, Australia	Jessica Dickons, G. Britain

100 INDIVIDUAL MEDLEY

Year	Gold	Silver	Bronze
1999	Martina Moravcova, Slovakia	Lori Munz, Australia	Oxana Verevka, Russia
2000	Martina Moravcova, Slovakia	Marianne Limpert, Canada	ALenka Kejzar, Slovenia
2002	Martina Moravcova, Slovakia	Gabrielle Rose, USA	Alison Sheppard, G. Britain
2004	Brooke Hanson, Australia	Shayne Reese, Australia	Martina Moravcova, Slovakia
2006	Brooke Hanson, Australia	H.-Maria Seppala, Finland	Martina Moravcova, Slovakia
2008	Shayne Reese, Australia	H.-Maria Seppala, Finland	Kirsty Coventry, Zimbabwe

200 INDIVIDUAL MEDLEY

Year	Gold	Silver	Bronze
1993	Allison Wagner, USA	Dai Guohong, China	Elli Overton, Australia
1995	Elli Overton, Australia	Martina Moravcova, Slovakia	Louise Karlsson, Sweden
1997	Louise Karlsson, Sweden	Martina Moravcova, Slovakia	Susan Rolph, G. Britain
1999	Martina Moravcova, Slovakia	Yana Klochkova, Ukraine	Lori Munz, Australia
2000	Yana Klochkova, Ukraine	Martina Moravcova, Slovakia	Marianne Limpert, Canada
2002	Yana Klochkova, Ukraine	Gabrielle Rose, USA	Oxana Verevka, Russia

	Gold	Silver	Bronze
2004	Brooke Hanson, Australia	Lara Carroll, Australia	Katie Hoff, USA
2006	Qi Hui, China	Kaitlin Sandeno, USA	Lara Carroll, Australia
2008	Kirsty Coventry, Zimbabwe	Mireia Belmonte, Spain	Hanna Miley, G. Britain

400 INDIVIDUAL MEDLEY

	Gold	Silver	Bronze
1993	Dai Guohong, China	Allison Wagner, USA	Julie Majer, Australia
1995	Joanne Malar, Canada	Nancy Sweetnam, Canada	Britta Vestergaard, Denmark
1997	Emma Johnson, Australia	Sabine Herbst, Germany	Joanne Malar, Canada
1999	Yana Klochkova, Ukraine	Joanne Malar, Canada	Lourdes Becerra, Spain
2000	Yana Klochkova, Ukraine	Nicole Hetzer, Germany	Katie Yevak, USA
2002	Yana Klochkova, Ukraine	Alenka Kejzar, Slovenia	Georgina Bardach, Argentina
2004	Kaitlin Sandeno, USA	Katie Hoff, USA	Lara Carroll, Australia
2006	Qi Hui, China	Alessia Filippi, Italy	Anastasia Ivanenko, Russia
2008	Kirsty Coventry, Zimbabwe	Hannah Miley, G. Britain	Mireia Belmonte, Spain

400 FREESTYLE RELAY

	Gold	Silver	Bronze
1993	China	Sweden	USA
1995	China	Australia	Sweden

	Gold	Silver	Bronze
1997	China	Germany	Sweden
1999	Great Britain	Holland	Australia
2000	Sweden	Germany	Great Britain
2002	Sweden	Australia	China
2004	USA	Sweden	Australia
2006	Holland	Australia	Sweden
2008	Holland	Australia	Great Britain

800 FREESTYLE RELAY

	Gold	Silver	Bronze
1993	China	Australia	USA
1995	Canada	Germany	Australia
1997	China	Sweden	Australia
1999	Sweden	Great Britain	Australia
2000	Great Britain	USA	China
2002	China	USA	Australia
2004	USA	Australia	Sweden
2006	Australia	China	USA
2008	Holland	Great Britain	Australia

400 MEDLEY RELAY

	Gold	Silver	Bronze
1993	China	Australia	USA
1995	Australia	Canada	USA
1997	China	USA	Australia
1999	Japan	Australia	Sweden
2000	Sweden	Germany	USA
2002	Sweden	USA	China
2004	Australia	USA	Sweden
2006	Australia	USA	China
2008	USA	Australia	Great Britain

Appendix L
Olympic Games: Years, Sites, and Dates

Year	Site	Dates
1896	Athens, Greece	6–15 April
1900	Paris, France	20 May–28 Oct.
1904	St. Louis, Missouri	1 July–23 Nov.
1906	Athens, Greece	22 April–2 May
1908	London, England	27 April–31 Oct.
1912	Stockholm, Sweden	5 May–27 July
1920	Antwerp, Belgium	23 April–12 Sept.
1924	Paris, France	4 May–27 July
1928	Amsterdam, Netherlands	17 May–12 Aug.
1932	Los Angeles, California	30 July–14 Aug.
1936	Berlin, Germany	1–16 Aug.
1948	London, England	29 July–14 Aug.
1952	Helsinki, Finland	19 July–3 Aug.
1956	Melbourne, Australia	22 Nov.–8 Dec.
1960	Rome, Italy	25 Aug.–11 Sept.
1964	Tokyo, Japan	10–24 Oct.
1968	Mexico City, Mexico	12–27 Oct.
1972	Munich, Germany	26 Aug.–11 Sept.
1976	Montreal, Canada	17 July–1 Aug.
1980	Moscow, Russia	19 July–3 Aug.
1984	Los Angeles, California	28 July–12 Aug.
1988	Seoul, South Korea	17 Sept.–5 Oct.
1992	Barcelona, Spain	25 July–9 Aug.
1996	Atlanta, Georgia	20 July–4 Aug.
2000	Sydney, Australia	14 Sept.–1 Oct.
2004	Athens, Greece	13–29 Aug.
2008	Beijing, China	8–24 Aug.
2012	London, England	27 July–12 Aug.
2016	Rio de Janeiro, Brazil	5–21 Aug.

Appendix M
Olympic Games: Most Overall Medals (Country)

Country	Number	Gold	Silver	Bronze
United States	489	214	155	120
Australia	168	56	54	58
East Germany	98	38	32	22
Great Britain	64	15	21	28
Hungary	63	23	23	17
Japan	62	20	21	21
Germany	59	13	18	28
Soviet Union	59	12	21	26
Holland	52	17	17	18
Canada	40	7	13	20
Sweden	35	8	14	13
France	33	4	11	18
China	27	7	15	5
West Germany	22	3	5	14
Italy	17	4	4	9
Russia	15	5	5	5
South Africa	12	4	2	6
Germany	12	1	5	6
Denmark	12	2	5	5
Austria	11	1	6	4
Brazil	11	1	3	7
Unified Team	10	6	3	1
Ukraine	10	4	5	1

Appendix N
Olympic Games: Most Gold Medals (Career)

Name	Number
Michael Phelps, United States	14
Mark Spitz, United States	9
Jenny Thompson, United States	8
Matt Biondi, United States	8
Kristin Otto, East Germany	6
Amy Van Dyken, United States	6
Gary Hall Jr., United States	5
Ian Thorpe, Australia	5
Aaron Peirsol, United States	5
Krisztina Egerszegi, Hungary	5
Tom Jager, United States	5
Don Schollander, United States	5
Johnny Weissmuller, United States	5

Appendix O
Olympic Games: Most Medals (Career)

Name	Number	Gold	Silver	Bronze
Michael Phelps, United States	16	14	0	2
Jenny Thompson, United States	12	8	3	1
Dara Torres, United States	12	4	4	4
Mark Spitz, United States	11	9	1	1
Matt Biondi, United States	11	8	2	1
Natalie Coughlin, United States	11	3	4	4
Gary Hall Jr., United States	10	5	3	2
Franziska van Almsick, Germany	10	0	4	6
Ian Thorpe, Australia	9	5	3	1
Alexander Popov, Russia	9	4	5	0
Dawn Fraser, Australia	8	4	4	0
Kornelia Ender, East Germany	8	4	4	0
Roland Matthes, East Germany	8	4	2	2
Inge De Bruijn, Holland	8	4	2	2
Petria Thomas, Australia	8	3	4	1
Shirley Babashoff, United States	8	2	6	0
Susie O'Neill Australia	8	2	4	2
Aaron Peirsol, United States	7	5	2	0
Krisztina Egerszegi, Hungary	7	5	1	1
Charles Daniels, United States	7	4	2	1
Pieter van den Hoogenband, Holland	7	3	2	2
Jason Lezak, United States	7	3	1	3
Amanda Beard, United States	7	2	4	1
Kirsty Coventry, Zimbabwe	7	2	4	1

Appendix P
Olympic Games: Most
Gold Medals (Single Olympiad)

Name	Number	Year
Michael Phelps, United States	8	2008
Mark Spitz, United States	7	1972
Michael Phelps, United States	6	2004
Kristin Otto, East Germany	6	1988
Matt Biondi, United States	5	1988
Amy Van Dyken, United States	4	1996
John Naber, United States	4	1976
Don Schollander, United States	4	1964

Appendix Q
Olympic Games: Most Medals (Single Olympiad)

Name	Number	Year	Gold	Silver	Bronze
Michael Phelps, United States	8	2008	8	0	0
Michael Phelps, United States	8	2004	6	0	2
Mark Spitz, United States	7	1972	7	0	0
Matt Biondi, United States	7	1988	5	1	
Kristin Otto, East Germany	6	1988	6	0	0
Natalie Coughlin, United States	6	2008	1	2	3
Kornelia Ender, East Germany	5	1976	4	1	0
Ian Thorpe, Australia	5	2000	3	2	0
Shane Gould, Australia	5	1972	3	1	1
Ines Diers, East Germany	5	1980	2	2	1
Dara Torres, United States	5	2000	2	0	3
Natalie Coughlin, United States	5	2004	2	2	1
Shirley Babashoff, United States	5	1976	1	4	0

Appendix R
Olympic Games: Men's Medal Winners

Note: If a year is not listed, the event was not contested.

50 FREESTYLE

	Gold	**Silver**	**Bronze**
1904	Z. Von Hamay, Hungary	J. Scott Leary, USA	Charles Daniels, USA
1988	Matt Biondi, USA	Tom Jager, USA	Gennadi Prigoda, S. Union
1992	Alex Popov, Unified Team	Matt Biondi, USA	Tom Jager, USA
1996	Alexander Popov, Russia	Gary Hall Jr., USA	Fernando Scherer, Brazil
2000	Gary Hall Jr., USA/	Not Awarded	P. v.d. Hoogenband, Holland
	Anthony Ervin, USA		
2004	Gary Hall Jr., USA	Duje Draganja, Croatia	Roland Schoeman, S. Africa
2008	Cesar Cielo, Brazil	Amaury Leveaux, France	Alain Bernard, France

100 FREESTYLE

	Gold	**Silver**	**Bronze**
1896	Alfred Hajos, Hungary	Efstathios Choraphas, Greece	Otto Herschmann, Austria
1904	Z. Von Halmay, Hungary	Charles Daniels, USA	J. Scott Leary, USA
1908	Charles Daniels, USA	Z. Von Halmay, Hungary	Harald Julin, Sweden
1912	Duke Kahanamoku, USA	Cecil Healy, Australia	Kenneth Huszagh, USA
1920	Duke Kahanamoku, USA	Pua Lealoha, USA	William Harris, USA

Year	Gold	Silver	Bronze
1924	Johnny Weissmuller, USA	Duke Kahanamoku, USA	Sam Kahanamoku, USA
1928	Johnny Weissmuller, USA	Istvan Barany, Hungary	Katsuo Takaishi, Japan
1932	Yasuji Miyazaki, Japan	Tatsugo Kawaishi, Japan	Albert Schwartz, USA
1936	Ferenc Csik, Hungary	Masanori Yusa, Japan	Shigeo Arai, Japan
1948	Walter Ris, USA	Alan Ford, USA	Geza Kadas, Hungary
1952	Clarke Scholes, USA	Hiroshi Suzuki, Japan	Goran Larsson, Sweden
1956	Jon Henricks, Australia	John Devitt, Australia	Gary Chapman, Australia
1960	John Devitt, Australia	Lance Larson, USA	Manuel Dos Santos, Brazil
1964	Don Schollander, USA	Robert McGregor, G. Britain	Hans Klein, W. Germany
1968	Michael Wenden, Australia	Ken Walsh, USA	Mark Spitz, USA
1972	Mar Spitz, USA	Jerry Heldenreich, USA	Vladimir Bure, S. Union
1976	Jim Montgomery, USA	Jack Babashoff, USA	Peter Nocke, W. Germany
1980	Jorg Woithe, E. Germany	Per Holmertz, Sweden	Per Johansson, Sweden
1984	Rowdy Gaines, USA	Mark Stockwell, Australia	Per Johansson, Sweden
1988	Matt Biondi, USA	Chris Jacobs, USA	Stephan Caron, France
1992	Alex Popov, Unified Team	Gustavo Borges, Brazil	Stephan Caron, France
1996	Alexander Popov, Russia	Gary Hall Jr., USA	Gustavo Borges, Brazil
2000	P. v.d. Hoogenband, Holland	Alex Popov, Russia	Gary Hall Jr., USA
2004	P. v.d. Hoogenband, Holland	Roland Schoeman, S. Africa	Ian Thope, Australia
2008	Alain Bernard, France	Eamon Sullivan, Australia	Jason Lezak, USA/ Cesar Cielo, Brazil

200 FREESTYLE

	Gold	Silver	Bronze
1900	Frederick Lane, Australia	Z. Von Halmay, Hungary	Karl Ruberl, Austria
1904	Charles Daniels, USA	Francis Gailey, USA	Emil Rausch, Germany
1968	Michael Wenden, Australia	Don Schollander, USA	John Nelson, USA
1972	Mark Spitz, USA	Steven Genter, USA	Werner Lampe, FRG
1976	Bruce Furniss, USA	John Naber, USA	Jim Montgomery, USA
1980	Sergej Kopljakow, S. Union	Andrej Krylow, S. Union	Graeme Brewer, Australia
1984	Michael Gross, FRG	Michael Heath, USA	Thomas Fahrner, FRG
1988	Duncan Armstrong, Australia	Anders Holmertz, Sweden	Matt Biondi, USA
1992	E. Sadovyi, Unified Team	Anders Holmertz, Sweden	Antti Kasvio, Finland
1996	Danyon Loader, N. Zealand	Gustavo Borges, Brazil	Daniel Kowalski, Australia
2000	P. v.d. Hoogenband, Holland	Ian Thorpe, Australia	Massi Rosolino, Italy
2004	Ian Thorpe, Australia	P. v.d. Hoogenband, Holland	Michael Phelps, USA
2008	Michael Phelps, USA	Tae Hwan Park, S. Korea	Peter Vanderkaay, USA

400 FREESTYLE

	Gold	Silver	Bronze
1896	Paul Neumann, Austria	Antonios Pepanos, Greece	Efstathios Choraphas, Greece
1904	Charles Daniels, USA	Francis Gailey, USA	Otto Wahle, Austria
1908	Henry Taylor, G. Britain	Frank Beaurepaire, Australia	Otto Scheff, Austria

Year			
1912	George Hodgson, Canada	John Hatfield, G. Britain	Harold Hardwick, Australia
1920	Norman Ross, USA	Ludy Langer, USA	George Vernot, Canada
1924	Johnny Weissmuller, USA	Arne Borg, Sweden	Andrew Charlton, Australia
1928	Alberto Zorrilla, Argentina	Andrew Charlton, Australia	Arne Borg, Sweden
1932	Buster Crabbe, USA	Jean Taris, France	Tsutomu Oyokota, Japan
1936	Jack Medica, USA	Shumpel Uto, Japan	Shozo Makino, Japan
1948	William Smith, USA	James McLane, USA	John Marshall, Australia
1952	Jean Boiteux, France	Ford Konno, USA	Per-Olof Ostrand, Sweden
1956	Murray Rose, Australia	Tsuyoshi Yamanaka, Japan	George Breen, USA
1960	Murray Rose, Australia	Tsuyoshi Yamanaka, Japan	John Konrads, Australia
1964	Don Schollander, USA	Frank Wiegand, E. Germany	Allan Wood, Australia
1968	Mike Burton, USA	Ralph Hutton, Canada	Alain Mosconi, France
1972	Bradford Cooper, Australia	Steven Genter, USA	Tom McBreen, USA
1976	Brian Goodell, USA	Tim Shaw, USA	Vladimir Raskatow, S. Union
1980	Vladimir Salnikov, S. Union	Andrej Krylow, S. Union	Ivan Stukolkin, S. Union
1984	George DiCarlo, USA	John Mykkanen, USA	Justin Lemburg, Australia
1988	Uwe Dassier, E. Germany	Duncan Armstrong, Australia	Artur Wojdat, Poland
1992	E. Sadovyi, Unified Team	Kieren Perkins, Australia	Anders Holmertz, Sweden
1996	Danyon Loader, N. Zealand	Paul Palmer, G. Britain	Daniel Kowalski, Australia
2000	Ian Thorpe, Australia	Massi Rosolino, Italy	Klete Keller, USA
2004	Ian Thorpe, Australia	Grant Hackett, Australia	Klete Keller, USA
2008	Tae Hwan Park, S. Korea	Zhang Lin, China	Larsen Jensen, USA

1,500 FREESTYLE

	Gold	Silver	Bronze
1896	Alfred Hajos, Hungary	Jean Andreou, Germany	Efstathios Choraphas, Greece
1900	John Jarvis, G. Britain	Otto Wahle, Austria	Zoltan Von Halmay, Hungary
1904	Emil Rausch, Germany	Geza Kiss, Hungary	Francis Gailey, USA
1908	Henry Taylor, G. Britain	Thomas Battersby, G. Britain	Frank Beaurepaire, Australia
1912	George Hodgson, Canada	John Hatfield, G. Britain	Harold Hardwick, Australia
1920	Norman Ross, USA	George Vernot, Canada	Frank Beaurepaire, Australia
1924	Andrew Charlton, Australia	Arne Borg, Sweden	Frank Beaurepaire, Australia
1928	Arne Borg, Sweden	Andrew Charlton, Australia	Buster Crabbe, USA
1932	Kusuo Kitamura, Japan	Shozo Makino, Japan	James Cristy, USA
1936	Noboru Terada, Japan	Jack Medica, USA	Shumpei Uto, Japan
1948	James McLane, USA	John Marshall, Australia	Gyorgy Mitro, Hungary
1952	Ford Konno, USA	Shiro Hashizume, Japan	Tetsuo Okamoto, Japan
1956	Murray Rose, Australia	Tsuyoshi Yamanaka, Japan	George Breen, USA
1960	John Konrads, Australia	Murray Rose, Australia	George Breen, USA
1964	Robert Windle, Australia	John Nelson, USA	Allan Wood, Australia
1968	Mike Burton, USA	John Kinsella, USA	Gregory Brough, Australia
1972	Mike Burton, USA	Graham Windeatt, Australia	Douglas Northway, USA
1976	Brian Goodell, USA	Bobby Hackett, USA	Stephan Holland, Australia
1980	Vladimir Salnikov, S. Union	Alexander Tschajew, S. Union	Max Metzer, Australia
1984	Mike O'Brien, USA	George DiCarlo, USA	Stefan Pfeiffer, FRG
1988	Vladimir Salnikov, S. Union	Stefan Pfeiffer, FRG	Uwe Dassier, E. Germany

Year		Silver	Bronze
1992	Kieren Perkins, Australia	Glen Housman, Australia	Joerg Hoffmann, Germany
1996	Kieren Perkins, Australia	Daniel Kowalski, Australia	Graeme Smith, G. Britain
2000	Grant Hackett, Australia	Kieren Perkins, Australia	Chris Thompson, USA
2004	Grant Hackett, Australia	Larsen Jensen, USA	David Davies, G. Britain
2008	Ous Mellouli, Tunisia	Grant Hackett, Australia	Ryan Cochrane, Canada

100 BACKSTROKE

Year	Gold	Silver	Bronze
1904	Walter Brack, Germany	Georg Hoffmann, Germany	Georg Zacharia, Germany
1908	Arno Bieberstein, Germany	Ludvig Dam, Denmark	Herbert Haresnape, G. Britain
1912	Harry Hebner, USA	Otto Fahr, Germany	Paul Kellner, Germany
1920	Warren Kealoha, USA	Pay Kegeris, USA	Gerard Blitz, Belgium
1924	Warren Kealoha, USA	Paul Wyatt, USA	Karoly Bartha, Hungary
1928	George Kojac, USA	Walter Laufer, USA	Paul Wyatt, USA
1932	Masaji Kiyokawa, Japan	Toshio Irie, Japan	Kentaro Kawatsu, Japan
1936	Adolph Kiefer, USA	Albert v.d. Weghe, USA	Masaji Kiyokawa, Japan
1948	Allen Stack, USA	Robert Cowell, USA	Georges Vallerey, France
1952	Yoshinobu Oyakawa, Japan	Gilbert Bozon, France	Jack Taylor, USA
1956	David Theile, Australia	John Monckton, Australia	Frank McKinney, USA
1960	David Theile, Australia	Frank McKinney, USA	Robert Bennett, USA
1968	Roland Matthes, E. Germany	Charles Hickcox, USA	Ron Mills, USA
1972	Roland Matthes, E. Germany	Mike Stamm, USA	John Murphy, USA

100 BACKSTROKE (continued)

Year	Gold	Silver	Bronze
1976	John Naber, USA	Peter Rocca, USA	Roland Matthes, E. Germany
1980	Bengt Baron, Sweden	Victor Kusnjetsow, S. Union	Vladimir Dolgov, S. Union
1984	Rick Carey, USA	Dave Wilson, USA	Mike West, Canada
1988	Daichi Suzuki, Japan	David Berkoff, USA	Igor Polianski, S. Union
1992	Mark Tewksbury, Canada	Jeff Rouse, USA	David Berkoff, USA
1996	Jeff Rouse, USA	Rodolfo Falcon, Cuba	Neisser Bent, Cuba
2000	Lenny Krayzelburg, USA	Matt Welsh, Australia	Stev Theloke, Germany
2004	Aaron Peirsol, USA	Markus Rogan, Austria	Tomomi Morita, Japan
2008	Aaron Peirsol, USA	Matt Grevers, USA	Arkady Vyatchanin, Russia/ Hayden Stoeckel, Australia

200 BACKSTROKE

Year	Gold	Silver	Bronze
1900	Ernst Hoppenberg, Germany	Karl Ruberl, Austria	Johannes Drost, Holland
1964	Jed Graef, USA	Gary Dilley, USA	Robert Bennett, USA
1968	Roland Matthes, E. Germany	Mitch Ivey, USA	Jack Horsley, USA
1972	Roland Matthes, E. Germany	Mike Stamm, USA	Mitch Ivey, USA
1976	John Naber, USA	Peter Rocca, USA	Dan Harrigan, USA
1980	Sandor Wladar, Hungary	Zoltan Verraszto, Hungary	Mark Kerry, Australia
1984	Rick Carey, USA	Frederic Delcourt, France	Cam Henning, Canada
1988	Igor Polianski, S. Union	Frank Baltrusch, E. Germany	Paul Kingsman, N. Zealand

	Gold	Silver	Bronze
1992	Martin Zubero, Spain	V. Selkov, Unifield Team	Stefano Battistelli, Italy
1996	Brad Bridgewater, USA	Tripp Schwenk, USA	Emanuele Merisi, Italy
2000	Lenny Krayzelburg, USA	Aaron Peirsol, USA	Matt Welsh, Australia
2004	Aaron Peirsol, USA	Markus Rogan, Austria	Razvan Florea, Romania
2008	Ryan Lochte, USA	Aaron Peirsol, USA	Arkady Vyatchanin, Russia

100 BREASTSTROKE

	Gold	Silver	Bronze
1968	Don McKenzie, USA	Vladimir Kossinski, S. Union	Nikolai Pankin, S. Union
1972	Nobutaka Taguchi, Japan	Tom Bruce, USA	John Hencken, USA
1976	John Hencken, USA	David Wilkie, G. Britain	Arvidas Juosaitis, S. Union
1980	Duncan Goodhew, G. Britain	Arsen Miskarow, S. Union	Peter Evans, Australia
1984	Steve Lundquist, USA	Victor Davis, Canada	Peter Evans, Australia
1988	A. Moorhouse, G. Britain	Karoly Guttler, Hungary	Dmitri Volkov, S. Union
1992	Nelson Diebel, USA	Norbert Rozsa, Hungary	Phil Rogers, Australia
1996	F. deBurghgraeve, Belgium	Jeremy Linn, USA	Mark Warnecke, Germany
2000	Domenico Fioravanti, Italy	Ed Moses, USA	Roman Sloudnov, Russia
2004	Kosuke Kitajima, Japan	Brendan Hansen, USA	Hugues Duboscq, France
2008	Kosuke Kitakima, Japan	Alexander Dale Oen, Norway	Hugues Duboscq, France

200 BREASTSTROKE

	Gold	Silver	Bronze
1908	Frederick Holman, G. Britain	William Robinson, G. Britain	Pontus Hanson, Sweden
1912	Walther Bathe, Germany	Willy Lutzow, Germany	Kurt Malisch, Germany
1920	Hakan Malmrot, Sweden	Tor Henning, Sweden	Arvo Aaltonen, Finland
1924	Robert Skelton, USA	Joseph De Combe, Belgium	Bill Kirschbaum, USA
1928	Yoshiyuki Tsuruta, Japan	Erich Rademacher, Germany	T. Yldefonzo, Phillipines
1932	Yoshiyuki Tsuruta, Japan	Reizo Koike, Japan	T. Yldefonzo, Phillipines
1936	Tetsuo Hamuro, Japan	Erwin Sietas, Germany	Reizo Koike, Japan
1948	Joseph Verdeur, USA	Keith Carter, USA	Robert Sohl, USA
1952	John Davies, Australia	Bowen Stassforth, USA	Herbert Klein, Germany
1956	Masaru Furukawa, Japan	Masahiro Yoshimura, Japan	Charis Junitschew, S. Union
1960	William Mulliken, USA	Yoshihiko Osaki, Japan	Weiger Mensonides, Holland
1964	Ian O'Brien, Australia	Georgi Prokopenko, S. Union	Chester Jastremski, USA
1968	Felipe Munoz, Mexico	Vladimir Kossinski, S. Union	Brian Job, USA
1972	John Hencken, USA	David Wilkie, G. Britain	Nobutaka Taguchi, Japan
1976	David Wilkie, G. Britain	John Hencken, USA	Rick Colella, USA
1980	Robertas Zulpa, S. Union	Alban Vermes, Hungary	Arsen Miskarow, S. Union
1984	Victor Davis, Canada	Glenn Beringen, Australia	Etienne Dagon, Switzerland
1988	Jozsef Szabo, Hungary	Nick Gillingham, G. Britain	Sergio Lopez, Spain
1992	Mike Barrowman, USA	Norbert Rozsa, Hungary	Nick Gillingham, G. Britain
1996	Norbert Rozsa, Hungary	Karoly Guttler, Hungary	Andrey Korneyev, Russia
2000	Domenico Fioravanti, Italy	Terence Parkin, S. Africa	Davide Rummolo, Italy

Year	Gold	Silver	Bronze
2004	Kosuke Kitajima, Japan	Daniel Gyurta, Hungary	Brendan Hansen, USA
2008	Kosuke Kitajima, Japan	Brenton Rickard, Australia	Hugues Duboscq, France

100 BUTTERFLY

Year	Gold	Silver	Bronze
1968	Douglas Russell, USA	Mark Spitz, USA	Ross Wales, USA
1972	Mark Spitz, USA	Bruce Robertson, Canada	Jerry Heidenreich, USA
1976	Matt Vogel, USA	Joe Bottom, USA	Gary Hall Sr., USA
1980	Par Arvidsson, Sweden	Roger Pyttel, E. Germany	David Lopez, Spain
1984	Michael Gross, FRG	Pablo Morales, USA	Glen Buchanan, Australia
1988	Anthony Nesty, Suriname	Matt Biondi, USA	Andy Jameson, G. Britain
1992	Pablo Morales, USA	Rafal Szukala, Poland	Anthony Nesty, Suriname
1996	Denis Pankratov, Russia	Scott Miller, Australia	Vladislav Kulikov, Russia
2000	Lars Frolander, Sweden	Michael Klim, Australia	Geoff Huegill, Australia
2004	Michael Phelps, USA	Ian Crocker, USA	Andriy Serdinov, Ukraine
2008	Michael Phelps, USA	Milorad Cavic, Serbia	A. Lauterstein, Australia

200 BUTTERFLY

Year	Gold	Silver	Bronze
1956	William Yorzyk, USA	Takashi Ishimoto, Japan	Gyorgy Tumpek, Hungary
1960	Mike Troy, USA	Neville Hayes, Australia	David Gillanders, USA

Year	Gold	Silver	Bronze
1964	Kevin Berry, Australia	Carl Robie, USA	Fred Schmidt, USA
1968	Carl Robie, USA	M. Woodroffe, G. Britain	John Ferris, USA
1972	Mark Spitz, USA	Gary Hall Sr., USA	Robin Backhaus, USA
1976	Mike Bruner, USA	Steve Gregg, USA	Billy Forrester, USA
1980	Sergey Fesenko, S. Union	Phillip Hubble, G. Britain	Roger Pyttel, E. Germany
1984	Jon Sieben, Australia	Michael Gross, FRG	Rafael Vidal, Venezuela
1988	Michael Gross, FRG	Benny Nielsen, Denmark	Anthony Mosse, N. Zealand
1992	Mel Stewart, USA	Danyon Loader, N. Zealand	Franck Esposito, France
1996	Denis Pankratov, Russia	Tom Malchow, USA	Scott Goodman, Australia
2000	Tom Malchow, USA	Denys Sylantyev, Ukraine	Justin Norris, Australia
2004	Michael Phelps, USA	Takashi Yamamoto, Japan	Stephen Parry, G. Britain
2008	Michael Phelps, USA	Laszlo Cseh, Hungary	Takeshi Matsuda, Japan

200 INDIVIDUAL MEDLEY

Year	Gold	Silver	Bronze
1968	Charles Hickcox, USA	Greg Buckingham, USA	John Ferris, USA
1972	Gunnar Larsson, Sweden	Tim McKee, USA	Steve Furniss, USA
1984	Alex Baumann, Canada	Pablo Morales, USA	Neil Cochran, G. Britain
1988	Tamas Darnyi, Hungary	Patrick Kulh, E. Germany	Vadim Yaroshuk, S. Union
1992	Tamas Darnyi, Hungary	Greg Burgess, USA	Attila Czene, Hungary
1996	Attila Czene, Hungary	Jani Sievinen, Finland	Curtis Myden, Canada
2000	Massi Rosolino, Italy	Tom Dolan, USA	Tom Wilkens, USA
2008	Michael Phelps, USA	Laszlo Cseh, Hungary	Ryan Lochte, USA

400 INDIVIDUAL MEDLEY

	Gold	Silver	Bronze
1964	Richard Roth, USA	Roy Saari, USA	Gerhard Hetz, W. Germany
1968	Charles Hickcox, USA	Gary Hall Sr., USA	Michael Holtaus, FRG
1972	Gunnar Larsson, Sweden	Tim McKee, USA	Andras Hargitay, Hungary
1976	Rod Strachan, USA	Tim McKee, USA	Andrej Smirnov, S. Union
1980	Aleksandr Sidorenko, S. Union	Sergey Fesenko, S. Union	Zoltan Verraszto, Hungary
1984	Alex Baumann, Canada	Ricardo Prado, Brazil	Rob Woodhouse, Australia
1988	Tamas Darnyi, Hungary	David Wharton, USA	Stefano Battistelli, Italy
1992	Tamas Darnyi, Hungary	Eric Namesnik, USA	Luca Sacchi, Italy
1996	Tom Dolan, USA	Eric Namesnik, USA	Curtis Myden, Canada
2000	Tom Doland, USA	Erik Vendt, USA	Curtis Myden, Canada
2004	Michael Phelps, USA	Erik Vendt, USA	Laszlo Cseh, Hungary
2008	Michael Phelps, USA	Laszlo Cseh, Hungary	Ryan Lochte, USA

400 FREESTYLE RELAY

	Gold	Silver	Bronze
1964	USA	Germany	Australia
1968	USA	Soviet Union	Australia

Year	Gold	Silver	Bronze
1972	USA	Soviet Union	East Germany
1984	USA	Australia	Sweden
1988	USA	Soviet Union	East Germany
1992	USA	Unified Team	Germany
1996	USA	Russia	Germany
2000	Australia	USA	Brazil
2004	South Africa	Holland	USA
2008	USA	France	Australia

800 FREESTYLE RELAY

Year	Gold	Silver	Bronze
1908	Great Britain	Hungary	USA
1912	Australia–New Zealand	USA	Great Britain
1920	USA	Australia	Great Britain
1924	USA	Australia	Sweden
1928	USA	Japan	Canada
1932	Japan	USA	Hungary
1936	Japan	USA	Hungary
1948	USA	Hungary	France
1952	USA	Japan	France
1956	Australia	USA	Soviet Union
1960	USA	Japan	Australia

1964	USA	Germany	Japan
1968	USA	Australia	Soviet Union
1972	USA	West Germany	Soviet Union
1976	USA	Soviet Union	Great Britain
1980	Soviet Union	East Germany	Brazil
1984	USA	West Germany	Great Britain
1988	USA	East Germany	West Germany
1992	Unified Team	Sweden	USA
1996	USA	Sweden	Germany
2000	Australia	USA	Holland
2004	USA	Australia	Italy
2008	USA	Russia	Australia

400 MEDLEY RELAY

	Gold	Silver	Bronze
1960	USA	Australia	Japan
1964	USA	Germany	Australia
1968	USA	East Germany	Soviet Union
1972	USA	East Germany	Canada
1976	USA	Canada	West Germany
1980	Australia	Soviet Union	Great Britain

1984	USA	Canada	Australia
1988	USA	Canada	Soviet Union
1992	USA	Unified Team	Canada
1996	USA	Russia	Australia
2000	USA	Australia	Germany
2004	USA	Germany	Japan
2008	USA	Australia	Japan

Appendix S
Olympic Games: Women's Medal Winners

Note: If a year is not listed, the event was not contested.

50 FREESTYLE

	Gold	Silver	Bronze
1988	Kristin Otto, E. Germany	Yang Wenyi, China	Katrin Meissner, E. Germany
1992	Yang Wenyi, China	Zhuang Yong, China	Angel Martino, USA
1996	Amy Van Dyken, USA	Le Jingyi, China	Sandra Volker, Germany
2000	Inge De Bruijn, Holland	Therese Alshammar, Sweden	Dara Torres, USA
2004	Inge De Bruijn, Holland	Malia Metella, France	Libby Lenton, Australia
2008	Britta Steffen, Germany	Dara Torres, USA	Cate Campbell, Australia

100 FREESTYLE

	Gold	Silver	Bronze
1912	Fanny Durack, Australia	Wilhelmine Wylie, Australia	Jennie Fletcher, G. Britain
1920	Ethelda Bleibtrey, USA	Irene Guest, USA	Frances Schroth, USA
1924	Ethel Lackie, USA	Marie Wehselau, USA	Gertrude Ederle, USA
1928	Albina Osipowich, USA	Eleanor Garatti, USA	M. Joyce Cooper, G. Britain
1932	Helene Madison, USA	W. den Ouden, Holland	Eleanor Garatti, USA
1936	H. Mastenbroek, Holland	J. Campbell, Argentina	Gisela Arendt, Germany

	Gold	Silver	Bronze
1948	Greta Andersen, Denmark	Ann Curtis, USA	M.–Louis Vaessen, Holland
1952	Katalin Szoke, Hungary	Johanna Termeulen, Holland	Judit Temes, Hungary
1956	Dawn Fraser, Australia	Lorraine Crapp, Australia	Faith Leech, Australia
1960	Dawn Fraser, Australia	Chris Von Saltza, USA	Natalie Steward, G. Britain
1964	Dawn Fraser, Australia	Sharon Stouder, USA	Kathleen Ellis, USA
1968	Jan Henne, USA	Susan Pedersen, USA	Linda Gustavson, USA
1972	Sandy Neilson, USA	Shirley Babashoff, USA	Shane Gould, Australia
1976	Kornelia Ender, E. Germany	Petra Priemer, E. Germany	Enith Brigitha, Holland
1980	Barbara Krause, E. Germany	C.n Metschuck, E. Germany	Ines Diers, E. Germany
1984	Carrie Steinseifer, USA/ Nancy Hogshead, USA	Not Awarded	A. Marie Verstappen, Holland
1988	Kristin Otto, E. Germany	Zhuang Yong, China	Catherine Plewinski, France
1992	Zhuang Yong, China	Jenny Thompson, USA	F. van Almsick, Germany
1996	Le Jingyi, China	Sandra Volker, Germany	Angel Martino, USA
2000	Inge De Bruijn, Holland	Therese Alshammar, Sweden	Dara Torres, USA/ Jenny Thompson, USA
2004	Jodie Henry, Australia	Inge De Bruijn, Holland	Natalie Coughlin, USA
2008	Britta Steffen, Germany	Libby Trickett, Australia	Natalie Coughlin, USA

200 FREESTYLE

	Gold	Silver	Bronze
1968	Debbie Meyer, USA	Jan Henne, USA	Jane Barkman, USA
1972	Shane Gould, Australia	Shirley Babashoff, USA	Keena Rothhammer, USA

Year			
1976	Kornelia Ender, E. Germany	Shirley Babashoff, USA	Enith Brigitha, Holland
1980	Barbara Krause, E. Germany	Ines Diers, E. Germany	C. Schmidt, E. Germany
1984	Mary Wayte, USA	Cynthia Woodhead, USA	A.Marie Verstappen, Holland
1988	Heike Friedrich, E. Germany	Silvia Poll, Costa Rica	M. Stellmach, E. Germany
1992	Nicole Haislett, USA	F. van Almsick, Germany	Kerstin Kielgass, Germany
1996	Claudia Poll, Costa Rica	F. van Almsick, Germany	Dagmar Hase, Germany
2000	Susie O'Neill, Australia	Martina Moravcova, Slovakia	Claudia Poll, Costa Rica
2004	Camelia Potec, Romania	Federica Pellegrini, Italy	Solenne Figues, France
2008	Federica Pellegrini, Italy	Sara Isakovic, Slovenia	Pang Jiaying, China

400 FREESTYLE

Year	Gold	Silver	Bronze
1920	Ethelda Bleibtrey, USA	Margaret Woodbridge, USA	Frances Schroth, USA
1924	Martha Norelius, USA	Helen Wainwright, USA	Gertrude Ederle, USA
1928	Martha Norelius, USA	Maria Johanna, Holland	Josephine McKim, USA
1932	Helene Madison, USA	Lenore Kight, USA	Jennie Maakai, S. Africa
1936	H. Mastenbroek, Holland	Ragnihild Hveger, Denmark	Lenore Kight, USA
1948	Ann Curtis, USA	Karen Harup, Denmark	Catherine Gibson, G. Britain
1952	Valerie Gyenge, Hungary	Eva Novak, Hungary	Evelyn Kawamoto, Japan
1956	Lorraine Crapp, Australia	Dawn Fraser, Australia	Sylvia Ruuska, USA
1960	Chris Von Saltza, USA	Jane Cederqvist, Sweden	Catherina Lagerberg, Holland
1964	Virginia Duenkel, USA	Marilyn Ramenofsky, USA	Terri Lee Stickles, USA

	Gold	Silver	Bronze
1968	Debbie Meyer, USA	Linda Gustavson, USA	Karen Moras, Australia
1972	Shane Gould, Australia	Novella Calligaris, Italy	Gudrun Wegner, E. Germany
1976	Petra Thumer, E. Germany	Shirley Babashoff, USA	Shannon Smith, Canada
1980	Ines Diers, E. Germany	Petra Schneider, E. Germany	C. Schmidt, E. Germany
1984	Tiffany Cohen, USA	Sarah Hardcastle, G. Britain	June Croft, G. Britain
1988	Janet Evans, USA	Heike Friedrich, E. Germany	Anke Mohring, E. Germany
1992	Dagmar Hase, Germany	Janet Evans, USA	Hayley Lewis, Australia
1996	Michelle Smith, Ireland	Dagmar Hase, Germany	Kristen Vlieghuis, Holland
2000	Brooke Bennett, USA	Diana Munz, USA	Claudia Poll, Costa Rica
2004	Laure Manaudou, France	Otylia Jedrzejczak, Poland	Kaitlin Sandeno, USA
2008	Rebecca Adlington, G. Britain	Katie Hoff, USA	Joanne Jackson, G. Britain

800 FREESTYLE

	Gold	Silver	Bronze
1968	Debbie Meyer, USA	Pam Kruse, USA	Maria Ramirez, Mexico
1972	Keena Rothhammer, USA	Shane Gould, Australia	Novella Calligaris, Italy
1976	Petra Thumer, E. Germany	Shirley Babashoff, USA	Wendy Weinberg, USA
1980	Michelle Ford, Australia	Ines Diers, E. Germany	Heike Dahne, E. Germany
1984	Tiffany Cohen, USA	Michele Richardson, USA	Sarah Hardcastle, G. Britain
1988	Janet Evans, USA	Astrid Strauss, E. Germany	Julie McDonald, Australia
1992	Janet Evans, USA	Hayley Lewis, Australia	Jana Henke, Germany

Year		Silver	Bronze
1996	Brooke Bennett, USA	Dagmar Hase, Germany	Kirsten Vlieghuis, Holland
2000	Brooke Bennett, USA	Yana Klochkova, Ukraine	Kaitlin Sandeno, USA
2004	Ai Shibata, Japan	Laure Manaudou, France	Diana Munz, USA
2008	Rebecca Adlington, G. Britain	Alessia Filippi, Italy	Lotte Friis, Denmark

100 BACKSTROKE

Year	Gold	Silver	Bronze
1924	Sybil Bauer, USA	Phyllis Harding, G. Britain	Aileen Riggin, USA
1928	Maria Braun, Holland	Ellen King, G. Britain	Joyce Cooper, G. Britain
1932	Eleanor Holm, USA	Philomena Mealing, Australia	Valerie Davies, G. Britain
1936	Nida Senff, Holland	H. Mastenbroek, Holland	Alice Bridges, USA
1948	Karen Harup, Denmark	Suzanne Zimmerman, USA	Judy Davies, Australia
1952	Joan Harrison, S. Africa	Geertje Wielema, Holland	Jean Stewart, N. Zealand
1956	Judith Grinham, G. Britain	Carin Cone, USA	Margaret Edwards, G. Britain
1960	Lynn Burke, USA	Natalie Steward, G. Britain	Satoka Tanaka, Japan
1964	Cathy Ferguson, USA	Christine Caron, France	Virginia Duenkel, USA
1968	Kaye Hall, USA	Elaine Tanner, Canada	Jane Swagerty, USA
1972	Melissa Belote, USA	Andrea Gyarmati, Hungary	Susie Atwood, USA
1976	Ulrike Richter, E. Germany	Birgit Treiber, E. Germany	Nancy Garapick, Canada
1980	Rica Reinisch, E. Germany	Ina Kleber, E. Germany	Petra Reidel, E. Germany
1984	Thersa Andrews, USA	Betsy Mitchell, USA	Jolanda deRover, Holland
1988	Kristin Otto, E. Germany	K. Egerszegi, Hungary	Cornelia Sirch, E. Germany

	Gold	Silver	Bronze
1992	Krisztina Egerszegi, Hungary	Tunde Szabo, Hungary	Lea Loveless, USA
1996	Beth Botsford, USA	Whitney Hedgepeth, USA	Marianne Kriel, S. Africa
2000	Diana Mocanu, Romania	Mai Nakamura, Japan	Nina Zhivanevskaya, Spain
2004	Natalie Coughlin, USA	Kirsty Coventry, Zimbabwe	Laure Manaudou, France
2008	Natalie Coughlin, USA	Kirsty Coventry, Zimbabwe	Margaret Hoelzer, USA

200 BACKSTROKE

	Gold	Silver	Bronze
1968	Pokey Watson, USA	Elaine Tanner, Canada	Kaye Hall, USA
1972	Melissa Belote, USA	Susie Atwood, USA	Donna Gurr, Canada
1976	Ulrike Richter, E. Germany	Birgit Treiber, E. Germany	Nancy Garapick, Canada
1980	Rica Reinisch, E. Germany	Cornelia Polit, E. Germany	Birgit Treiber, E. Germany
1984	Jolanda deRover, Holland	Amy White, USA	Aneta Patrascoiu, Romania
1988	Krisztina Egerszegi, Hungary	K. Zimmerman, E. Germany	Cornelia Sirch, E. Germany
1992	Krisztina Egerszegi, Hungary	Dagmar Hase, Germany	Nicole Stevenson, Australia
1996	Krisztina Egerszegi, Hungary	Whitney Hedgepeth, USA	Cathleen Rund, Germany
2000	Diana Mocanu, Romania	Roxana Maracineanu, France	Miki Nakao, Japan
2004	Kirsty Coventry, Zimbabwe	Stanislava Komarova, Russia	A. Buschschulte, Germany
2008	Kirsty Coventry, Zimbabwe	Margaret Hoelzer, USA	Reiko Nakamura, Japan

100 BREASTSTROKE

	Gold	Silver	Bronze
1968	D. Bjedov, Yugoslavia	G. Prozumenshchikova, S. Union	Sharon Wichman, USA
1972	Catherine Carr, USA	G. Prozumenshchikova, S. Union	Beverly Whitfield, Australia
1976	Hannelore Anke, E. Germany	Ljubow Russanova, S. Union	Marina Koschewaja, S. Union
1980	Ute Geweniger, E. Germany	Elwire Wassilkowa, S. Union	Susanne Neilsson, Denmark
1984	Petra van Staveren, Holland	Anne Ottenbrite, Canada	Catherine Poirot, France
1988	Tania Dangalakova, Bulgaria	A. Frenkeva, Bulgaria	Silke Horner, E. Germany
1992	E. Rudkovskaya, Un. Team	Anita Nall, USA	Samantha Riley, Australia
1996	Penelope Heyns, S. Africa	Amanda Beard, USA	Samantha Riley, Australia
2000	Megan Quann, USA	Leisel Jones, Australia	Penelope Heyns, S. Africa
2004	Luo Xuejuan, China	Brooke Hanson, Australia	Leisel Jones, Australia
2008	Leisel Jones, Australia	Rebecca Soni, USA	Mirna Jukic, Austria

200 BREASTSTROKE

	Gold	Silver	Bronze
1924	Lucy Morton, G. Britain	Agnes Geraghty, USA	Gladys Carson, G. Britain
1928	Hilde Schrader, Germany	Mietje Baron, Holland	Lotte Muhe, Germany
1932	Claire Dennis, Australia	Hideko Maehata, Japan	Else Jacobsen, Denmark
1936	Hideko Maehata, Japan	Martha Genenger, Germany	Inge Sorensen, Denmark
1948	Petronella van Vliet, Holland	Beatrice Lyons, Australia	Eva Novak, Hungary

Year	Gold	Silver	Bronze
1952	Eva Szekely, Hungary	Eva Novak, Hungary	Helen Gordon, G. Britain
1956	Ursula Happe, FRG	Eva Szekely, Hungary	E.-Marie Elsen, E. Germany
1960	Anita Lonsbrough, G. Britain	Wiltrud Urselmann, FRG	Barbara Goebel, E. Germany
1964	G. Prozumenshchikova, S. Union	Claudia Kolb, USA	Svetlana Babalina, S. Union
1968	Sharon Wichman, USA	D. Bjedov, Yugoslavia	G. Prozumenshchikova, S. Union
1972	Beverly Whitfield, Australia	Dana Schoenfield, USA	G. Prozumenshchikova, S. Union
1976	Marina Koschewaja, S. Union	Marina Jurtschenja, S. Union	Ljubow Russanova, S. Union
1980	Lina Kaciusyte, S. Union	Svetlana Warganova, S. Union	Julija Bogdanova, S. Union
1984	Anne Ottenbrite, Canada	Susan Rapp, USA	Ingrid Lempereur, Belgium
1988	Silke Horner, E. Germany	Huang Xiaomin, China	A. Frenkeva, Bulgaria
1992	Kyoko Iwasaki, Japan	Lin Li, China	Anita Nall, USA
1996	Penelope Heyns, S. Africa	Amanda Beard, USA	Agnes Kovacs, Hungary
2000	Agnes Kovas, Hungary	Kristy Kowal, USA	Amanda Beard, USA
2004	Amanda Beard, USA	Leisel Jones, Australia	Anne Poleska, Germany
2008	Rebecca Soni, USA	Leisel Jones, Australia	Sara Nordenstam, Norway

100 BUTTERFLY

Year	Gold	Silver	Bronze
1956	Shelley Mann, USA	Nancy Ramey, USA	Mary Sears, USA
1960	Carolyn Schuler, USA	M. Heemskerk, Holland	Janice Andrew, Australia

	Gold	Silver	Bronze
1964	Sharon Stouder, USA	Ada Kok, Holland	Kathleen Ellis, USA
1968	Lyn McClements, Australia	Ellie Daniel, USA	Susan Shields, USA
1972	Mayumi Aoki, Japan	Roswitha Beier, E. Germany	Andrea Gyarmati, Hungary
1976	Kornelia Ender, E. Germany	Andrea Pollack, E. Germany	Wendy Boglioli, USA
1980	Caren Metschuck, E. Germany	Andrea Pollack, E. Germany	C. Knacke, E. Germany
1984	Mary T. Meagher, USA	Jenna Johnson, USA	Karin Seick, W. Germany
1988	Kristin Otto, E. Germany	Birte Weigang, E. Germany	Qian Hong, China
1992	Qian Hong, China	C. Ahmann-Leighton, USA	Catherine Plewinski, France
1996	Amy Van Dyken, USA	Liu Limin, China	Angel Martino, USA
2000	Inge De Bruijn, Holland	Martina Moravcova, Slovakia	Dara Torres, USA
2004	Petria Thomas, Australia	Otylia Jedrzejczak, Poland	Inge De Bruijn, Holland
2008	Libby Trickett, Australia	Christine Magnuson, USA	Jessicah Schipper, Australia

200 BUTTERFLY

	Gold	Silver	Bronze
1968	Ada Kok, Holland	Helga Linder, E. Germany	Ellie Daniel, USA
1972	Karen Moe, USA	Lynn Colella, USA	Ellie Daniel, USA
1976	Andrea Pollack, E. Germany	Ulrike Tauber, E. Germany	R. Gabriel, E. Germany
1980	Ines Geissier, E. Germany	S. Schonrock, E. Germany	Michelle Ford, Australia
1984	Mary T. Meagher, USA	Karen Phillips, Australia	Ina Beyermann, FRG
1988	Kathleen Nord, E. Germany	Birte Weigang, E. Germany	Mary T. Meagher, USA
1992	Summer Sanders, USA	Wang Xiaohong, China	Susie O'Neill, Australia

	Gold	Silver	Bronze
1996	Susie O'Neill, Australia	Petria Thomas, Australia	Michelle Smith, Ireland
2000	Misty Hyman, USA	Susie O'Neill, Australia	Petria Thomas, Australia
2004	Otylia Jędrzejczak, Poland	Petria Thomas, Australia	Yuko Nakanishi, Japan
2008	Liu Zige, China	Jiao Liuyang, China	Jessicah Schipper, Australia

200 INDIVIDUAL MEDLEY

	Gold	Silver	Bronze
1968	Claudia Kolb, USA	Susan Pedersen, USA	Jan Henne, USA
1972	Shane Gould, Australia	Kornelia Ender, E. Germany	Lynn Vidali, USA
1984	Tracy Caulkins, USA	Nancy Hogshead, USA	Michelle Pearson, Australia
1988	Daniela Hunger, E. Germany	Elena Dendeberova, S. Union	Noemi Lung, Romania
1992	Lin Li, China	Summer Sanders, USA	Daniela Hunger, Germany
1996	Michelle Smith, Ireland	Marianne Limpert, Canada	Lin Li, China
2000	Yana Klochkova, Ukraine	Beatrice Caslaru, Romania	Cristina Teuscher, USA
2004	Yana Klochkova, Ukraine	Amanda Beard, USA	Kirsty Coventry, Zimbabwe
2008	Stepahanie Rice, Australia	Kirsty Coventry, Zimbabwe	Natalie Coughlin, USA

400 INDIVIDUAL MEDLEY

	Gold	Silver	Bronze
1964	Donna deVarona, USA	Sharon Finneran, USA	Martha Randall, USA
1968	Claudia Kolb, USA	Lynn Vidali, USA	S. Steinback, E. Germany

Year			
1972	Gail Neall, Australia	Leslie Cliff, Canada	Novella Calligaris, Italy
1976	Ulrike Tauber, E. Germany	Cheryl Gibson, Canada	Becky Smith, Canada
1980	Petra Schneider, E. Germany	Sharron Davies, G. Britain	Agnieszka Czopek, Poland
1984	Tracy Caulkins, USA	Suzanne Landells, Australia	Petra Zindler, W. Germany
1988	Janet Evans, USA	Noemi Lung, Romania	Daniela Hunger, E. Germany
1992	Krisztina Egerszegi, Hungary	Lin Li, China	Summer Sanders, USA
1996	Michelle Smith, Ireland	Allison Wagner, USA	Krisztina Egerszegi, Hungary
2000	Yana Klochkova, Ukraine	Yasuko Tajima, Japan	Beatrice Caslaru, Romania
2004	Yana Klochkova, Ukraine	Kaitlin Sandeno, USA	Georgina Bardach, Argentina
2008	Stephanie Rice, Australia	Kirsty Coventry, Zimbabwe	Katie Hoff, USA

400 FREESTYLE RELAY

	Gold	Silver	Bronze
1912	Great Britain	Germany	Austria
1920	USA	Great Britain	Sweden
1924	USA	Great Britain	Sweden
1928	USA	Great Britain	South Africa
1932	USA	Holland	Great Britain
1936	Holland	Germany	USA
1948	USA	Denmark	Holland
1952	Hungary	Holland	USA
1956	Australia	USA	South Africa

	Gold	Silver	Bronze
1960	USA	Australia	Germany
1964	USA	Australia	Holland
1968	USA	East Germany	Canada
1972	USA	East Germany	West Germany
1976	USA	East Germany	Canada
1980	East Germany	Sweden	Holland
1984	USA	Holland	West Germany
1988	East Germany	Holland	USA
1992	USA	China	Germany
1996	USA	China	Germany
2000	USA	Holland	Sweden
2004	Australia	USA	Holland
2008	Holland	USA	Australia

800 FREESTYLE RELAY

	Gold	Silver	Bronze
1996	USA	Germany	Australia
2000	USA	Australia	Germany
2004	USA	China	Germany
2008	Australia	China	USA

400 MEDLEY RELAY

	Gold	Silver	Bronze
1960	USA	Australia	Germany
1964	USA	Holland	Soviet Union
1968	USA	Australia	West Germany
1972	USA	East Germany	West Germany
1976	East Germany	USA	Canada
1980	East Germany	Great Britain	Soviet Union
1984	USA	West Germany	Canada
1988	East Germany	USA	Canada
1992	USA	Germany	Unified Team
1996	USA	Australia	China
2000	USA	Australia	Japan
2004	Australia	USA	Germany
2008	Australia	USA	China

Appendix T
Olympic Games: Men's Diving Medal Winners

Note: If a year is not listed, the event was not contested.

PLATFORM DIVING

	Gold	Silver	Bronze
1904	George Sheldon, USA	Georg Hoffmann, Germany	Frank Kehoe, USA/
			Al Braunschweiger, Germany
1908	Hjalmar Johansson, Sweden	Karl Malmstrom, Sweden	Arvid Spangberg, Sweden
1912	Erik Adlerz, Sweden	Albert Zurner, Germany	Gustaf Blomgren, Sweden
1920	Clarence Pinkston, USA	Erik Adlerz, Sweden	Harry Prieste, USA
1924	Albert White, USA	David Fall, USA	Clarence Pinkston, USA
1928	Peter Desjardins, USA	Farid Simaika, Egypt	Michael Galitzen, USA
1932	Harold Smith, USA	Michael Galitzen, USA	Frank Kurtz, USA
1936	Marshall Wayne, USA	Elbert Root, USA	Hermann Stork, Germany
1948	Samuel Lee, USA	Bruce Harlan, USA	Joaquin Capilla, Mexico
1952	Samuel Lee, USA	Joaquin Capilla, Mexico	Gunther Haase, Germany
1956	Joaquin Capilla, Mexico	Gary Tobian, USA	Richard Connor, USA
1960	Bob Webster, USA	Gary Tobian, USA	Brian Phelps, G. Britain
1964	Bob Webster, USA	Klaus Dibiasi, Italy	Thomas Gompf, USA
1968	Klaus Dibiasi, Italy	Alvaro Gaxiola, Mexico	Edwin Young, USA
1972	Klaus Dibiasi, Italy	Richard Rydze, USA	Giorgio Cagnotto, Italy
1976	Klaus Dibiasi, Italy	Greg Louganis, USA	Vladimir Aleynik, S. Union

	Gold	Silver	Bronze
1980	Falk Hoffmann, E. Germany	Vladimir Aleynik, S. Union	Dave Ambartsumyan, S. Union
1984	Greg Louganis, USA	Bruce Kimball, USA	Li Kongzheng, China
1988	Greg Louganis, USA	Xiong Ni, China	Jesus Mena, Mexico
1992	Sun Shuwei, China	Scott Donie, USA	Xiong Ni, China
1996	Dmitri Sautin, Russia	Jan Hempel, Germany	Xiao Hailiang, China
2000	Tian Liang, China	Hu Jia, China	Dmitri Sautin, Russia
2004	Hu Jia, China	Matt Helm, Australia	Tian Liang, China
2008	Matthew Mitcham, Australia	Zhou Luxin, China	Gleb Galperin, Russia

THREE-METER SPRINGBOARD

	Gold	Silver	Bronze
1908	Albert Zurner, Germany	Kurt Behrens, Germany	George Gaidzik, USA/ Gottlob Walz, Germany
1912	Paul Gunther, Germany	Hans Luber, Germany	Kurt Behrens, Germany
1920	Louis Kuehn, USA	Clarence Pinkston, USA	Louis Balbach, USA
1924	Albert White, USA	Peter Desjardins, USA	Clarence Pinkston, USA
1928	Peter Desjardins, USA	Michael Galitzen, USA	Farid Simaika, Egypt
1932	Michael Galitzen, USA	Harold Smith, USA	Richard Degener, USA
1936	Richard Degener, USA	Marshall Wayne, USA	Alan Greene, USA
1948	Bruce Harlan, USA	Miller Anderson, USA	Samuel Lee, USA
1952	David Browing, USA	Miller Anderson, USA	Bob Clotworthy, USA

Year	Gold	Silver	Bronze
1956	Bob Clotworthy, USA	Donald Harper, USA	Joaquin Capilla, Mexico
1960	Gary Tobian, USA	Samuel Hall, USA	Juan Botella Medina, Mexico
1964	Kenneth Siztberger, USA	Francis Gorman, USA	Lawrence Andreasen, USA
1968	Bernard Wrightson, USA	Klaus Dibiasi, Italy	James Henry, USA
1972	Vladimir Vasin, S. Union	Giorgio Cagnotto, Italy	Craig Lincoln, USA
1976	Phil Boggs, USA	Giorgio Cagnotto, Italy	Aleksandr Kosenkov, S. Union
1980	Aleksandr Portnov, S. Union	Carlos Giron, Mexico	Giorgio Cagnotto, Italy
1984	Greg Louganis, USA	Tan Liangde, China	Ronald Merriott, USA
1988	Greg Louganis, USA	Tan Liangde, China	Li Deliang, China
1992	Mark Lenzi, USA	Tan Liangde, China	Dmitri Sautin, Russia
1996	Xiong Ni, China	Yu Zhuocheng, China	Mark Lenzi, China
2000	Xiong Ni, China	Fernando Platas, Mexico	Dmitri Sautin, Russia
2004	Peng Bo, China	Alexandre Despatie, Canada	Dmitri Sautin, Russia
2008	He Chong, China	Alexandre Despatie, Canada	Qin Kai, China

SYNCHRONIZED 10-METER PLATFORM

Year	Gold	Silver	Bronze
2000	Igor Lukashin/ Dmitri Sautin, Russia	Hu Jia/ Tian Liang, China	Jan Hempel/ Heiko Meyer, Germany
2004	Tian Liang/ Yang Jinghui, China	Leon Taylor/ Peter Waterfield, G. Britain	Matt Helm/ Robert Newbery, Australia

| 2008 | Lin Yue/ Huo Liang, China | Patrick Hausding/ Sascha Klein, Germany | Gleb Galperin/ Dmitriy Dobroskok, Russia |

SYNCHRONIZED THREE-METER SPRINGBOARD

	Gold	Silver	Bronze
2000	Xiong Ni/ Xiao Hailiang, China	Alexandre Dobroskok/ Dmitri Sautin, Russia	Robert Newbery/ Dean Pullar, Australia
2004	Thomas Bimis/ Nikolaos Siranidis, Greece	Andreas Wels/ T. Schellenberg, Germany	Steven Barnett/ Robert Newbery, Australia
2008	Wang Feng/ Qin Kai, China	Dmitri Sautin/ Yuriy Kunakov, Russia	Illya Kvasha/ Oleksiy Prygorov, Ukraine

Appendix U
Olympic Games:
Women's Diving Medal Winners

Note: If a year is not listed, the event was not contested.

10-METER PLATFORM

	Gold	Silver	Bronze
1912	Greta Johnson, Sweden	Lisa Regnell, Sweden	Isabelle White, G. Britain
1920	Stefanie Clausen, Denmark	Beatrice Armstrong, G. Britian	Eva Olliwier, Sweden
1924	Caroline Smith, USA	E. Becker-Pinkston, USA	Hjordis Topel, Sweden
1928	E. Becker-Pinkston, USA	Georgia Coleman, USA	Laura Sjoqvist, Sweden
1932	Dorothy Poynton Hill, USA	Georgia Coleman, USA	Marion Roper, USA
1936	Dorothy Poynton Hill, USA	Velma Dunn, USA	Kathe Kohler, Germany
1948	Victoria Draves, USA	Patricia Elsener, USA	B. Christoffersen, Denmark
1952	Pat McCormick, USA	Paula Myers, USA	Juno Irwin, USA
1956	Pat McCormick, USA	Juno Irwin, USA	Paula Pope, USA
1960	Ingrid Kramer, E. Germany	Paula Pope, USA	Ninel Krutova, S. Union
1964	Lesley Bush, USA	Ingrid Kramer, E. Germany	Galina Alekseeva, S. Union
1968	M. Duchkova, Czechoslovakia	Natalya Lobanova, S. Union	Ann Peterson, USA
1972	Ulrika Knape, Sweden	M. Duchkova, Czechoslovakia	Marina Janicke, E. Germany
1976	E. Vaytsekhovskaya, S. Union	Ulrika Knape, Sweden	Deborah Wilson, USA
1980	Martina Jaschke, E. Germany	Servard Emirzian, S. Union	Liana Tsotadze, S. Union
1984	Zhou Jihong, China	Michele Mitchell, USA	Wendy Wyland, USA
1988	Xu Yanmei, China	Michele Mitchell, USA	Wendy Williams, USA

	Gold	Silver	Bronze
1992	Fu Mingxia, China	Y. Mirochina, Unified Team	Mary Ellen Clark, USA
1996	Fu Mingxia, China	Annika Walter, Germany	Mary Ellen Clark, USA
2000	Laura Wilkinson, USA	Li Na, China	Anne Montminy, Canada
2004	Chantelle Newbery, Australia	Lao Lishi, China	Loudy Tourky, Australia
2008	Chen Ruolin, China	Emilie Heymans, Canada	Wang Xin, China

THREE-METER SPRINGBOARD

	Gold	Silver	Bronze
1920	Aileen Riggin, USA	Helen Wainwright, USA	Thelma Payne, USA
1924	E. Becker-Pinkston, USA	Aileen Riggin, USA	Caroline Fletcher, USA
1928	Helen Meany, USA	Dorothy Poynton-Hill, USA	Georgia Coleman, USA
1932	Georgia Coleman, USA	Katherine Rawls, USA	Jane Fauntz, USA
1936	Marjorie Gestring, USA	Katherine Rawls, USA	Dorothy Poynton-Hill, USA
1948	Victoria Draves, USA	Zoe-Ann Olsen-Jensen, USA	Patricia Elsener, USA
1952	Pat McCormick, USA	Madeleine Moreau, France	Zoe-Ann Olsen-Jensen, USA
1956	Pat McCormick, USA	Jeanne Stunyo, USA	Irene MacDonald, Canada
1960	Ingrid Kramer, E. Germany	Paula Pope, USA	Elizabeth Ferris, G. Britain
1964	Ingrid Kramer, E. Germany	Jeanne Collier, USA	Mary Willard, USA
1968	Susanne Gossick, USA	Tamara Pogosheva, S. Union	Keala O'Sullivan, USA
1972	Micki King, USA	Ulrika Knape, Sweden	Marina Janicke, E. Germany
1976	Jennifer Chandler, USA	Christa Kohler, E. Germany	Cynthia Potter, USA
1980	Irina Kalinina, S. Union	Martina Proeber, E. Germany	Karin Guthke, E. Germany

1984	Sylvie Bernier, Canada	Kelly McCormick, USA	Christina Seufert, USA
1988	Gao Min, China	Li Qing, China	Kelly McCormick, USA
1992	Gao Min, China	Irina Lashko, Unified Team	Brita Baldus, Germany
1996	Fu Mingxia, China	Irina Lashko, Russia	Annie Pelletier, Canada
2000	Fu Mingxia, China	Guo Jingjing, China	Dorte Lindner, Germany
2004	Guo Jingjing, China	Wu Minxia, China	Yuliya Pakhalina, Russia
2008	Guo Jingjing, China	Yuliya Pakhalina, Russia	Wu Mingxia

SYNCHRONIZED 10-METER PLATFORM

	Gold	**Silver**	**Bronze**
2000	Li Na/ Sang Xue, China	Emilie Heymans/ Anne Montminy, Canada	Rebecca Gilmore/ Loudy Tourky, Australia
2004	Lao Lishi/ Li Ting, China	Natalia Goncharova/ Yulia Koltunova, Russia	Blythe Hartley/ Emilie Heymans, Canada
2008	Chen Ruolin/ Wang Xin, China	Briony Cole/ Melissa Wu, Australia	Paola Espinosa/ Tatiana Ortiz, Mexico

SYNCHRONIZED THREE-METER SPRINGBOARD

	Gold	Silver	Bronze
2000	Vera Ilina/ Yuliya Pakhalina, Russia	Fu Mingxia/ Guo Jingjing, China	Ganna Sorokina/ Olena Zhupina, Ukraine
2004	Wu Mingxia/ Guo Jingjing, China	Vera Ilina/ Yuliya Pakhalina, Russia	Irina Lashko/ Chantelle Newbery, Australia
2008	Guo Jingjing/ Wu Mingxia, China	Yuliya Pakhalina/ A. Pozdnyakova, Russia	Ditte Kotzian/ Heike Fischer, Germany

Appendix V
Michael Phelps' Individual World Records

Date	Site	Event	Time
30 March 2001	Austin, Texas	200 Butterfly	1:54.92
24 July 2001	Fukuoka, Japan	200 Butterfly	1:54.58
15 August 2002	Fort Lauderdale, Florida	400 Individual Medley	4:11.09
6 April 2003	Indianapolis, Indiana	400 Individual Medley	4:10.73
29 June 2003	Santa Clara, California	200 Individual Medley	1:57.94
22 July 2003	Barcelona, Spain	200 Butterfly	1:53.93
24 July 2003	Barcelona, Spain	200 Individual Medley	1:57.52
25 July 2003	Barcelona, Spain	100 Butterfly	51.47
25 July 2003	Barcelona, Spain	200 Individual Medley	1:56.04
27 July 2003	Barcelona, Spain	400 Individual Medley	4:09.09
9 August 2003	College Park, Maryland	200 Individual Medley	1:55.94
7 July 2004	Long Beach, California	400 Individual Medley	4:08.41
14 August 2004	Athens, Greece	400 Individual Medley	4:08.26
17 August 2006	Victoria, British Columbia	200 Butterfly	1:53.80
20 August 2006	Victoria, British Columbia	200 Individual Medley	1:55.84
17 February 2007	Columbia, Missouri	200 Butterfly	1:53.71
27 March 2007	Melbourne, Australia	200 Freestyle	1:43.86
28 March 2007	Melbourne, Australia	200 Butterfly	1:52.09
29 March 2007	Melbourne, Australia	200 Individual Medley	1:54.98
1 April 2007	Melbourne, Australia	400 Individual Medley	4:06.22

Date	Site	Event	Time
29 June 2008	Omaha, Nebraska	400 Individual Medley	4:05.25
4 July 2008	Omaha, Nebraska	200 Individual Medley	1:54.80
10 August 2008	Beijing, China	400 Individual Medley	4:03.84
12 August 2008	Beijing, China	200 Freestyle	1:42.96
13 August 2008	Beijing, China	200 Butterfly	1:52.03
15 August 2008	Beijing, China	200 Individual Medley	1:54.23
9 July 2009	Indianapolis, Indiana	100 Butterfly	50.22
29 July 2009	Rome, Italy	200 Butterfly	1:51.51
1 August 2009	Rome, Italy	100 Butterfly	49.82

Bibliography

INTRODUCTION

Each section of this bibliography is specific to a topic covered within the *Historical Dictionary of Competitive Swimming*. The bibliography covers individual athletes, the strokes of the sport, development of training methods and innovations, specific competitions such as the Olympics and World Championships, and noncompetitive developments within the sport, such as the impact of doping and drug use.

CONTENTS

I. HISTORICAL WORKS

Besford, Pat. *Encyclopedia of Swimming.* New York: St. Martin's Press, 1971.
Meuret, Jean-Louis, and Cornelio Marculescu. *HistoFINA*: Volume 1. Lausanne, Switzerland: FINA Press, 2007.

Olsen, Jamie Fabos. *USA 2008 Olympic Swim Team Media Guide*. Colorado Springs, Colo.: USA Swimming, 2008.

Thomas, Stephen. "History's Fastest Swims." *Swimming World* (Jan. 2007): 16–17.

II. SWIMMING STROKES

Ryan, Frank. *Backstroke Swimming*. New York: Viking Press, 1974.

Ryan, Frank. *Breaststroke Swimming*. New York: Viking Press, 1974.

Ryan, Frank. *Butterfly Swimming*. New York: Viking Press, 1974.

Ryan, Frank. *Swimming Skills: Freestyle, Butterfly, Backstroke, Breaststroke*. Harmondsworth, England: Penguin Books, 1978.

III. DIVING

Louganis, Greg. *Breaking the Surface*. New York: Random House, 1994.

Miller, Doris I. *Biomechanics of Competitive Diving*. Indianapolis, Ind.: USA Diving, 2007.

O'Brien, Ronald F. *Ron O'Brien's Diving for Gold*. Champaign, Ill.: Human Kinetics, 1992.

O'Brien, Ronald F. *Springboard and Platform Diving*. Champaign, Ill.: Human Kinetics, 1992.

Veckers, B. *Fundamentals of Springboard Diving*. Boston: American Press, 1989.

IV. EXPLORATION OF TECHNIQUE AND DEVELOPMENT

Colwin, Cecil. *Breakthrough Swimming*. Champaign, Ill.: Human Kinetics, 2002.

Counsilman, James E. *The Science of Swimming*. Englewood Cliffs, N.J.: Prentice-Hall, 1968.

Evans, Janet. *Janet Evans' Total Swimming*. Champaign, Ill.: Human Kinetics, 2007.

Hines, Emmett W. *Fitness Swimming*. Champaign, Ill.: Human Kinetics, 2008.

Lynn, Alan. *Swimming: Technique, Training, Competition Strategy*. Ramsbury, Marlborough: Crowood Press, 2006.

Maglischo, Ernest W. *Swimming Faster: A Comprehensive Guide to the Science of Swimming.* Palo Alto, Calif.: Mayfield Publishing, 1982.

Price, Robert G. *The Ultimate Guide to Weight Training for Swimming.* Cleveland, Ohio: Price World Enterprises, 2003.

Rutemiller, Brent. "Who Rules the Pool?" *Swimming World* (June 2008): 6–8.

Scholander, Don. *Inside Swimming.* Chicago: Regnery, 1974.

Sweetenham, Bill, and John Atkinson. *Championship Swim Training: Workouts and Programs from the World's #1 Coach.* Champaign, Ill.: Human Kinetics, 2003.

Whitten, Phillip. *The Complete Book of Swimming.* New York: Random House, 1994.

V. OLYMPIC GAMES AND WORLD CHAMPIONSHIPS

Barney, David E., and Robert K. Barney. "A Centennial View of Aquatics." *Swimming World* (July 2004): 22–25.

Blundell, Nigel, and Duncan Mackay. *The History of the Olympics.* London: PRC Publishing, 1999.

Bud Greenspan's Favorite Stories of Olympic Glory. Dir. Bud Greenspan. Prod. Nancy Beffa. TV Special. Showtime, 2001.

Ingram, Bob. "Parity in the Pool." *Swimming World* (Sept. 1992): 34–37.

LaMondia, Susan. *First to the Wall, 100 Years of Olympic Swimming.* East Longmeadow, Mass.: FreeStyle Publications, 1999.

Lohn, John. "Encore to Athens." *Swimming World* (Sept. 2005): 12–17.

Mallon, Bill, and Ian Buchanan. *Historical Dictionary of the Olympic Movement.* Lanham, Md.: Scarecrow Press, 2006.

Mullen, P. H. *Gold in the Water: The True Story of Ordinary Men and Their Extraordinary Dream of Olympic Glory.* New York: St. Martin's Press, 2001.

Schoenfield, Al. "Munchen 1972—The Olympics." *Swimming World* (Oct. 1972): 5–8.

VI. MICHAEL PHELPS

Adelson, Eric. "Ripple Effect." *ESPN The Magazine* (1 March 2004): 44–50.

Gosman, Mike. "The Kid." *Swimming World* (June 2001): 26–27.

Lohn, John. "Without Peer." *Swimming World* (Sept. 2003): 24–29.

Lohn, John. "The Genius Behind the Masterpiece." *Swimming World* (Jan. 2009): 18–21.

McMullen, Paul. "Eyes Focus on Phelps and His Future." *Baltimore Sun* (20 Sept. 2000).

McMullen, Paul. *Amazing Pace: The Story of Champion Michael Phelps from Sydney to Athens to Beijing.* New York: Rodale, 2006.

Phelps, Michael, and Alan Abrahamson. *No Limits: The Will to Succeed.* New York: Simon & Schuster, 2008.

Schaller, Bob. *Michael Phelps: The Untold Story of a Champion.* New York: St. Martin's Press, 2008.

Solotaroff, Paul. "How Do You Improve on Greatest Ever?" *Men's Journal* (July 2007): 82–84, 148–149.

VII. INDIVIDUAL ATHLETES AND COACHES

Agh, Norbert. "The Road to Glory." *Swimming World* (April 2001): 28–31.

Chaykun, Harry. "He Won Gold, Then Swam Away." *Delaware County Daily Times* (22 Feb. 1999): 54.

Commings, Jeff. "Then and Now." *Swimming World* (June 2009): 12–13.

Cowley, Michael. "Hanson Loses Desire to Keep Chasing." *Sydney Morning Herald* (21 Nov. 2007).

Denniston, Dave. "A Dual Responsibility." *Swimming World* (April 2006): 10–11.

English, Ben. "Hackett Fails His History Test." *The Australian Online* (17 Aug. 2008).

Kroll, Chuck. "Remembering George Haines." *Swimming World* (June 2006): 8.

Lohn, John. "The Next Great American Distance Star?" *Swimming World* (Jan. 2003): 21–24.

Lohn, John. "Sabbatical Is the Answer for Hansen." *Delaware County Daily Times* (30 Jan. 2009): 76.

Lord, Craig. "The Price of Glory." *Swimming World* (Sept. 2001): 24–27.

Lord, Craig. "Thorpe Topples Out and Loses Place at Olympics." *Times Online* (29 March 2004).

Mason, Emily. "Still Kicking." *Swimming World* (Nov. 2005): 8.

Morales, Tito. "Swimming the Good Life." *Swimming World* (Oct. 2004): 22–26.

Muckenfuss, Mark. "A Year of Records." *Swimming World* (May 1987): 24–39.

Mullen, P. H. "No Quann-dary Here." *Swimming World* (June 2000): 34–37.

Nakayama, Chiemi. "Japan's Pocket Rocket: Focused on Athens." *Swimming World* (Jan. 2004): 24–27.

Nessel, Lee. "From Out of the Shadows." *Swimming World* (March 1997): 31–33.

Silver, Michael. *Golden Girl: How Natalie Coughlin Fought Back, Challenged Conventional Wisdom, and Became America's Olympic Champion.* New York: Rodale, 2006.

Thomas, Stephen. "The Empire Strikes Back." *Swimming World* (May 2006): 21–23.

Thompson, Larry. *Swimmers: Courage and Triumph.* Fort Lauderdale, Fla.: ISHOF Press, 2007.

Torres, Dara, and Elizabeth Weil. *Age Is Just a Number: Achieve Your Dreams at Any Stage in Your Life.* New York: Broadway Books, 2009.

Whitten, Phillip. "Thorpedo Torpedoed." *Swimming World* (May 2004): 6.

VIII. DOPING AND DRUG USE

Jeffery, Nicole. "Ian Thorpe May Sue French Newspaper over Drug Claim." *The Australian Online* (25 June 2008).

Lord, Craig. "Chinese Takeout." *Swimming World* (Nov. 1994): 60–61.

Whitten, Phillip. "Proof of East German Drug Use." *Swimming World* (Dec. 1994): 51.

Whitten, Phillip. "Why Are People Saying All Those Nasty Things About a Nice Irish Girl Like Michelle Smith?" *Swimming World* (Jan. 1997): 31–32.

IX. COUNTRIES

Jeffery, Nicole. "The Aussie Galaxy." *Swimming World* (July 2006): 11–14.

Lohn, John. "Return to Glory." *Swimming World* (April 2006): 13–15.

Olsen, Jamie Fabos. *USA 2008 Olympic Swim Team Media Guide.* Colorado Springs, Colo.: USA Swimming, 2008.

X. WEB SITES OF INTEREST

www.beijing2008.cn   Official Web site of the 2008 Beijing Olympic Games.

www.fina.org   Official Web site of the Fédération Internationale de Natation, the international governing body for the five aquatic sports: swimming, diving, water polo, synchronized swimming, and open-water swimming. This site also provides Web addresses for the majority of the national federations that compete in the FINA competition.

www.ishof.org Official Web site of the International Swimming Hall of Fame. Includes biographies of individuals inducted into the Hall of Fame.

www.isoh.org Official Web site of the International Society of Olympic Historians (ISOH).

www.olympic.org Official Web site of the International Olympic Committee. Includes lists of all Olympic medal winners, biographical information on numerous athletes, and details of the Olympic movement.

www.rowdygaines.com Official Web site of three-time Olympic gold medalist Rowdy Gaines, whose competitive career has been followed by a career in broadcasting and philanthropy in the sport.

www.santaclaraswimclub.org Official Web site of the Santa Clara Swim Club, one of the most storied club programs in the United States and host of the annual Santa Clara International Swim Meet.

www.sports-reference.com Web site with Olympic section of all athletes who have competed in the Olympic Games.

www.swimming.org.au Official Web site of Swimming Australia, the governing body of the sport in that country. Includes archived results of national and international competition and biographical information of Australian athletes.

www.swimmingworldmagazine.com Web site of *Swimming World Magazine*. Includes archived articles from magazine issues from 1960 to the present.

www.swimnews.com Official Web site of *Swim News*, a Canadian-based swimming magazine. Includes up-to-date world rankings and results, news articles, and columns.

www.usaswimming.org Official Web site of United States Swimming. Includes archived results of national and international competition and biographical information of U.S. athletes.

XI. CD COLLECTION

Complete issues of *Swimming World Magazine*: 1960–2008. This collection contains PDF files of every issue of *Swimming World* published from its inception through December 2008. Included are hundreds of features, meet recaps, results, and training tips.

About the Author

John Lohn is the senior writer for *Swimming World Magazine* and the former deputy sports editor of the *Delaware County Daily Times*. His interest in swimming was sparked in 1998 when he began covering future Olympic gold medalist Brendan Hansen. From that introduction to the sport, a passion for swimming developed. He has written for *Swimming World* on a regular basis since 2000, becoming the magazine's senior writer in 2006. His work appears monthly in the magazine and more frequently on the magazine's Web site, www.swimmingworldmagazine .com. During the past decade, he has covered the 2000, 2004, and 2008 United States Olympic Trials and several U.S. National Championships. He covered the 2008 Olympic Games in Beijing, documenting the historic accomplishments of Michael Phelps for *Swimming World*'s print product, in addition to providing coverage for the magazine's Web site. He has also covered the World Championships and has been a guest on the ESPN shows *The Hotlist* and *Pregame* from the 2007 World Championships in Melbourne. Additionally, he has provided analysis on the sport for several radio programs and also international newspapers and magazines. He is a graduate of La Salle University in Philadelphia and an avid golfer and traveler, especially cruising.